NORTH CAROLINA
STATE BOARD OF COMMUNITY COLLEGES
DISCARD
LIBRARIES
CRAVEN COMMUNITY COLLEGE

D1037323

NORTH CAROLINA
STATE BOARD OF COMMUNITY COLLEGES
LIBRARIES
CRAVEN COMMUNITY COLLEGE

DISCARD

CONSERVING BUILDINGS

CONSERVING BUILDINGS
Guide to Techniques and Materials

Martin E. Weaver
with F. G. Matero

40641

JOHN WILEY & SONS, INC.
New York / Chichester / Brisbane / Toronto / Singapore

All photos taken by author except for Chapter 10, taken by
Frank G. Matero and photo on page 4, taken by Mary Bramley.

In recognition of the importance of preserving what has been
written, it is a policy of John Wiley & Sons, Inc., to have books
of enduring value published in the United States printed on
acid-free paper, and we exert our best efforts to that end.

Copyright © 1993 by John Wiley & Sons, Inc.

All rights reserved. Published simultaneously in Canada.

Reproduction or translation of any part of this work
beyond that permitted by Section 107 or 108 of the
1976 United States Copyright Act without the permission
of the copyright owner is unlawful. Requests for
permission or further information should be addressed to
the Permissions Department, John Wiley & Sons, Inc.

This publication is designed to provide accurate and
authoritative information in regard to the subject
matter covered. It is sold with the understanding that
the publisher is not engaged in rendering legal, accounting,
or other professional services. If legal advice or other
expert assistance is required, the services of a competent
professional person should be sought. *From a Declaration
of Principles jointly adopted by a Committee of the
American Bar Association and a Committee of Publishers.*

Library of Congress Cataloging in Publication Data:

Weaver, Martin E., 1938–
    Conserving buildings : guide to techniques and materials /
Martin E. Weaver with F.G. Matero.
        p.   cm.
    Includes bibliographical references (p.   ) and index.
    ISBN 0-471-50945-0
    1. Buildings—Conservation and restoration—Technique.
2. Building materials.   I. Matero, F.G.   II. Title.
NA105.W43   1992
720′.28′8—dc20   91-48263
                                                  CIP

Printed in the United States of America

10 9 8 7 6 5 4 3 2

This book is dedicated to my daughters Alex, Helen, Mika, and Laura with confidence that their generations will have the good sense to stop the pollution of our environment and to preserve our heritage for the future.

PREFACE

The conservation of buildings has developed both as a science and as a profession particularly since the early 1970s. Through such organizations as the Association for Preservation Technology, North American practitioners have made significant contributions in this developing field. This book represents the first attempt to produce a major text which is both a comprehensive study on the technology of building conservation and a survey of North American practice.

Some years ago a reviewer of a "comprehensive" book on the maintenance of historic buildings commented that he tended to be acutely suspicious of any work which claimed to be comprehensive on such a vast topic. I have tried to keep this caution in mind and have based this book both on nearly thirty years of professional practice all over the world and on twenty-two years of university lecturing on the technology of historic building materials and their conservation.

After being advised by my father who was a Scotland Yard detective that he did not recommend crime investigation as a profession, I made my first steps toward a career in conservation in England in 1957 when there were no university courses in the conservation of historic buildings. At that time the field was more commonly known by a rather grander title as "the conservation of historic monuments and sites."

After studying architecture at the Architectural Association School of Architecture, attending lectures at the Institute of Archaeology, and working on archaeological excavations in the United Kingdom, Greece, and Iran I worked for six years as a restoration architect with the Historic Buildings Division of the Greater London Council. The early interest in forensic science combined with studies in architecture, archaeology, and continuous practical experience to provide the basis for an investigative and technical approach to building conservation which has proved to be both fascinating and rewarding.

Since 1967 I have lectured at many universities on practically all aspects of the conservation of historic building and sites. Among these lectures, those given for the master's degree students of the Restoration Department at the Middle East Technical University in Ankara, Turkey and of the Historic Preservation Program at Columbia University in New York, have been perhaps the most important in that they have allowed me to focus particularly on building conservation as a subject to be taught, understood, and analyzed.

Another process which has been most helpful to me has been the writing of technical articles on conservation for general and professional audiences who may have not had a scientific education. Typical articles have appeared in the now defunct *Canadian Heritage* magazine, *Construction Specifier*, the journal of the Construction Specification Institute of the USA, and the *Bulletin of the Association for Preservation Technology*. This is a process which I enjoy and I have found that such writing provides powerful incentives first to gain a clear understanding oneself and then to write so that the essentials and the interest of the topic can be clearly conveyed to the reader.

It is a common thread in all these studies that first the nature of materials and systems must be understood as must the nature of the processes of their deterioration. This complex understanding then leads to the development and application of conservation technology.

No matter how long or how deep the university education of the aspiring practitioner, there are also the twin essential requirements of field experience and a knowledge of materials and their ways which can only be gained by working with them with the hands. This poses something of a Catch 22 situation because it is difficult to obtain the practical field experience without practice, but prior experience is naturally preferred by clients and potential employers.

I hope that this book will enable readers to share some of my field experience and some of my joy in knowing materials and working with them. I should, however, add a cautionary note that this is not a recipe book full of all the answers and shortcuts.

Each case in building conservation is unique although it may have certain features in common with other cases. The conservator can never afford to skimp on field investigations because the critical and unique features may be missed. New problems appear all the time, one never stops learning, and there are very few shortcuts. The only proper method is to approach each conscientiously with an open mind and let the physical evidence speak for itself. The following quotation appears on the door of one of my favorite bookshops in New York and it is a very apt motto for us:

The mind is like a parachute, it only works when open.

Many years ago when I was first lecturing at Columbia University I first met Frank Matero. Thus began a long friendship and what developed into a process of constant professional exchange and renewal from which I have had much pleasure. It is also a process which I value most deeply. When I first started to write this book, Professor Frank Matero was Director of Columbia University's prestigious Center for Preservation Research. Under his direction the Center developed a well deserved reputation as being one of North America's finest architectural conservation practices. I am delighted that I was able to persuade him to join me to produce part of this book and that we have been able to publish for the first time extracts from some of the conservation case files from the Center. These projects and treatments represent the state of the art as far as North American practice is concerned and much of the data are simply not available elsewhere. All of these projects were carried out by teams and the members are credited in the acknowledgment section of the text.

As I write this introduction early in 1991 we have taken up new roles and entered a new and most interesting stage in the development of North American building conservation. I have just been appointed Director of Columbia University's newly reorganized Center for Preservation Research and Professor Matero is the Director of the University of Pennsylvania's architectural conservation laboratory.

New York, New York   Martin E. Weaver
June 1992

ACKNOWLEDGMENTS

Any work of this size and scope inevitably relies heavily on the accumulated knowledge and experience of many others working in the field, both through their writings and through personal contacts. I would like to take this opportunity to thank all my professional colleagues for their long and fruitful friendships and regret that a faulty memory and the passage of time may cause some omissions which I would otherwise regard as inexcusable.

I must first thank Leslie my wife for her patience with me during the long gestation period for this book. I am only too aware how many times home and family have come second to "the book"! She has also worked long hours at the computer keyboard on parts of the manuscript when I did not have time or the requisite skills to use my own computer. At Columbia University, Mary Jacobs, my assistant, has also helped enormously with computer work on material which has originated from the Center for Preservation Research. Barry Burton, my research assistant and laboratory manager at the Center, has also made a fundamental contribution by showing me how our computers can be used to manipulate the manuscript and to transform many disparate parts on different systems into one cohesive whole. It was a wonderful and at times nerve-wracking experience to see the book actually emerging.

Among my many professional colleagues around the world I would particularly like to thank the following individuals for their unstinted help, data, and suggestions on many occasions: Sir Bernard Feilden; John Fidler; Nicola Ashurst; Norman Weiss; Ian Hodkinson; Morgan Phillips; Hugh Miller; Lee Nelson; Eric Jokinen; Alan Spry; Jan Rosvall; Nils Marstein; Jon Brenner; Fran Gale; Joe Payer; Nick Veloz; Shelley Sass; Lorraine Schnabel; and Tom Rudder.

I am enormously grateful to Jonathan Rath who produced the excellent line illustrations on his computer in Ottawa and who was such a pleasure to work with.

I would also like to acknowledge my gratitude to John F. S. Pryke of the famous British firm of Pynford's. Part of his crack classification system is illustrated in the text, and he is quoted in the chapter on foundations. I have known John for many years and have benefitted greatly from his generous sharing of his wide knowledge and experience on structural surveys and conservation.

The following conservators were members of the teams involved in the conservation projects described in the extracts from the case files of the Center for Preservation Research: Frank G. Matero (normally project director); Norman R. Weiss; Lee Dassler; Joel Snodgrass; Shelley Sass; Joan Berkowitz; Glen Bornazian; Melissa Meighan; Mary Hardy; Antonio Rava; Phoebe Tudor; Mary Jablonski; Caroline Fenton; Robert Koestler; Maria Ruiz de Anton.

CONTENTS

CHAPTER 1

A GENERAL INTRODUCTION TO THE CONSERVATION OF BUILDINGS

"Conservation" can be defined as preservation from loss, depletion, waste, or harm. From early beginnings which included the controversial "restorations" of great historic buildings which so outraged John Ruskin in the nineteenth century, the field expanded to encompass the more scientific preservation of a heritage of great and small older buildings for the use and enjoyment of our own and future generations.

The period since the Second World War has seen not only a rapid development of the technology of conservation but also a matching development of the philosophy and ethics of conservation. In this same period, the term "conservation" has been adopted to refer specifically to the professional use of a combination of science, art, craft, and technology as a preservation tool. The conservation of historic buildings or buildings of heritage value has thus developed into an extremely complex process involving a team of many professionals, specialists, trades, and craftsworkers.

In the 1970s a number of specialists who had trained primarily in the United Kingdom and Europe, worked on the development of the conservation of historic buildings and sites for the Canadian government. They developed an organized approach to the management of the conservation process which has been a major Canadian contribution to this field. Their conservation process is divided into six or seven distinct phases beginning with a phase in which the initial decision is made to conserve the building or resource and a conservation "dossier" is created. The continuously documented process then moves through phases of research, analysis, and design to physical conservation measures and ultimately to continuing conservation or maintenance. It can readily be appreciated that such a process is cyclical in nature, a never-ending process exactly like that of painting the great steel bridges which are also a part of our heritage. It does not really matter whether we use precisely this process or some variation. It is imperative, however, that the process is organized and carefully managed so that all relevant disciplines, skills, and individuals are involved at every appropriate stage.

Each action involving a physical intervention on the resource or a commitment to such an intervention must first be carefully considered and tested against the highest professional and technical standards before the actual intervention takes place. Permanent records must remain of the states of the resource before and after conservation; of the decision-making process which led to that conservation; and of the reasons for the decisions.

Conservation processes are continuously threatened by the infatuation of our society with the latest products and mysteries of science and technology. All too often it is discovered that physical and chemical changes in the latest "wonder" products have seriously and adversely affected historic building materials to which they have been applied in the name of preservation! Once the original materials have been thus treated and damaged the processes are found to be irreversible and the products can not be removed without destroying the very resource which was to be preserved. To guard against the harmful consequences of insufficient knowledge leading to a misuse of technology and to ill-considered actions, professional conservators have adopted codes of ethics and guidelines which are in themselves a mark of the growing maturity of their profession. The following guideline is significant in this context:

> . . . The conservator shall endeavour to use only techniques and materials which, to the best of current knowledge, will not endanger the cultural and physical integrity of the cultural property. Ideally, these techniques and materials should not impede future treatment or examination. Whenever possible, the conservator shall select the techniques which have the least adverse effect on the cultural property. Similarly, the conservator shall use materials which can be removed most easily and completely. (IIC-CG, 1989)

There are two fundamental problems associated with the use of modern technology and materials to eradicate and prevent present and future deterioration. First, in order to eradicate and prevent deterioration, the materials, phenomena, processes, and their micro- and macro-environments must be totally understood. Second, it must be possible to determine the future behavior of the original materials and of the new materials which are added to them in the conservation process.

The first can be an incredibly complex, difficult, and expensive process. The second involves an attempt to forecast the future by means of accelerated tests designed to simulate the "aging" of original and new materials separately and in combination. Processes of deterioration can be a function of the passage of time; of the quantities and impact velocities of harmful substances to which materials are exposed; and of the environments in which they are exposed. The environments are normally considered in terms of temperature, pressure, ultraviolet radiation, light levels, and relative humidity. In order to speed up the processes so that we don't have to wait around a hundred years or so for that most reliable of all tests, the "test of time," it is customary to increase the severity of exposure. This may be done, for example, by increasing quantities of pollutants and raising temperatures, radiation levels, pressures, or humidity levels.

We are only now beginning to understand the complexities of deterioration processes in polluted urban environments which are dependant upon incredibly complex combinations of chemicals, environmental factors, and synergistic and catalytic reactions. From this understanding comes the disturbing but sure knowledge that our artificial aging tests are at best imperfect and at worst useless or grossly misleading. These inherent problems necessitate a continuing reliance on field observation and investigation of materials and deterioration phenomena in combination with an intelligent use of technology, materials, and data from the widest possible range of sources, many of which may have little or nothing to do with historic buildings. It is also necessary to return at intervals and to reevaluate the results of past conservation treatments.

Many of the best conservators also follow conservative practices involving the use of traditional and well-proven technology and materials. Even that approach may prove to be inadequate in the face of changing modern environments which have introduced pollutants and combinations of materials totally alien to any past traditions, crafts, or cultures; and in which those "tried and proven" technologies and materials may fail miserably. It may also be found that materials and techniques which have been used without question for long periods are in fact ineffective and that while they are not necessarily harmful neither are they in any way beneficial.

As a classic example of this phenomenon, the use of water repellents on restored or even new masonry has often been continued only because no water appeared to have penetrated other masonry following similar treatments. The good performance of the other examples may have had nothing whatsoever to do with the water repellent.

Similarly, certain plaster conservation techniques which still appear regularly in conservation texts, were found by Professor Hodkinson of Queen's University, Kingston, Ontario, and me to be almost totally useless. Almost unbelievably nobody had been curious enough to be bothered to try the methods and then to cut sections through the plaster and find out what had happened!

In the next chapter I have tried to offer some guidance on investigation techniques for old buildings and in exercising practical curiosity.

REFERENCE

Code of Ethics and Standards of Practice. (1989). International Institute for Conservation-Canadian Group. Ottawa. Revised edition. IIC-CG.

CHAPTER 2

INVESTIGATING OLD BUILDINGS

The process of investigating old buildings can range from the brief and inadequate to the opposite extreme of being almost endless and superfluous. Obviously our goal lies somewhere in between.

Many of the most significant contributions to building investigation and survey work in North America have originated from or have been commissioned by government organizations such as the Canadian Parks Service and the United States National Park Service. While this work has been of fundamental importance, there have been occasions when the equipment and resources brought to bear upon a problem have been so costly or so exotic that they are totally beyond the budgets of normal professional practices and even municipalities.

As examples of this we have the use of wonderfully sophisticated stereophotogrammetry by the Heritage Recording Unit of the Canadian Parks Service and incredible combinations of advanced scientific equipment and specialists which have been assembled to "crack" the conservation problems of tiny buildings at Colonial Williamsburg and at St. Vital, Manitoba. While these examples may be justifiable in the final analysis the lesson which must be learned from them is that to be effective, investigations must be practical and they must secure only the information strictly necessary for the conservation of the resource. Interesting as it may be, the collection of more and more information becomes unnecessary and uneconomic. Much more important, however, is the fact that unnecessary expenditures at this stage may consume funds required for essential conservation work.

The conservator is faced with a balancing act which requires the constant reevaluation of conservation goals, requirements, and available budgets. Practical experience demonstrates again and again that insufficient research and planning lead to projects running over budget and to poor conservation practice.

In the chapters which follow, investigative processes in the field and in the laboratory are reviewed for each group of materials and associated systems.

MEASURING HISTORIC BUILDINGS AND STRUCTURES

Surveying, measuring, and recording have a number of functions which can affect the selection of techniques, scale, and degree of detail required. We record historic buildings or structures for the future just in case by some unfortunate chance they happen to be badly damaged or even destroyed in a disaster. We should then have sufficient information to restore them or at least to describe them for future generations. Such records may require a very high level of accuracy and great detail.

We may also survey and measure a structure in order to prepare conservation contract documents which will convey our intentions and requirements to contractors, trades, or craftsworkers.

Measurements may also be required for structural survey records to establish the current state of a structure so that we can detect any changes which occur with the passage of time or because of external forces acting upon that structure. This group includes the use of tell-tales, micrometers, and strain gauges to record and measure the magnitude of structural movements, cracks, bulges, and other distortions.

RECORDING FOR POSSIBLE FUTURE USE

Recording in case of future disaster is usually best carried out by means of stereophotogrammetry. The entire structure can be recorded by stereo pairs of photographs with all appropriate measurements and scales in the photographs. Technical data on the camera, including focal length, must also be recorded. Many of the variations on this process are described in more detail in such works as Ogleby and Rivett (1985), UNESCO/ICOMOS (1981), and Borchers (1977).

Great care must be exercised in the selection of an appropriate scale since this affects the number of photographs which will be required and hence the degree of detail which will be recorded. For practical purposes, it is recommended that the scale should be no smaller than 1:50 or $\frac{1}{4}''$:1'. A scale of 1:25 or $\frac{1}{2}''$:1' is a common choice.

The ideal feature of this type of recording is that once the stereo pairs are taken they can simply be stored in an appropriate archive. They do not have to be immediately processed and converted into drawings.

SURVEYING AND RECORDING FOR CONTRACT USE

Probably the most common use of surveying and recording techniques is in the preparation of contracts. Practical experience has shown that combinations of photographs, hand measurement, and drawings can be compiled into photo-drawings which are reproducible. As can be seen from the examples, the prints from these reproducibles present the contractor with the best combination of various forms of data to explain exactly what is required and exactly where. I currently take photographs on site using 35-mm color print film. The resulting prints are then cut and mounted to produce composite images or "mosaics." These are then reproduced by laser scanning and printing on transparencies. The transparencies in their turn are cut to size and set in matching sized holes cut with a scalpel into polyester or mylar drawing film. They are secured in place with a good quality transparent self-adhesive transparent tape. Additional transparencies, drawings, and specification notes are added and then the whole photo-drawing is ready for reproduction. When carrying out conservation studies or surveys on masonry buildings, I prefer to have photo-mosaics previously prepared so that prints from them can be taken on site and annotated with coded symbols to show various defects.

Author with photomosaic. Photo: Mary Bramley.

Details which are of special interest can be photographed to a much larger scale and resulting transparencies included in the photo-drawings. Some specialists use rectified photography to produce images which are reproduced to predetermined scales and with perspective distortion eliminated or minimized by the use of perspective-corrected lenses, rising and tilting front cameras, or by subsequent rectification of the images. A useful discussion of this subject is to be found in Chambers (1973). Such surveys with annotated photo-drawings form an ideal basis for contract documents with a minimum of interim steps in the production process.

STRUCTURAL SURVEY RECORDS

Annotated photo-drawings or photo-mosaics make ideal structural survey records. Additional information is required on the actual dimensions of cracks and of the directions of movements which caused the cracks to open. It is important that crack dimensions are measured in the direction of movement. As can be seen from the diagrams, the reading of cracks with associated directions of movement is analogous to having two pieces of a jig-saw puzzle. In order to get the two pieces together so that their matching profiles interlock, the pieces must be moved in a certain direction. When looking at a crack one simply draws a series of parallel lines in these directions linking matching profiles and this gives the direction of movement. Signs of localized crushing associated with the cracking should also be closely examined since these reveal where masonry masses are being pushed together and where others are being pulled apart.

Although structural surveys should involve qualified structural engineers, the conservator is frequently going to encounter evidence of structural problems when no engineer is present and in situations where it is unlikely that anybody is going to be able to return for a second look until much later in the project when it may be too late.

CATEGORIES OF STRUCTURAL CRACKS

With the above in mind it is worth noting that structural cracking falls into two categories.

The first category is one where the cracking has no effect on the structure, or at least only an aesthetic effect. This category is often classified in four classes: less than 0.10 mm; 0.10–0.30 mm; 0.30–1.00 mm; and 1.00–2.00 mm. This category ranges from fine hairline cracks which may be very difficult to see, up to the 2.00 mm cracks which can be seen in a clear light from a few meters or yards away.

These cracks are very often caused by initial shrinkage in new materials or by thermal expansion and contraction movements over a long period.

The second category is also divided into four classes. The use and serviceability of the building will be affected in the first three classes and in the fourth there is an increasing risk of the structure becoming dangerous.

The classes in the second category commence at 2.00–5.00 mm; at the upper limit doors and windows may stick, draughts and moisture may penetrate through walls, and arches may crack and loosen.

Class of Crack	(A) Crack Size in mm.	(B) Physical Maximum Width in mm. (Full Scale)
P 0	Less than 0.1	0.1
P 1	0.1 to 0.3	0.3
P 2	0.3 to 1.0	1.0
P 3	1.0 to 2.0	2.0
P 4	2.0 to 5.0	5.0
P 5	5.0 to 15.0	15.0
P 6	15.0 to 25.0	25.0
P 7	Greater than 25.0	> 25.0

A) Crack size is to be assessed in direction of movement.
B) Crack width is shortest distance between edges.

A = Crack Size
B = Crack Width
A = B When there is no displacement along the line of the crack, that is, there is tensile failure but **no** shear movement.

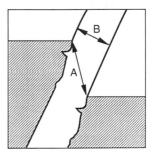

Figure 1. Pynford classification of visible damage to walls.

The next class is 5.00–15.00 mm. Cracks in this class are associated with serious structural damage. Doors and windows may be jammed, walls cracked right through, and severe shear patterns may develop with, for example, diagonal cracking in ceilings, falling plaster, and collapsing arches. At the upper limits tilework and other slab finishes may fall off the building and plumbing and service pipes may be broken. This class is clearly associated with structural movement patterns which can usually be traced to settlement of posts, columns, footings, plates, and sleeper walls; or to the bending of beams or trusses.

The next class is 15.00–25.00 mm. Cracks in this class are extremely serious and are easily discerned, usually with clear patterns of movement and often the cracks are grouped. In older buildings arches, sections of masonry wall, and thin structural features such as chimney stacks and pinnacles may collapse or show signs of movement and impending failure. Distortions, bulges, and horizontal movements at bearing points can be seen with the naked eye. Cracking in this class may also be caused by sudden changes or the removal of supports, usually associated with subsidences associated with mining, collapsing excavations, and landslips.

The final class is comprised of cracks which are greater than 25.00 mm. Cracking in this class can be regarded as evidence of a dangerous structure. The dimensions of such cracks can increase suddenly and without further warning and total or partial structural collapse may result. This class of cracking is particularly dangerous in old masonry buildings where walls may consist of two or more wythes which are imperfectly bonded together. A sudden failure of one wythe can lead to an immediate and extreme overloading of the remaining wythes which will have too high a slenderness ratio and will collapse as a result.

When studying and documenting structural cracks it is important not only to know the dimensions and direction of movement but also which of the following conditions apply:

- The movement has ceased and the crack has ceased to open. Usually this is associated with the occurrence of early foundation settlement which has ceased now that underlying soils are fully compacted.
- The movement is cyclic or intermittent so that the cracks open and close as soils expand and contract with the cycles of wet and dry seasons; or as subterranean water levels go up and down with tidal fluctuations.
- The movement is continuing so that the crack continues to open. If a graph is plotted with time as the abscissa (horizontal x axis) and crack width as the ordinate (vertical or y axis), the resulting plot is a rising straight line. In such cases it is possible to forecast when the crack will be sufficiently large to make the structure dangerous.
- The movement is accelerating so that the crack continues to open but the acceleration makes it difficult or impossible to forecast when the crack may become large enough to make the structure dangerous.

When carrying out structural inspections or crack surveys, particularly in poorly lit interiors, it may be helpful to use strong raking light to highlight surface irregularities and distortions.

ACCESS TO STRUCTURES FOR INVESTIGATIONS

Effective surveys and inspections of the exteriors of buildings are largely dependent on the type of access which the conservator or surveyor has to the actual surface of the building. At the lowest and most inaccurate end of the scale is the survey which depends on a visual inspection from the ground. For slightly better results, the surveyor uses high powered binoculars. For the most effective inspections, the surveyor must be able to actually touch the surface of the building. Indeed in some cases, such as terracotta-faced buildings, it may be necessary for the surveyor to "sound" every single terracotta unit in certain critical areas (see Chapter 6). In order to have this close access it is necessary to use hydraulic platforms, cranes with telescopic booms, fire department ladder trucks, swing stages, or scaffolding.

Although it is very expensive, scaffolding undoubtedly provides the most secure and satisfactory means of carrying out an investigation. However, it must be properly designed for the job to give safe and close

Scaffold on Langevin Building, Ottawa. Built for roof repairs but used for wall survey.

access to all surfaces without the surveyor having to lean out or swing dangerously from stages which are just too far away from the surface to be inspected. All too often the surveyor has little choice in the matter but is pressed to use a scaffold which has been erected for another purpose, such as repairing a roof.

I carry out a large number of inspections from cranes which may sometimes be capable of reaching heights of over 250 ft. In such cases the best conditions are given by a glass fibre reinforced plastic "bucket" or pair of buckets attached to the end of the boom or a jib extension to the boom. The closed sides of the buckets afford some protection from cold winds and help to prevent the accidental dropping of tools and measuring equipment. On no account should surveys be carried out from baskets suspended at the end of steel cables. In certain places this practice is actually illegal. The

Crane with personnel buckets.

baskets tend to rotate and swing in such a way that they may crash into the side of the building causing structural damage and even knocking fragments off so that they fall with great risk to life and limb. The steel cables also tend to cut into projecting portions of the structure such as overhanging cornices.

In some cases it may be necessary for inspections to be carried out from swing stages. In Chicago the detailed inspection of the exterior masonry of the famous Rookery Building was carried out from swingstages during the day, and the same swingstages were used at night by the masonry cleaning contractors. In cities where municipal regulations require that cleaning operation are carried out at night, such an arrangement may be very economical and logical.

It is patently obvious that any inspection which requires working high above the ground in crane buckets or on swingstages can be dangerous for the surveyor unless proper safety precautions are observed.

I have found that a number of crane companies no longer supply safety belts because of the insurance risks associated with implied responsibilities if any accident should occur.

The law, however, normally requires that any person carried in a bucket or basket at the end of a crane boom or jib must not only wear a safety belt or harness of approved standard design, but also that the safety belt or harness shall be attached securely to the structure of the end of the crane by means of a lanyard with approved catches at both ends. Persons using swingstages must be similarly attached to special safety lines.

In these circumstances, if the surveyor is likely to be carrying out a number of such surveys then it makes good sense for the surveyor to acquire a personal safety belt and lanyard. It is also worth noting that old belts and lanyards which have unknown histories, may have been subjected to stresses and deterioration which have already brought them close to breaking. The sudden stresses caused by an accident could cause a life-threatening failure. If the surveyor arrives on the site to carry out an inspection and is handed a safety belt and lanyard, these should be carefully inspected for any signs of metal corrosion, cracking, abrasion, heat damage, and decay or fraying of leather or fabric. If any of these are found, the belt and/or lanyard should be rejected and the inspection abandoned until satisfactory replacements are supplied. The surveyor should also check to establish whether local regulations require the use of a full body harness rather than just a belt and lanyard. If a fall occurs the sudden shock on a simple waist belt can cause internal or spinal injuries. The full body harness has shoulder and thigh straps in

Crane basket hits terracotta facade.

addition to a belt and this combination spreads the weight evenly, avoiding these injuries.

I have also encountered a number of scaffolds which were totally unsatisfactory for inspection purposes and indeed were in some cases unsafe. Some of these scaffolds were erected by apparently reputable firms but somehow irregularities had escaped correction. How can the surveyor deal with such cases? Obviously experience is of paramount importance, especially when there are life-safety considerations, but equally obviously it takes a long time to gain the experience and the surveyor has to begin somewhere.

A PREUSE CHECKLIST FOR ACCESS SYSTEMS

The following short checklist may be helpful:

- If vertical access is by means of ladders they should be properly locked to the scaffold and should be rigged on the inside of the scaffold. The ladders should be arranged so that vertical runs are of no more than about three "lifts" at a time and so that there are landings to reduce the height of any accidental fall. I worked from one scaffold where a continuous vertical ladder 90 ft high was attached to the outside of the scaffold with no guards and in such a way that a single slip could cause a fatal fall.

Any ladders which must be erected on the outside of a scaffold should have a tubular cage guard designed to prevent climbers falling backward off the ladder.

- The scaffold boards should be properly tied down and guard boards or kick boards should be provided.

The former precaution is not simply to prevent boards from being dislodged by winds but is also necessary to ensure that treading on one end of a board does not cause the other end to lift, tipping the unfortunate surveyor off the scaffolding.

- The scaffold should be effectively secured or tied back to sound parts of the structure. This is usually best done with substantial noncorroding ringbolts and noncorroding expanding anchors in the masonry. The scaffolding is then attached to the ringbolts with heavy twisted wire strops.

When an inspection is being carried out to determine the structural state of the building and the state of deterioration of the materials, it can be extremely difficult to find sound parts of the structure to which the scaffold can be tied back.

Before commencing any survey or inspection from a scaffold I customarily inspect all the tie-backs from the bottom of the scaffolding upward.

Unsafe ladders, Edmonton, Alberta.

church tower, the critical stonework was found to consist of a thin veneer of ashlar over loose rubble. The poor state of the supporting structure was revealed in the course of the inspection and necessitated the dismantling of the scaffold. This problem occurred despite the fact that following good practice, cores had been diamond-drilled through the masonry to establish its composition and condition. By great misfortune the only core drilled through the masonry in that vicinity missed the small fragments of stone and instead went through the only large stones present. The core thus gave a totally false impression of solidity. A further complication arose from the fact that the scaffold obstructed access because it was partly standing on the structure which required inspection.

In one instance I climbed about 80 ft up to the apex of some scaffolding, only to find that the scaffolding was "tied back" with a loop of old rope to a stone pinnacle which was loose!

- The ends of scaffold tubes should be padded and protected with plywood pads so that no damage occurs to masonry surfaces.
- Where scaffolding starts from a roof, the top of a tower, or some other part of the structure above ground level, great care should be taken to ensure that the structure of the building is capable of supporting the load of the scaffold without causing damage. On a recent project in Ontario it was found that where scaffolding enclosing a stone spire was supported by stonework at the top of the

Unsafe scaffold tied back to loose stonework.

In another case the scaffolding was "supported" by the ridge of a lower roof in such a way that the roof was seriously overloaded. Upper parts of the same scaffolding were actually supported by a balcony and wrought iron work which were suspected of being unsound.

- The scaffolding should not sway or wobble. Particular care should be taken when climbing on or using scaffolding which has been partially dismantled or altered for some reason. An otherwise stable scaffolding system can be rendered totally unstable by the removal of a critical brace or tie to facilitate access or to "speedup" the work.
- The load-bearing capacities of the scaffolding stages, boards, and structure as a whole should be carefully checked to see if they meet all requirements. This can be particularly important if stonework is expected to be dismantled onto the scaffold.

THE INSPECTION KIT

Conservators develop their own preferences for what equipment and material they take with them on the site, up the scaffolding, or in the bucket of the crane. The following items might be regarded as standard (see also each chapter for special equipment associated with various types of investigations):

- Prints of photo-mosaics or of drawings upon which to mark coded information on defects. The drawings should be conveniently folded or better still printed on separate sheets which require minimal folding.

The strong winds which are normally found high on the outside of buildings make the control of large sheets of paper virtually impossible.

- A notebook or notepaper.
- A clip board or small patent plastic drawing board to provide a firm support for the drawings or prints.
- Clips and rubber bands to assist in holding down the drawings or prints.
- A 35-mm camera with close-up, zoom, and normal lenses.
- Spare film for the camera.
- A pocket microscope preferably with a graticule for measuring objects in the field of view.

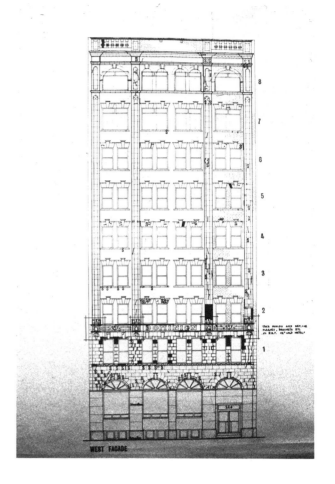

Quebec City coded drawing of terracotta facade.

- Measuring tapes and folding rods.
- Polyethylene bags and screw-top plastic vials for samples. (I normally use polyethylene "Ziplok" freezer bags which are conveniently sealed with their own built-in seals.)
- Scalpels and other small tools for taking samples.
- A "permanent marker" felt pen for writing on the plastic bags and vials to record, site, location, and date.
- Pens and pencils.
- pH test strips of the nonbleed variety with a plastic dropper bottle of distilled water.
- Assorted tools depending on the nature of the structure but probably including a heavy rubber mallet, a small thin steel pry-bar with a nail-lifting slot, a long thin bladed screwdriver with an impact resistant handle, a pair of pliers with cutters, and

Typical survey kit.

a small pair of "tin-snips" or sheet metal shears.
- A pair of powerful binoculars preferably with a zoom capacity.
- A small tape recorder or electronic voice recorder.
- A laptop computer. Standardized formats for surveys can be used with laptop computers which are actually taken on site so that data are stored directly. Ideally this method avoids or minimizes the costs and risks of errors associated with every transfer of data from handwritten material to electronic or machine-readable form.

The above list is not an exhaustive one but the surveyor or investigator will require a large bag to contain all this material. I use a large, light-weight bag made of heavy-duty woven nylon with three zippered compartments and a shoulder strap.

When the surveyor is working from scaffolding, the large bag should be hauled up separately by rope. If the surveyor climbs ladders with the bag slung from a shoulder, there is a risk of the bag catching in a projection and causing the surveyor to be pulled off the ladder.

REFERENCES

Borchers, P.E. (1977). *Photogrammetric Recording of Cultural Resources*. Washington: National Park Service, United States Department of the Interior.

Burns, J.A. (ed.), et al. (1989) *Recording Historic Structures*. Washington: National Park Service, United States Department of the Interior.

Chambers, J.H. (1973). *Rectified Photography and Photo Drawings for Historic Preservation*. Washington: National Park Service, United States Department of the Interior.

Ogleby, C. and Rivett, L.J. (1985). *Handbook of Heritage Photogrammetry*. Canberra: Australian Heritage Commission, Australian Government Publishing Service.

UNESCO/ICOMOS (1981). International Committee on Architectural Photogrammetry. *Optimum Practice in Architectural Photogrammetry Surveys*. The published papers of the CIPA Symposium, Paris, September 1980.

CHAPTER 3

THE STUDY OF BUILDING MATERIALS

Any building conservation project depends to a large extent on studies of the original building materials and particularly on their methods of manufacture, the sources and extraction of their raw materials, and their deterioration generally and specifically in the instance under study.

So important are these studies that conservators are developing standard scientific approaches to them. In many instances, the conservator or conservation scientist adopts and adapts tests and standards which have been developed for other purposes. Such tests and standards may be primarily oriented toward new materials rather than old materials which we may wish to keep for their cultural and historical values rather than simply replacing them.

This process is not without its problems, and in fact a number of methods or approaches developed in recent years have subsequently been found to have been unreliable or inadequate. The examination of historic mortar samples is a excellent example of this type of problem. In a paper entitled "Chemical Techniques of Historic Mortar Analysis," the Canadian conservation scientists Costain and Stewart (1982) reported on their studies on the problems of improving analytical techniques for studies on historic mortars.

They concluded that while the majority of the current tests provided somewhat unreliable results, some provided results which were misleading or simply incorrect.

Chapters of this book are devoted to each of the major building materials. Each chapter contains a study of the nature of the material, its chemical and physical structure, and its behavior. This is followed by a study on the sources of the raw materials, processing, and manufacture. Each chapter is completed by a section on the deterioration of the material, followed by a section on appropriate conservation techniques and materials.

Special techniques of examination and testing of the materials alone and in systems are discussed in the appropriate contexts.

Any book of this nature which discusses materials' testing and standards cannot fail to refer to the invaluable and vast resources contained in the works of the American Society for Testing and Materials. Their standards for materials and for test methods are also given in their appropriate contexts.

REFERENCE

Costain, C. and Stewart, J. (1982). Chemical Techniques of Mortar Analysis. *Bulletin of the Association for Preservation Technology* XIV.1: 11–16.

CHAPTER 4

RESTORING AND REPAIRING OLD WOODEN STRUCTURES

Any approach to the problem of restoring or repairing an old wooden structure must be systematic.

First we must discover the nature of the structural system and the species of woods which were used for the various structural elements. Some woods were chosen for their durability, while others were simply used because they were there. Armed with the knowledge of where the structural timbers are and of what species they are made we can then find out what, if anything, is wrong with them. Finally when we have this knowledge, and only then, can we proceed to design and specify appropriate treatments.

HISTORIC TIMBERWORK

When the European settlers first came to North America they found a wonderful new world which, even if it wasn't actually flowing with milk and honey, was endowed with the most incredible resources of great trees which could be harvested for building everything from modest houses to great wooden warships.

Even by the seventeenth century many of Europe's forests had been seriously depleted by expanding settlement, industry, agriculture, and by an unceasing requirement for fuel. In England, this serious depletion had been noted in a report published by John Norden, Surveyor of His Majesty's English Forests in 1607. In the eighteenth and nineteenth centuries the rapid growth of the Industrial Revolution and the Napoleonic Wars created even greater demands, and inevitably shortages of timber, particularly oak for building ships' frames and pine for masts and spars. To the timber-starved settlers then the incredible richness of the North American forests seemed like a wonderful inex-

haustible resource. A thriving industry quickly began to produce timber for the European market and for home consumption.

Much of the first settlers' timber had to be sawn laboriously by hand with great pit saws but water- and wind-powered sawmills were introduced in the seventeenth century. While most of the earliest mills powered a single vertical reciprocating blade, gang saws consisting of a number of blades in a frame were certainly in existence in the Netherlands in the seventeenth century. There is no reason to assume that the Dutch did not use them in the wind-powered sawmills which they built in New York as early as 1623. A water-powered mill in Exeter, New Hampshire, in 1650 alone produced 80,000 boards and planks. These were of undefined lengths but were probably at least 10 ft long which means a probable annual production of at least 800,000 board ft. By the middle of the nineteenth century the industry was producing vast amounts of sawn lumber primarily from steam-powered mills. Steam power was first applied to sawmilling in the United States in 1803 in New Orleans, but the mill was burned down by displaced sawyers. By 1812–1813 steam-powered sawmills were becoming relatively common, with three in the Mississippi Territory alone. Steam-powered sawmills were developed at the same time in Canada and documentation exists for the sale of one in 1818 in Quebec.

With the full resources of steam power and improved quality blades, the production figures from the sawmills by the mid-nineteenth century are staggering even by today's standards. An account as early as 1832 described a steam-powered sawmill as having 28 perpendicular saws and two circular ones cutting each day an average of 18,000 to 20,000 ft, plank measure (2-in.

Timber sawn by a sawmill with a reciprocating blade, Ontario, ca. 1830.

planks). Nine mills in Ottawa in 1876 produced 1,500,000 board ft in 24 hours. Mills often ran 24 hours a day for six months of the year. Normal small mill production was about 20,000 board ft per 24 hours. In 1887 George Benson Hall's mills at Quebec were said to be the largest in the world and produced in one season the huge quantity of 75,000,000 (seventy five million) ft of pine deals (3-in. plank). The "season" probably lasted about 100 days! The incredible growth of this industry would have been totally impossible without an equally incredible forest resource. The huge production made it possible for timber cross sections in buildings to be more than generous and for timber use to verge on the prolific.

In today's world of timber shortages and the desperate struggles for the preservation of ever-shrinking forests in British Columbia and the Amazon Basin, it is hard to comprehend just how wonderful those North American forests were.

In 1833 Samuel Thompson wrote of the glorious forests near Georgian Bay in Canada. "I once saw a white or wainscot oak that measured fully twelve feet in circumference at the butt, and eighty feet clear of branches. This noble tree must have contained somewhere about seven thousand square feet of inch boarding." Thomas Fowler, also writing at about that time, described near Coburg (Ontario) "towering pines . . . frequently above a hundred feet high . . . contained six twelve feet logs without a branch." In this golden age of timber it was possible to find high-quality "first growth" mature pine in a single stick 120 ft long and with a diameter of 42 in. at a distance of 40 ft from the butt (Richardson, 1974).

Samuel Sloan, the American architect writing in 1852 of U.S. timbers, described white oak trees as being often 6 ft in diameter and 75–80 ft high; hemlock trees as being 70–80 ft high with diameters of 6 to 9 ft for two-thirds of that height; Southern yellow pine 80 ft high and 18 in. in diameter; and finally white pine as being sometimes 180 ft high and 6 ft in diameter with only about half an inch of sapwood!

Knowing the quality and quantity of the resource and the almost astronomical production quantities, it becomes much easier to comprehend the standard use of masses of oversized timbers.

A QUESTION OF SPECIES

In order to understand how the wood has behaved and is behaving in an old structure it is necessary to know which species were used and to understand how this affects the durability of the woods. Usually the selection of one type of wood as against another was dependant upon the closest available and hence most economical species. Large timbers are heavy and were hard to move over primitive roads if waterways were not available. In Europe and Britain where there was no alternative, the timber often had to be hauled long distances and was much more expensive as a result. In

North America, the opposite was true and timber was frequently very close to the user.

Despite the richness of the resources in, say, Ontario and New York State, in some areas the resources were not so good and the closest available species might not have been durable. In this way poplar, aspen, and maple were used in some historic structures. These woods are among the least durable species and fall in the third or worst of the three standard categories of "durable," "moderately durable," and "normally nondurable."

Depending first on the most easily available species and only second on the most durable or suitable species, the woods most commonly chosen from the times of the earliest historical settlements for structural timbers were white pine (*Pinus strobus*) and white oak (*Quercus alba*).

The majority of the other species used are described in the following list. The dates refer to significant historically documented early uses and the types are arranged alphabetically, without reflecting any preferred order of use. D means durable; M, moderately durable, and N, normally nondurable:

Birch, white (*Betula papyrifera*) N. Beams and column caps, Nova Scotia, 1830.

Cedar, eastern white (*Thuja occidentalis*) D. Boards in New England 1659; and house and ship building in Ontario and Quebec circa 1830.

Cedar, red (*Thuja plicata*) D. West Coast Indian pre-European contact for house timbers and poles; and then for all cultures and all structural uses in British Columbia, Oregon, and Washington, subsequently used everywhere.

Chestnut, sweet (*Castanea dentata*) D. New England, 1712.

Cypress (*Taxodium distichum*) D. South and Southwest United States, for example, New Orleans, 1852.

Fir, balsam (*Abies balsamea*) M. Rafters, door frames, knees in Nova Scotia, 1830s.

Fir, Douglas (*Pseudotsuga menziesii*) M. Logwork 1805 Oregon; structural timbers and shipbuilding from 1890s on.

Hemlock, eastern (*Tsuga canadensis*) D. Column caps, beams, mine timbering, and piles in Ontario and Nova Scotia, 1820s and 1830s.

Larch (*Larix decidua*) Also known as the European larch, M. For groundsills, New England, 1663.

Larch, western (*Larix occidentalis*) M.

Locust, black (*Robinia pseudoacacia*) D. Sleepers 1852, groundsills.

Maple, Manitoba (*Acer negundo*) Also known as box elder and ash leaved maple, N. Beams, framing; 1840s in Manitoba.

Maple, sugar (*Acer saccharum*) N. House framing, ships keels, and foundation timbers for locks and mills if they were to remain wet, Ontario and Quebec, 1840s.

Oak, black (*Quercus velutina*) N. Used interchangeably with red oak.

Oak, burr (*Quercus macrocarpa*) D. 1852.

Oak, live (*Quercus viginiana*) M. Knees, 1852.

Oak, red (*Quercus rubra*) N. Less satisfactory substitute for white oak, 19th century.

Osage-orange (*Maclura pomifera*) D.

Pine, red (*Pinus resinosa*) Also known as Norway pine, M. United States, 1852. Occasionally framing and shipbuilding, Ontario and Quebec, 1820s on.

Pine, southern yellow (*Pinus palustris*) Also called longleaf pine, M. Framing, beams, shipbuilding, particularly south of Virginia but used in the North as well, 1852.

Poplar, tulip (*Liriodendron tulipifera*) N. Heavy framing in western United States, 1852 but noted as nondurable.

Redwood (*Sequoia sempervirens*) D. Structural timbers.

Sassafras (*Sassafras albidium*) D.

Spruce, white (*Picea glauca*) N. Rafters, columns, beams, and shipbuilding from 1830s; but heartwood only because the sapwood was of such inferior durability.

Tamarack (*Larix laricina*) M. In 1830s, knees in both ships and buildings.

Walnut, black (*Juglans nigra*) D. Occasional use for log houses and framing where stands of walnut were sufficiently large; used in preference to ash in New England in 1634; and Ontario 1825–1850.

The reader is cautioned that when these historic uses occurred and when the durability ratings were assessed, the timbers in question were first growth, mature specimens and their durability may far exceed that of many timbers available today. Although it may be possible to match the species by scientific name, the timber obtained may be second growth, immature, and with a high sapwood content, thus making it distinctly less durable. ("First growth" or "virgin growth" are the terms used to define the original growth or stands of mature trees. "Second growth" defines timber that has grown after the removal, whether by cutting, fire, wind, or other agency of all or a large part of the previous stand.)

HISTORIC TIMBER STRUCTURES

Frame Structures

When the first European settlers arrived their first permanent structures tended, not surprisingly, to be based upon the carpentry traditions of their countries of origin.

Thus the English and French built timber framed houses with substantial, squared timbers joined together by means of tenons set in mortises and secured with pegs, very much in a continuation of regional styles and of a long medieval tradition which itself extended back at least to Roman morticed and tenoned structural frames. They built primarily in oak but also used chestnut for framing and white pine for long beams. Their delight at thus being able to build again with cheap plentiful oak was particularly commented upon after the problems of shortages and costs in Europe.

To build a frame house out of oak, for example, the laborious squaring of the timbers and then the cutting of mortices and tenons which had to be accurate, took a long time and required highly skilled carpenters. These carpenters from England and Europe brought with them not only carpentry traditions but also skills and their specialized tool kits. The amount of timber used was actually recorded in one instance in the seventeenth century as being about eight tons for a house.

Siegfried Giedion writing in 1939 stated that early in the nineteenth century, the "balloon frame" was "invented" in the United States. This was supposed to be a new system of construction, which used more closely spaced, uniform, sawn, much smaller cross sections of softwoods and was fixed together by nailing with no mortices and tenons. There is some argument as to exactly who "invented" the system and when, but the honors for the first balloon-framed building in the United States usually go to St. Mary's church in Chicago in 1833 or a Chicago warehouse in 1832. A great fire had destroyed much of the city and the need for speedy reconstruction to provide shelter before the onset of winter gave the necessary impetus for the development and massive adoption of the method.

It seems clear that Giedion's statement was inaccurate and it has been shown by Peter Bell working in Australia on the houses of the North Queensland mining settlements, that systems of light stud framing connected with nails were used long prior to 1833 in Eng-

land and most probably in the United States as well. Indeed it could be claimed that the light stud system started to be developed in Elizabethan England. Certainly there are many surviving eighteenth century examples in the South of England.

All these claims and counterclaims notwithstanding, it is clear that the speedy development of the system in the United States was made possible by the incredible production of the fast growing sawmilling industry and the industrialization of iron nail production. The main feature which distinguished the American development of the system was the absence of carpentered joints with mortices, tenons, and dovetails, and the wholesale use of nails for all joints.

The result of the new "invention" was indisputable; suddenly it was no longer necessary for skilled carpenters to be involved in all frame construction. A farmer and his son could practically build a frame house between them.

After some nineteenth century problems with fires in balloon-framed structures, an improvement was evolved called the "platform frame" in which horizontal timbers cut across the gaps between the vertical studs at the upper floor levels and prevented fires spreading quickly up the interior of the walls from the point of origin into the roof.

Obviously the old system of framing was not dropped immediately and indeed for some forms of buildings it never did totally disappear. Barns are among the structures which continued to be occasionally built with this system. Hand wrought frame houses are of course now being built again in an interesting revival which appears to have sprung from concerns for the environment and the "back to nature" movements in the 1970s and 1980s.

LOG STRUCTURES

In the United States, some of the early Swedish (1638) and German settlers (1710) built log structures occasionally in white oak but more usually in white pine or less commonly red pine. After this it was normal practice for many settlers from Europe to build a log house, and much less commonly settlers from England, Scotland, and Ireland either had a log house built for them or tried their own hand at building one.

In the nineteenth century there arose the strange and utterly false idea that all the early settlers built log structures as soon as they arrived in North America (Shurtleff, 1939)!

This curious idea seems to have been born in the

eighteenth century with the American revolution and with the creation of mystiques of mankind returning to nature. In the political dynamics of new nationhood, the log cabin came to symbolize the, home of a nineteenth century Adam repossessing the Garden of Eden (Rempel, 1980). In the symbol's greatest days it was thus the preferred birthplace of all politicians. It was an "American ideal" made true by great men like Abraham Lincoln having come from humble and respectable origins. "From log cabin to White House" was the dream which could come true for every American. For those who followed the mystique there was no difficulty in extending it to assume that all American forebears had been good, simple, honest folk and that by association they too must have been born or at least lived in log cabins. It took a lot of research by Shurtleff and historian Fiske Kimball among others to dispose of this ridiculous idea.

Depending on the national origins of their builders, log structures varied in the forms of their corner joints, the cross sections of the logs, and the ways in which door and window openings were handled. Interested readers are referred to an invaluable book covering a wealth of these European forms and variations (Phleps, 1982).

To this essentially European traditional basis can be added log structures which were evolved by the military and the fur trading companies in North America.

UNUSUAL TIMBER STRUCTURES

Two other less common historic forms of timber structure may be of interest. These are stackwall or "plank-on plank" and cordwood construction.

In the former case the structural walls are built of a solid stack of planks which are usually about 6 in. wide, laid flat and arranged so that they overlap at the corners from alternate directions forming a kind of comb joint. Alternate planks were sometimes staggered a little under an inch to provide keys for stucco on the outside and plaster on the inside of the building. In cordwood construction which is also known as "log-butt" and "stovewood" construction, the structural walls are usually about 1 or 2 ft thick and are actually formed from a solid pile of short log-butts in the round laid in lime mortar. From the outside the wall appears as a mass of round log ends. Corners might be made with a heavy timber crib, with long and short quoinwork in blocks of squared timber like a stone masonry corner or with a vertical 8-in.-square post at the corner.

FURTHER READING

For frame structures depending on the national/regional background, *Bulletin of the Association for Preservation Technology*, various issues.

Bicknell, A.J. and Comstock, W.T. *Victorian Architecture.*

Stack plank construction, Ontario, ca. 1840.

New York, 1873. Facsimile edition by American Life Foundation, Watkins Glen, N.Y., 1975.

Cummings, Abbott Lowell. *The Framed Houses of Massachusetts Bay, 1625–1725*. Cambridge, MA: The Belknap Press of Harvard University Press, 1979.

Hewett, C.A. *English Historic Carpentry*. City: Phillimore, 1980.

Sloan, Samuel. *The Model Architect*. Philadelphia: ES Jones, 1852. Modern facsimile edition by Da Capo Press Inc., New York, 1975.

THE NATURE OF WOOD

In any text of this nature space limitations prevent any detailed study of the physiology and chemistry of wood, but a brief summary is appropriate in this context.

Wood is a natural polymeric or macromolecular material composed of the following substances; cellulose, 40–50%, hemicellulose, 25–35%, lignin, 20–30%; and extractives, which can vary from 5–30%, depending on species, time of year, and other variables. Minerals such as silica, calcium, potassium, and phosphates may comprise 0.3–3.0% of the wood substance.

In tropical hardwoods, the lignin contents are frequently higher and the wood is correspondingly more rigid and less resilient. The timber industry considers woods as being either softwoods or hardwoods. Softwoods are derived from coniferous trees such as pines and firs. Hardwoods are derived from deciduous or broad leaved trees such as oak, maple, and walnut. This typology causes much confusion, because some hardwoods are extremely soft, the classic example being balsa wood (*Ochroma* spp.) which is a South American hardwood but is the lightest and softest wood in the world.

The structure of the wood is formed of cells of various sizes and shapes.

Hardwoods and softwoods have cells of distinctly different natures and arrangements or distributions which make it possible to identify the various species. The longitudinal cells which carry nutrients and water in softwoods are called tracheids, while in hardwoods, the large cells are called vessels and small ones fibres. Softwoods may also contain occasional longitudinal resin ducts. Both hardwoods and softwoods contain horizontal groups of cells which form rays radiating from the pith or heart of the tree out to the cambium or growth layer of cells beneath the bark. The ray cells are called parenchyma or parenchymal tissue and function as nutrient storage. Cell growth occurs in the cambium or cambial layer where new wood is added to the outside of the sapwood and new cells to the inner side of the phloem or inner bark layer. As the tree matures, cells on the inner side of the sapwood die and are slowly transformed in a number of ways, including the creation of extractives from nutrients stored in the parenchyma, color changes, and the pits or "valve-like"

Softwood microstructure.

connections between the cells close off. These changes result in the formation of heartwood which is less permeable because of the closed pits and more durable because of the decay resistance conferred by the extractives which include such natural fungicides as thujaplicin and other phenolic compounds.

In each growing season the tree adds first a layer of "earlywood" which tends to contain mostly cellulose, then second a layer of "latewood" which may contain more lignin.

Earlywood used to be known as springwood and latewood was called summerwood, while the two together were called an "annual ring." This system can be used for trees which grow in temperate climates but does not work for tropical trees which may have more than one combination of early and latewood rings per year. The old "annual ring," and "springwood" and "summerwood" terms therefore tend to have been dropped.

Readers wishing to read more about wood chemistry, physiology, pathology and the identification of species are recommended to refer to Panshin and De-Zeeuw (1970).

MOISTURE CONTENTS AND SHRINKAGE

When a tree is felled the wood has a moisture content averaging from 60 to 200% (based upon the oven-dry weight of the wood). Incense cedar sapwood has been measured at 219% and western red cedar sapwood at 249%. Longleaf pine heartwood has been measured at 31%. Water at this point is contained in the cell walls (bound water) and in the lumens or central spaces within the cells (free water). The free water may be lost without any dimensional changes taking place in the wood. When all the water from the lumens has gone, the wood is described as being at "fibre saturation point" which varies from about 24 to 32%, depending on species. As the moisture content is lowered still further for use in buildings or furniture, shrinkage occurs in the wood. Wood is an anisotropic material which means in this context that it does not shrink equally in all directions. Shrinkage tangential to the growth rings is largest; then about half as much as that radially and only negligibly in length. (Actual values vary from species to species but for white oak, radial shrinkage has been measured at 5.6% and tangential shrinkage at 10.5%).

Transverse and volumetric shrinkage for the various domestic species have been measured by methods described in ASTM Designation D143-83. Standard Methods of Testing Small Clear Specimens of Timber.

These differences in shrinkage rates mean that certain cross sections of timber are less dimensionally stable than others, the most stable being "quarter sawn" or "edge grain" sections where the growth rings are perpendicular to the long sides. The least stable sections are "flat sawn" or "tangentially sawn" where the long sides are tangential to the growth rings. The latter tend to cup with their outer edges curling outward. Wood in service constantly tends to adjust its moisture content to reach a balance with the ambient relative humidity. This balanced state at a certain ambient temperature is referred to as the equilibrium moisture content or EMC. Over a period of several hundred years, the actual total dimensional changes in response to EMC changes become slightly less.

For new construction, wood moisture contents are normally selected as follows: (these values are only approximate)

for rough exterior carpentry work	25%
for general joinery work	15%
for furniture, doors panelling	12%
for panelling and other work near heat sources or in centrally heated areas	down from 8%

In restoration and repair practice the existing moisture contents of the wood to be repaired may be even lower than 8%, particularly in the cold dry areas of Canada and the northern United States. Conservators usually prefer to store the wood which will be used for restoration and repair work in the building in such a way that the old and new woods come to the same or similar equilibrium moisture contents before the work is carried out.

WOOD DETERIORATION

Wood is a remarkably resilient material with great strength in relation to its density. Wood may be so light and soft that large blocks can be lifted by a child, as is the case with balsa wood. Wood may also be so hard and dense that it is difficult to cut even with a sharp chisel and will not float in water as is the case with lignum vitae. The latter species is so tough that it has been used in bearings for propellor shafts. The woods that were traditionally used in buildings are not normally as soft as balsa or as hard as lignum vitae but they could be as soft as eastern white cedar or as hard as white oak or black walnut.

If any of this wide range of wood types was used in buildings in such a way that they could become damp, or worse still remain damp for long periods, then they often deteriorated swiftly from a wide range of causes.

The presence of moisture in too large a quantity is usually the key to wood preservation problems.

Let us examine a list of the factors which can cause deterioration in wood "in service" in a building as part of its structure, its finishes, or its furniture. The factors may be grouped as follows.

PHYSICAL, CHEMICAL, AND MECHANICAL FACTORS

The following physical, chemical, and mechanical factors may be important in the deterioration of wood in heritage buildings:

- Growth-related defects in the wood itself.
- Problems related to the seasoning or drying processes.
- Problems related to the conversion process from the log to the dimensioned timber.
- Loss of strength due to high moisture content in the wood. Commencing at oven-dry weight static bending strength is reduced 2% for every 1% increase in moisture content; the modulus of rupture is reduced 4% for every 1% increase in moisture content; and compression strength parallel to the grain is reduced 6% for every 1% increase in moisture content.
- Problems related to the failure of the wood fibers under load or stresses induced by excessive or too rapid shrinkage; and shrinkage where the wood is restrained. Surface-, end-, and through-checking are typical results of this type of problem.
- Abrasion or wear from foot and vehicular traffic or work processes; wind-blown dusts, sands, gravels; cables and ropes swinging back and forth in the wind; water; ice abrasion; animals chewing on the wood or tearing at it with their claws; and repeated wear from hardware.
- Photodegradation of the wood surface caused by exposure to sunlight and ultraviolet radiation. Ultraviolet radiation can damage the surface layers of the wood to a depth of a few micrometers at a time. Lignin is made soluble in water and can thus be leached out, leaving loosened fibers and the silver-gray appearance familiar from driftwood on sunny beaches. The ultraviolet radiation will pass through many clear finishes such as polyurethane lacquers and will cause surface degradation under the lacquer, leading to a adhesion failure of the

Mold growth under polyurethane lacquer.

coating. Such failures are often evident because of the growth of molds in the tiny "greenhouse" environment formed between the wood and the clear coating.

- Thermal degradation of the wood caused by exposure to elevated temperatures for prolonged periods. At temperatures ranging from 131 to 149°F (55 to 65°C) depolymerization of the cellulose and hemicellulose commences. Cellulose burns at 451°F (233°C). At about 480°F (250°C) charring occurs in the absence of air, the cell walls volatilize, and the wood burns in the presence of air. Without reaching the temperature necessary for combustion, thermal degradation can still cause severe strength losses. Douglas fir tested at 215°F (102°C) for 335 days had its modulus of resistance reduced by 45% and the modulus of elasticity by 17%. The

Timber charred by contact with an electric light bulb, Lower Fort Garry, Manitoba.

same results were observed after testing the wood at 320°F (160°C) for seven days. Thus it can be seen that the degradation is a function of both time and temperature.

• Damage caused by repeated cycles of expansion related to hydration and dehydration of crystals of water-soluble salts deposited in the wood.

• Chemical degradation or hydrolysis caused by concentrated acids or alkalis.

• Problems related to inadequacies in original struc-

Brittle fracture of floor beam partly caused by thermal degradation, Ukrainian log house, Alberta.

Salt damage, two examples from salt fish warehouses.

tural design, or caused by the failure of original structural elements.

- Problems related to the failure of original weathering details.
- Problems related to structural inadequacies caused by later alterations to original designs involving the removal of elements or parts of elements. Such alterations may be intentional or may occur as a result of accidents such as vehicle impacts.
- Problems related to structural inadequacies caused by changes in loading and additions to the original structure.

BIODETERIORATION

This is a huge group with causes ranging from bacteria at the smallest end of the scale up to large mammals and even trees.

BACTERIA

Certain bacteria may thrive in wood in anaerobic conditions under water. They attack the pit membranes of pits between the wood cells and by destroying them can open up the cell structure to water penetration, thus causing wood to become waterlogged and liable to further degradation.

Normally the bacteria do not cause major degrada-tion of the wood but a number of cases have been noted where timber piles in freshwater lakes in North America have been severely damaged by bacteria after decades of immersion.

Typical species of bacteria which have been isolated in pine and tamarack piling in the Milwaukee River include 10 different species of *Pseudomonas*, five of *Bacillus*, nine of *Clostridium*, and three of *Alcaligenes*. Of these, the commonest by far was *Pseudomonas flourescens* Migula.

FUNGI

Fungi, molds, and sapstains or "bluestains," are all related and cause varying degrees of decay. The following conditions must exist for a fungal attack to take place:

1. A source of infestation. The air is full of spores which require certain conditions to germinate. Some buildings contain millions of spores and even fungal hyphae remaining in masonry from previous outbreaks.
2. A suitable food supply—nontoxic wood, cellulose, hemicellulose, lignin, and stored nutrients in parenchymal tissue.
3. Sufficient moisture to permit spores to germinate and then for the fungus to develop. The wood rotting basidiomycete fungi require wood mois-

Fruiting body and spores in a humid poorly ventilated basement.

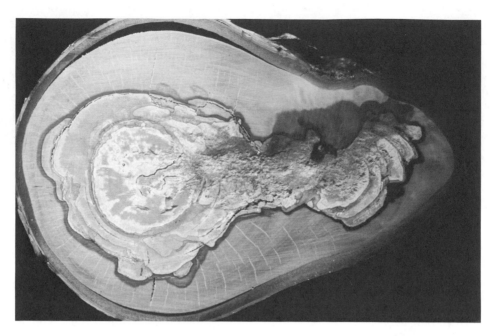

White rot damage in birch caused by fungus *Fomes igniarius*.

ture contents to be 35–50% for them to thrive. If the moisture content is below fiber saturation point, that is, about 25%, growth will be minimal.

4. A source of air. In other words, for the fungi to thrive the wood must be wet but cannot be submerged in water.

5. The temperature must be suitable for fungal growth, that is, the optimum for most fungi is 77–90°F (25–32°C). At freezing point the fungus lies almost dormant and at above 150°F (65°C), the fungus is killed. Obviously the maintenance of such a high temperature in wood in a building for a period long enough to actually kill all fungi would be impractical. Indeed one might risk thermal degradation of the wood.

Brown rot showing typical cubical deterioration of deteriorated wood.

TYPES OF FUNGI

The fungi which attack wood in service can be divided into four groups, primarily by the appearance of the wood during the attack.

White Rots

The species of this group of fungi leave the wood as a whitish-cream colored mass of stringy and punky useless fiber remains. The zone under attack also contains and is bordered by fine dark brown lines. Incipient attack consists of small lens-shaped pockets which gradually extend to the entire body of the timber. The wood usually retains its dimensions until it collapses. White rots prefer hardwoods but I have seen them attacking softwoods, in painted pine fence rails, for example. Species include: *Coriolus versicolor* (L. ex Fr.) Quel., see also *Trametes versicolor* (L: Fr.); *Fomes igniarius*

Soft rot damage; note little or no color change.

(L. ex Fr.) Gill, also known as *Phellinus igniarius* (L. ex Fr.) Quel.; *Phanerochaete chrysosporium* Burds.

Brown Rots

These are also known as brown cubical rots because the wood under attack typically breaks up into small cubes or brick-shaped, brown colored crumbling wood. Brown rots prefer softwoods but do attack hardwoods. Brown rot fungi consume the cellulose and hemicellulose, leaving only the brown crumbling lignin components of the cells, and thus giving the attacked wood its distinctive color. Species include: *Serpula lacrymans* (Schum. ex Fr.) SF Gray, which used to be known as *Merulius lacrymans* [or *lacrimans*] (Wulf ex Fr.) Fr. This fungus is apparently not commonly reported in the United States but is more common in Canada. This may not be too significant because many outbreaks are not reported or examined by mycologists. *Gloeophyllum trabeum* (Pers. ex Fr.) Murrill, used to be known as *Lenzites trabea* (Fr.); *Poria placenta* (Fr.) used to be known as *Poria monticola* Murr., see also *Postia placenta* (Fr.); M. Lars and Lomb; *Poria vaillantii* (DC. ex Fr.) Cooke; *Poria vaporaria* (Pers.). Some of the brown rot fungi such as *Serpula lacrymans* (Wulf ex Fr.) Fr. are also known as dry rots or "true dry rots."

These terms have caused a great deal of confusion but they are relevant in the building conservation context. The dry rot fungi are capable of penetrating brick and stone masonry. They can also produce water by their own metabolic processes and can then transport this water to the wood by means of specialized tissues termed rhizomorphs. In this way, they can help to maintain the necessary moisture contents for attacks to be sustained. Thus to a certain degree "dry" wood is not necessarily safe from these fungi. They are definitely the most difficult to eradicate, particularly because of the survival of fungal strands or hyphae in adjacent masonry even after affected wood has been removed.

Soft Rots

These species are sometimes referred to as microfungi because they move through and attack the wood by way of the cell walls rather than by way of the larger lumens or voids in the middle of the cells. Soft rot fungi consume the cellulose of the S2 or middle layer of the cell wall, leaving the rest of the wall to collapse. Lignin is occasionally also degraded but much more slowly. Only very wet wood is attacked and the surface is checked into small squares or cubes. There is a slight brownish or grayish discoloration of the attacked wood which is softened and suffers extreme strength losses.

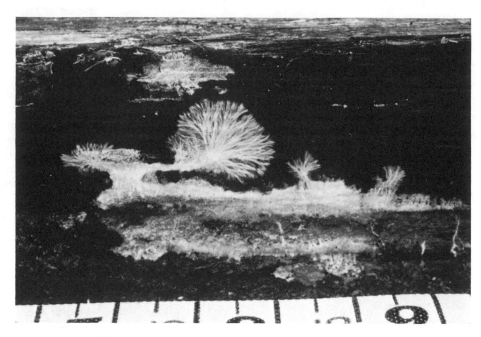

Cellar rot damage; note blackened appearance of wood.

External surfaces appear to be attacked first. Species include *Chaetomium globosum* (Kunze), *Paecilomyces* spp., and *Allescheria terrestris* (Apinis).

Cellar Rot, Wet Rot, or Black Rot

Cellar rot will only grow in extremely damp conditions with 40–50% wood moisture content and cannot extend beyond these areas as the dry rots can. The attacked wood has a very dark brown or black appearance and cracks predominantly along the grain. The wood has been described as "looking burned." Fungi of this species are those most commonly found in old wooden boats and ships. Both hardwoods and softwoods are attacked. A typical species is *Coniophora cerebella* (Pers.) Duby, or cellar fungus, now known as *Coniophora puteana* (Schum. ex Fr.) Karst.

MOLDS

Molds are in fact types of fungi which are visible as colored powdery deposits on the surface of wood under attack. Most of these represent only a superficial growth on the surface which can be removed by brushing, shallow planing or sanding. Orange pink stains can be caused by molds of the *Penicillium* spp.; purplish stains by the *Fusarium* spp.

Perhaps the most important feature of the presence of molds lies in the fact that they signal that the moisture content of the wood is high and that therefore an attack by more damaging fungal species could occur.

SAPSTAINS

More deep seated stains may affect the whole of the sapwood of softwoods. This group are known as sapstains or "bluestains" from the predominant color of the affected wood. The *Ceratocystis* spp. are typical examples of this type which discolor softwoods. Sapstain has no significant effect on the main strength characteristics of the wood but may increase permeability and slightly reduce toughness.

INSECTS

Wood in service in North America may be attacked by a wide range of insect species at various points in their life cycles. The species include beetles; carpenter ants; termites; woodwasps; and carpenter bees.

Insects have their own class within the scientific classification system of all living organisms. Using the common furniture beetle as an example, the system is as follows:

Kingdom	Animalia
Phylum	Arthropoda
Class	Insecta

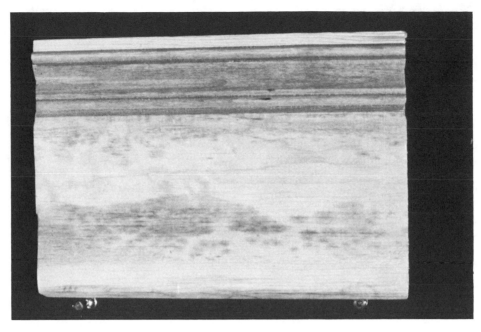

Molds on section of baseboard.

Order   Coleoptera
Family   Anobiidae
Genus   *Anobium*
Species   *Anobium punctatum* (DeG.)

The third part of the species name is the name of the scientist who first described the species in print. In practice, this is often shortened, for example, "DeG."

standing for De Geer. If the name appears in parentheses, this means that this was not the first or original genus in which this insect was described.

The life cycle consists of four main stages which are as follows:

- The egg stage; the female beetle lays the eggs on the surface of the wood. The eggs are laid either

Blue sapstain in pine log end.

singly or in masses and they hatch after a period of several days.

- The larva or larval stage; the egg hatches into a larva. (Plural larvae.) As the larva grows bigger it sheds its skin or molts and a larger larva emerges. Each growth or molt stage is referred to as an instar. There are usually at least three instar stages.
- The pupa; the last instar stage molts and changes into a pupa. This is called the "resting stage." The pupa looks like a pale mummified adult beetle.
- The adult; the pupa molts and a young adult emerges which is not fully hardened or colored. This stage lasts only a few hours and is called teneral. The exoskeleton hardens and becomes fully colored and the result is a fully grown adult.

The actual insects responsible for the damage often remain invisible, or are not seen by the casual observer. In the absence of the actual culprits the conservator uses the following evidence to commence the identification process:

- The form of the frass or wood boredust and excreta which may be found in the galleries or tunnels.
- The diameter and form of the exit holes or flight holes bored by the young adult insects as they emerge onto the surface of the wood. Diameters may vary from about $\frac{1}{16}$ up to $\frac{3}{4}$ in. The holes may be circular or elliptical.
- The form of the galleries or tunnels.
- The presence or absence of frass in the galleries or tunnels.

The most serious damage to timber is usually caused by species of insects in the three orders Coleoptera (beetles), the Isoptera (termites), and the Hymenoptera (ants and bees).

Preservationists and pest control specialists distinguish between insect species which attack wood in service, that is, wood in a building or bridge, and so on; and insects which "do not reinfest," that is, do not attack wood in a building again and again until it is destroyed.

Coleoptera or Beetles

Within the order of Coleoptera there are four families which are primarily responsible for damage to wood in older buildings. The Anobiidae family includes the species *Annobium punctatum* (DeG.) or the common furniture beetle and *Xestobium rufovillosum* (DeG.) or

Insect damage in barn post; note small piles of frass. The diagonal batten is a different species of wood and is not attacked.

I Actual size

Figure 2. Furniture Beetle, *Anobium Punctatum*.

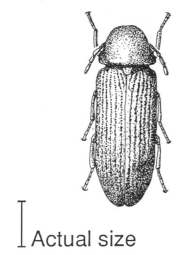

Actual size

Figure 3. Eastern Death-watch Beetle.

Actual size

Figure 5. Drugstore Beetle, *Stegobium Paniceum.*

the death watch beetle. The latter was apparently not indigenous to North America but was introduced most probably from the United Kingdom late in the nineteenth century or early in the twentieth. Also included in this family are *Ernobius mollis* (L.) and *Stegobium paniceum* (L.) or the drugstore beetle. The latter has been described as "eating anything but cast-iron." Although this may sound like an exaggeration, this beetle is recorded as having eaten through tin-foil and lead sheet. It has also been known to bore a straight hole through a whole shelf-load of books and through the wooden shelves as well! *Hadrobregmus gibbicollis* (LeC.), another Anobiid, is very active in Douglas fir in British Columbia where it has been found in both house and bridge timbers. *Coelostethus quadrulus* (LeC.) is also found in Douglas fir and has reduced beams to a fine powder. *Ptilinus pectinicornis* (L.) and *Ptilinus ruficornis* Say. are distinctive Anobiids with

large "pectinate" (branched or "antler-like") antennae. The larvae attack hardwoods and may damage interior woodwork or structural timbers. The *Trichodesma* spp., of which there are seven examples in North America, are distinguished by a dense covering of hair and tufts of bristles. *Trichodesma gibbosa* (Say) has been noted as attacking joists and studs in the east of the United States.

The Lyctidae or true powder post beetles, include *Lyctus brunneus* (Steph.), the brown powder post beetle, and *Lyctus plannicolis* LeC. or the southern lyctus beetle. *Lyctus linearis* (Goeze), the European lyctus, is their European counterpart. A family of beetles producing similar damage are the powder post borers or Bostrichidae which include Stout's bostrichid, a native of California and Oregon, *Polycaon stoutii* LeC. This beetle has been noted emerging through a polished veneered table top after having eaten its way through

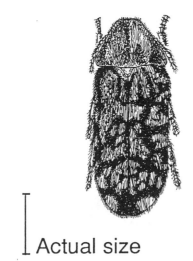

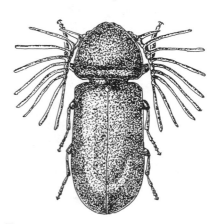

Actual size

Figure 4. Death-watch Beetle, *Xestoblum Rufovillosum.*

Actual size

Figure 6. Death-watch Beetle, *Ptilinus Ruficornis.*

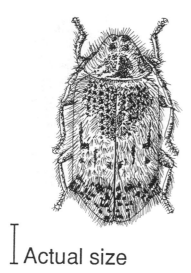

I Actual size

Figure 7. Death-watch Beetle, *Trichodesma Gibbosa*.

the native fruitwoods underneath. The Lyctidae prefer hardwoods and are a special pest in maple flooring. They have been found in magnolia, sweetgum, black gum, birch, persimmon, locust, elm, poplar, sycamore, and cherry, but they prefer oak, ash, hickory, maple, walnut, and bamboo.

The Cerambycidae or longhorned beetles, so named for their very long antennae, include the old house borer, *Hylotrupes bajulus* (L.), which is a common scourge of softwoods in Europe and North America. The subfamily Cerambycinae include a number of sawyer beetles such as *Monochamus titillator* (Fab.), the southern pine sawyer beetle, and *Tetropium cinnamopterum* Kirby, the eastern larch borer. Although these latter species usually attack dead or felled lumber, they will also attack telephone poles, log struc-

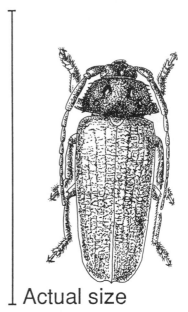

I Actual size

Figure 9. Long-horned Beetles: Ponderous borer, *Ergates Spiculatus*.

tures, bridges, and so on. The largest beetle attacking wood in North America, the ponderous beetle, *Ergates spiculatus* LeC. (about $2\frac{3}{8}$ in. or 60 mm long) belongs to the subfamily Prioninae or tooth-necked long horns. It feeds on Douglas fir and pines and inhabits all of the western United States. Beetle collectors are wary of the long horns because they bite. The wharf borer (*Nacerdes melanura*) also belongs in this group. As the popular name suggests, this beetle prefers moist marine environments and is found particularly in coastal buildings in both Canada and the United States. The adult beetle is 0.8–1.25 cm long and will infest moist and preferably rotting timber. The beetle is not a major economic problem because it only attacks wood

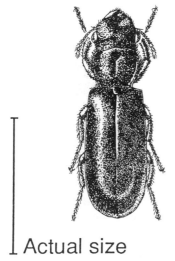

I Actual size

Figure 8. Branch and twig borers: Stout's Bostrichid, *Polycaon Stoutii*.

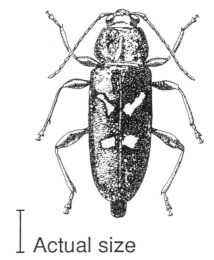

I Actual size

Figure 10. Old House Borer, *Hylotrupes Bajulus* (L.).

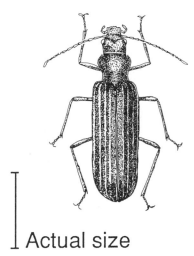

Actual size

Figure 11. False Blister Beetles: Wharf Borer, *Nacerdes Melanura* (L).

Actual size

Figure 13. Powder Post Beetles: Southern Lyctus Beetle, L. *Planicollis.*

which is already rotting. The adult beetles will occasionally emerge in very large numbers, tend to move to light, and will crawl all over persons and objects causing considerable annoyance.

Ambrosia beetles and pinhole borers of the Platypodidae family attack recently felled hardwoods and softwoods. Their damage is frequently seen in wood in buildings where it causes a lot of unnecessary anguish. The various species do not reinfest. The boreholes and emergence holes are distinctive and are small, 0.5–3.0 mm in diameter, and are stained black by a tiny fungus with which the larvae live in a symbiotic relationship.

The Buprestidae, or metallic borers, such as *Buprestis aurulenta* L. are also known as flat headed borers from the anvil-shaped heads of the larvae. These very beautiful iridescent bronze and golden brass colored beetles may have very long life cycles and some larvae are recorded as continuing mining operations 15–20 years after the eggs were first laid on dead or

dying wood! Thus although the Buprestids normally attack trees, logs, and sawn timber while the wood is green, they may emerge long after the wood has been used in a building. At least in theory this species does not reinfest. Occasionally, however, cases are reported of Buprestids emerging from infested firewood and attacking house timbers. Hardwoods and softwoods are attacked as are heartwood and sapwood.

Weevils of the Curculionidae family such as *Hexarthrum ulkeyi* are found in wood which is already under attack by fungi and thus are not a major economic pest. Their emergence holes are very small, 0.5–2.0 mm in diameter, and may be slightly oval with ragged edges. Weevils are easily recognized by the snout-like projection on their heads—hence their popular name "snouted beetles".

Termites, the Isoptera

There are three principal types of termite which attack wood in service in North America. The subterranean

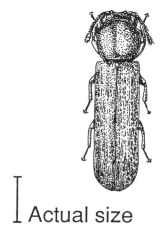

Actual size

Figure 12. Powder Post Beetles: *Lyctur Brunneus.*

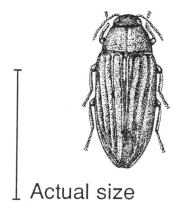

Actual size

Figure 14. Metallic Wood Boring Beetles: *Buprestis Aurulenta.*

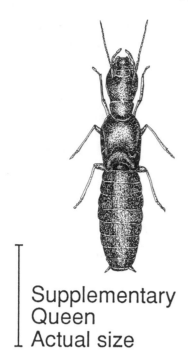

Supplementary
Queen
Actual size

Figure 15. Eastern Subterranean Termite, *Reticulitermes Flavipes* (Kollar).

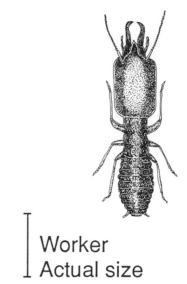

Worker
Actual size

Figure 17. Eastern Subterranean Termite, *Reticulitermes Flavipes* (Kollar).

termite *Reticulitermes flavipes* (Kollar) is probably the most destructive and widely distributed species in North America. This termite extends into Canada and attacks are well established in southern British Columbia and southern Ontario including parts of Toronto. Apart from Alaska most probably no states in the United States are totally without attacks. Attacks most often occur in moist or wet wood close to or in contact with the ground. Both hardwoods and softwoods are

attacked. Varieties of subterranean termites such as *Coptotermes formosanus* S. have been reported attacking wood and books in Hawaii, and *C. formosanus* has also been accidentally introduced into Florida. Damp wood termites of the *Zootermopsis* spp. attack only wet or decayed wood which is usually in such bad condition that their destructive role is almost redundant. These species are known in southern British Columbia, Washington and Oregon particularly.

The dry wood termite, *Kalotermes* spp., for example, *Cryptotermes brevis* W., does not attack in the colder northern latitudes but is common in California, southern Florida, and Hawaii. Its attacks may readily be identified by the tiny hard brown fecal pellets which are left in large numbers in the galleries. These pellets closely resemble poppy seeds and have six slight indentations in their sides and measure 0.75×0.5 mm.

Hymenoptera: Ants, Bees, and Wasps Carpenter Ants, Formicidae

Two principal species of carpenter ants are active in North America even into sub-Arctic areas and will completely destroy large parts of timbers in buildings. The two principal species are *Camponotus pennsylvanicus* De Geer and *Camponotus ferrugineous*. The carpenter ants do not eat the wood but excavate large chambers for their colonies in timbers while they feed elsewhere. The galleries have a cleanly "sandblasted" appearance and no frass remains in them. All the frass is ejected and forms large piles of coarse "sawdust" beneath the wood under attack. After a colony has

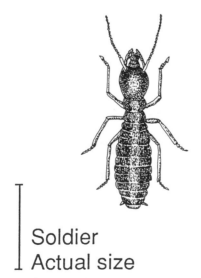

Soldier
Actual size

Figure 16. Eastern Subterranean Termite, *Reticulitermes Flavipes* (Kollar).

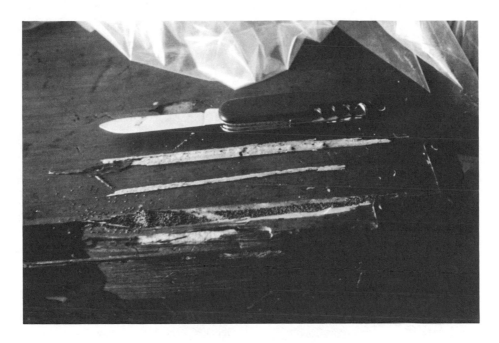

Fecal pellets and the damage of the dry wood termite in an imported antique Japanese chest.

been in existence for about two years winged reproductive forms may be observed.

These shed their wings after mating and the discarded wings may be found all around the vicinity of a colony. These large shiny black ants are about $\frac{1}{2}$ in.

long and are often seen walking around foraging for food.

Bees, Xylocopa spp. Carpenter bees such as *Xylocopa virginica* Drury attack wood which is soft and easy to cut, such as redwood, cedar, and white pine. Attacks typically consist of large cleanly cut holes over 10 mm in diameter in exterior timbers in well lit areas

Queen
Actual size

Figure 18. Carpenter Ant, *Camponotus Pennsylvanicus* (De Geer), *Camponotus Ferrugineus* (Fab.).

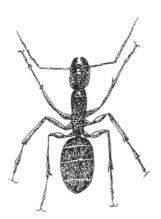

Small Worker
Actual size

Figure 19. Carpenter Ant, *Camponotus Pennsylvanicus* (De Geer), *Camponotus Ferrugineus* (Fab.).

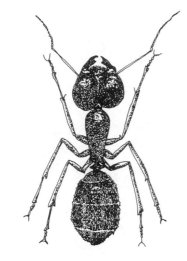

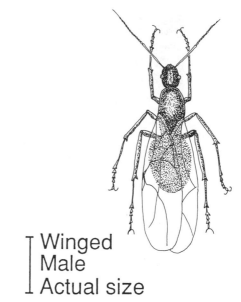

I Winged Male Actual size

Figure 22. Carpenter Ant, *Camponotus Pennsylvanicus* (De Geer), *Camponotus Ferrugineus* (Fab.).

I Large Worker or "Soldier" Actual size

Figure 20. Carpenter Ant, *Camponotus Pennsylvanicus* (De Geer), *Camponotus Ferrugineus* (Fab.).

such as barge boards and fascias. Behind the large holes, lie 150–200 mm long horizontal galleries, about 25 mm below the surface.

***Wasps, the* Siricidae.** Woodwasps of the *Siricidae spp.* usually only attack dead or dying trees but have

been known to attack logwork or rusticwork. Both types of course still retain their bark and the wasps presumably are confused into believing that these are in fact dead or dying trees. The *Siricidae* are also known as "horntails" from the very distinctive long spines which project from the ends of their abdomens.

MARINE BORERS

Marine borers as the name implies only attack wood in marine or saline waters. The marine borers mainly belong to two phyla. The molluscs, primarily Teredo borers or *Bankia* spp. are commonly called "shipworms." The crustaceans, principally Limnoria and Sphaeroma are commonly known as "gribble." Both can reduce wood from structural timbers to useless junk in a matter of months. Another group of wood boring molluscs are the Pholads which clearly resemble clams. The Pholads, such as the Martesia and Xylophaga, are capable of doing great damage to timbers by repeated attacks, boring holes approximately 1 in. in diameter. Their activities in North American waters appear to be mainly limited to the Gulf of Mexico.

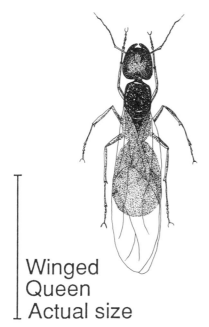

Winged Queen Actual size

Figure 21. Carpenter Ant, *Camponotus Pennsylvanicus* (De Geer), *Camponotus Ferrugineus* (Fab.).

PLANTS

Plants can damage wood in a number of ways including: by discoloration; by retaining moisture or preventing drying of the wood; by abrasion, for example, as

Teredo borer damage.

branches are blown back and forth by the wind; and by prying and splitting, for example, when seeds germinate in cracks in old timbers and then the growing tree stem splits the surrounding timber.

The following list is arranged in order of increasing size and severity:

- Algae; a sign of high humidity and moisture content.
- Lichens; as algae and moisture retaining.
- Mosses; as lichens.
- Small plants; as lichens and mosses.

Limnoria damage.

- Bushes and shrubs; moisture retaining and mechanical damage.
- Trees; moisture retaining and mechanical damage.

ANIMALS

Animals damage wood in the following ways:

- Birds; woodpeckers; primarily boring into wood searching for insect larvae. Hollow structures may "fool" woodpeckers and cause them to attack wood which does not contain insects.
- Rodents and small mammals; damage is usually caused by chewing to gain access to building interiors for food or nesting.

Door damaged by the claws of a very large dog.

Woodpecker damage.

- Large mammals; damage is usually caused by cribbing or biting typical of horses, or licking by cows.

THE TIMBER DEFECTS SURVEY

The above long list of defects or problems may occur singly but more usually will occur in groups since many of them share a common cause—water. On the basis of experience, building conservation specialists commonly develop their own survey techniques. No matter which checklist is used, or in what order a survey is carried out, all defects surveys must be thorough and full. Symptoms and signs must be carefully searched out and recognized for what they are. Causes and defects must then also be recognized and traced from the symptoms. Defect occurrences usually follow patterns and there are critical locations which should always be checked carefully.

The following checklist may be helpful, but not definitive. Readers are encouraged to develop their own with specific approaches and details to suit the structures and materials with which they deal.

1. Carefully examine every timber which is embedded in a masonry wall, for example, beam ends, floor joist ends and bond timbers. Do not trust apparently hard outer surfaces. Probe and test for moisture contents which would favor decay and insect attacks. Fungal decay will occur if the wood is at or above fiber saturation point which is around 25–30%, depending on species. Insect attacks also typically occur at high moisture contents but in a large number of cases I have found that a 13% moisture content often appears to be a critical starting point.

2. Examine timber lintels and places where timber lintels may occur. They can bend and cause local cracks to open in the adjacent structure. If water is then admitted via the cracks the lintel is severely weakened by the presence of the moisture and will bend even more.

3. Examine the backs of door linings and the backs of sash window casings. Decay and insect attacks often occur in hidden favorable environments in such locations.

4. Carefully examine areas which could be affected by water entering through cracks which exist in the external walls.

5. Examine all timbers near the ground which could be affected by rising damp or splashes from adjacent paving or other surfaces.

6. Examine all timbers in contact with the ground, for example, ground plates, sill plates, door sills, floor joists and beams, floor boards, and column bases.

7. Examine all timbers which may be affected by leaks in the roof, particularly under valleys and just above the eaves where ice-dams may occur. Watch for water stains and traces of mould or fungal attacks, and so on, on the inside of the roof.

8. Look carefully in all locations where water can lodge on ledges and in cracks, for example, on horizontal surfaces and in horizontal checks and splits in exposed timbers.

9. Check any places where sapwood may have been used, for example, laths, battens, floor and roof boarding, and sheathing. Many wood-de-

Timber lintel only begins bending under load when it is wet, Ohio.

stroying insects prefer to attack sapwood. The sapwood may also have a higher moisture content and lack the fungitoxic extractives present in heartwood thus making it also subject to attack by fungi.

10. Look into all joints and crevices and on rough timber surfaces; these are favored spots for female beetles to deposit their eggs.

11. Examine all exposed timbers which can suffer from abrasion, for example, door sills, doors, frames, corner posts. Any locations where there may be a lot of pedestrian or vehicle traffic are potential trouble spots.

12. Examine all fixed furniture, for example, lined cupboards and panelling which may be in con-

Upper and lower sides of boarding from a floor with an unventilated crawspace.

tact with damp floor or walls; especial care must be taken to survey this type of woodwork in basements.

13. Look for signs of unventilated spaces beneath wooden floors at ground level, for example, blocked vents and earth piled against external walls to and above ground floor level.

14. Check infill panels in half-timbered or framed structures; and horizontal filler logs between vertical timbers in Red River frame or Hudson's Bay frame structures. Infill panels will often crack away from the main structure because of differential expansion and other movements. The cracks will admit water.

15. Look for open joints in timber structures but do not wedge them shut or fill the gaps with inelastic materials. The gaps may well close again with changes in humidity and serious damage

may occur if the wood is prevented from attaining its original dimensions, for example, joints may be strained, mortice and tenon joints smashed, or pegs or pins snapped. Use elastic gap sealants for temporary repairs but remember they do not last for ever.

16. Check the performance of any rubber, plastic, or other forms of gap sealants. They may have failed and water may again be entering the structure.

17. Watch for metals in contact with timbers such as oak in the presence of moisture. Oak and some other timbers are acidic and in the presence of moisture will cause corrosion in certain metals, for example, tannic acid from oak attacks lead. Other wood acids may attack aluminum and zinc.

18. Look for water stains and signs of water entering a building especially anywhere near roofing, rainwater pipes, downspouts and gutters, flashings, copings, parapets, chimneys, dormers, and any other place where the roof is penetrated by or abuts some other architectural features.

19. Carefully examine junctions between different structures, for example, between house and summer kitchen; house and porch; church tower and nave; and original building and later addition. Different foundations may lead to differential movement and the development of cracking which will then admit water or overstress structural timbers.

20. Check any woodwork which may be exposed to high temperatures and hence thermal degradation, for example, next to flues and radiators, and under sheet metal roofing.

21. Check all glued woodwork to see if the adhesive is sound or failing.

22. Check all hollow columns and posts to establish whether the interior is properly ventilated and that no condensation is forming inside. The existence of vents is not proof of ventilation! Vents are often blocked by paint, insects, or other debris.

23. Check all exterior miter joints. Such joints are subject to opening and closing as tangential and radial shrinkage and expansion occur. The miter joints will then be prone to leak.

REPAIR AND RESTORATION

The selection of repair, conservation, and restoration techniques and materials must always be dependant upon the nature and extent of the deterioration of the original wood or the structural system. There are a number of golden rules and essential principles to follow when doing any such work:

1. **Golden Rule**: First remove the source(s) of the trouble! Reseal the leaking roof, gutter, eavestrough, or ventilate and drain the wet basement. Remove causes of overloading.

2. Retain as much original work as is practically possible and disturb the original work as little as is practically possible.

3. Repair in such a manner that the original aesthetic effect is not impaired. Do not make labored reproductions of the old. The U.S. furniture conservator Walter Angst (1980) of the Smithsonian Institution's Conservation Analytical Laboratory invented the additional term and principle—"never improvorst" an object (improvorsting = "improving" for the worse) that is, never repaint, recarve, rechase, remodel, reengrave, and so forth, an object. There is a sharp distinction between a bona-fide restoration and "improvorsting" an artifact.

4. When repairing roofs and floors, pay special attention to the effects of your work on ceilings beneath, especially plaster ones.

5. Do not alter the balance of stresses—avoid overloading other parts of the structure when repairing.

6. Approach the straightening of deformed structures with great care. It is too easy to snap, shear, or deform joints, tenons, dowels, pegs, and so on without knowing. Later troubles can easily be caused in this way. Securing or stabilizing may be all that is required.

7. Make sure that the timbers which you are leaving exposed were meant to be exposed. Many subsequent problems have been caused by the stripping of exterior boards, stucco, and paint from timbers. Often the stripping is done in the mistaken belief that this was how "the original was supposed to be seen."

WOOD RESTORATION AND CONSERVATION

Wood in older buildings can be conserved for two purposes and it is essential to define which is required. The first and most common purpose is to enable the wood to continue to function as a load-bearing structural member in the building or in furniture.

The second and less common purpose is to simply

enable the wooden object to carry its own weight, possibly with some assistance from supports. The latter is normally only found to be a problem of museum objects which will remain in a protected environment such as a showcase.

The various restoration and conservation techniques may be grouped under partial or complete replacement, mechanical reinforcement, consolidation by impregnation, and reinforcement and consolidation.

PARTIAL OR COMPLETE REPLACEMENT

If old timbers are very badly deteriorated, they can be totally replaced or, if some parts are still sound enough these may be retained and patches or "Dutchmen" inserted. The guiding principle should be to retain as much original material as possible. Such repairs are usually referred to as "replacements in kind." This term is often misused or not understood in all its implications. To replace "in kind" should mean that new and old wood should be accurately matched according to all the following criteria:

1. Species.
2. Quality; first growth or second growth.
3. Cut; quarter sawn or flat sawn or mixed.
4. Color.
5. Grain direction and figure or pattern.
6. Tool marks.
7. Finish.

Where old wood is being partly replaced the new wood is then carefully inset into the old where the unsound wood has been neatly chiselled away and usually undercut. Synthetic resin adhesives are frequently used to secure the new piece in place.

MECHANICAL REINFORCEMENT

The wood may be reinforced with dowels or pegs of wood, metal, or glass fiber reinforced plastic. Clamps or wedges such as "butterfly clamps" may be inset, for example, across checks or splits, but great care must be taken not to restrain wood to such a degree that it is not free to shrink when it loses moisture. If this occurs, the wood will tear itself apart.

Structural timbers can be splinted with new timbers, plywood, structural steel, or plastic, connected by gluing, screwing, or bolting. Failed or weak connections can be improved or replaced by special brackets, angle irons, fishplates, stirrups, and hangers. Failed tenons can be replaced by splicing-in complete new tenons. The addition of metal shear rings and timber connectors can be used to improve shear resistance at pinned or bolted joints.

Missing areas of wood can be "filled" with gap-

Spliced-on beam ends, Lower Fort Garry, Manitoba.

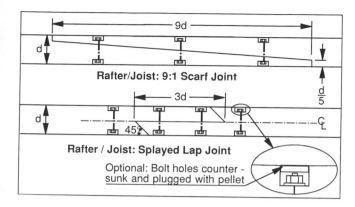

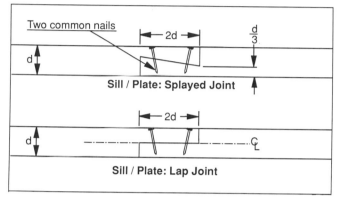

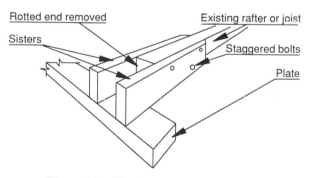

Figure 23. Wood splice joints.

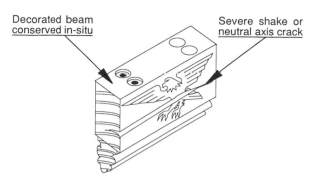

Figure 25a. Timber: structural repairs.

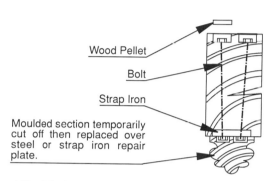

Figure 25b. Timber: structural repairs, section through decorated beam.

Figure 24a. Wood splice joints: sisters.

Note:

Treat all surfaces and flood bolt holes with wood preservative before assembly.

Mating surfaces should be coated with high strength waterproof adhesive or epoxy having good gap filling qualities, however; a proper close fitting joint is essential for mechanical strength.

Use galvanized bolts and flat washers.

Optional: countersink bolts and plug holes.

Any sill or plate joint must be supported by foundation or stud respectively, at joint.

Figure 24b. Wood splice joints: general notes.

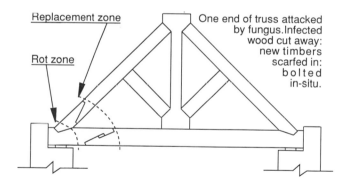

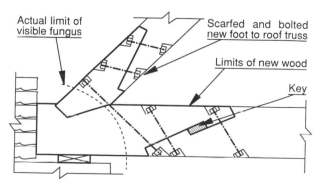

Figure 26. Timber: structural repairs.

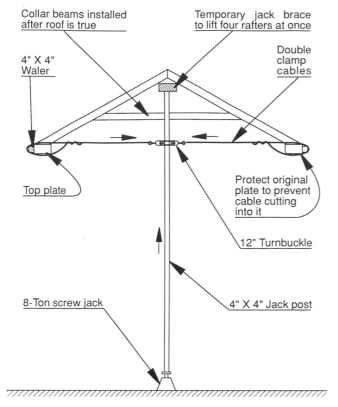

Figure 27. Turnbuckle and screw jack remove sag from roof.

fillers or ''plastic'' repairs consisting of synthetic resins and wood powder or sawdust or other fillers. Such fillers may be commercially manufactured or may be custom made for the job. An interesting patching or filler compound formulation discussed by Morgan Phillips involves the use of 100 parts by weight epoxy resin (Dow DER 331); 96 parts by weight polysulfide polymer (Thiokol LP-3); 12 parts by weight fumed silica (Cabot Corporation Cabosil) and 36 parts by weight phenolic resin microballoons (Union Carbide). The combined fillers weigh 24% of the total weight of the resin/polymer combination. The resulting mix is semiflexible and can be carved, sanded, and planed. Caution is needed; some fillers shrink or can be hard to work. Others may break down or melt at normal temperatures, for example, in hot sunshine.

CONSOLIDATION BY IMPREGNATION

Where old wood has become powdery or friable because of insect or fungal attacks, thermal degradation or burning, for example, the remaining materials can be bonded together again by impregnating the wood with a low viscosity synthetic resin or molten wax.

The synthetic resins may also be used with fillers to bulk them where gaps also exist. The resins can be introduced *in situ* via drilled holes using large hypodermic syringes or bulk loading guns.

Spliced-in tenons to repair ballusters, S.P.N.E.A.

Consolidants should meet the following important criteria:

1. They should penetrate deeply into the wood.
2. They should cure or harden without shrinkage.
3. They should bond well to the wood.
4. They should not adversely affect the wood by chemical or other reactions.
5. They should be reversible or removable without harming the wood.
6. They should remain stable with aging and not undergo further chemical reactions, for example, no discoloration in ultraviolet radiation and no embrittlement through loss of plasticizers.
7. They should remain where they are placed and not be subsequently removed by moisture.
8. They should not cause aesthetically unacceptable changes in surface appearance, for example, high gloss shine caused by resin migrating back to surface with solvents.

The epoxy resins suffer from the major drawback that, for practical purposes they are irreversible. The acrylic resins based on methyl methacrylate can be manipulated to satisfy most of the criteria.

REINFORCEMENT SYSTEMS AND CONSOLIDATION

There are two methods which use synthetic resins plus steel reinforcement to reinstate old structural timbers and enable them to carry loads again. These two methods which both use epoxy resins are the WER System which was developed in Canada, and the BETA System which was developed in the Netherlands. The former was developed late in the 1970s by Paul Stumes who was then a restoration engineer with Parks Canada, the federal government historic preservation agency.

Neither system should be used indiscriminately, particularly because the epoxies are for practical purposes, irreversible.

The following list is an adaptation of one Stumes has presented as a series of cases in which the application of the WER System (and hence similar systems) may be considered when wood is severely deteriorated:

• If the timber is painted, carved, or otherwise of artistic value.
• If some historic event or person is intimately associated with the timber.

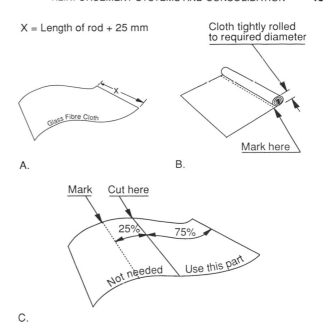

Figure 28. Making F. R. P. reinforcing rods.

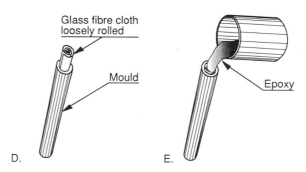

Figure 29. Making F. R. P. reinforcing rods (*continued*).

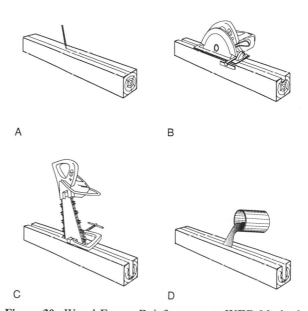

Figure 30. Wood Epoxy Reinforcement: WER Method.

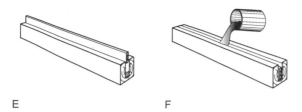

E   F

Figure 31. Wood Epoxy Reinforcement: WER Method (*continued*).

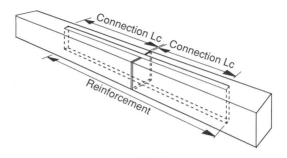

Figure 33b. Rejoining cut beam.

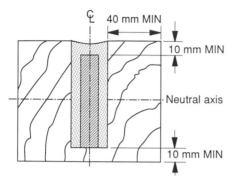

Figure 32a. Wood Epoxy Reinforcement: single plate installation.

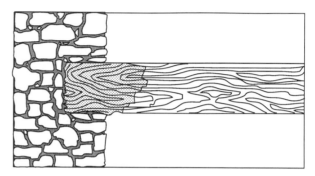

Figure 34a. Decayed construction using the BETA system.

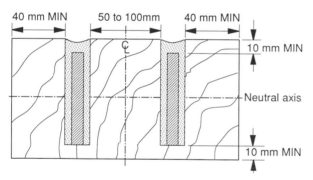

Figure 32b. Wood Epoxy Reinforcement: double plate installation.

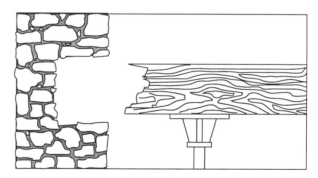

Figure 34b. Decayed parts and supporting stonework removed.

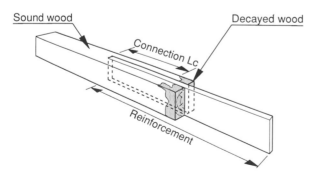

Figure 33a. Replacing missing beam end.

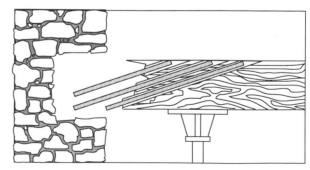

Figure 34c. Holes drilled, BETA system glass fiber reinforced plastic rods inserted.

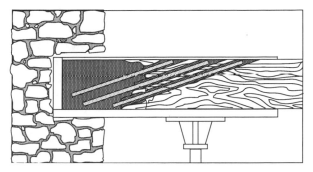

Figure 34d. Forms constructed, BETA system epoxy mortar poured.

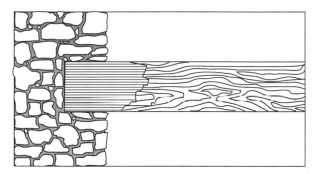

Figure 34e. Forms removed, stonework replaced; restoration complete.

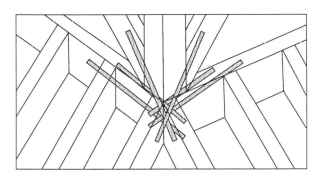

Figure 35a. Restoration at complicated timber connection (BETA).

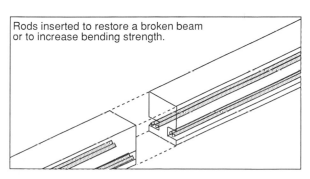

Rods inserted to restore a broken beam or to increase bending strength.

Figure 35b. Longitudinal reinforcement (BETA).

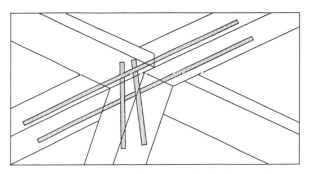

Figure 35c. Joint truss/tie-beam/wall plate (BETA).

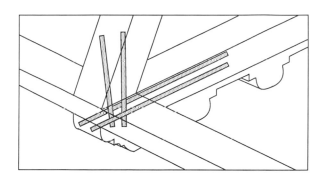

Figure 35d. Joint truss/console (BETA).

- If the timber is significant because of its age or because it is an original part of a structure.
- If it represents an important part in the development or history of the structure.
- Where the replacement of the element would unduly disturb the surrounding fabric.
- If the replacement would be too expensive or impractical although otherwise justifiable.

Application of such methods is not recommended in the following cases:

- If it interferes beyond reasonable limits with the visual integrity of the element or the resource.
- If it defaces important artistic works.
- If it destroys a large segment of the original fabric and hence significantly compromises the authenticity of the resource.
- If it does not meet a safety standard or code requirement.
- If the installation will adversely affect surrounding structures.

Perhaps Stumes' most significant note is as follows . . . "We should not forget that there is a constant progress in the technology of monument conservation. Every year new methods are developed for the rehabilitation of previously unsalvageable objects. A ten year pause is insignificant in the hopefully eternal life of a historic monument.'' The WER and BETA methods are compared in the illustrations.

PESTICIDES AND PRESERVATIVES

Disclaimer

It may be unusual to commence with a disclaimer addressed to the reader but you are advised that you alone are responsible for determining whether a given pesticide or preservative can be legally, appropriately, or safely purchased and/or applied by you, or whether its use is restricted to professional pest control operators. The purpose of this section is to inform the reader about pesticides and preservatives generally. The legal usage status and controls of pesticides and preservatives are subject to change at any time as is the state of medical knowledge. It is clearly impossible for a work such as this to be totally comprehensive or definitive.

ONLY the pesticide or preservative CONTAINER LABEL can be depended upon to inform you of the restrictions and legal use controls relevant to a particular substance at its date of manufacture. The current situation must be verified with the relevant local, regional, and national government agencies. Neither the author nor the publisher is responsible in any way for any accidental poisonings of humans or any other form of life that may be claimed to have occurred or to have been threatened as a result of recommendations made in this work.

Caution!

Having read the disclaimer it is easier to understand why many architects, engineers, contractors, and even preservationists are intimidated by the subject of pesticides and preservatives and their uses in existing buildings. Since the subject is highly technical in nature and deals with poisonous substances, caution and reluctance are understandable and certainly wiser than uninformed dabbling in what can be a highly dangerous field.

The uses of pesticides and preservatives are today increasingly restricted and controlled by law at national, state, or provincial levels and even at the municipal level. As an ordinary unlicensed individual, you may not be allowed to purchase, mix, or apply certain substances to eradicate pests; and even if you are a licensed pest control specialist, uses may be heavily restricted.

Many formulae for pesticides and preservatives are given here for both restricted and unrestricted use. Their disposal is also strictly regulated and controlled. Public health authorities and other relevant regulatory bodies should be consulted in all cases. The inclusion here of any substance and any information given, in no way relieve the readers from their legal responsibilities.

In the United States, since October 1977 all pesticides have been classified by the Environmental Protection Agency (EPA) into two categories:

1. ''Restricted usage'' refers to pesticides which can only be applied legally by certified pest control operators or by someone working directly under their control.
2. ''General usage'' pesticides may be applied by anyone at any time.

Further control of sales, transportation, applications, and disposal, and so on, may be controlled by state or local government.

In Canada, the Pest Control Products Act is administered by Agriculture Canada, the responsible federal government department. This act controls the registration and labeling of pesticides. Their sale, distribution, application, transportation, storage, and disposal are regulated by provincial legislation such as the Pesticide Control Act of British Columbia. There are indications that the federal controls may be improved since it is seen to be something of a conflict of interest to have one federal agency responsible both for promoting and controlling the use of pesticides.

It is also worth noting that other legislation may exist which at first would not seem to affect the use of pesticides but may in fact be of considerable importance. Typical of this kind are laws protecting endangered species such as certain types of bat. The bats feed on insects and if the insects already have pesticides in their systems the bats may suffer cumulative poisoning. Thus the pesticide user may be guilty of killing protected species.

This problem actually occurred in the United Kingdom and the general use of insecticides other than those based on pyrethroids has virtually ceased as a result.

The Insect Pests

The insect pests which we may wish to eradicate or control in our buildings are of three types:

- Those which attack wood in the structure or in the furniture and decorations.
- Those which attack textiles and textile fibers; fur and hair in furniture, decorations and clothes.
- Those which infest a building, feeding upon stored foodstuffs, spoiling materials, and spreading disease.

The first type includes carpenter ants and termites, and wood-destroying beetles including anobiids, lyctids, cerambycids, and buprestids (see also Weaver, 1990).

The second type includes moths and carpet beetles which destroy textiles, such as the webbing clothes moth; the casemaking clothes moth; the varied carpet beetle; the furniture carpet beetle and the black carpet beetle. The hide or leather beetle prefers to eat hides and skins but will thrive on smoked meat and cheese; one relation called the larder beetle will honeycomb wooden beams and will tunnel through upholstery, penetrating even lead and tin. The drugstore beetle has been described as eating anything but cast iron! Its normal diet has been noted to include many human foodstuffs, leather, wool, hair, manuscripts, books, drugs, shelf-loads of books, and even an ancient Egyptian mummy. It too can pierce lead sheet and tin-foil. The cigarette beetle will not only eat stored tobacco products but is a serious pest of books, eating both the binding and the pages! They have been found eating many human foodstuffs but also attack plant collections and upholstered furniture involving flax tow and straw. They have even been noted as having eaten pyrethrum insecticide powders strong enough to kill cockroaches (Story, 1985).

The third type include cockroaches, crickets, silverfish and firebrats, ants, lice, fleas, and ticks. Of these the German cockroach is in fact the most common insect pest in buildings in the United States, outnumbering its close relations, the American cockroach and the Oriental cockroach. The latter two do not breed as fast, are both larger, and consequently find it more difficult to hide in small crevices. Cockroaches may not only eat human foodstuffs but they also have the unpleasant habits of vomiting, depositing feces, and secreting fluid from abdominal glands which can cause severe staining and unpleasant odors. They may also cause fires by chewing insulation off wiring and otherwise interfering with electrical equipment. They will also eat books, papers, leather, hair, wallpaper, animal skins, and upholstery. Materials soiled with sweat are particularly favored!

As may be seen from the above lists some of the insects attack wood while others attack a bewildering range of materials other than wood. There are yet others which attack both wood and other materials. I have included them all here since pesticidal and preservative treatments are usually of general application.

The Nature of the Problem

In this work there are two terms which are often used interchangeably and incorrectly by the general public and even by professionals who really should know better.

A "pesticide" is a substance which is used to eradicate an infestation by some undesirable animal, insect, or other organism which in this case is causing damage to a heritage structure and perhaps its contents. This term is derived from two Latin words: *pestis*; meaning a plague, disease, or contagion; and *cidere*; meaning to cut or to kill.

A "preservative" is a substance which is used to protect wood, for example, against future attacks. Some preservatives can be used as pesticides to treat attacks which have already occurred, but many will not stop an attack which is already in progress. Some preservatives can only be used under specially controlled conditions of heat and pressure which cannot be duplicated on wood which remains in a structure. Chromated copper arsenate treatments are a good example of the latter.

Increasing legal controls on the use of toxic substances are a sign of growing public awareness and concern following the publication of pioneering environmental works on the consequences of poorly controlled use of pesticides, such as Rachel Carson's *The Silent Spring* in 1962.

In the last decade particularly there has been a steadily increasing pressure to develop pest control technology and new pesticides and preservatives of lower toxicity. The ideal form of pest control being one which involves no use of toxic substances.

Is There an Ideal Pesticide or Preservative?

Ideally pesticides and preservatives should have the following characteristics: They will:

- be cheap;
- be safe to the user;
- kill insect and fungi at all stages of their life cycles, for example, insect adults, larvae and eggs; and fungal spores and mycelium;
- be fast working;
- retain killing power long enough to kill the maximum amount of pests;

C.C.A. treatment; the wood has a characteristic pale green color.

• be specific to the target pests rather than being "broad spectrum" toxins which can kill or injure a very large range of living organisms including mammals, birds, and fishes;
• be easy to apply.

They won't:

• leave or form harmful residues;
• break down or loose their effectiveness in storage;
• be absorbed by and build up in animal or plant tissue;
• injure nontarget animals or plants;
• corrode or damage building materials, equipment, furnishings, or valuable artifacts.

NO INSECTICIDE OR PRESERVATIVE CURRENTLY IN EXISTENCE COMPLETELY SATISFIES ALL THESE REQUIREMENTS.

THE DEVELOPMENT OF THE USE OF CHEMICALS AGAINST PESTS

The ancient Chinese were probably the first to use toxic chemicals which prevented attacks by insects and fungi which cause wood deterioration. The Chinese painted their buildings brilliant red using the pigment vermillion or cinnabar which is red mercuric sulfide.

The red color was apparently used for luck and to avert evil. The red certainly averted the evil of wood deterioration because mercury compounds are extremely toxic and prevented attacks.

The ancient Chinese are also credited with first uses of arsenic and pyrethrum to control insect pests of crops.

The ancient Romans used lead sheet to protect the wooden hulls of their ships against the ravages of marine borers and used surface charring in an attempt to protect wood which was to be partly buried. They also discovered that they could control insects by burning sulfur.

By the seventeenth century ships' hulls were being protected by layers of copper sheet which not only prevented attacks by marine borers but also the accumulation of seaweed and barnacles.

The Vikings pioneered the use of wood extractives to act as preservatives for their wooden ships and buildings. Because of the regular use of pine tar in Norway since medieval times, we still have woodwork from the eleventh century surviving outdoors and in excellent condition, for example, at the World Heritage Church at Urnes. The pine tar is still made by the original process of destructive distillation from pine stumps and root stocks.

A long series of decay problems in wooden ships of the British Royal Navy, including one where the bottom literally fell out of the large 100 gun warship, *Royal George* in 1782, prompted research into potential pre-

Urnes stave church, Norway; Norwegian pine preserved for over 700 years by cyclical applications of wood tar.

servatives and methods of getting them to penetrate into wood. With the growth of the railways early in the nineteenth century there also came a need for preservatives to protect the wooden ties or sleepers.

The first patent for a modern type of chemical treatment which used heat and pressure to force the preservative deep into the wood was issued in England in 1838 for Bethell's Process. Creosote with ammonia removed and the addition of crude iron acetate (then called "pyrolignite") was forced into the wood at about 120°F and at pressures of 150–200 psi in a large iron pressure vessel now called a "retort." The treatment was popular for railroad ties and poles.

The nineteenth century also saw a rapid growth in the enthusiastic use of wood preservatives containing increasingly toxic inorganic chemicals in aqueous solutions. The principal chemical compounds were copper

sulfate (e.g., Margary's Process, pat. 1837); iron acetate (Boucherie's Second Process); chloride of zinc (Burnettizing, pat. 1837); and perhaps the most dangerous of them all, "corrosive sublimate of mercury" or mercuric chloride, a violent poison which is fatal in doses of as little as 1 or 2 g. Its use as a preservative and primarily as a fungicide was patented as Kyan's Process or Kyanizing in 1832 in England. Kyanizing was used in 1848 at Lowell, Massachusetts.

Many of these substances were not only highly toxic to man, other mammals, and most other organisms, but also corroded all nails, screws, and other metalwork in the vicinity. Associated efflorescent salts and acid hydrolysis could also severely disrupt the structure of the wood. Concern over extremes of toxicity led to a Swedish ban on this use of mercuric chloride late in the nineteenth century, although such use continued much later elsewhere.

The requirements for the protection of personnel, wood, leather, and textiles against insects and fungi, particularly in the tropics in the Second World War led to the large-scale development of preservatives and pesticides based on organic chemicals. The widespread use of broad spectrum pesticides such as DDT started at this time and led 20 years later to Rachel Carson's eloquent pleas.

The Catch 22 Question of Assessing Toxicity

Toxicity can be assessed or measured by a number of systems but obviously one can't test-rate unknown but potentially acutely poisonous substances on humans! An additional problem lies in the fact that substances may be dangerous or harmful in many ways. Without considering other forms of life, practically every pesticide or preservative is either toxic to man or can cause harmful short-term effects such as eczema or allergic reactions.

Reactions to long-term exposures are even more complex and can be extremely difficult to assess primarily because of the difficulty of isolating the effects of exposure to one substance from those of exposure to others.

One approach to rating toxicity is the "LD 50" system. Tests are carried out on large groups of laboratory animals, such as rats.

Carefully measured doses are administered, usually orally, and when 50% of that group dies the results are then expressed as the number of milligrams per kilogram of the animal's body weight required for a fatal dose.

An LD 50 rating of more than 5000 mg/kg is considered relatively nontoxic. An LD 50 of between 500 and 5000 mg/kg is slightly toxic. Between 50 and 500 mg/

PATENT PRESERVATIVE SYSTEM.

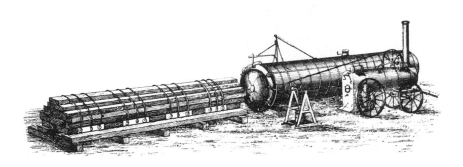

Mess.rs John Bethell and C.os Timber preserving Apparatus.

In 1838 Bethell's process was the first to use heat and pressure to impregnate wood with creosote.

kg is moderately toxic, and any LD 50 of less than 50 mg/kg is very toxic. Remember that a low number conveys extreme toxicity while a very high number means low toxicity!

The LD 50 system rates toxicity in terms of the amount of a substance necessary to produce a fatal dose either immediately or as a result of longer term accumulation. One must be aware that this does not take into account other harmful effects which may occur after exposures to smaller amounts. Such effects may range from mild discomfort to hay fever, eczema and asthma right on up to birth deforming (teratogenic), carcinogenic (cancer causing), mutagenic (causing mutations) and spontaneous miscarriage effects some of which may even be transmitted from an affected subject to a partner!

As if all this was not complicated enough we must also remember that pesticides and preservatives are commonly diluted with, dissolved in, or combined with other substances. These other substances may also be toxic or be hazardous in other ways. For example, methanol and acetone which can both be used as solvents are both moderately toxic, highly flammable liquids and form explosive vapors! They may thus be the most dangerous part of a formulation which has an active ingredient which is only slightly toxic!

In case I should be accused of exaggerating the question of toxicity, and to put the data into perspective,

here are LD 50 ratings for some more or less familiar substances:

Aspirin or acetylsalicylic acid: LD 50 orally in mice, rats; 1.1, 1.5 g/kg (note, 1g = one gram or 1000 mg).

Sodium chloride or common table salt: LD 50 orally in rats; 3.75 g/kg.

Caffeine: LD 50 orally in mice, hamsters, rats, rabbits; mg/kg 127, 230, 355, 246 (in males) 137, 249, 247, 224 (in females).

Nicotine: (used as a fumigant and insecticide) extremely toxic with an LD 50 rating in mice (mg/kg) 0.3 intravenous, 9.5 intraperitoneal, and 230 orally.

Cocaine: LD 50 intravenous in rats; 17.5 mg/kg or extremely toxic (All data *Merck Index*, 1983).

Insecticides

Insecticides may be classified both by the way in which they affect the target insect and by their type. Thus we have:

- contact insecticides;
- fumigants or respiratory insecticides;
- residual insecticides;
- stomach insecticides.

There are two basic types, inorganic and organic insecticides. The latter have a subtype known as the "botanicals" which are plant products which may be used with synergists or activators, or they may be synthetic versions of plant products.

Contact insecticides have the characteristic ability to penetrate the integument or outer "skin" of the insect and to attack its nervous system or other life functions. Such insecticides are typically in the form of dusts or wettable powders.

Fumigants or respiratory insecticides enter the insect via the trachea and other parts of the respiratory system. They usually paralyze the oxygen system and prevent respiration.

Long-lasting insecticides which leave a layer of toxic material on surfaces are called residual insecticides. Insects subsequently contacting these surfaces may take up toxins in a number of ways and frequently they act as nerve poisons. Some residuals such as chlordane also act as fumigants by emitting vapors.

Stomach insecticides mostly enter during feeding or via the mouth when the insect is cleaning or grooming itself or other insects.

Inorganic Insecticides

Inorganic insecticides based upon inorganic chemicals tend to have been less commonly used than the organics since the Second World War. Some of them are now receiving more attention because they can be a part of formulations which can be used to target specific species.

Sodium fluoride is an extremely toxic inorganic chemical used in dusts to control cockroaches, silver fish, and ants. It has been used with pyrethrum (a botanical) as a dust and is believed to act as a stomach and contact insecticide. It is also toxic to fungi and is used in aqueous solutions as a fungicide. LD 50 orally in rats is 0.18 g/kg (*Merck Index*, 1983). Somewhat unusually, sufficient data exist from actual cases of human poisoning to establish that death may result from doses of 5–10 g and severe symptoms may result from ingestion of less than 1 g.

Lethal poisoning cases commence with muscular weakness and tremors and proceed to convulsions, collapse, dyspnea (difficulty in respiration), and total respiratory and cardiac failure. EPA regulations require that when sold as an insecticide, sodium fluoride must be tinted Nile Blue.

Borax is effective when used as a dry powder to control ants and cockroaches. It acts as both a contact and a stomach insecticide. Borax or sodium borate has a LD 50 orally in rats of 5.66 g/kg (*Merck Index*, 1983).

Silica aerogels, also known as amorphous-fumed silica, and diatomaceous earth are commonly mixed with pyrethrins as dusts. They cause water loss and extreme dehydration leading to the death of affected insects. In dry conditions, they last almost indefinitely. Classified as nontoxic or only slightly toxic to humans, the particles or dusts may be so light that they float in clouds and may be inhaled. The silica aerogels are not believed to cause silicosis but the dust of diatomaceous earth is described as causing fibrosis of the lungs (Lewis, 1991).

Organic Insecticides

The first of this constantly expanding group of compounds for us to consider are the organic phosphates or organophosporous compounds. This group contains two of the most toxic chemicals known; parathion with an LD 50 orally in female and male rats of 3.6 and 13 mg/kg, respectively and phosdrin with an LD 50 orally in female and male rats of 3.7 and 6.1 mg/kg. These ratings are in the "extremely toxic" category.

Acephate is a residual insecticide which is used for cockroach control. It is marketed under the registered tradename Orthene and is described by Hamm (1982) as being of low toxicity. Lewis (1991) lists it as HR.3 or moderately toxic. LD 50 orally in rats is 700 mg/kg (*Merck Index*, 1983).

Chlorpyrifos is a broad spectrum insecticide with moderate toxicity, LD 50 orally in rats of 145 mg/kg (*Merck Index*, 1983). It has wide use as a spray, a paint-on lacquer, and as granules. It is particularly good for cockroach control. It is marketed under various tradenames including Dursban, Lorsban, and Killmaster. Lewis (1991) reports that there is experimental evidence that it is a teratogen.

DDVP (dimethyl dichlorovinyl phosphate) or Dichlorvos as a liquid used in sprays at recommended concentration of 0.2–0.5% by weight is of low mammalian toxicity and kills many crawling insects. It is used at a 20% concentration in resin strips against flying insects. Registered trade names include Vapona, No-Pest strips, Nuvan, and Dedevap. It is noted as being a cholin esterase inhibitor which means that like some other phosphorus-containing insecticides and nerve gases it can interfere with the functioning of brain, nerve, and red blood cells. (*Merck Index*, 1983) In its normal form, DDVP is classified as being moderately toxic but it has an LD 50 orally in male and female rats of 80 and 56 mg/kg (*Merck Index*, 1983) which is very close to being highly toxic. Lewis (1991) reports that it has produced teratogenic and mutagenic effects in experiments. Extreme caution should be exercised with the impregnated strips which should not be used in confined spaces.

Diazinon is used at a 0.5–1.0% concentration as a liquid to kill a very wide range of insects including the very resistant cockroach. Lewis (1991) reports that diazinon has been found to be teratogenic, to produce reproductive effects, and that there are data on human mutation caused by it. It is classified as being HR 3 or moderately toxic with an LD 50 of 350 mg/kg. Trade names include Basudin, Spectracide, Nucidol, and Sarolex. Dimethoate is used for the control of flying insects but its strong odor limits its indoor use. Trade names include Cygon, De-fend, Dimetate, and Roxion. It is rated as moderately toxic (Lewis, 1991) and there are reported human mutation data [LD 50 orally in rats; 250 mg/kg (*Merck Index*, 1983)]. It is noted as being a cholin esterase inhibitor (*Merck Index*, 1983)

Fenthion is a residual insecticide of moderate mammalian toxicity used at a 2% concentration, especially against cockroaches and is marketed as Baycid, Baytex, Entex, Lebaycid, and Rid-a-bird. It is rated as moderately toxic HR 3 (Lewis, 1991) but with some experimental evidence of mutagenic, teratogenic, and reproductive effects. [LD 50 orally in male and female rats; 215 and 245 mg/kg (*Merck Index*, 1983)]. It is noted as being a cholin esterase inhibitor (*Merck Index*, 1983).

Malathion is usually used at a 2% concentration in many organic solvents, and is marketed as Cythion, Carbophos, Sumitol, and Malathiozol. Lewis (1991) reports that malathion is rated moderately toxic HR3 and that it is a questionable carcinogen and that human mutation data have been reported [LD 50 orally in female and male rats; 1000 and 1375 mg/kg (*Merck Index*, 1983)].

Propetamphos, is a low odor, broad spectrum residual insecticide which is particularly effective against cockroaches and fleas. It is marketed as Safrotin. Lewis (1991) lists it as being moderately toxic HR3 [LD 50 orally in rats; 75 mg/kg (*Merck Index*, 1983)].

Ronnel or fenchlorfos is used as a liquid in organic solvents, often in a spray form at 0.2–0.5% concentrations. Usually used for flea and cockroach control, it is also marketed as Korlan, Nankor, and Trolene. Lewis (1991) reports that it is rated as HR3 or moderately toxic and that teratogenic and reproductive effects have been observed experimentally (LD 50 orally in male and female rats; 1250 and 2630 mg/kg) and it is noted as a cholin esterase inhibitor (*Merck Index*, 1983).

The second group to be considered are the carbamates.

Bendiocarb is used as a wettable powder in 1% dusts as a broad spectrum contact and residual insecticide.

Very low odor and vapor permit its use in sensitive areas such as hospitals. Marketed as Dexa-Klor, Ficam, and Ubicid, this product is rated as HR3 or moderately toxic (Lewis, 1991) [LD 50 orally in mammals; 35–100 mg/kg (*Merck Index*, 1983)].

Carbaryl is soluble in many organic solvents and is used as a contact insecticide against many insects. Marketed as Sevin, it is particularly effective against bees and wasps. Lewis (1991) rates it as HR3 or moderately toxic but with experimental teratogenic and reproductive effects noted. There is inadequate evidence of carcinogenic activity, but human mutation data exist [LD 50 orally in rats; 250 mg/kg (*Merck Index*, 1983)].

Dimetilan which is marketed under the trade name Snip is used in fly bands and impregnated strips. Hamm (1982) rates dimetilan as highly toxic and describes its use as being primarily to kill flies and flying insects by slowly emitting toxic vapor from impregnated plastic or resin strips [LD 50 orally in rats; 25 mg/kg (*Merck Index*, 1983)].

Propoxur has its prime use in aerosols and has good "knockdown" and killing properties. It is used as a 1% emulsion (not being soluble in organic solvents) at a 25% concentration for baits and at 70% for wettable powder. A 1% emulsion is used against cockroaches. Market products include Baygon, Blattanex, Suncide, and Undene. Its quick flushing action and long residual life make propoxur a very useful general-purpose insecticide but it is particularly effective against cockroaches, ticks, and other difficult insect species. It is very useful against arachnids or spiders. Hamm (1982) described it as highly toxic. The LD 50 rating for male and female rats orally is 83 and 86 mg/kg (*Merck Index*, 1983).

The third group are the chlorinated hydrocarbons.

Chlordane, the first of this group, acts as a stomach, contact, residual, and fumigant poison. It can be used in many forms and is insoluble in water but soluble in a wide range of organic solvents. It is used in dusts at a 5% concentration and in liquids based upon an emulsion concentrate containing 47–49% by weight chlordane. It has for some years been the main pesticide used for the control of subterranean termites and carpenter ants. Although chlordane is classified as being of moderate toxicity, since 1975 the EPA has restricted its use primarily to subsurface ground control for subterranean termites. This restriction is because its stability and long-term residual effects ensure that it stays a threat to man and animals through the food and water chains. Registered trade names include Belt, Octachlor, Ortho-Klor, and Velsicol 1068. The *Merck Index* (1983) lists the LD 50 rating as 343 mg/kg i.p. (intraperitoneal) in male rats. West (1983) gives an oral LD 50 of 439 mg/kg.

Heptachlor is related to chlordane and was used for ant control but because of its relatively high mammalian toxicity is now used largely for subterranean termite control in insensitive areas. Registered trade names include Drinox and Heptamul. It is more volatile and hence its vapor makes it more effective as a fumigant than the other members of this group [LD 50 rating orally in male, and female rats; 100 and 162 mg/kg (*Merck Index*, 1983)].

Lindane is a contact, stomach, residual and fumigant poison with a relatively fast knockdown. It is used in the form of emulsions, solutions, wettable powders, and dusts as a broad spectrum insecticide; and in sprays at 0.1–0.5% by weight concentration. In a 1% solution in oil or water it is used for the control of anobiid beetles, lyctids, and other wood boring beetles. Lindane is also known as gamma BHC or gamma HCH and is marketed under such tradenames as Gammexane and Kwell. Moderately toxic, lindane is more stable in heat than other insecticides and thus can be used around radiators and other heaters and without losing effectiveness. Its LD 50 orally in male and female rats is 88 and 91 mg/kg (*Merck Index*, 1983). Its volatility makes it less effective residually.

The fourth group are the botanicals which, as we have noted, are based upon plant products or are synthetic versions of such products. They are often combined with synergists or activators, thus piperonyl butoxide is mixed with pyrethrin or synthesized pyrethroids. The first of the botanicals is pyrethrum (active ingredient pyrethrin) which is produced from the dried and powdered flowers of the *Chrysanthemum cinerariaefolium* (formerly of the genus *pyrethrum*). Essentially non-toxic to man and other warm blooded animals, it is added to synergists to produce a fast knockdown at low concentrations. The LD 50 is 1.2 g/kg orally in rats (*Merck Index*, 1983). Pyrethrin, the active substance in pyrethrum along with pyritol, chrysanthimine, cinerin, and jasmolin, break down rapidly when exposed to sun and air.

Piperonyl butoxide is marketed as Butacide and has an LD 50 orally in female and male rats of 6150 and 7500 mg/kg. It is used as a synergist with both pyrethrin and rotenone.

Pentachlorophenols or PCPs are chlorinated hydrocarbons which have been used extensively as fungicides, wood preservatives, and herbicides in addition to being used as insecticides. After many years of what has amounted almost to careless use as a broad spectrum biocide, concerns arose that their toxicity and related health effects made it necessary to restrict their use. The problems are partly related to the fact that treated wood continues to emit toxic vapor over a very long period and that such vapors can build up to dangerous levels in interiors. In Canada and many areas in the United States it is now illegal to use pentachlorophenols for the treatment of wood inside buildings or in any location where the treated wood could come into contact with foodstuffs or allow PCPs to get into the food chain. The LD 50 rating orally in male and female rats is 146 and 175 mg/kg (*Merck Index*, 1983). It is noted that this substance is more toxic in organic solvents and LD 50 ratings of 50 mg/kg have been quoted for some PCP compounds.

PCPs can also contain small quantities of dioxin as an impurity or contaminant associated with their manufacture.

Dioxin or TCDD (tetrachlorodibenzo-*p*-dioxin) has LD 50 rating orally in male and female rats of 0.022 and 0.045 mg/kg, which puts this material in a category of its own as a toxic substance (*Merck Index*, 1983) The *Merck Index* describes it as "Extremely potent, low molecular weight toxin." It is also noted as causing a wide range of other toxic effects including teratogenicity, chloracne, vascular lesions, carcinogenicity, and delayed death. It was the infamous toxin associated with the Seveso industrial disaster in Italy in 1976 and has also been implicated as the causative agent of the various symptoms of the Vietnam veterans and others exposed to the defoliant "Agent Orange" (*Merck Index*, 1983).

Fumigants

Fumigants are defined as being in a vapor or gaseous phase and not present in an aerosol. The molecular state gives fumigants good penetration and allows them to clear quickly. There are other requirements which are set out in detail in Hector Monro's now unfortunately out-of-print *Manual of Fumigation for Insect Control* (Rome, 1969, UNFAO).

Until recent years ethylene oxide and methyl bromide were preferred fumigants particularly for use in chambers in museums. Fumigation of buildings was carried out with a number of extremely dangerous gases including hydrogen cyanide and methyl bromide. Recent research has revealed that residues of ethylene oxide remain in objects and are released slowly over a long period. The gas has also been found to be a carcinogen even in tiny amounts and the EPA consequently lowered the permissable exposure level to $\frac{1}{2}$ ppm for an eight-hour day. This being very difficult to measure and all other considerations taken into account, the use of ethylene oxide has tended to be dropped in favor of such gases as sulfuryl fluoride which is marketed as Vikane. This odorless gas is used with 20 ppm of another fumigant gas, chloropicrin, which has a biting pungent odor and is used as a warning agent. Chloropicrin is a lacrymatory or tear gas and has been used as a war gas and for law enforcement.

Sulfuryl fluoride has also come into wide use as a fumigant for buildings being used for such sensitive locations as fast food outlets.

Fumigation may be used to control severe or problematic cases of insect and fungal infestation but treatments may have to be repeated in order to eradicate all stages of the pests' life cycles. All fumigation is extremely hazardous except under proper, careful control and consequently all operations are strictly limited to licensed specialists and controlled by law.

Current Trends

In the United Kingdom apparently conservation legislation protecting once threatened British bat species directly resulted in the banning of a broad range of insecticides which might otherwise have accumulated in and killed the bats because of their insect diets. Insects which have already been exposed to poisons might not actually die immediately and thus the toxins in them can enter the ecological system.

Fungicides and Fungicidal Treatments

In recent years it has been confirmed that the fungicide pentachlorophenol has been responsible for the introduction of unacceptably high levels of toxic substances into the food chain. In consequence, pentachlorophenol has been banned in Canada for all uses inside buildings and its use elsewhere is limited to locations where livestock cannot be exposed to it. Some similar limitations have been applied in the United States. The banning of this substance has left a major lacuna in the range of fungicidal treatments known to be effective for *in-situ* use against a broad range of fungi.

The most effective fungicidal treatments which leave the wood safe for us to handle are those in which the chemical compound is introduced into the wood by means of a combination of heat and pressure in a retort or pressure vessel. The wood preservation industry in North America has understandably largely focused on a variety of "pressure treatments" and the products which can be employed in such treatments. The need of the conservator for an effective fungicide which can be used for *in-situ* treatments has not really been recognized, nor do adequate long-term test data exist for the few *in-situ* treatments which have been developed.

Pressure treatments can be considered in two groups:

- chemical compounds soluble in water.
- chemical compounds soluble in organic solvents.

Some types of chemicals can occur in slightly different forms which are soluble in either water or organic solvents, for example, orthophenylphenol. Water soluble chemical compounds may become fixed, which means they combine chemically with the wood substances. Other compounds may be leached out again as moisture passes in and out of the wood. Generally the water soluble compounds leave the surface clean but need drying after treatment. Wood treated with fungicides in organic solvents may have a "dirty" surface and may require cleaning with more organic solvents before it can be painted or glued.

In the former category the most popular treatment in North America is with CCA Type C, or chromated copper arsenate. This treatment is sometimes described as Wolmanizing and the treated wood is a pale green color. Up until several years ago ethylene oxide and methyl bromide were preferred fumigants for chamber fumigation in museums. Ethylene oxide (EtO) kills both fungi and insects and had a TLV-TWA (threshold limit value–time weighted average) of 100 ppm for eight hours per day five days per week for the life of an individual. It was then discovered that EtO has been identified as a carcinogen and OSHA, the Occupational Safety and Health Administration in the United States, consequently lowered the effective TLV–TWA to less than $\frac{1}{2}$ ppm. Sulfuryl fluoride is now used instead of ethylene oxide but it does not kill fungal spores. (A specific product for sulfuryl fluoride is "Vikane" from Dow Chemical.) The highly toxic fumigants Chloropicrin and Diazomet (tetrahydro-3,5-dimethyl-2H-1,3,5-thiadiazine-2-thione) and Vapam (sodium N-methyldithiocarbamate) have been shown to be highly effective against brown rot fungi but these two fumigants are so toxic that they cannot be used for the treatment of timbers within structures or in poorly ventilated areas. Chloropicrin has been found to be more effective when it is introduced via small holes in the wood and the timber is then wrapped in polyethylene sheet.

Copper napthenate is bright green and is not nearly as fungitoxic as, say, chloropicrin, but it has a much lower LD 50 rating and is therefore preferred for applications where its color is not a problem. Zinc napthenate is even less toxic but has the advantage of being colorless. Both products are soluble in organic solvents.

In *Canadian Heritage Magazine*, June 1980, p. 49, I described a water-repellent preservative mixture for wood which uses orthophenyl phenol as the active pesticidal ingredient instead of pentachlorophenol which has been probably the most commonly used, and misused, wood preservative in the world. It is of interest to compare their LD 50 rating figures. Orthophen-

Copper napthenate treated timber; the wood has a characteristic strong green color.

ylphenol is only slightly toxic at LD 50 2480 mg/kg (rats oral) while pentachlorophenol is very toxic at LD 50 50 mg/kg (rats oral). Aspirin for comparison is slightly toxic at 1750 mg/kg (rats oral).

Complications arise, as if this were not complicated enough, when one dissolves the chemical in organic solvents or carriers, such as methanol or methyl hydrate which also has an unsavory but well-deserved reputation as a poison. Such solvents may also be highly flammable or even explosive in vapor form.

The on-going search for effective fungicides of low mammalian toxicity has led to increased interest in the use of borax compounds such as sodium borate, sodium metaborate and disodium tetraborate. The LD 50 for rats is 4500–6000 mg/kg for borax. Borax and the other borates have long been known as mild antiseptic fungicides and as broad spectrum herbicides. The crystals effloresce at low RH and borates are highly soluble in water. Although they have been found to be effective in large-scale treatments against some fungi, their solubility in water raises doubts about their residual effects. Once they have been redissolved there are potential further problems with their efflorescent salts which have been shown to be capable of destroying adjacent masonry materials. There are also a number of reported instances of borates which were used as combination fire-retardants and fungicides for cellulose fiber insulation, going into solution in condensation and the resulting solution then acting as an electrolyte in the galvanic corrosion of electrical conduits of mixed metals.

Pest Control or Pest Management

In his excellent work *Approaches to Pest Management in Museums*, which was published by the Smithsonian Institution in 1985, Keith O. Story presented a series of control options which are discussed here.

- If barriers can be placed between the insects and their target foodstuffs, then infestations may be controlled; thus one uses containers which the insects can't get into.
- Most insect pests may be controlled or killed outright by heat at temperatures ranging from 105°F up to 130°F. Such temperatures may harm delicate objects and adhesives, for example; thus potential ill effects must be studied.
- Non-heat forms of radiation can be used including gamma radiation which has shown considerable success as a safer alternative to fumigation with ethylene oxide gas, for example; x rays; ultraviolet radiation; electrical energy, and microwave radiation.

Most have associated problems but gamma radiation particularly may offer a solution with no residual effects and potential damage limited to a small range of materials if the equipment is properly operated.

- It has been found that if the temperature is lowered quickly to about 0°F most insects will be killed. A temperature "shock effect" which is sometimes very effective may be achieved by lowering the temperature, quickly raising it then lowering it again—carpet beetles and clothes moths may be killed in this way.

- Parasites, diseases, and predators which naturally prey on the target species may be used to control infestations. However, there are serious problems in trying to use such methods indoors. The new predators may also thrive in their new environments and become pests themselves!

- An extraordinary range of miscellaneous nonchemical methods can be employed often at low cost and with no risk of "collateral damage." Such methods include lowering moisture contents of building materials and furnishings; the use of sticky traps and light traps; using screening and other barriers to prevent insects entering buildings; sealing off or physically removing centers of infestation; physically removing the pests themselves by vacuuming, brushing, and dry cleaning; cleaning fabrics to remove substances such as perspiration which attracts cockroaches; removing or sealing garbage, food remains, and empty soft drink bottles which pests can feed on; using ultrasound to repel insects; and last but not least, special management and policies such as more effective cleaning programs at more frequent intervals, or not using cut flower displays in certain parts of museum houses because of the fresh insect populations introduced by large bunches of flowers.

- Conventional insecticides and fumigants are discussed in this section in considerable detail. Among the biggest problems are those of toxicity to nontarget species, especially man. The LD 50 rating system is discussed as are the low toxicity pesticides such as pyrethrum. Unfortunately individuals may react in different ways even to this least toxic of pesticides. A very large percentage of people are allergic to pyrethrum and although some just sneeze the most severely affected may go into anaphylactic shock and can die if no treatment is immediately available.

Many pesticides, particularly fumigants, may cause damage to various materials ranging from furs and feathers to brass, silver, cellophane, and leather. These additional potential corrosive or other damaging effects must be carefully checked before proceeding with treatments of interiors with contents of furnishings and objects. The fumigants are all powerful biocides and have mostly been used at one time or another as war gases or for law enforcement, for example, tear gas;

they present considerable problems in terms of the use and operation of facilities.

Again it must be stressed that fumigants are normally used in buildings only for severe or difficult infestations and their use must be left to licensed pest control operators. As has been noted fumigation treatments may not kill all the stages of an insect's life cycle in one operation and thus more than one treatment is normal.

An atmospheric gas which can be vented into the atmosphere without significant health or pollution hazard is a very attractive form of pest control. It has been found that carbon dioxide at a concentration of 60% held for four days at a temperature of 70°F (21°C) or higher will kill all life stages of most pests. However, the problems of the "greenhouse effect" may mean that the addition of further carbon dioxide to the atmosphere may be unacceptable.

Nonconventional or low toxicity pesticides which may only be in the experimental stages of their development present at least a prospect of increasingly popular alternatives to the organophosphate and organochlorine compounds. Available products include the botanicals such as pyrethroids, for example, resmethrin and permethrin; "inert" dusts and powders such as silica aerogels; and various repellants and attractants. Currently only in the experimental stages are antijuvenile hormones, for example, compactin, fluoromevalonate, which cause the premature development of dwarf nonviable adult insects; and various inhibitors of growth, chitin, egg laying, and feeding.

Some conventional chemicals may be used in nonconventional ways, for example, pyrethroids in packaging, and propoxur in insecticidal adhesive tapes.

Pheromones are chemical "message carriers" secreted by insects and used by them to modify the behavior of other insects of their species. Pheromones can act as mass stimuli to breeding, feeding, conflict, and many other insect activities. They are currently synthesized and produced commercially and are used to make poisoned bait traps more attractive; for example, periplanone B, a sex pheromone, is used to make American cockroaches feed on poisons.

Finally the most promising pest control method today is the use of combinations of methods in an "integrated pest management program." I have recently been involved in a major study on a famous heritage building in Texas containing historic wallpapers and textiles and a valuable collection of antiques and works of art. An integrated pest management program formed a central part of the multidisciplinary conservation study on the building, gardens, grounds and contents. This is clearly the way of the future.

REFERENCES

Angst, W. (1980). *Ethics in Scientific Furniture Conservation*. Proceedings of the Furniture and Wooden objects Symposiums, July2–3, Ottawa.

Hamm, James G. (1982). *The Handbook of Pest Control*. New York: Frederick Fell Publishers, Inc.

Lewis, Richard J. (1991). *Hazardous Chemicals Desk Reference*, 2nd ed. New York: Van Nostrand Reinhold.

Mallis, A. et al. K.O. Story (ed.) (1982). *Handbook of Pest Control*, 6th ed. Cleveland: Franzak & Foster Co.

Miller, A.V. et al (eds) (1980). *Handbook for Pesticide Applicators and Pesticide Dispensers*. Victoria, British Columbia: BC Ministry of the Environment.

Panshin, A.J. and DeZeeuw, C. (1970). *Textbook of Wood Technology*. New York: McGraw-Hill.

Phelps, Hermann (1982). *The Craft of Log Building*, translated ed. Ottawa: Lee Valley Tools, Ltd.

Richardson, A.J.H. "Indications for Research in the History of Wood Processing Technology". *Bulletin of the Association for Preservation Technology*. Vol. VI, No. 3 35–146. Ottawa. 1974. The Association for Preservation Technology.

Story, Keith O. (1985). *Approaches to Pest Management in Museums*.

Shurtleff, Harold R. (1939). *The Log Cabin Myth*. Glouster, MA: Harvard University Press.

Washington D.C. (1985). The Conservation Analytical Laboratory, Smithsonian Institution.

Weaver, Martin. (1980). *Getting the Bugs Out; Poisons Pesticides and Preservatives Canadian Heritage Magazine*, Ottawa, August, 45–48.

Weaver, M. (1990). Restoring Structural Wood. *Construction Specifier*, July, pp. 115–126.

West A.S. (principal author) (1983). *The Manual of Pest Control*, 5th ed. Ottawa: Canada Department of National Defence.

Windholz, Martha et al. eds. (1983). *The Merck Index, An Encyclopedia of Chemicals, Drugs, and Biologicals*, 10th ed. Rahway, NJ: Merck & Co., Inc.

CHAPTER 5

RESTORING STONEWORK

RESEARCH

Many of our finest heritage buildings were built of stone or in more recent years were faced with a stone veneer over a steel or concrete frame. When the stonework deteriorates its restoration can pose many problems, especially for those who have not been trained in the conservation of buildings or those who have not had any experience in dealing with such materials and systems. This is the first of two sections to examine the whole process of stone restoration.

When the first European settlers came to North America they tended to use stone which could be simply picked up from the surface close to the site of the building. Sometimes stones were used just as they were and sometimes they were roughly squared. As more time became available for building purposes, stone was quarried from shallow excavations into hillsides or into river cliffs. The density and therefore great weight of stone made it difficult to move long distances over the primitive early roads. Thus a stone was often selected primarily for its accessibility and only secondarily for its durability. Stones were often quarried from sedimentary rock formations of limestone or sandstone. This was because the stone split very readily into roughly rectangular blocks which needed little or no further work to be used in coursed rubble work. From the beginning of the nineteenth century the quarries got larger and deeper and steam power was used both to cut larger stone blocks from their beds and to lift the blocks from the deeper quarries. Initially stones were carried long distances by boat or barge on various waterways, but by the middle of the century, the railroads were also being used to move large quantities of stone. While earlier public and commercial buildings

tended to be built using stones from the same state or province, gradually the opening up of North America combined with the poor performances of some stones led to the development of certain major sources of excellent and more durable stones, particularly Ohio sandstones, Indiana limestones, and Vermont and Quebec granites. The earlier small quarries either ran out of usable stone or they were abandoned because of poor quality, inaccessibility, and flooding, or because they were simply uneconomic to run.

The stone industry flowered again for certain quarries in the early twentieth century and then faded, first with the growth of the use of architectural terracotta and then with the use of reinforced concrete. In more recent years technological advances particularly in the development of diamond sawing and flame cutting and finishing have started a new revival of interest in the use of stone as a beautiful and durable natural material.

When we are faced with deteriorated stonework in an old building, it is the current scientific practice to ask a series of questions and obtain answers by means of a combination of documentary and scientific research. The following list of questions with possible sources and methods for obtaining answers may be helpful.

What General Types of Stone Occur in the Masonry? For example, the stones may be of igneous, sedimentary, or metamorphic origin, such as granite, syenite, gabbro, calcareous sandstone, quartzite, limestone, dolomite, gneiss, and slate. The actual types are usually best recognized from experience and some spot tests, but records may exist. Extreme caution should be exercised with such sources because the actual

Small quarry close to 19th century Ontario house.

stones used were often not the same as the ones described in the specifications.

Where Did the Original Stone Come From and From What Specific Geological Formation? What historical data exist on the stone, for example, early geological reports and chemical analyses of the stone?

Is this stone still available? If not, are there any similar stones which could be used as substitutes for restoration and/or repairs? In North America the primary sources for the historical information are the state geological surveys in the United States and William A Parks' *Report on the Building and Ornamental Stones of Canada*. The five volumes of this report were pub-

House built from very local stone.

Canadian historical building stones include: a. Wallace olive grey sandstone, Nova Scotia; b. Sackville red sandstone, New Brunswick; c. Deschambault limestone polished and bush hammered, Saint Marc des Carrieres, Quebec; d. Queenston dolomite limestone, Ontario; e. Tyndall mottled magnesian limestone, Manitoba; f. Nepean sandstone, Ontario; g. Adare "marble", dolomite, Ontario.

This group of granites from the United States shows the great diversity which is to be found even within such a small selection. (a) and (e) are Stoney Creek granites from Rhode Island. (c, c1) Grey Tapestry granite from the Baretto Granite Corp. New Hampshire. (f) is a Cold Spring Granite Co., Spring Green (i, j1, j2) are Westerly blue, light and pink granites from Rhode Island. (l) is a Cold Spring Texas Red granite. (m) is a Barre blue grey granite from Vermont.

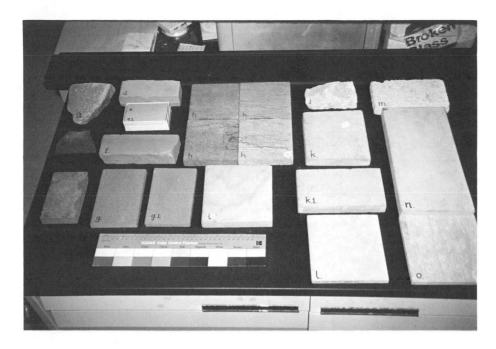

Similarly this group of sandstones and limestones from the United States again illustrates rich diversity. (b) and (c) are Bluestones from the Catskills, New York State. Two samples marked (e, e1) are Scioto sandstones from Ohio. Four examples marked (h) are Briar Hill sandstones from Ohio. (i) is a Berea sandstone from South Amherst, Ohio. (k, k1) and (n) are Indiana limestones with various finishes. (m) is a Texas shellstone, a fossiliferous limestone.

lished in Ottawa, Ontario, by the Department of Mines, in the first two decades of this century. Contemporary stone trade journals such as *Stone Magazine* or *Through the Ages* often described the stones used in major commercial and public buildings but such sources should be treated with caution since their articles were often based on press releases and these were not necessarily based on up-to-date information. To locate the same quarries if they still exist may take a lot of detective work but once again state and provincial geological and mineral resource agencies are among the best sources. Some stone supply companies may be able to match stones which are no longer available, by going to other sources and even to other countries.

What was the Geological and Mineralogical Nature of the Stone?

What are the current chemical constituents of the stone? Current natural constituents and contaminants will need to be distinguished from each other. Once again this information comes partially from the state geological surveys and from Parks' *Report*. The documentary research is usually backed up by x-ray fluorescence (XRF) and x-ray diffraction (XRD) analyses to determine the chemical constituents of the stone both qualitatively and quantitatively.

Scanning electron microscopy (SEM) is frequently used with XRF microprobe to show the actual structure of the stone, for example, with pollutant salts lodged in eroded fissures in the deteriorated stone surface. A great deal of the identification of minerals such as quartz and feldspar may also be accomplished by examining thin sections of the stone under a petrological microscope with transmitted light and polarized light. Thin sections are cut with a diamond saw and are mounted on glass slides where they are abraded down to a thickness of about 7 or 8 μm using water and carborundum papers. Once the microscopic analyses have been made, the information so gained can be passed on to the conservators. Why is this information so critical? The deterioration of stones can only be understood when one knows the chemical constituents of the stone, the cohesion between the crystals or grain structure of the stone, and the nature of pollutant salts and other substances deposited on and within the stone. The possibilities of chemical and physical transformation of crustal layers, for example, can also be understood only in the context of the chemical constituents of the stone. The stone can not even be cleaned without a basic knowledge of the chemical constituents. For example, if chemical cleaning methods are to

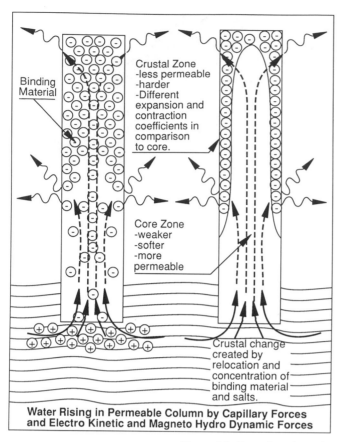

Biological Activity

Trees - Shrubs Plants - Grasses Mosses - Lichens Fungi - Algae Bacteria	Insects Marine borers Burrowing animals Birds

Aesthetic *Staining and* *discolouration* - Mud deposits - Algae - Fungi - Birds - Insects **Solution:** **Removal of binders** - Root secretions - Bird droppings **Formation or** **deposition of** **soluble salts** - Bacteria - Bird droppings	**Mechanical** *Splitting and prying apart* *Root action* *Abrasion;* *Moving branches* *Boring of holes* - Tree roots - Tree branches - Plant and lichen roots - Marine borers - Burrowing animals - Insects - Birds **Retention of moisture** **in or on surfaces** - Trees - Plants - Mosses

Figure 36. Deterioration of masonry material and structures.

be used, acidic cleaners tend to destroy stones based on carbonates and strong alkalis often tend to react with ferrous iron to form highly undesirable ferric hydroxide staining.

Does the Stone have a Pronounced "Grain," Bedding Plane, or Similar Structure? If pronounced grain or bedding planes are present, how was the stone placed in the structure in relation to them? Are any stone blocks delaminating because of incorrect orientation of the bedding planes? Usually there are standard orientations for the bedding planes in any masonry. The blocks are laid so that the bedding planes are perpendicular to the direction of loading.

In normal ashlar work the bedding planes should be parallel to the ground. In copings, projecting cornices, and belt courses, the bedding planes are arranged to lie vertically and at right angles to the face of the wall. In arches the bedding planes are so arranged that they are at right angles to the face of the wall and parallel to a line through the center of each voussoir to the center of the relevant arc of the arch.

In cases where the stone was laid with its bedding planes vertically and parallel to a major exposed face the stone tends to delaminate and peel away layer by

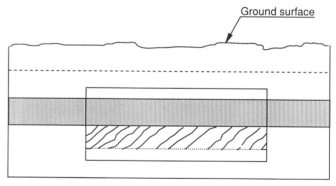

Figure 37a. Bedding planes: side view.

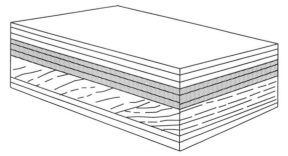

Figure 37b. Bedding planes: perspective view of removed section.

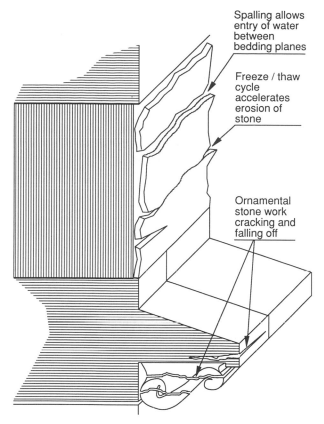

Spalling allows entry of water between bedding planes

Freeze / thaw cycle accelerates erosion of stone

Ornamental stone work cracking and falling off

Figure 38. Incorrect orientation of bedding planes.

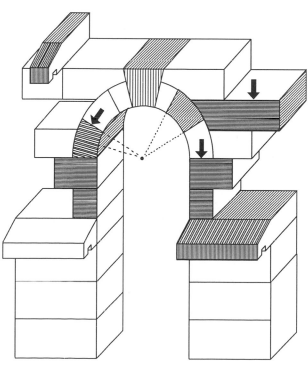

Figure 39. Correct orientation of bedding planes.

Face bedding problems.

layer. This fault is referred to as "face bedding." Projecting cornices often tend to lose carved details and particularly modillions from their undersides where such details crack away along the bedding planes.

How were the Stone Units or Blocks Placed in the Walls? Is the masonry solid or are there inner and outer wythes separated by rubblework and/or cavities? How are the inner and outer wythes bonded together? Are the inner and outer wythes made from different types or qualities of stone?

Where the inner and outer wythes are insufficiently bonded together the outer wythe frequently buckles outward under load, first developing a major bulge and then possibly even collapsing. The buckling will often occur because of differential loading on the inner and outer wythes.

Bulging wall face caused by loss of internal mortar.

efflorescence. When they occur in or below the surface they are termed subflorescence or cryptoflorescence.

The most common salts appearing as contaminants in masonry are sulfates, chlorides, nitrates and phosphates. Sulfates and chlorides are often associated with acid precipitation and air pollution. Nitrates also come from air pollution but being highly soluble in water tend to be easily removed by any water passing through the masonry. Traces of actual nitrates are thus not often found in the stone although they may well have been present and have actually caused damage. If they are found in any quantity nitrates usually are found to have come from some other source, e.g., from an industrial storage facility or from "saltpetre" used historically in making gunpowder. If the salts are causing severe damage to the stone they may have to be removed by washing and by poulticing. Chlorides may be associated with severe corrosion in metals embedded in, or in contact with wet masonry. Chlorides are particularly dangerous to iron and steel, copper, bronze, aluminum and even to some forms of stainless steel.

Were Metal Clamps, Dowels or Other Forms of Fixings or Connectors Used in the Masonry and if so Were They Made of Iron or Steel Which has Corroded and Expanded, Shattering the Surrounding Masonry? Such corroded metal work is often most conveniently cored out using diamond-tipped coring bits of appropriate diameters. I have worked on the restoration of the 1858 Oswego, New York, Customs' House where thousands of dollars worth of damage had been caused by corroding cramps shattering sandstone blocks. In this case the cramps were originally set in molten sulfur or "brimstone" which contributed to the corrosion when acid rain penetrated to the wrought-iron cramps. In such cases all traces of the sulfur must be removed in addition to the corroded iron.

What are the Nature and Condition of the Mortar in Which the Stones Were Laid? Earlier mortars tend to be based on lime rather than hydraulic cements. Lime mortars are acid soluble and tend to be very badly damaged by acidic rainwater and snow melt water if leaks and cracks are left unattended for years. Ultimately the lime is removed and only wet sand remains. The deposition of sheets of redeposited carbonates on external surfaces of walls and on the soffits of arches are sure indicators that lime is being removed from within the wall and that the wall is being seriously weakened in the process.

How are the Mortar Joints Finished or Pointed? Careful note should be taken of the overall appearance of the original pointing mortar; the color,

Are the Stones Wholly or Partly Water Soluble? For example, alabaster or crystalline calcium sulfate is partially water soluble. Are the stones wholly or partly acid soluble? Carbonate rocks such as limestone and marble are soluble in acids. Do the stones show any signs of having been partially dissolved? Stones which are partially soluble in water and acids such as acid rain will often hold up remarkably well until an open mortar joint, an eavestrough, or a rainwater pipe leaks into the masonry on a prolonged basis. Then the stones may be totally destroyed. In such situations, remedying leaks and carrying out limited repairs to mortar and some stones may greatly extend the life of the stone masonry.

Are there Accumulations of Water-soluble Salts on or in the Surface of the Stones? Powdery deposits of crystals of various salts on the surface are termed

Acid soluble stone; note the damage to left face which was exposed to the rain.

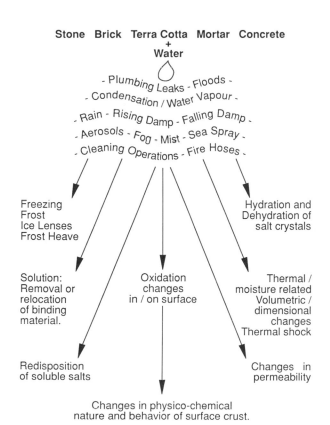

Figure 40. Deterioration of masonry materials and structures.

profile, and texture of the finished joints; and the grain sizes, colors, and shapes of aggregates. Examination of sand and mortar samples under a microscope at a magnification of about 20 to 30 with a built-in graticule to measure particle sizes is a most helpful part of the process here.

How were the Stone Surfaces Finished? What are the correct terms for these finishes, for example, punched, tooled, boasted, bush hammered?

What is the Crushing or Compressive Strength of the Stone Both When Dry and When Wet? (ASTM C 170-87 Standard Test Method for Compressive Strength of Natural Building Stone.)

What is the Modulus of Rupture of the Stone Both When Dry and When Wet? (Adapted from ASTM C 99-87 Standard Test Method for Modulus of Rupture of Natural Building Stone.) In the cases of some sandstones, the strengths even of fresh samples are actually halved when the stones are wetted.

The performance of the stone should be compared with the relevant ASTM Standards:

C 503-85   Standard Specification for Marble Building Stone;
C 568-79   (Reapproved 1985) Standard Specification for Limestone Building Stone;
C 615-85   Standard Specification for Granite Building Stone;

Oswego Custom House, iron cramps set in sulfur corroded and shattered stone masonry.

C 616-85   Standard Specification for Sandstone Building Stone;

C 629-80   (Reapproved 1985) Standard Specifcation for Slate Building Stone;

C 406-84   Standard Specification for Roofing Slate.

What are the Absorption and Bulk Specific Gravities of the Stone? (ASTM Standard Test Method C 97-83 Absorption and Bulk Specific Gravity of Natural Building Stone.)

What are the Capillary Characteristics of the Stone? These may generally be calculated from the uptake of distilled water by the stone sample from surface contact with an inert wetted pad or permeable medium. The amount of water absorbed is calculated against the dry weight of the sample and plotted against

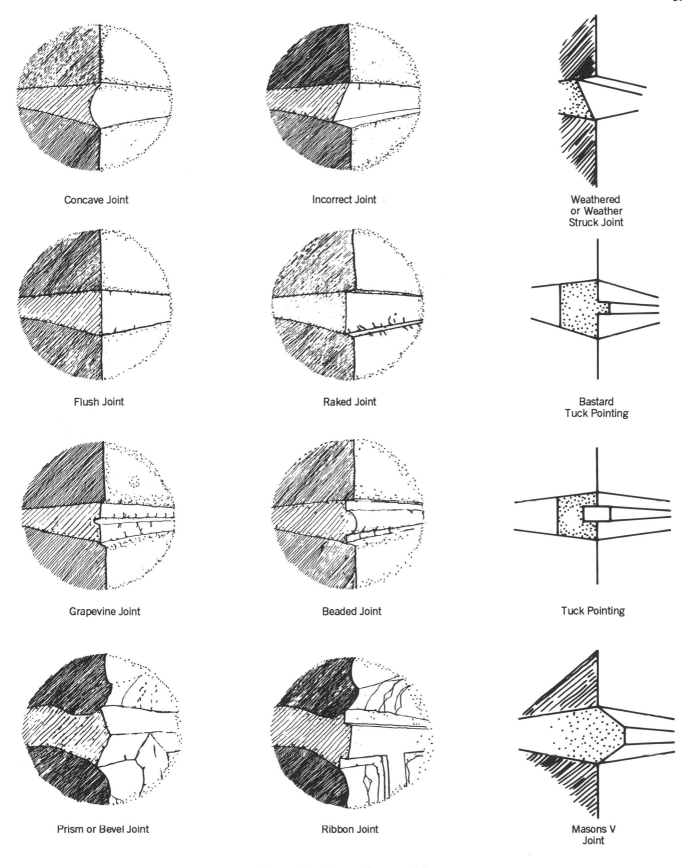

Figure 41a. Types of mortar joints.

STONE WORK

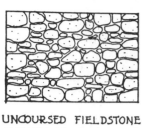
UNCOURSED FIELDSTONE ROUGH OR ORDINARY.

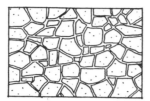
POLYGONAL, MOSAIC OR RANDOM.

COURSED

Laid of stratified stone fitted on job. It is between rubble & ashlar. Finish is quarry face, seam face or split. Called rubble ashlar in granite.
SQUARED-STONE MASONRY.

TYPES OF RUBBLE MASONRY

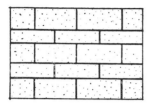
RANGE. Coursed

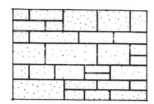
BROKEN RANGE.

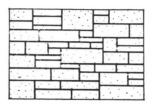
RANDOM RANGE. Interrupted coursed

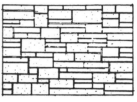
RANGE. Coursed (long stones)

TYPES OF ASHLAR MASONRY
This is stone that is sawed, dressed, squared or Quarry faced.

ELEVATIONS SHOWING FACE JOINTING FOR STONE.

Draft line

For both hard and soft stones. Rock or Pitch Face.

Smooth, but saw mark visible. All stones. Sawed Finish (Gang).

More marked than sawed. Soft stones. Shot Sawed (Rough).

Smooth finish with some texture. Soft stones. Machine Finish (Planer).

Tooled margin

May be coarse, medium or fine. Usually on hard stones. Pointed Finish.

After pointing on hard stones. Pean Hammered.

For soft stones. Bush-hammered.

All stones. Used much on granite. 4 to 8 cut in ⅞". Patent Bush-hammer.

For soft stones. Drove or Boasted.

Random For soft stones. Hand Tooled.

Tool marks may be 2 to 10 per inch. Machine Tooled.

For soft stones. Tooth-chisel.

Random For soft stones. Crandalled.

Textured by machine For Limestone Plucker Finish.

Very smooth. For Limestone. Done by machine. Carborundum Finish.

Smooth All stones. May use sand or carborundum. Rubbed (Wet).

Very Smooth Marble, granite. For interior work. Soft stones. Honed (rubbed first).

Very smooth Has high gloss. Marble and granite. Polished (honed first).

STONE FINISHES.
Seam face and split face (or Quarry face) not shown as they are not worked finishes.

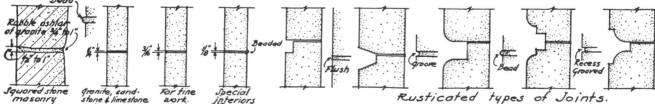
Bead
Rubble ashlar of granite ¾ to 1"
Squared stone masonry
¼ granite, sandstone & limestone ashlar. general use.
⅜ For fine work. Limestone
⅛ Special interiors
Beaded Flush
Groove
Bead
Recess Grooved
Rusticated types of Joints.

STONE JOINTS

TYPES, FINISH AND JOINTING OF STONE MASONRY.
A perch is nominally 16'6" long, 1'0" high & 1'6" thick = 24¾ cu.ft. In some localities 16'½ & 22 cu.ft. are used.

Figure 41b. Stone faces and finishes. (From *Architectural Graphic Standards*, 5th ed., (1956), John Wiley & Sons, Inc., New York.)

Mortar turned to sand by prolonged penetration of acid rain, St. Mary's Cathedral, Kingston, Ontario.

Two different types of sandstone weathering differently on the corner of a tower. The Ohio sandstone on the right is suffering from "alveolar erosion" caused by wind vortices and the increased deposition of water soluble salts caused by higher evaporation rates at the corner.

Sandstone and marble in a small area show the influences of microclimates on stone deterioration. Note how the sandstone surface is blistering as sulfate salts expand in and under the surface below the moulding where the rain does not wash the salts away. A little lower down where the acidic precipitation can wash the surface, the carbonates of the marble are being dissolved away.

Red sandstone blocks in a wall show what at first looks like ''face bedding'' problems, until close inspection reveals that the surface is exfoliating on all faces. The problem is caused by extreme physical and chemical changes in the surface crust.

A major structural crack passes through a block of limestone at an angle. Close inspection of the limestone blocks also reveals networks of microcracks which are being penetrated by acid rain. Ultimately these will cause the blocks to fall apart.

time. From these measurements, a capillary curve may be plotted.

What is the Extent and Nature of the Pore System Within the Stone?

Two methods may be used to determine these parameters—water uptake at atmospheric temperature and pressure (ATP) and under vacuum; and mercury intrusion porosimetry (MP or MIP). Mercury porosimetry is limited by the fact that certain assumptions have to be made as to the geometry of the pores; and because the size of the mercury molecule limits measurement to pores of over 32 Ångstrom units diameter or greater. MP will however permit us to determine the total porosity and the relative amounts of pores of known diameters. This permits us to calculate the relative amounts of micropores to macropores. There is some argument currently as to the critical pore diameter or size below which frost or salt damage would be likely to occur. Current observations suggest that the cutoff point is at about 5 to 8 μm. Below that size the damage occurs on a regular basis. Below 1–2 μm pore diameter the damage is almost inevitable. Above that size the pores can dry out and disruptive internal pressures usually do not develop.

THE CONSERVATION OF STONEWORK

Restoration versus Conservation

In the preservation of old buildings the term "restoration" has the specific meaning of recreating their ap- pearance or condition at some specific point in the past. "Conservation" means stabilizing and prevent- ing or retarding further deterioration. This part of this chapter examines all the conservation options for his- toric stone masonry including replacement or substitu- tion, consolidation, dismantling, and reerection and re- pairs. The principal problems are also reviewed with their solutions. Clearly, if a building was built with a stone which was selected without proper regard for its durability and which subsequently swiftly deteriorated because of its poor qualities, there would be little point in carefully finding exactly the same poor stone and recreating all the problems all over again. Replacement with more stone from the original source should be considered in cases where a basically durable stone has deteriorated only, for example, because of abnormal exposure to acid rain and air pollution, or because of lack of maintenance of the building leading to severe leaks in roofs, flashings, and rainwater disposal sys- tems. Since many of the original quarries or sources have closed down or have been worked out of stone, it may be necessary to find a replacement from elsewhere giving a close match in strength, color, texture, and chemical composition to the original stone which will remain in the structure. In my experience, matching the above qualities is not usually difficult but matching original dimensions in terms of bed-depth may be a serious problem. I have had many cases where the de- sired limestones and sandstones were simply not avail- able in blocks of sufficiently large vertical dimensions

Figure 42. Stone repair: photographic montage.

for the bedding planes to be correctly oriented. Because of this potential problem anyone seeking stone for restoration work is well advised to check and double check that the bed depth or thickness of the quarried strata are sufficiently large to allow for the supply of sawn stone of the desired vertical dimensions.

Obtaining the Stone

When obtaining stone for restoration work the ideal situation is for the experienced restorer or conservator to go to the quarries and select the material for the specific project. At the same time the restorer presents standards in the specifications for the job in order to ensure that the stone is of the requisite quality.

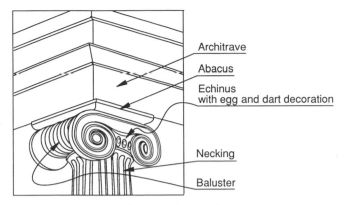

Figure 43a. Architectural details.

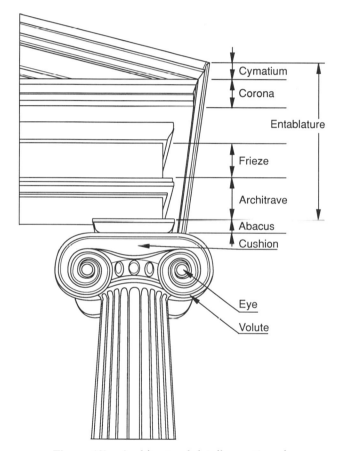

Figure 43b. Architectural details *continued*.

the quarry with dimensioned drawings with the bedding plane orientations clearly marked for all units individually. On the basis of this information, the quarry can supply accurate estimates for price and delivery times. Even in cases where the restorer is working through an intermediate stone dealer it is still advisable for the restorer to follow all these procedures. The restorer should also quote all the appropriate ASTM stone

The Use of Substitutes

In cases where deicing salts have caused severe damage to sandstones used for paving, staircase treads and at the bases of buildings adjacent to the sidewalk it may be necessary to consider using a limestone for replacement work. Limestones are often much more resistant than sandstones to attacks by salts. But on no account should sandstones be replaced by limestones where the runoff from the limestone will cause carbonates to be redeposited in the adjacent sandstone units. The original sandstones can be destroyed as a result of such substitutions, particularly in polluted environments. The substitution of more durable stones in conditions of extreme weathering and pollutant exposure is prudent but it is recommended that acid-resistant stones of igneous or metamorphic origin should be employed instead of limestones. As an example of this process, a fine grained granite of similar color to a disintegrating original sandstone was used for restoration work on the base of the National Assembly Building in Quebec.

Avoiding Bedding Plane Problems

The restorer must pay careful attention to the correct orientation of bedding planes in original work and in new work. Obviously if the original units are in good condition and showing no signs of problems despite incorrect orientation of the bedding planes, then they should be left alone. If, however, definite face bedding problems are occurring the offending unit should be carefully cut out and, if possible, turned so that the orientation is corrected. This will not often be possible and the unit may have to be totally replaced. In my experience bedding plane problems generally occur in certain sandstones which tend to split very readily on planes where thin clay layers occur. Some of the Quebec limestones of the Trenton and Chazy formations also tend to split along fine horizontal crack lines. In some sandstones the inexperienced practitioner may be confused by "contour scaling" or the loss of the crustal layer through oxidation crust formation and other causes. Although at first gance this phenomenon may be confused with face bedding problems, further inspection will immediately reveal that the losses are not parallel to one plane but also proceed at right angles to that plane.

Deicing salt damage in sandstone next to staircase.

Stone Veneers and Double Walls

In cases where veneers of stonework or outer wythes have become detached from backing masonry or inner wythes, it is first necessary to establish their stability. If it is clear that stonework of the outer wythe is actually moving outward and could become unsafe, then there are a number of possible approaches to the restoration of the masonry. It is essential that the cause of the problem be established so that it can be remedied first. I have known of a number of cases where thick stone walls had their inner and outer wythes moving apart and major structural cracking and bulging occurring. In nearly all of these cases the problems were the

Contour scaling in red sandstone.

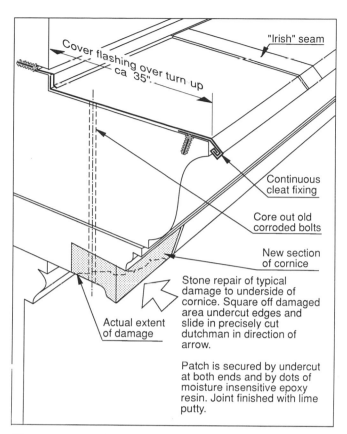

Figure 44a. Detail of flashing of main cornice: Vieux Palais de Justice, Montreal, Quebec.

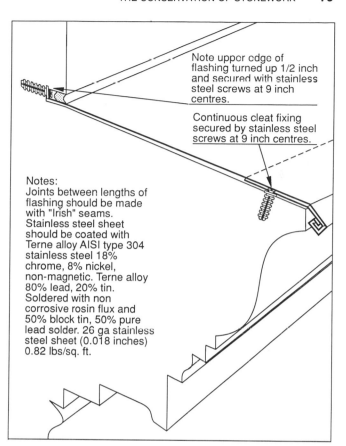

Figure 44c. New stainless steel flashing on belt course.

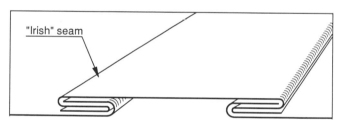

Figure 44b. Detail of flashing of main cornice.

result of acid precipitation penetrating into the interior of the wall via open joints and defective flashings or roofing. The excessive quantities of water had removed most of the lime from the mortar leaving only wet sand. Obviously in all such cases the sources of unwanted water must first be eliminated by repointing joints and replacing flashings and roof finishes.

Once the cause of the bond failure has been eliminated the wythes can be stabilized either by the injection of a liquid grout into the core of the wall to replace the deteriorated mortar, or by drilling holes with diamond-tipped coring bits through the outer wythe into a stable core or masonry backing and then inserting stainless steel tubular injection anchors set in cementitious grout or threaded stainless steel rods which are set in a moisture insensitive epoxy resin-based grout. Various combinations of these techniques may also be used. I use AISI Type 316 stainless steel for such conservation work because of its very high corrosion resistance. In locations where the problems have clearly been caused by acid recipitation and air pollution it is a false economy to use anything other than such corrosion-resistant material despite its expense.

Any subsequent restoration necessitated by the failure of less durable materials will immediately cost a great deal more than was saved by their use.

Dismantling and Rebuilding

In extreme cases of bulging wythes and in other cases where stonemasonry is unstable, the stonework may have to be carefully taken down and totally rebuilt. Such rebuilding should be preceded by numbering and recording so that the stonework can be restored exactly

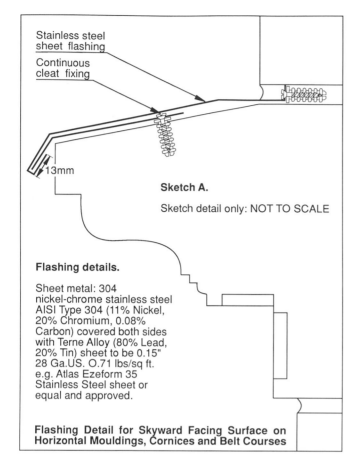

Stainless steel
sheet flashing

Continuous
cleat fixing

13mm

Sketch A.

Sketch detail only: NOT TO SCALE

Flashing details.

Sheet metal: 304
nickel-chrome stainless steel
AISI Type 304 (11% Nickel,
20% Chromium, 0.08%
Carbon) covered both sides
with Terne Alloy (80% Lead,
20% Tin) sheet to be 0.15"
28 Ga.US. O.71 lbs/sq ft.
e.g. Atlas Ezeform 35
Stainless Steel sheet or
equal and approved.

**Flashing Detail for Skyward Facing Surface on
Horizontal Mouldings, Cornices and Belt Courses**

Continuous Cleats:
Same metal and thickness as sheet metal specified above. Make cleats at least 38mm wide and folded into stainless steel flashings 13mm as shown. Any seams in the sheet metal flashing are to be formed as double locked cross welts. The upper edge of the flashing is to be secured with No. 8 stainless steel screws set in lead plugs at 450mm centres.

The cleat is to be secured with No. 8 s.s. screws set in lead plugs at 300mm centres. The upper edge of the flashing is to be covered with a neatly struck fillet of 1:1:6 mortar finished with a slightly concave profile. (all parts by volume white non-staining Portland Cement: hydrated lime: sand)

Figure 45. Flashing details.

as it was. Temporary numbering in chalk is placed on the faces of the stone units for photographic recording. When the stonework is dismantled the permanent numbers are painted onto faces which will be hidden in the rebuilding. I normally use exterior quality latex paints for this numbering. A system of temporary and permanent numbering avoids the difficult problem of removing paint from the finished faces of the stone units. Special attention should be paid to recording the thickness of joints so that they can be reproduced. Without this precaution the masonry can never be accurately rebuilt. I usually specify the use of timber or plywood templates or profile boards which are cut to match the vertical profiles of the masonry at various critical points.

When the stonework is being rebuilt the blocks should be set on soaked hardwood wedges so that they are in their correct positions and so that the mortar has time to cure without the blocks settling out of position. When the mortar has cured, the wedges will have shrunk and can be removed. The resulting holes can be filled with mortar.

Refinishing, Inserts, Repairs, or Consolidation?

Where stones have been dissolved by water or acidic solutions they may simply be reduced in thickness or may have lost binding material to such an extent that they are liable to crumble and fail under load. In the former case the restorer must judge whether the surface loss in any way endangers the continued survival of the stone. If it is merely an aesthetic problem, the stone should be left as it is. Where the remaining surface has a totally unacceptable appearance, it may be redressed or retooled if the original unit is thick enough. If redressing produces too large a setback, the stone block can be carefully cut free and can be advanced and reset. Redressing is not a technique for use in all situations but should be reserved for cases of severe surface deterioration in otherwise sound blocks. Any new stone units which are set into old salt-infested stonework must be isolated from that work by having their back surfaces coated with an appropriate waterproof coating such as a sanded bitumen paint. The coatings should be kept away from surfaces which will be exposed and it is generally recommended that they are stopped about one inch short of the face to avoid staining problems.

When stones naturally containing ferrous compounds are placed in masonry in contact with large volumes of fresh concrete it is also necessary to coat their backs or the face of the concrete in order to prevent reactions with the strong alkalis in the concrete. Indiana limestone is a good example of a stone which suffers from ''alkali staining'' in just this way. The rust-colored stains are, in fact, formed by ferric hydroxide resulting from a reaction between calcium hydroxide in the concrete and iron ions in the stone.

When fragments of a stone block have spalled off or where critical drip edges have weathered away, it may be necessary to insert a patch into the original stone. The hole in the stone is carefully squared off, with the sides undercut to assist in holding the patch in place. The patching may then be carried out with a piece of matching stone which is carefully cut to match the hole and set in position with dots of a moisture-insensitive epoxy resin. The small gap between the patch and the

Stabilized and restored voussoired stone beam; before and after views, 1840's Gatehouse, Kingston Penitentiary, Ontario.

original stone is then "pointed" or filled with a lime putty or similar mortar to match the stone. As in wood conservation such patches are known as "Dutchmen."

Plastic Repair or Dentistry?

Small chips and spalls may also be patched with "plastic" repairs. A plastic repair is usually a mortar/synthetic resin composite mixed with stone dust and other materials to form a stable patch matching the original in color and texture and which can be placed in position and shaped. It will then cure and harden in place adhering to the prepared surface at the desired location. The adhesion of the patch is additionally ensured by the insertion of threaded stainless steel rods, teflon, or nylon rods or other noncorroding reinforcement into the old stone and through the patch. Any resins used in such mortar repairs must be nonreemulsifiable which

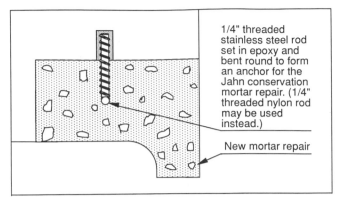

1/4" threaded stainless steel rod set in epoxy and bent round to form an anchor for the Jahn conservation mortar repair. (1/4" threaded nylon rod may be used instead.)

New mortar repair

Figure 46. Mortar repair: detail of new patch.

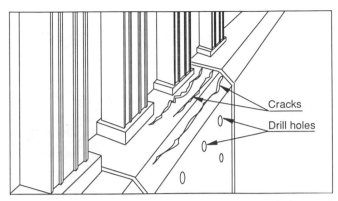

Cracks

Drill holes

Figure 49a. Stone repairs: perspective view of damaged stone.

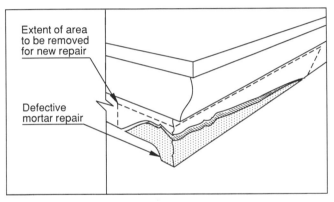

Extent of area to be removed for new repair

Defective mortar repair

Figure 47. Mortar repair: Vieux de Palais Justice, Montreal, Quebec.

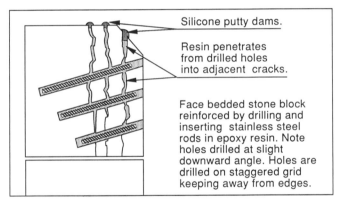

Silicone putty dams.

Resin penetrates from drilled holes into adjacent cracks.

Face bedded stone block reinforced by drilling and inserting stainless steel rods in epoxy resin. Note holes drilled at slight downward angle. Holes are drilled on staggered grid keeping away from edges.

Figure 49b. Stone repairs: section.

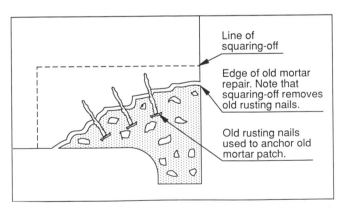

Line of squaring-off

Edge of old mortar repair. Note that squaring-off removes old rusting nails.

Old rusting nails used to anchor old mortar patch.

Figure 48. Mortar repair: detail of old patch.

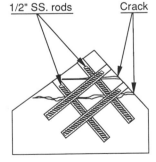

1/2" SS. rods   Crack

Cracked blocks are repaired by drilling across crack lines or planes and so arranging holes that each crack has at least one pair of holes crossing it from different sides to form a "dovetail". 1/2" diameter stainless steel rods are set in holes with their ends below surface by about 1 1/2". Note use of modelling clay dams to prevent epoxy resin leaking out onto surface.

Figure 49c. Stone repair: section of typical coping block.

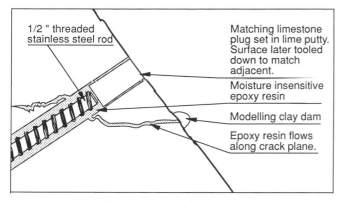

Figure 49d. Stone repair: enlargement of section.

1/2 " threaded stainless steel rod

Matching limestone plug set in lime putty. Surface later tooled down to match adjacent.

Moisture insensitive epoxy resin

Modelling clay dam

Epoxy resin flows along crack plane.

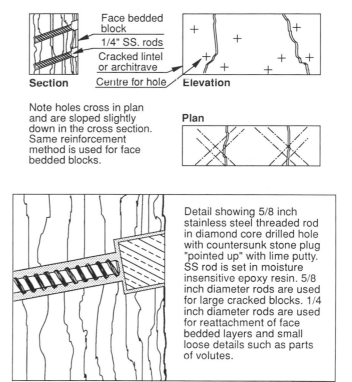

Face bedded block

1/4" SS. rods

Cracked lintel or architrave

Section   Centre for hole   **Elevation**

Note holes cross in plan and are sloped slightly down in the cross section. Same reinforcement method is used for face bedded blocks.

Plan

Detail showing 5/8 inch stainless steel threaded rod in diamond core drilled hole with countersunk stone plug "pointed up" with lime putty. SS rod is set in moisture insensitive epoxy resin. 5/8 inch diameter rods are used for large cracked blocks. 1/4 inch diameter rods are used for reattachment of face bedded layers and small loose details such as parts of volutes.

Figure 50. Repair of cracked stone lintels and architraves.

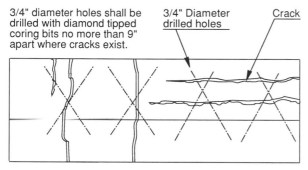

3/4" diameter holes shall be drilled with diamond tipped coring bits no more than 9" apart where cracks exist.

3/4" Diameter drilled holes

Crack

Figure 49e. Stone repair: side view of typical coping block.

means that when moisture passes through the patch, as it inevitably will, it will not reemulsify the resin and remove it.

Even when synthetic resins are used in such patches, experienced restorers avoid forming thin "feather" edges in the patches because these tend to be brittle and easily break away. Most restorers prefer to leave stones alone when the surface losses are nonthreatening, first because restoration is unnecessary but second because the weathered surface of the stone is a part of its history, character, and authenticity.

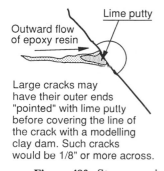

Lime putty

Outward flow of epoxy resin

Large cracks may have their outer ends "pointed" with lime putty before covering the line of the crack with a modelling clay dam. Such cracks would be 1/8" or more across.

Where blocks are badly cracked with loose sections the detached parts shall be reattached with Sikadur Hi Mod two component epoxy resin. The same resin may be injected down holes where steel rods are to be inserted, It will then flow out back along crack lines as shown. Henley, Twin Bridges Heritage Stonework Conservation. Sketch #1

Figure 49f. Stone repair: enlargement of crack.

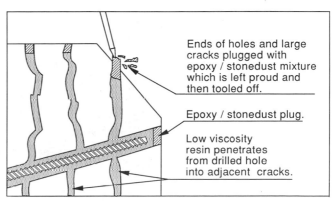

Ends of holes and large cracks plugged with epoxy / stonedust mixture which is left proud and then tooled off.

Epoxy / stonedust plug.

Low viscosity resin penetrates from drilled hole into adjacent cracks.

Figure 51. Stone repairs: section enlargement.

Consolidants

Where the loss of binding or cementing materials is causing the stone to crumble, the use of stone consolidants may be considered. Although sandstones, limestones, and some architectural ceramics may be treated with stone consolidants, sandstones with calcareous and argilaceous binders are perhaps the stones most frequently subject to binder or cement loss. The latter have been successfully consolidated with alkali silicates or with various types of alkoxysilanes and synthetic resins such as ethyl silicate, triethoxymethylsilane, or trimethoxymethylsilane. Although these two types of products are the most common, acrylic copolymers, epoxies, polyurethanes, and microcrystalline waxes have had some recorded successes in specific applications. For normal use on the exterior of buildings products of German origin of both types are available in North America. Bagrat silicates and Pro-SoCo's Conservare alkoxysilanes are the two major product ranges with proven long-term good performances. Consolidation with epoxy/solvent systems rather than pure low viscosity resins is the subject of apparently successful laboratory tests at the Getty Conservation Institute (personal communication). The lack of the frequently problematic darkening and reverse flow of the resin to the surface has been achieved by various means including solvent-saturated atmospheres in plastic film enclosures.

The history of the development of stone consolidants is marked with a long series of failures which have involved subsequent total losses of treated surfaces, severe discoloration, heavy soiling caused by the sticky nature of the treated surface, and many other problems caused particularly by entrapped moisture.

Early attempts to use resins with solvents were continuously dogged by the problem of the resin returning to the surface with the solvent as the latter evaporated. This typically caused darkening of the surface and sometimes an unpleasantly glossy, slick surface because of the resin concentration.

Consolidants will not function as grouts, void fillers, or means of reattaching flaking, exfoliating, or spalling surface layers. Spot use of moisture-insensitive epoxy resins may be appropriate for such purposes.

There have been many failures of historic stones which have been found to have been associated with earlier treatments with paraffin wax and/or beeswax. The "Caffal Process" or "Obelisk Process" which was still in use in the 1920s was based on the use of hot paraffin wax. This process was used on many New York landmarks, including "Cleopatra's Needle" in Central Park, and contributed to the deterioration of the stones.

This core from some historic concrete has been coated with an epoxy resin which has consolidated the concrete but has radically changed its appearance making it darker, yellow and glossy.

Cleopatra's Needle, Central Park, New York, showing deteriorated face.

Salts and Their Removal

Harmful accumulations of water-soluble salts are best dealt with by poulticing techniques which use "inert" powders which may be mixed with water to form a stiff paste with about the consistency of runny peanut butter or stiff cream. The stiff paste is applied to a lighly wetted surface and then left to dry. In excessively dry or sunny conditions, the evaporation of moisture from the surface of the poultice may be helpfully retarded by covering the poultice with a sheet of polyethylene. The moisture from the poultice soaks into the stone, dissolves the salts, and returns to the surface with them in solution. When the moisture evaporates into the atmosphere, the poultice dries out and the salts are left behind in the temporary surface provided by the poultice, which is then removed. The process may be repeated a number of times to complete the removal of the salts. Suitable poultice materials include diatomaceous earth (available, for example, as Celite which is manufactured by Johns Manville); fullers earth, and kaolinite.

Corroded Metal Elements

Where iron or steel cramps or dowels have corroded and shattered surrounding stonework through the expansion of their corrosion products, it is essential to remove the corroded remains and sulfur settings where these exist. A new cramp or dowel of a noncorroding metal such as an appropriate type of stainless steel may then be substituted for the original.

I have found that the easiest way to remove such corroded remains which may be jammed into the stone, is to drill them out with water-cooled diamond-tipped coring bits. Problems with mortars and repointing raise many major issues which are discussed in Chapter 7.

Poultice of diatomaceous earth and water being used to remove salts.

Repairs of cramp shattered stonework, Oswego, NY.

Median Monument, Queen Elizabeth highway bridge. St. Catherine's, Ontario. Further surface exfoliation was prevented by treating the stone surface with a water repellent.

Water Repellents

A final problem concerns stones which are excessively permeable or which have extensive networks of such small diameter pores or capillaries that they are subject to moisture-related problems. The water or moisture may be eliminated at its source or in some cases the stone surface may be treated with a water repellent or hydrophobic substance.

Water repellents, like stone consolidants, have a long history of unfortunate failures behind them. In situation where there are concentrations of water-soluble salts trapped behind the coating of water repellent, the latter may actually cause the destruction of the stone. In practice, only if and when all other methods for keeping water out of stonemasonry have been tried and found unsatisfactory, then there may be a case for the use of a water repellent. I have been consulted on a large number of cases of stone surface failures which have been traced to the use of silicone and less commonly metallic stearate water repellents. There have, of course, been thousands of examples of treatments with water repellents which have caused no problems but scientific research and field observations have suggested that in a large percentage of these cases there was, in fact, no need for the treatment in the first place. It should be clear, however, that water repellents have proved their value in certain specific applications, particularly where rain and spray are being driven through thin and permeable stonework in very exposed locations. Where such stonework is by the sea and the interior surfaces are powdering and crumbling, then the repellent should be applied to the exterior surface only. Stone window mullions and tracery are particularly prone to this problem.

I worked on a case where an oligomeric alkylalkoxysilane from the Conservare range of products was used to protect the surfaces of some vintage bridge pylons and median monuments built of dolomite. Fast moving trucks and cars constantly bombarded the surfaces of the stone with high velocity sprays of polluted water from puddles, causing deep penetration of pollutants and consequent damage. The additional feature of the alkali resistance of the selected repellent makes it an almost essential conservation material in this case because it will not be affected by the alkalis in fresh mortar or concrete used in the restoration work. Conservators generally agree that most water-repellent treatments are carried out unnecessarily and have added what may have been a substantial cost for no particular benefit. Most water repellents break down after a number of years and cease to function. Unfortunately, they do not break down evenly and can cause unsightly blotches and patches on surfaces as they deteriorate. Having broken down, water repellents then require replacement but difficulties of access usually prevent this essential maintenance.

BUILDING AND MONUMENTAL STONES OF THE UNITED STATES

Anyone who examines stones from existing buildings and monuments will at some point encounter a stone which they do not recognize. If they then go on to search for reference works to help them to identify not only the type of stone but its original source and even sources for replacements and repairs, they will most likely encounter some problems. The surveys and publications of the United States Geological Survey and the various state Geological Surveys will normally have described all of the stones and their sources in terms of counties, nearby towns, and even individual quarries. However, these publications may have appeared back in the nineteenth century, and there are hundreds of them. Clearly if one is starting with a totally unknown stone which comes from an old building in New York, for example, one cannot search every survey in the country for its source. There are no comprehensive works which are designed specifically for the needs of the restorer or conservator of buildings and monuments. The following schedules of names and descriptions are a first attempt at remedying this lacuna. Obviously such a short study cannot be comprehensive for all periods and for the whole of the United States, but it may be found to be helpful for the eighteenth and nineteenth centuries in the eastern part of the country. Seventeenth century stone sources were normally very small and very close to the building in which the stone was to be used. This could well mean that the "quarry" has never been identified let alone studied and the stone subjected to petrographic analysis.

NAMES AND DESCRIPTIONS OF STONES

Granites

Connecticut, New London County: Granite and gneiss. From 1643–1648, at East Lyme and Niantic the quarries produced an even-grained pinkish gray granite, marketed in the 1930s as "Golden Pink Niantic." At Groton the quarry produced a fine grained greenish gray granite; Millstone Quarry produced fine grained dark gray. Waterford granite is buff gray but light gray when hammered. It takes a fine polish and has been sold as "Connecticut White." Windham County produces a biotite granite gneiss quarried near Oneco. The "Oneco" granite is a fine-grained dark bluish gray stone.

Georgia, Elbert County: Elberton Granite, Elberton Blue, Elberton Gray, Oglesby Light Blue, Oglesby Dark Blue. Fine grained bluish gray biotite granite with black and dark gray grains, also a light gray medium grain granite.

Massachusetts: Quincy Granite, Medium Dark and Extra Dark Quincy Granite. A hornblende pyroxene granite quarried in and around Quincy, the general color ranges from a medium or bluish gray, to a very dark bluish gray all with blue or blue black spots (from 1825 at Bunker Hill Quarry). An unusual variety is known as "Goldleaf" and is characterized by yellowish and reddish specks of iron oxide derived partly from the oxidation of the unusual mineral aenigmatite (a titano-silicate of ferrous iron and sodium with aluminum and ferric iron). Quincy granites are unusual in that they do not contain mica.

Massachusetts: Rockport Granite, Moose-A-Bec Granite, Rockport. Hornblende granite of which the Rockport Gray and Sea Green are medium to coarse grained, hard, tough and durable taking a high polish; they are colored gray or olive green spotted with black. The Moose-a-Bec is a dark reddish gray, biotite granite with white and pinkish feldspars and smaller spots of black biotite. Example: Soldiers and Sailors World War Memorial, Pittsfield, MA.

Maine, Deer Island, Crotch Island: Goss Pink, Stonington Pink. Knox County: Vinalhaven Hurricane Island and Fox Island Granite. Coarse-grained gray biotite granite with pink to lavender; widely used for buildings and bridges. Contains orthoclase, microline, oligoclase, smoky quartz, and biotite. Crotch Island quarry opened in 1870. Compressive strength 23,620 lb/in^2. Example: St. John the Divine, New York.

Minnesota: Rainbow Granite, Minnesota Rainbow, and Cold Spring Rainbow Granite. A coarse grained red, pink, dark gray, or deep green background with swirling gneissic bands and knots of black. Takes and holds a fine polish. Weight 185 lb/ft^3. Crushing strength 23,000 lb/in^2. Modulus of rupture 3042 lb.

Minnestoa: St. Cloud, Rockville Pink, Minnesota Pearl Pink Granite. Medium grained pinkish gray, red, and fine grained gray; and coarse grained pink with gray quartz and biotite granites. Weight 175 lb/ft^3. Crushing strenght 20,000 lb/in^2. Modulus of rupture 2000 lb. SiO_2 62.15%; $A10_3$ 19.41%; Lime 2.27%; Phosphorus 0.13%.

New Hampshire: Milford Granite. Fine, medium, and coarse grained light gray, and pink granites with coarse black grains; a quartz monzonite. Examples: Columbia University Campus such as base of Low Library, New York.

New Hampshire: Concord Granite. Fine to medium grained light gray biotite-muscovite granite with the soft brownish color of the muscovite. The potassium feldspar crystals are very small giving the granite a fine grain. A second variety known in 1927 as Swenson's Antique Granite was colored warm buff and gray and was said to be reminiscent of old ivory in color. Examples: Concord State House 1816–1819 and Old State's Prison, Concord, 1812. Essex County Hall of Records, Newark, NJ.

North Carolina: Mount Airy Granite. Medium grained even textured light gray to white biotite granite, used for buildings and monuments. Biotite has some tendency to segregate in streaks. Quarry opened 1889, first shipment 1890. Examples: columns capitals and panels, Municipal Building, New York. SiO_2 70.70%; Al_2O_3 16.50%; Fe_2O3 2.34%; MgO 0.29%; CaO 2.96%; Na_2O 4.56%; K_2O_3 .45%; FeS_2 0.09%. Weight 165 lb/ft^3. Crushing strength 23,068 lb/in^2.

Rhode Island: Westerly Blue, Dark Pink, and Light Pink Granite. Fine grained gray, bluish gray, and brown granites, typically all with "pepper and salt" appearance caused by fine black grains. A medium coarse grained variety is colored a reddish gray speckled with black; this stone is a medium red when polished. From ca. 1847. Examples: Declaration of Independence Monument, Boston, MA.

Rhode Island: Westerly Granite. A very fine grained white granite when hammered but a clear dark blue when polished.

Virginia: Petersburg Granite. Medium grained gray; used for buildings and monuments.

Virginia: Richmond Granite. Fine grained, light gray biotite granite; used for buildings and monuments.

Vermont: Barre. Fine textured, medium grained white to light and medium dark gray biotite granite; used for all purposes. There is also a dark blue gray used for polishing only and a light gray for hammered work. The first quarries at Barre operated ca. 1814. The dark Barre granite consists of about 65% feldspars, 27% quartz, and 8% mica. This is the largest producer of granite in the United States.

Marbles: Including Orthomarbles and Metamarbles

Alabama, Talladega County: Alabama Marble. A fine grained white marble with variations of more or less creamy color and two varieties with either fine pencil like grayish veins or heavier veins of a greenish or dark gray with orange or pink clouded borders to the veins. Example: Interior, United States Custom House, New York, (Cass Gilbert) 1899–1907; and the Arkansas State Capitol.

Colorado, Yule Creek: Leadville Quarries, upper part medium grained white calcitic marble; lower part dolomitic (primarily 1886–1940). Examples: Tomb of the Unknown Soldier and the Lincoln Memorial.

Georgia, Tate District, Tate and Marble Hill: Murphy Marble. Medium to coarse grained predominantly calcitic white, rose to deep pink, veined and mottled with greenish black actinolite and hornblende. In 1927, the Georgia Marble Company advertised that their White and Silver Grey Georgia Marbles were unexcelled for sculpture work exposed to the weather, the marble being unaffected by even the most severe weather. Examples: New York Stock Exchange is Georgia White; Buckingham Fountain, Grant Park Chicago is Georgia Pink. Columns and monoliths 30 ft long by 4 ft diameter. $CaCO_3$ 98.96%; $MgCO_3$ 0.13%; AlO 0.22%; SiO 0.61%; Loss 0.08%. Weight 165 lb/ft^3. Water absorbtion after 24-hr immersion 0.028%.

New York: Catskill Marble. Fossiliferous limestone dark brown in color with crinoids. Very hard and dense. Used in buildings and engineering works.

New York, Duchess County: South Dover, Dover White. Medium grained very white dolomitic marble used extensively for fine building work (by 1815).

New York: Tuckahoe. White coarse grained dolomitic marble. Once extensively used for building work.

Tennessee: Knoxville District, East Tennessee. A wide range of thick bedded Palaeozoic crystalline limestones which take a high polish and are known as Holston orthomarble; the predominant colors are pinks but there is a range from light gray and pinkish gray, via deep pink and red to a deep chocolate brown.

Usually used for interiors, the names of the Tennessee marbles are usually descriptive of the distinguishing features in a polished state, for example, Dark Cedar Tennessee (dark chocolate with fossil fragments), Appalachian Dark Chocolate, and Appalachian Roseal (fine grained grayish pink with splotches of white, pink, rich red, and black). Many varieties contain fossils which may range from indistinct fragments to very large straight shelled cephalopods as large as seven feet long. The United States Government opened the first quarries in 1838 for interior marble for the U.S. Capitol. In 1934 Bowles noted that Tennessee marble accounted for 35.5% of the total value of marble produced in the country.

Vermont: Clarendon marble. A number of varieties for both exterior and interior use, light in color generally with a white background with gray and green clouded and veined varieties; there is also a green veined cream and a cream with golden vein and blue. Example; Exterior, State Educational Building, Albany NY. Crushing strength 14,000 psi. Water absorbtion with immersion 0.01%.

Vermont: Pittsford District. Medium to coarse grain light bluish gray. Example: Scott Fountain, Belle Isle, Detroit made from single 65-ton block.

Vermont: Rochester Quarry. Serpentine marble, "Verde Antique" deep green with light green and almost white veining.

Vermont: Danby Quarry, Dorset Mountain. Close grained white with soft clouding of grey and green; occasional tints of light tan or "gold" (since 1907).

Vermont: Imperial Quarry Danby, Dorset Mountain. Close grained white with gray and beige markings; white with bold gray green veining (since 1907).

Limestones

Indiana or Bedford Limestone. Termed Salem limestone by the geological surveys of Indiana and Illinois, and Spergen limestone by the U.S. Geological Survey, a calcarenite or detrital limestone composed of oolites, fossil shells, and carbonate detritus. The stone occurs in massive beds; and single blocks 60 ft, long, 12 ft high, and 4 ft thick are commonly available. This stone comprises 60% of the dimension limestone produced in the United States. Production commenced in 1929.

Indiana limestone is gray or bluish gray below groundwater level but pale buff to light grey as it is exposed and weathered. Stylolites or "crowsfeet" may occur. These resemble graph lines in appearance and are present along bedding planes and locally throughout the rock. They consist of black shaly bituminous matter and occasional pyrites and other ferruginous material. They are not usually large enough to cause weathering and staining problems. Brown staining may result from contact with alkalis and organic matter, for example, ferric hydroxide staining from concrete.

Bedford Blue: 1.15% SiO_2; 1.91% Fe_2O_3; 53.25% CaO; 1.23% MgO; 42.40% CO_2.

Bedford Buff: 0.77% SiO_2; 0.63% Fe_2O_3; 3.0% Al_2O_3; 52.85% CaO; 1.18 MgO; 41.54% CO_2.

Weight per cubic foot: 140.3–152.4 lb/ft$_3$. Compressive strength: Buff 9012 psi; Blue 10,823 psi. Shear strength: Buff 1222 psi; Blue 1016 psi.

Tennessee: Holston orthomarble (see **Marbles**).

Sandstones

Connecticut: Portland Brown Stone. A medium to fine textured Upper Triassic sandstone of uniform reddish brown color, with flakes of muscovite parallel to the bedding planes. Quarries at Portland opened in 1665. Examples: Morris-Jumel Mansion, ca. 1765, New York; Cooper Union Building, New York 1859; Church of the Ascension, Fifth Ave and 10th St. New York, 1841. Also quarried at Middletown, Middlesex County, CN. Crushing strength 13,980–15,020 lb/in.^{2}. Specific gravity 2.35. Ratio of absorbtion 1:40. Silica 70.11%; alumina 13.49%; Fe_2O_3 4.85%; lime 2.39%; magnesia 1.44%; soda and potash etc. 7.37.

Massachusetts: East Longmeadow Sandstone. Upper Triassic sandstone evenly fine-grained brick red to reddish brown in color. Iron oxide cementing quartz grains. Examples: St. George's Church, Stuyvesant Sq. and East 16th St. New York, 1848: Bobst Library, New York University, 70 Washington Sq., New York, 1973.

New Jersey: New Jersey Brownstone. An Upper Triassic compact sandstone fine to coarse grained, thickly bedded with and without distinct lamination. The stone is arkosic with a cement of silica and sometimes iron oxide. The colors vary but include white–gray–brown and red. Examples: Trinity Church, Broadway and Wall St., New York, 1846; Villard Houses, Madison Ave. between 59 and 61 Sts., 1884. Quarries; Passaic, Belleville, North Arlington, Pleasantdale, Patterson, Little Falls and Osborne and Marsellis. The stone and hence the quarries extend in a belt 32 miles wide along the Delaware River above Trenton, and from the Palisades on the Hudson to the Ramapo River at Suffern NY.

New York: New York Bluestone, Genesee Valley Bluestone. A fine grained dense even gray-blue sandstone. Genesee Valley Bluestone is quoted in Sweet's in 1927 as having a crushing strength of 19,970 lb/in.^{2}. Weight

150 lb/ft³. Silica 76.50%; alumina 14.75%; Fe_2O_3 6.35%; water 2.00%. The Genesee Valley Quarry opened in 1899 at Ambluco in Wyoming County, NY. Massive use for paving but also used for ashlar and bed courses. Extremely durable and wear resistant. An analysis for a sandstone from this region and known as Bigelow bluestone (also known as Ulster bluestone) by F.L. Nason and published by Dickinson in 1893 was as follows: Minerals: quartz and feldspar, quartz grains angular, some feldspar grains fresh and others almost completely decomposed; cementing material silica; no carbonate of lime and very little iron oxide.

New York, Catskills: Saugerties Bluestone. A fine grained dense, even gray-blue sandstone of the Upper Devonian period, with fine large slabs, some containing fossil brachiopods. Extensive quarrying for paving slabs for New York City all through the nineteenth century. The old quarries now contain Harvey Fite's famous monumental sculpture Opus 40 which was built 1939–1976. The grain structure is extremely fine and compact. Freshly broken surfaces are bluish gray but weathered surfaces oxidize to a grayish brown.

New York: Medina Sandstone. Upper Silurian fine-grained sandstone, quartz grains with minor amounts of kaolinized feldspar; colors gray to red and variegated. Locations: western New York with major deposits in Orleans County at Medina, also in Niagara County at Lockport, for example, and Monroe County at Brockport. The deposits extend into Canada where the stone was also extensively quarried.

New York: Potsdam Sandstone. An Upper Cambrian fine to medium grained sandstone with angular grains of clear quartz in a siliceous cement. The colors range from light pink to light red and reddish brown and there is also a variegated type. Sources: northern New York, Racquette River Valley, Lawrence County, northern Adirondacks. Potsdam Quarry since 1856.

Ohio, Cuyahoga County, Lorain County, northern Ohio: Berea, South Amherst Quarries. The Mississippian sandstone commonly occurs as fill in deep ancient channels cut in underlying shales. Some of the quarries at South Amherst are 235 ft deep. The colors and types vary but a typical Berea is light gray medium- to fine-grained protoquartzite with silica and some clay cement. Honey or buff colored variations exist with a coarser grain version with fine rust colored banding. In polluted environments rust-colored staining may be found to consist of individual rusting grains of ferric compounds (from ca. 1840.) Examples: carved stone-

work of the Ottawa Parliament Buildings, East Block, 1859; Oswego, NY, Custom House 1858.

Ohio: Massilon Sandstone, Middle Pottsville; Glenmont, Holmes County, Briar Hill; Ohio. The type consists of a wide variety of sandstones which tend to be cross-bedded and poorly sorted with grain sizes varying from fine to coarse. Typical dimensioned stone is buff to light ochre in color with darker rust colored and even dark red-brown fine irregular bands or veins. The latter are usually left in relief as the stone weathers. One variety of Briar Hill Sandstone is a warm Indian Red in color. Briar Hill Sandstone's chemical analysis is as follows: silicon dioxide 95.00%; aluminum oxide 2.75%; iron oxide 0.60%; calcium oxide 0.30%; magnesium oxide 0.25%; loss in ignition 1.10%. Absorbtion 6% by weight. Crushing strength 4000–6000 lb/in.².

Pennsylvania: Pennsylvania Brownstone. An Upper Triassic, fine-grained, even textured, reddish brown to purplish brown sandstone with fine angular quartz grains in a cement of clay and iron oxide. Principal quarry was at Hummelstown, Dauphin County from 1867.

Pennsylvania: Delaware Valley Sandstone, Lumberton Quarry, Lumberville, Bucks County. A variety of sandstones with colors ranging from buff and light bluish gray to dark gray to brown. Lumberton Quarry has operated since 1852. Used as ashlar but also as split face fieldstone and rubble.

SOURCES

Bates, Robert L. *Geology of the Industrial Rocks and Minerals.* New York: Dover, 1969.

Bowles, Oliver. *The Stone Industries, Dimension Stone, Crushed Stone, Geology, Technology, Distribution, Utilization.* New York: McGraw-Hill, 1934.

Briar Hill Stone Company Stone Literature and Samples, Glenmont, Ohio, 44628

Building Stone Institute. *Stone Catalog.* New York. Various years. Building Stone Institute.

Center for Preservation Research, Columbia University, New York. Historic Building Stones Collection.

Dickinson, Harold T. Quarries of Bluestone and Other Sandstones in the Upper Devonian of New York State. *New York State Museum Bulletin*, Albany 1903. University of the State of New York.

Indiana Limestone Institute. *Research and Development in Indiana Limestone.* Chicago: 1968. Unpublished Report.

Lent, Frank A. *Trade Names and Descriptions of Marbles,*

Limestones, Granites and Other Building Stones Quarried in the United States, Canada and Other Countries. New York: Stone Publishing Company, 1925.

Matero, F.G. and Teutonico, J.M. The Use of Architectural Sandstone in New York City in the 19th Century. *Bulletin of the Association for Preservation Technology*, Vol. XIV, No. 2, 1982.

McKee, Harley J. *Introduction to Early American Masonry, Stone, Brick, Mortar and Plaster.* Washington: 1973. National Trust for Historic Preservation and Columbia University, 1973.

Radford, William A. (ed.) *Radford's Cyclopedia of Construction.* Chicago: Radford Architectural Company, 1909.

Sweet's Architectural Catalogue. Twenty Second Annual Edition. 1927–1928. Section A.

Vermont Marble Company. *Marble and Granite: Marble Color Selector and Use Guide.* Proctor, ND: Vermont Marble Company.

STONE CONSERVATION CASE HISTORIES

The following extracts from case histories and specification notes are taken from the files of the Center for Preservation Research, Columbia University, New York. They are included here to illustrate the form and contents of a series of typical conservation projects. They also illustrate precisely how typical technical problems are handled both in terms of techniques and materials, and how the specifications are written.

A CHURCH IN NEW YORK

Purchase of scaffolding by the Church, in an amount determined by the dimensions of the Tower and Spire, could be extremely cost-effective. The Church should pay a contractor for dismantling and reerection as the project proceeds, but could sell the (now used) scaffolding upon completion of the work, recovering a considerable percentage of the cost. Consideration should also be given to the advance purchase of some materials, such as colored sands and replacement stone, that could become difficult to secure in the later years of the work.

Final contract documents should be distributed to a short list of qualified restoration contractors for negotiated bidding. Submittal requirements must include the identification of all proposed subcontractors, a list of references and of recent reviews, a proposed work schedule, and price. It may be appropriate to make an initial award (perhaps as early as summer, 1987) for a demonstration contract involving only 2 or 3 bays of the Church, or the Soldier's Monument, as an opportunity for full-scale field-testing of all methods. This would permit final reevaluation of many important aspects of the project, including coordination and supervision needs, contractor competence, safe storage, handling and disposal of commercial projects, impact upon Church operations, total cost, and visual aesthetics.

Proper execution of the full project, which we estimate as 3 to 5 years in duration, will require close collaboration of the Church and its consultants in the matter of supervision. Technical judgments will certainly need to be made at all stages of the work; there must be established a mechanism to do so quickly and intelligently. Complete familiarity with the condition of the Church, with earlier restoration efforts, and with the materials and techniques being utilized by the contractor is necessary for all persons involved in on-site decision-making.

VII.2. Specific Operations

VII.2.1. Cleaning

Preliminary cleaning tests were carried out on June 25, 1986, on the Monument in the northeast corner of the Churchyard. The Monument, built shortly after completion of the Church, is said to be of the Little Falls sandstone, and has a treatment history that is similar to that of the Church. Testing was done on the north face (see Appendix B, Fig. 17), and the northeast corner. Acidic products conventionally used for the cleaning of sandstone did not remove the soiling effectively, because of the presence of organic coatings (the earlier treatments) that prevent the cleaners from coming into direct contact with the stone surface.[1]

The most complete series of tests was done to evaluate the possibility of alkaline degreasing, followed by acidic cleaning.[2] Four commercially manufactured alkaline products were tested. These were:

Heavy Duty Paint Stripper (HDPS);
Limestone Prewash (LP);

---

[1] Pressure washing without chemical treatment was also found to be ineffective. This surely would have been the case with water spraying, and with steam. Abrasive methods were ruled out as excessively damaging and dangerous. For a review of available techniques, see Ashurst, John, "Cleaning and surface repair," in *Conservation of Historic Stone Buildings and Monuments* (N.S. Baer, ed.). Washington: National Academy Press, 1982; also Weiss, Norman R., *Exterior Cleaning of Historic Masonry Buildings*. Washington: U.S. Dept. of the Interior, 1975.

[2] This two-step approach has become more common in recent years. We are currently involved in the cleaning of the General Electric Building, which is brick and terra cotta, by such a method. Earlier evaluation on sandstone and slate gravestones was done by us in the Trinity Churchyard, at King's Chapel Burying Ground, Boston, and the Ancient Burying Ground, Hartford. Some basic principles of chemical cleaning have been summarized by Heller, Harold L., "The chemistry of masonry cleaning," *Bulletin of the Association for Preservation Technology*, IX (2), 2–9 (1977).

766 Prewash; and
T-792 Alkaline Prewash[3]

The stone surface was prewetted only for the Limestone Prewash. All application was by brush. Air temperature was about 65 F, with some wind. Application time was 1 hour. The products were fully rinsed with water @ 500 psi. Restoration Cleaner (RC), diluted 1 part water to 2 parts concentrate, was then applied by brush, reapplied (and scrubbed) after 5 minutes, then rinsed fully @ 500 psi. (This was repeated in small areas within some of the test panels.) Surface pH was measured to ascertain that complete neutralization had taken place.

Performance of all systems was generally good, with the LP slightly worse than the others. The cleaning effect is dramatic; no loss of stone, etching, efflorescence or discoloration was observed. There appeared to be some drying or absorption of the 766 and the T-792 after 20–25 minutes, which lead to a procedural modification in the second set of tests, carried out on the Church, on November 7, 1986.

These later tests were done at the junction of elevations 18 and 20, that is, the southeast corner of the Chapel, where surfaces of both the Little Falls and the East Longmeadow sandstones could be cleaned. Air temperature was approximately 50 F. The 766 and the T-792 were tested again, with prewetting of the walls for about 2 minutes. Both were applied for only $\frac{1}{2}$ hour. (The HDPS and the LP were eliminated from the testing program for several reasons, including the greater difficulty of handling these products, especially on the higher elevations of the Church.) Another product, 859, an organic solvent-based stripper, was also tested here, with an application time of 15 minutes, and no prewetting.

All three were rinsed; the RC was then applied, diluted as in the earlier tests. After 5 minutes, a second application of the RC was made, then rinsed @ 500 psi.

Greater variation was seen in these tests, largely because of the shorter dwell time of the prewashes. In some areas, the 859 actually outperformed the other prewashes, but full interpretation of the several panels done in this location suggests that the T-792 may be the most generally useful product. It appears that prewetting will be possible with the T-792, which handled very well under these conditions. Supplemental use of the 859 for areas that resist cleaning seems feasible once such areas have dried.

Our recommendation, based on these test results, is that removal of surface coatings and heavy soiling can

[3] All are manufactured by ProSoCo, Inc., P.O. Box 1578, Kansas City, Kansas 66117. For product descriptions, see manufacturer's literature, including "Masonry cleaning weatherproofing and restoration products," and "Restoration products," both printed 1985.

be done by use of ProSoCo's T-792 Alkaline Prewash (prewetting, applied for 1 hour, rinsed @ 500–1000 psi with a broad fan nozzle, minimum 6 gpm flow rate), followed immediately by RC (diluted as described earlier, applied for 5 minutes, then re-applied, scrubbed and rinsed). Tarpaulins may need to be used to protect the public, especially at the east and west ends of the Church, where the work will be near property lines, and control of pedestrians is thus not entirely possible. Windows will also require protection with polyethylene sheeting and/or a strippable masking material; of special concern are the clerestory windows, which are not double glazed.

We believe that, in this instance, cleaning is of more than cosmetic value. Thorough removal of the soiled wax (and silicone) layer constitutes an important measure for the preservation of the stone, as it should effectively reduce moisture entrapment. It is, moreover, necessary to eliminate this coating prior to any further conservation treatment, most especially impregnation with a consolidant (see section VII.2.4. of this report)

BURIAL GROUND PHASE I

5.2.2. ADHESIVE REPAIR AND REATTACHMENT

Fragmented markers should be repaired before pieces become lost. For smaller fragments a structural adhesive, such as a 2-part water insensitive polyamid epoxy resin, is adequate. For the majority of repairs at the Burial Ground, Sikadur Hi Mod Gel alone and in conjunction with threaded nylon pins was employed. In previous stone fragment repairs in other northeastern cemeteries, this has provided excellent bonding and continued performance.

For adhesive repair, fragments should be cleaned as described for masonry and dried thoroughly. For surface preparation, the contact edges should be swabbed with a suitable solvent system such as denatured alcohol followed by acetone to ensure clean, degreased, dry surfaces. All joints should be dry tested for fit before the adhesive is applied. Surfaces should be aligned with a straight edge to maintain original plane. The adhesive should be mixed in quantities readily applied within the setting time. It should be applied thinly and evenly to both surfaces to be joined, leaving an adequate margin ($\frac{1}{4}$ in.) toward the outer edges to prevent surface exposure. The surfaces should be immediately joined and held in position until the initial set has occurred (approximately 15 minutes). It may be necessary to secure the individual pieces to be joined with clamps or other means to insure complete immobilization during the curing set. Any excess adhesive visible at the cracks should be mechanically removed in its gel state but before it hardens as it will discolor and degrade when exposed to sunlight.

On those stones where areas of loss exist along narrow

breaks, a fill of two parts white Portland Cement: one part hydrated lime (by volume) should be applied. The fill may be colored to match the stone by the addition of alkali-stable cement pigments in very small quantities (no more than 10% of the total binder component). Larger losses of stone along breaks require the addition of an appropriate aggregate to control shrinkage (see patching information below).

For most breaks, it is necessary to provide reasonable alignment by working on a horizontal support. Improperly aligned joins are unsightly. A sheet of plywood may be placed on sawhorses to provide a suitable work table on site. For tablets which have been deformed, temporary support of the deformation configuration must be constructed to achieve joint alignment and reduce stress at the joint. Masons' shims of various sizes are useful for this localized support.

For larger fragments or joins which require structural reinforcement, flexible threaded nylon or threaded stainless steel pins may be used, depending on the degree of strength or flexibility required. The diameter of the pin should not exceed one quarter the width of the stone. The length of the pin should be eight times the width of the drilled hole. Holes should be drilled with a masonry bit one-eighth inch larger than the diameter of the pin to be used. To determine the proper alignment of the pin holes, one edge is predrilled to the proper depth and its holes are filled with a colored chalk or crayon. Carefully assemble the adjacent section and the chalk will mark the respective location for pinning. These markings can then be rechecked using an adjustable scale such as that on a carpenters combination square. The second section should be drilled to the proper depth and angle using an adjustable carpenters angle for comparison, and then all holes should be cleaned of dust and debris with compressed air. Edges and holes should be swabbed with appropriate solvents such as denatured alcohol followed by acetone and allowed to dry. A dry assembly is essential to verify the hole placements and alignment of the fragments. Adhesive should be applied as described above and packed into holes before inserting pins, taking care to prevent excess from travelling to the surface of the stone.

Where original and replacement iron base pins were found, their removal or stabilization was considered essential for the future survival of the stones. This was achieved by either drilling the iron pins out and replacing them with threaded nylon rod as described above or by cleaning them down to bare metal (removing all corrosion) and priming them with a single-component, aluminum-pigmented moisture-cured urethane primer (Tnemec 50-330 Poly-Ura-Prime) before reuse. The latter option was only selected when removal was too difficult or dangerous to the stone and pins were found to be in relatively sound condition. Even broken tab assemblies were reattached by inserting nylon pins rather than recreating the same faulty design. Under no circumstances were markers completely adhered to their raised bases with structural (epoxy) adhesives, as this was considered too rigid and irreversible.

5.2.3. CLEANING

The decision to clean should be based on a genuine necessity to clean as all masonry cleaning subjects the stone to potential hazards. A monument which is darkened with soiling and biological growth is not only disfigured but also susceptible to accelerated masonry deterioration and therefore requires cleaning. A lightly soiled monument with legible details however, may not require a major cleaning. All cleaning methods must be tested in a discreet location for each stone before full-scale treatment. The gentlest methods should be tested first and if acceptable, should be chosen so as to avoid unnecessary damage to the stone.

5.2.3.1. Water Cleaning

Water cleaning is the gentlest, safest, and least expensive method of cleaning masonry especially for marbles and limestones. Most general surface soiling and some biological growth is easily removed with water. All open joints must be repaired to prevent penetration of quantities of water into the masonry. The water used should have a low metals content to avoid staining. Usually a potable water supply is adequate; however, the use of a particulate filter is advisable to secure against latent metallic staining.

Water can be applied at low pressure (up to 500–600 psi) and may be supplemented by gentle scrubbing with soft nonmetallic bristle brushes. However, cleaning with pressurized water and scrubbing should not be considered if the surface of the stone displays fragile condition.

Since black crusts, resulting from a carbonate stone's interaction with acid rain, are partially water soluble, they may be removed with a slow water misting soak. A perforated garden hose should be set up horizontally parallel to the surface to deliver water at city water pressure for 24 hours. Cleaning is done from top to bottom in this technique. As large amounts of water are used in this treatment, it is especially important that all joints and seams are watertight to prevent the introduction of water to the interior of the masonry and that drainage from the site is provided. Slight staining can sometimes develop on certain stones possessing iron-containing minerals which can react to form brown or yellow oxide stains.

5.2.3.2. Chemical Cleaning

For organic stains below the surface of the stone which are not removed by a water wash, the application of a bleaching poultice has proven to be very effective on porous stones such as marble. A low concentration solution of technical grade calcium hypochlorite (1.5–6%) is mixed into an inert clay body, such as kaolin and attapulgite clays. This paste is then spread over the stone or in localized areas to a thickness of no less than $\frac{1}{4}$ in. and left on for 10–30 minutes. The paste is then removed using nonabrasive tools such as wood or rubber spatulas and the stone is rinsed thoroughly with clean water. No odor of calcium hypochlorite should remain after rinse.

Poultice applications may be repeated if staining remains.

5.2.3.3. Abrasive Cleaning

Abrasive cleaning involving any grit or aggregate applied under pressure should not be used on soft stone types such as those found in the Burial Ground. This technique is considered too aggressive and can cause irreversible damage. It may lead to accelerated weathering by pitting the surface, thus opening the masonry to increased moisture penetration and atmospheric reactivity and subsequent deterioration.

5.2.3.4. Metallic Stain Removal

For removal of iron staining resulting from the corrosion of pins and braces, a saturated solution of ammonium citrate with glycerin and buffered with ammonium hydroxide to a pH of 8.5 should be used locally in a poultice application as described above under chemical cleaning. In this case the poultice should be covered with plastic for 48 hours. After the plastic has been removed and the poultice has completely dried, the remaining material should be removed with dry brushing and nonabrasive tools. The area should then be thoroughly rinsed with clean water.

As above, poultice applications may be repeated if some staining remains.

5.2.4. CONDITION

Consolidation treatment should be carefully considered for individual stones only by a professional conservator. If consolidation is considered viable, it must be tested before a full-scale treatment program is attempted. Previous research and test data suggest the use of organo-silicates as promising stone consolidants. The model treatments done on site using an ethyl silicate (Conservare Stone Strengthener H and OH, manufactured by Wacker-Chemie and distributed by ProSoCo) have shown to increase abrasion resistance and water repellency without significantly reducing water vapor permeability or changing color and texture. Consolidation of friable fragments is necessary prior to reattachment in order to insure adequate joint adhesion at the break. In all cases consolidation should be preceded by cleaning where a hydrophobic consolidation system is selected, as cleaning will be difficult later on. Mortar repairs must be installed prior to treatment and allowed to cure for 1–2 weeks before application of the consolidant.

For stones of manageable size, the first choice of application is the immersion method, however, for stones in place or of sufficient size and/or weight, a spray application method is satisfactory.

5.2.5. GROUTING

Conservators, masons, and others in the allied building trades are often confronted with the problem of stabilizing exfoliating or delaminating masonry and plaster. When details of historic fabric such as decorative carving, tombstone inscriptions, or painted mural surfaces are endangered, reintegration or reattachment is central to their conservation. Grouting—the injection of fluid mortars or synthetic adhesive materials at low pressure—has been successful as an effective, easily duplicated, safe and inexpensive technique for reintegrating detaching and unsound material, particularly when used for nonstructural historic masonry. The majority of commercially available grouting products today have properties which render them unacceptable for use on historic fabric including flexural, tensile, and compressive strengths which may exceed 2000–10,000 psi each.

Lower strength and more vapor-permeable formulations are available either commercially (Jahn M-40, from Cathedral Stone) or can be formulated using (by volume) 2 parts white portland cement: 1 part (Type S) hydrated lime: 3 parts aggregate (equal amounts of fine banding sand and ceramic eccospheres); either of these formulations are suitable, both are used and recommended by Center for Preservation Research for this type of grouting. Formulations should be premixed dry and then well mixed with water to the consistency of heavy cream. Cavities to be grouted are first cleaned of debris with compressed air and then water flushed. Cracks and fissures are dammed with nonstaining potter's clay and the grout injected by gravity through tubes or with low pressure syringes. After voids are completely filled and delaminations attached, the work is covered with wet burlap or plastic for slow cure. Capping of the grouted areas with mortar mixes (see Patching) where necessary is done to deter water infiltration and visually reintegrate the losses.

All masonry work should be executed under optimum weather conditions to ensure the success of the repairs. No work should be executed nor cured during freezing weather (below 40°F). To prevent too rapid drying in temperatures over 85°F, particularly of thin finishes such as mortar repairs and washes, masonry work may require repeated misting and protection from the sun with damp burlap sacking.

A NEW YORK CHURCH

1. INTRODUCTION

The Center for Preservation Research (CPR) conducted an investigation of exterior stonework of a Church in New York, beginning in April 1986. The investigation was undertaken at the request of the Director of Administration, in preparation for up-coming restoration work. The Church was designed in the Gothic style popular for ecclesiastical architecture at the turn of the century. Construction was completed in 1914. The church has an asymmetrical form with a main tower at one corner. A parish house of the same materials and style adjoins the church.

Because of some difficulties recently encountered during exterior cleaning of the parish house, an in-depth investigation of conditions of the stonework of the church was requested. The investigation included a review of records of past preservation treatments, onsite and laboratory examination of materials, and small-scale tests of cleaning methods. The following report summarizes data obtained and provides recommendations for restoring the original appearance of the Church.

2. MATERIALS

The principal material used in the construction of the Church is Bowling Green limestone, an oolitic limestone from Warren County, Kentucky. Beds are generally 10–22 feet thick; freshly quarried stone contains oil (from petroleum deposits) which gives the stone a murky appearance. Upon exposure to the weather, the oil evaporates leaving the stone with a white or nearly white appearance. Oolites stand out conspicuously and are rounded or elongated in shape. The primary mineral is calcite. Occasionally iron pyrite is present.

Bowling Green limestone is known as "the aristocrat of limestones" because of its color, uniformity, strength, and ease of working. The stone is also known for its good weathering qualities; original tool marks are often retained long after construction.

Sculpture of the entries is of Indiana (Bedford) limestone. This stone consists mainly of somewhat rounded shell fragments cemented together with calcite. Its color and texture are similar to that of Bowling Green limestone.

3. PREVIOUS TREATMENTS

3.1 Fluorosilicate Treatment

Church records state that in 1928–1929, Nicholson and Galloway, Inc. applied a solution of "Magnesium-Silicon-Fluorite" to stonework of the Church for the purpose of hardening the stone. Church records suggest that soiling and discoloration of the stonework were present at the time of treatment.

The fluorosilicate or "fluate" treatment for preserving stone was first proposed by J.L. Kessler in France in 1883. Reports of the treatment were initially enthusiastic. A report from 1918 states that Kessler's method is "free from all objectionable features possessed by other methods proposed or adopted for preservation of building stones." The treatment was thought to harden the surface of the stone and impart resistance to frost damage. However, as early as 1921, others described difficulties encountered with the treatment: the formation of a hard surface film on treated stone resulted in subsequent flaking, scabbing, and scaling.

Success of the treatment is based on the reaction of magnesium fluorosilicate with calcium carbonate (calcite) of which this limestone is primarily composed.

Because the pH of the solution is low, the evolution of carbon dioxide gas accompanies its reaction with limestone. The calcium fluoride and silica are deposited as a superficial, often spongy, layer. Unfortunately, deterioration often continues underneath this crust. Today, conservators of art and architecture are generally negative about the long-term benefits of fluorosilicate treatment.

3.2 Plexi-Seal Treatment

Proposals were made by Plexi-Seal Protection Corp. during 1971–1974 to apply a coating of Plexi-Seal to stonework of the church and parish house. According to product data, the coating used was a partially cross-linked polyester material. (In a recent telephone conversation, J.S. Wyner, the President of Plexi-Seal Protection Crop., stated that the coating also contained an acrylic resin.) Plexi-Seal is supposed to provide masonry substrates with a protective coating that will reduce damage caused by water intrusion. Correspondence indicates that the coating was applied to elements of the main tower, "frontal areas" of buttresses, the northwest rear wall at the third floor level, and to the parish house facade. In addition, a modified acrylic latex formulation of Plexi-Seal was added to mortar used in patching and repointing. Limitations of this type of treatment include its inability to achieve more than superficial penetration and the risk of drastically reducing water vapor permeability. With some building materials, the latter can result in damage from the entrapment of water and soluble salts. Fortunately, it does not appear that the Plexi-Seal coating has accelerated deterioration of the stonework of the Church.

However, the mottled appearance of stonework of the parish house after its recent cleaning appears to be the direct result of this "preservation" treatment. In addition, patching and repointing executed in the early 1970s is considerably darker than adjacent stonework. Discoloration of the Plexi-Seal coating strongly suggests that it is not resistant to ultraviolet radiation.

4. EXISTING CONDITIONS

The existing condition of exterior stonework was surveyed during several site visits. In those locations where closeup examination was not possible (e.g., upper areas of the main tower), inspection was made from the ground and roof levels with the aid of binoculars.

Stonework of the Church is generally in good condition. As surface erosion has been moderate, carved ornamental details are still relatively crisp and arrises sharp in most locations. Tool marks are still visible in many locations. A notable exception is the limestone of the turret where weathering has been severe.

A number of vertical and diagonal cracks were noted along the water table level of the church. As was earlier stated, these are patched with a now-darkened cementitious material. Repairs to limestone blocks can also be seen from the turret roof. Discoloration of the patching material in this location is similar to that noted on the crack repairs at the water table level.

A further description of several exterior masonry conditions (general soiling, coating residues, and localized stainings) provided in the paragraphs below. Deterioration mechanisms are discussed.

4.1. General Soiling

Dark soiling is present on exterior limestone in areas that are protected from direct contact with rainwater. This soiling pattern is typical for limestones and other calcareous stones. Although the condition was noted throughout, the pattern is perhaps most pronounced on the south elevation at street level. The mechanism resulting this condition is described below.

Acidic gases absorbed from the atmosphere by rainwater, cause it to be reactive with limestone and other calcareous stones. Sulfur dioxide, which (under typical atmospheric conditions) forms both sulfurous and sulfuric acid when dissolved in water, is perhaps the most destructive of these pollutant gases. In addition to the direct dissolution of calcium carbonate (calcite), the reaction of sulfur dioxide with limestone results in the formation of calcium sulfate dihydrate (gypsum) on the surface of the stone. As gypsum is more soluble in water than is calcium carbonate, the exposed surface becomes eroded when washed by the rain. Where this

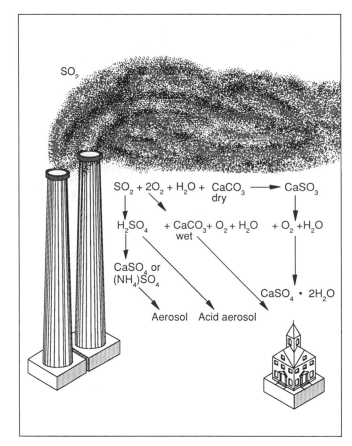

Figure 52. Air pollutants.

surface is protected from the flow of rainwater, the continued transormation of calcium carbonate into calcium sulfate dihydrate results in the formation of a "crust" of gypsum. Particulate matter becomes entrapped in the network of gypsum crystals, giving the surface of protected areas a blackened appearance.

At the Church, there is often an intermediate brownish-colored zone between the blackened gypsum crust and white, rainwashed stone. It is possible that this phenomenon is related to previous preservation treatments. In several locations leaching of calcium carbonate by rainwater has resulted in particularly heavy deposits of gypsum. Thick "framboidal" crusts can be seen at window tracery, decorative moldings of the entries, and ornamental carving of the turret.

Of particular note is alveolar erosion of the gypsum crust best seen at the turret. The reason for this differential deterioration is still uncertain. Possible causative factors are external conditions such as greater exposure to winds and heterogeneity of materials imposed by preservation treatments.

4.2. Coating Residues

Much of the stonework of the parish house is somewhat discolored with streaking and mottling. It appears that the recent cleaning of the parish house by Nicholson and Galloway, Inc. using the water method did not completely remove coating residues from the limestone surface. The appearance of the stonework as well as information from church records indicate that the residues are probably from the Plexi-Seal treatment of the early 1970s.

Stonework at the tops of buttresses and below the carved ornament of the turret display mottling that is similar in appearance of the dark-colored staining on brickwork at the northwest corner suggests the presence of a coating on the stonework above. Church records support the use of Plexi-Seal in these locations. Mottling, however, is not apparent on the main tower, where, according to Wyner, the coating was also applied.

Stonework of the entries also appears to have a coating residue. In these protected locations, mottling is less apparent. There is discoloration throughout with efflorescence visible above the doorway at the southeast entry.

4.3. Localized Staining

Metallic staining present on exterior masonry is of two types. Blue-green copper stains are present below the flashing on the inner wall below the turret and at the tracery of the clerestory level at the north facade. Solubility of the copper corrosion products in rainwater has resulted in this staining.

The reddish-brown color of stains below air conditioning units on the south elevation of the church and parish house suggests its ferrous source. However, there is no obvious source of similar colored staining on the limestone at the southwest corner of the clerestory level. Here, the staining may be related to the mineralogical composition of the limestone.

5. LABORATORY TESTS

Core drilling samples were obtained May 13 using $1\frac{1}{4}''$ diameter carbide tipped bit. Locations were as follows:

   A. northwest corner at stair landing
   B. parish house turret, north side
   C. clerestory, south side below turret

Each sample was examined by Robert Koestler using a scanning electron microscope. Results of the examination are highlighted below.

Calcium fluoride and amorphous silica were seen on all samples, undoubtedly dating from the 1928–1929 treatment. Examination of the samples suggests that the treatment may have contributed to etching of calcite grains. The presence of silica deposits on the surface of gypsum crystals of sample C indicates that the surface was somewhat weathered at the time of treatment. It appears that the Plexi-Seal treatment, seen on sample A, may have contributed to flaking of the surface crust.

6. ON-SITE TESTS

After the review of records of previous treatments and a thorough inspection of existing conditions, locations representative of typical substrate conditions were designated for on-site testing. Small-scale tests of several cleaning methods were conducted *in situ* during May and early June. Because metallic staining is not visible from the street level, no on-site tests were carried out to treat this condition. Materials and methodologies are described below.

6.2. General Soiling

6.2.1. Chemical Cleaning Tests
Because of the difficulties encountered during the cleaning of the parish house stonework and the records of previous fluorosilicate and Plexi-Seal treatments, it was feared the water washing would not be effective in removing general soiling from limestone. Chemical cleaning tests were executed on the clerestory level of the street facade using both commercial products and custom formulations.

The following commercial products were applied according to the manufacturers' instructions:

Limestone Prewash, diluted 1 part concentrate to 3 parts water (ProSoCo, Inc.)
T-792 Prewash (ProSoCo, Inc.)
Limestone Restorer (Deidrich Chemical)

Dwell times were approximately 1 hour. After thoroughly rinsing the surface, Limestone Afterwash (ProSoCo, Inc), prediluted 1:3, was applied. After 3–5 minutes, the surface was again thoroughly rinsed.

Results: With each of the above, there was some lightening of the surface. Complete removal of general soiling, however, was not effected in any of the test areas. In addition to the above commercial products, the following custom formulations were tested:

AB-57
D-10

Each was applied as a poultice and covered with polyethylene for the first 48 hours. The poultice was then allowed to dry (approximately 72 hours) and removed with dry brushing followed by water rinsing.

Results: Removal of general soiling was good with AB-

57 and moderate with D-10. However, the success of AB-57 may be due in part to the reaction of EDTA with the limestone rather than the removal of soiling from its surface.

6.2.2. Water Washing

Water washing is generally thought to be simplest, safest, and least expensive method for removing general soiling (gypsum crust) from limestones and other calcareous stones. The effectiveness of this method relies on the fact that the gypsum crust in which the dirt is incorporated is several times more soluble than is calcium carbonate. Thus, by partial dissolution, water loosens the gypsum crust and the material trapped within the network.

Water washing was tested at the southwest corner and at the north side of the passageway below the turret at the clerestory level of the street facade. A perforated garden hose using water at city pressure was aimed at soiling for approximately 24 hours.

Results: In both test areas, dark-colored soiling was successfully removed after a 24-hour water wash. In the passageway, some mottling was noticeable after drying was completed. The success of the small-scale tests suggests that the fluorosilicate treatment was probably applied to a weathered surface. (This determination is supported by the laboratory examination using the scanning electron microscope.) Water washing appears to penetrate the superficial crust of any surviving treatment residue, solubilizing the gypsum below.

6.3 Coating Residues

Tests to remove coating residues were first carried out on the parish house at the first story level.

The following commercial products (all ProSoCo, Inc.) were applied according to the manufacturers' instructions:

Limestone Prewash
T-792 Prewash
509 Paint Stripper
Heavy Duty Paint Stripper

Dwell times were approximately 1 hour. After thoroughly rinsing the surface, Limestone Afterwash (ProSoCo, Inc.), prediluted 1:3, was applied to all but the test where 509 Paint Stripper was used. After 3-5 minutes, the surface was again thoroughly rinsed.

Tests using the Limestone Prewash and the Heavy Duty Paint Stripper were also executed on the stonework of the southeast entry.

Results: At the parish house test areas, the yellow-colored mottling appears to be very resistant to chemi-

cal cleaning methods. The most effective product tested in this location was the Heavy Duty Paint Stripper.

At the southeast entry, the Heavy Duty Paint Stripper was only moderately successful after one application. In this location, however, removal of coating residues was easily accomplished using the Limestone Prewash. Success in the test area suggests that this product can be diluted for full-scale cleaning.

7. RECOMMENDATIONS

7.1. General Soiling

General soiling can be effectively removed from the stonework of most areas using the water wash method. Washing equipment should include manifolds, hoses and sprinkler heads capable of delivering a fine mist of water to *all* soiled surfaces. Equipment should be set up horizontally parallel to the topmost area of a wall. When washing is completed, the equipment should be lowered in a straight line to the lowest point. [Editor's note: all such equipment shall contain no ferrous materials which could corrode and cause rust staining.]

The time period required for the removal of general soiling (washing cycle) should be determined during on-site tests conducted by the contractor. After completion of the washing cycle, light brushing using natural bristle brushes or low pressure rinsing should be used to complete the cleaning operation.

In some areas, where soiling persists, supplemental cleaning may be required after water washing. Wherever necessary, chemical cleaning should be executed using the materials and procedures described in the section below (5.2. Coating Residues). To remove framboidal crusts, it may be necessary to supplement water washing with chemical and/or mechanical methods. The latter should be performed using blunt masonry chisels. Care should be taken to avoid damaging adjacent masonry surfaces.

As the water wash method necessitates the use of a considerable amount of water, it is important to guard against its intrusion to interior spaces. The contractor should inspect the condition of all interior surfaces before cleaning begins. Monitoring of the condition of materials should continue through full-scale operations. Cleaning should be *immediately* stopped upon any sign of dampness.

7.2. Coating Residues

Chemical cleaning will be necessary in areas where coating residues persist. In addition to stonework of the entries, it is expected that supplemental cleaning will be required on topmost areas of the turret and, possibly, on some elements of the main tower.

It is hoped that the Limestone Prewash can be used in a 1:3 dilution (concentrate to water). This may be possible if limestone surfaces are pre-washed with water just prior to chemical cleaning. Tests conducted by the contractor on stonework of the southeast entry will determine the feasibility of this modification. Chemical cleaning should be carried out by the procedure described below.

1. Prewet a 4' section of limestone
2. Brush apply Limestone Prewash (prediluted 1 part concentrate to 3 parts water) to prewetted wall surface.
3. After allowing the cleaner to remain on the surface for approximately 1 hour, immediately flood the entire section with water, removing all alkaline cleaner from the surface.
4. Immediately apply Limestone Afterwash (prediluted 1:3) and allow to remain on the surface for 3–5 minutes.
5. Immediately flood the entry section with water, removing all acidic cleaner from the surface. Complete rinsing operation using pressure washing equipment.

Cleaning should *not* be conducted when the air temperature is below 40°F. The contractor should follow the manufacturer's recommended procedures for protecting surrounding nonmasonry surfaces during all phases of the cleaning operations. Workers should utilize protective safety glasses, gloves, clothing, and so on, as specifically recommended by the manufacturer.

7.3. Metallic Staining

Should metallic staining become apparent after the completion of general cleaning operations, remedial treatment may be desirable in some locations. The following recommendations are based on recent experiences with removing metallic stains from calcareous stones.

For copper stains, a 20% solution of ammonium carbonate should be used in poultice application. The poultice should be covered with plastic and allowed to remain on the surface for approximately 48 hours. After drying is complete, all remaining poultice material should be removed with dry brushing. The area should then be thoroughly rinsed.

For iron stains, a solution of ammonium oxalate or ammonium citrate should be applied in the manner described above. In both cases, small-scale tests should precede full-scale operations.

NOTES

1. Information about Bowling Green limestone was obtained from *The Building Stones of Kentucky* by Charles Henry Richardson (Frankfort, KY: The Kentucky Geological Society, 1923) and *Physical Properites of the Principal Commercial Limestones Used for Building Construction in the United States* by D.W. Kessler and W.H. Sligh (Technologic Papers of the Bureau of Standards, 21, No. 349, 497–590, July 23, 1927).
2. Cecil H. Desch, The Preservation of Building Stone, *J. Soc. Chemc. Ind.* 37 (April 30, 1918): 118T.
3. Noel Heaton, The Preservation of Stone, *J. Roy. Soc. Arts* 70 (1921): 124–139.

MUNICIPAL BUILDING
MASONRY STONEWORK

Description

According to the drawings and specifications (see Appendix A) the stonework of the North and South Entrance Halls and the main stairwells was built as planned using a "Light Botticino marble dressed rubbed to a half polish." This light buff colored Italian marble became increasingly popular by the end of the century as evidenced by its widespread use in many public interiors of the period. Largely composed of calcium carbonate, its color is due to secondary mineral impurities—limonite or hydrous iron oxide. The veneer ashlar and all trimmings appear to have been installed as specified with metallic anchors to the backing wall and with dowels connecting adjoining pieces (top to bottom). All work was set in a white cement mortar with narrow $\frac{1}{8}$-in. bedding joints.

Accent stone was used in the lunettes above the arched elevator openings and in the floor pavement. Although the lunette fields were of a gypsum plaster imitation stone (see Plasterwork), the roundels within were built as specified with "grey and yellow sienna marble" dressed as the Botticino walls.

The floor pavement design called for a more complicated mix of different colored stone and cast bronze circular insets of the seal of the City. The design specified and built was a patterned background of "light and dark Pink Knoxville Marble," geologically a crystallized limestone with small circular and diamond-shaped inset panels of "Oriental and Verde Antique Vermont Marble." Larger square and circular panels placed along the center axis were to be of various granites, "Cape Ann, Ascutney Green, Jersey Pink, and Stoney Creek." This was all executed as planned with the exception of the cast brass inlays which were never installed.

Also as specified, the risers, treads, and platforms of

the entrance hall stairs were constructed of a ''Pink Knoxville Marble'' similar to the main pavement.

CONDITION

Only a general qualitative survey of the stonework was made to identify the major problems and to assist in setting up a treatment test program. In general the stonework of both lobbies appears to be in good condition. Overall soiling, observed as a gritty yellowish to brown film, occurs on most surfaces, except where it has been harshly removed by recent chemical cleaning along the lower walls. Both soiled and cleaned surfaces are dull in luster. This soiling is most likely the combined result of greasy air-borne particulates from fossil fuel combustion (automative exhaust and heating fuel), cigarette smoke, and body oils. The latter is most noticeable along the pier edges and lower walls of the stairwells due to high pedestrian traffic. No previous coatings appear to be present judging from a lack of surface anomalies; however, their presence sometimes can be difficult to ascertain.

An unusual white mottling of the Botticino marble occurring along hairline cracks, geological joints and veining, and construction joints is most prominent on the exterior walls, especially in the stairwells. This is most likely related to the transmission of water vapor or liquid through these openings and possibly the transport and deposition of water soluble salts. It is also possible these areas may appear lighter than the surrounding soiled surfaces because they have been kept clean by the migrating moisture. No salt fretting or spalling is evident except on the second floor landing of the South Hall stairwell.

In addition to these discolorations, localized stains from pressure tape adhesive, signage, chewing gum, and graffiti are also present. Previous fills, some of discolored adhesive resins, and many new losses from abrasion and impact are visible across much of the lower walls and arises. Isolated stress cracks exist as well.

MASONRY TESTING PROGRAM

In July and November of 1989, a small-scale testing program was conducted on the stonework and plaster ceilings to ascertain the most appropriate methods for restoration.

Cleaning tests of approximately 6 × 12 in. were performed on heavily soiled Botticino marble in the south stairwell and on the lower panel of the Directory and on a representative stair riser and tread of ''Knoxville

marble,'' all in the South Entrance Hall. Paint removal tests and restoration of the original plasterwork finish were also attempted in the northeast corner vault and lunette in the North Entrance Hall.

These tests and their results are outlined below:

0 No visible effect
+ Visible cleaning
− Negative or adverse effect

TEST AREA: SOUTH WALL OF SOUTH STAIRCASE SOUTH ENTRANCE HALL

X water scrub / 0
1 Ammoniated Triton X [20% 3*M* Ammonium hydroxide + 80% Triton X (Now Union Carbide) nonionic detergent (10 drops/gallon of water] /0
A Lacquer thinner
cotton pad applied/0
B Petroleum ether (technical grade)
cotton pad applied/0
C Denatured alcohol (technical grade)
cotton pad applied/0
D Sure Klean Marble Poultice with water (ProSoCo)
dwell time: 48 hours with scrub rinse/—surface alteration
E Sure Klean Marble Poultice (ProSoCo) with additive
dwell time: 48 hours with scrub rinse/—surface alteration
F Ammoniated Stripper (Manhattan Floor Supply) full-strength
dwell time: 20 minutes with scrub and water rinse/ + +
G Ammoniated Stripper (Manhattan Floor Supply) diluted 1 part concentrated: 10 parts water.
dwell time: 20 minutes with scrub and water rinse/ +
H Sure Klean Liquid Marble Cleaner (ProSoCo) diluted 1 part concentrate: 2 parts water
dwell time: 3–5 minutes with scrub and water rinse/ +
I Sure Klean 859 Stripper (ProSoCo) full strength
dwell time: 10 minutes with scrub and water rinse/ + +
ISC Sure Klean Interior Stone Cleaner (ProSoCo) prewet, diluted 1 part concentrate: 2 parts water
dwell time: 3–5 minutes, scrub and water rinse/ +
Z Control

The results of these tests suggest that the surface soiling is most effectively removed with alkali and alkali-solvent mixtures. Test panels F and I both displayed the best cleaning leaving the stone a cool buff color. Test panel E displayed an unacceptable rough texture and whitish color alteration. The results of test panel D appeared to be effective in removing surface grime, however, its application as a poultice would not be as efficient or cost effective as a single application of the Ammoniated Stripper (F) or 859 Stripper (I). The Liquid Marble Cleaner and the Interior Stone Cleaner were not as effective in removing the white mottling as the Ammoniated Stripper (full strength and dilute) or the 859 Stripper.

In addition to the above cleaning tests, a small panel of Botticino marble was resurfaced with wet abrasive/acidic polishing by a professional stonemason. This technique both cleaned and restored a luster finish to the marble.

CHAPTER 6

ARCHITECTURAL CERAMICS

BRICKS

Fired or burned bricks have been used on a large scale for buildings since at least the early third millenium B.C. when a facing of fired clay bricks was used on the great Ziggurat at Ur in about 2100 B.C. In later times the Romans and the Byzantines brought fired clay brick architecture to a state of fine achievement. In the early medieval period in parts of Europe clay brick use fell off to such a degree that in England, for example, the use of fired brick was comparatively rare even as late as the early sixteenth century. In some instances, Roman bricks were quarried from ancient sites and used in medieval buildings.

In Persia, northern Italy, Flanders, the Netherlands, and the Baltic region of Germany superb brick buildings were erected all through the medieval period.

It has been suggested that the greatest stimulus to the steadily increased use of fired brick all over Europe at the end of the sixteenth century and all through the seventeenth and eighteenth centuries, was the rapid growth first of towns and cities and then of industry. The increasingly densely populated centers and the bigger and better warehouses had one feature in common—the need for more fire- and vermin-resistant construction.

In Canada the first use of fired clay bricks occurred in 1605 at the French Habitation at Port Royal, Nova Scotia where Champlain erected a timber fort with accommodation and storage buildings of heavy timber framing and logwork. Bricks made from locally dug clay were fired on the site and were used in the construction of the fireplaces and chimneys. Fired clay roofing tiles were imported from Spain and were used on stone buildings by the Basque whalers who settled at Red Bay, Labrador, Canada in the sixteenth century. The latter use is almost certainly the earliest example of architectural ceramic imports to North America from Europe.

The first Dutch settlers in New Amsterdam were well used to fine brick buildings and bricklayers and brickmakers were among the earliest Dutch and English settlers in the first decade of the seventeenth century in what was to become the United States.

Fired bricks were made at Jamestown Virginia in 1610. While the English often built half-timbered or timber-framed buildings they usually used fired clay bricks for chimneys and hearths, particularly where no suitable stones were readily available. The Dutch on the other hand often built mainly in brick in the familiar forms of the Netherlands with decorative stepped and ornamented gables.

The sizes and qualities of bricks have been controlled by various laws and regulations in America since the seventeenth century.

Materials

Clay, the principal material in fired bricks, is composed of a mass of fine particles derived from the erosion and chemical breakdown of igneous rocks. The most common clay minerals are kaolinite, illite, montmorillonite, and chlorite. The crystals of these clay minerals typically have a finely layered structure which enables them to absorb water and consequently to expand on wetting. Montmorillonite is particularly noted for the latter characteristic. Often when clays are dug straight from the ground they are found to be too "plastic." This means that while they can be readily molded and formed with the hands or in molds, they shrink se-

99

verely on drying and can warp, twist or crack. Worse still they may not dry completely before being fired and as a result may generate steam and explode in the kiln destroying all the ceramics around them.

To reduce plasticity, sand may be added to the clay. Early colonial brickmakers often used a mix of about 30% sand to 70% plastic clay.

This in turn raises the firing temperature necessary to produce good quality bricks. Then a small quantity of for example crushed limestone may be used as a "flux" to lower the melting points of the silica in the sand and the silicates in the clays. Some excellent mixtures of clay and sand occur naturally and are ideal for the manufacture of fired bricks. These naturally occurring mixes are called "brick-marls." A second source of "ready-mixed" clay and possibly some sands are the so-called "brick shales." A shale is a rock which has been formed naturally in the earth's crust by heat and pressure from mud or barely consolidated mud known as "mudstone."

The first steps in early brick manufacture were digging the clay then "weathering" or laying the lumpy clay mass out in the open to break down and crumble (see also reference to "blunging" in manufacture of terracotta). "Tempering" was the next step and involved mixing the clay with sand and water. At first this was done crudely and often ineffectively by hand but later horses or oxen were used to drive a heavy roller or wheel round in a ring-pit, cutting and mixing the brick materials. By the 1850s first horse-driven and then steam-driven "pug mills" had been introduced. In these, a vertical shaft studded with iron or steel blades revolved in a large tub to repeatedly slice and thoroughly mix the clay and the other materials. The mechanized pug-mills made possible the advent of the evenly colored and textured smooth "pressed" bricks of the second half of the nineteenth century.

The colors of early bricks varied greatly because their makers had no idea of the chemistry of the process which controlled colors. The normal brick colors of red or orange are derived from the iron compound ferric oxide, usually present at about 5–6% of the clay content. The presence of lime produces cream, yellow, or greenish bricks; magnesia and alumina produce buff bricks. Ferrous oxide can produce colors ranging from green to black and manganese may produce brown or even purple colors.

Different firing temperatures and improperly or incompletely mixed clays all led to color variations even in a single brick. These variations and irregularities of form often tend to give early bricks a distinctive character and charm.

From the seventeenth century until the nineteenth and in some instances even into the twentieth, bricks were molded by hand-packing the clay mix into single or double wooden molds. With increased production needs wooden molds were at first protected by iron or brass sheet and later the molds were made from cast iron.

Multiple molds for six, twelve bricks, or more at one time were made in presses powered by horses in the 1840s. By the middle of the century, steam engines were used to mix the clays and other materials, and to power extrusion machines to drive large impellors which could force the clay mix through a nozzle or die and extrude a continuous ribbon or prism of regular section. The ribbon was then cut into individual bricks by multiple wires held in a rotating frame.

Although brick making machines were in use in the 1830s, they were not commonly in use in the United States until the 1870s and even then the machines were often English. Machine mixing, pressing, and extrusion processes produced more homogeneous, evenly textured bricks with fine sharp regular edges or arrisses, which are characteristic of the latter part of the nineteenth century.

After the molding or extrusion process the bricks usually had to be laid out to dry. In the earlier or more primitive processes they were laid out under rough shelters made of scraps of wood and with straw thatch roofs. These shelters were known as hovels, the English generic term for a crude shelter. A dry clay process was introduced in the United States in the 1870s. In this process, a high pressure was used to press the bricks in a metal mold. Bricks made by this method did not require drying but could be fired immediately.

The main method of firing the early bricks was the clamp or scove kiln. The latter term is mentioned in 1973 by Harley J. McKee in his excellent *Introduction to Early American Masonry*. The term "scove" is Cornish and is to be found in mining texts at least as early as the eighteenth century. "Scove" was used to describe a particularly rich ore of either lead, tin, or copper with more than 50% metal.

Such rich scove ores could be smelted by simply piling the ores and firing them. In brick-making, the clamp or scove-kiln was basically a large rectangular pile of unfired bricks with slightly battered sides that was built over a series of parallel flues packed with fuel. The early fuel was usually wood or brushwood or even straw. Coal was not commonly used until the last quarter of the nineteenth century and was sometimes responsible for introducing sulfates into the bricks.

The base and flues were built from old fired bricks which were rejects from earlier firing operations. The outside of the clamp was usually plastered over with a mixture of mud and straw to help insulate the clamp and retain heat to produce a more even "burn" or fir-

Over-fired brick from Louisbourg, Nova Scotia. ca. 1730.

ing. Screens of reed or straw matting, burlap, or canvas might also be erected around the clamp to prevent sudden windstorms from causing excessively fast burning of the fuel with resultant high temperatures and melting and fusing of the adjacent bricks into a large solid mass.

The usual high firing temperature for a good well-burned brick was about 1,800°F (982°C) but bricks at the top of the clamp or on the outsides well away from the flues were often underfired and would soften and crumble in a return to the clay state if exposed to prolonged wetting.

If they were not rejected, such bricks were either used for interior partitions or in other locations where they might be expected to remain dry. If they were

Beehive kiln, Hamilton, Ontario, built about World War I.

rejected they could be used for rubble and in the construction of clamp bases. Over-fired bricks would tend to a glassy state and would be distorted and twisted as they started to melt and flow. Slightly overfired bricks next to the flues might have "glazed" dark ends and these were sometimes used to produce decorative effects and patterns such as chevrons or lozenges.

McKee cites contemporary sources noting that in Philadelphia in 1684, clamps produced 40 to 50,000 bricks at one time consuming half a cord of wood. Improvements in kiln design led first to firing bricks in single, occasionally roofless rectangular chambers with the fuel burning in a chamber beneath; then in the nineteenth century to the beehive or round down-draft kilns. In the latter the heat and hot gases were drawn down over the bricks, producing a more even firing with better fuel economy. Greater improvements in fuel economy later in the nineteenth century were facilitated by the use of multiple kiln chambers linked by a complex system of damper-controlled flues. With the appropriate use of the damper controls, waste heat was used to dry bricks prior to firing; then the bricks were fired; and finally, recently fired bricks were cooled by fresh air being sucked into their hot kiln chambers. All these processes were carried out with a single continuous firing operation. The first of these mass-production firing processes used the Hoffmann Kiln which was circular in plan and had as many as 12 kiln chambers. This was later superceded by Warren's Patent Kiln or the Improved Hoffmann Kiln in which the kiln became long and rectangular with 14 or more chambers.

In the 1920s the Tunnel Kiln was introduced. This too is a continuous process but rather than have the drying, firing, and cooling operations moving round a series of chambers, the stack of bricks proceeds down a long tunnel on a slowly moving steel wagon. At the beginning of the tunnel the fresh bricks are slowly dried and then temperatures rise to firing point, cooling off again as the wagon proceeds to the end of the tunnel. This process is still used and produces the highest quality bricks.

Despite the steady increase in the knowledge of what was necessary to make a good quality brick, many historic bricks were made from clay mixes which were far from ideal but were used simply because they were readily to hand.

Many researchers and would-be restorers of historic brick buildings are told that the bricks used "were brought in by ship from England" or that they were "English bricks." Unless such stories are substantiated by documentary evidence one must be extremely sceptical about them. In many such cases the supposedly "imported bricks" are of such poor quality that locally made bricks would have been superior and there would have been no point in importing.

In passing, it should be noted that "English brick" was a term used to describe any bricks which conformed to legal brick sizes in England. Such bricks did not have to be made in England but could have been made in Virginia, for example.

Bricklaying and Bonds

Historic brickwork in North America was normally laid in a bed of lime-based mortar. Brick walls were and are still built in multiples of the width of a brick that is, $4\frac{1}{2}$ in. If the wall was thick enough, the outer and inner faces were laid first followed by the middle, one course at a time. The bricklayer first laid a bed of mortar with a trowel and added a dab of mortar against the end of the adjacent brick. The new brick was then "shoved" or pressed into place with a sliding action so that the mortar was pushed against all surrounding brick faces. In poorer quality work, the brick was dropped into place and the open vertical joints were "slushed" or filled with a more liquid mortar. Generally speaking the best work used relatively dry mortar mixes which were pushed home with considerable force. In English trade slang which was also used in North America, shoving was preferable to slushing.

The strength of the brick masonry depended upon both the adhesive and cohesive qualities of the mortar and upon the bond. The bond consists of various systems of overlapping the individual bricks from course to course and connecting the inner and outer faces of the wall with "through-bricks" or "bond-bricks." The walls were nominally 9, $13\frac{1}{2}$, 18, or 21 in. in thickness, these being multiples of the width of a brick plus one or more joints. With an enormous number of variations historic North American bricks might average $8\frac{3}{8}$ to 9 in. in length (the stretcher face) by 4 to $4\frac{1}{2}$ in. in width (the header face) by $2\frac{1}{8}$ to 3 in. in thickness.

Typical bonds found in England were also used in colonial brickwork but variations on stretcher bonds were also developed from what was known as a "Liverpool bond." The usual bond was "Flemish bond" in which headers alternate with stretchers in all courses, overlapped in such a way that there are no continuous vertical joints. In "English bond," continuous courses of headers alternate with continuous courses of stretchers. "Liverpool bond" consisted of three courses of stretchers alternating with a single course of headers. Various "American Common" bonds varied the number of stretcher courses between the single course of headers with four, five, or even six courses of stretchers. The stretcher bond variations could be laid more quickly but the strength of the wall was reduced by the decreasing frequency of header or bond courses to tie the two faces together. When no headers appear on the surface this is called "stretcher bond," and the conservator must take care to establish whether the outer wythe is a single wythe veneer over a timber structure or a possibly inferior brick interior wythe. The bonding or tie system which attaches the veneer must also be carefully checked.

Some stretcher bonds were built with an improved strength by laying "bond" bricks diagonally into triangular recesses formed by clipping off the back corners of adjacent stretchers. Such single diagonal bond bricks might occur at 18-in. intervals in one course and then again in further courses after four courses of plain stretcher bond. The total wall thickness of a typical example of this kind from Ontario in the 1870s was about $13\frac{1}{2}$ in.

In "gauged work" or "rubbed work" specially in made oversized bricks were employed. They were made with a softer brick which could be rubbed down to tapered or other special shapes. The precisely shaped bricks were then usually laid with much thinner joints filled with pure lime mortar or lime "putty" with a little fine sand. The joints in this fine work might be a little as $\frac{1}{8}$ in. thick.

Other special brick forms to produce accurate voussoirs for arches, for example, were obtained by forming them in special molds and are known generically as "molded bricks." One final group of special bricks were made with a slightly softer and sandier texture than usual and were sculpted with chisels and rasps after they were built into rough forms. These were used in what was referred to as "carved" or "cut" brickwork.

The dividing line between molded brickwork and terracotta is a very fine one indeed and it could be argued that they were really one and the same thing, except that the molded bricks tended to be small, evenly sized units.

The Deterioration of Historic Brickwork

Until the latter part of the nineteenth century historic bricks in North America tended to be relatively soft and porous. Although this might at first be thought to cause problems of durability, generally the pore and capillary diameters were well in excess of what is known today to be the critical limit of 1 μm or below. Paradoxically it is the higher strength, denser bricks with their pore diameters of 1 or 2 μm or less, which have been found to deteriorate most rapidly.

Failures in historic brickwork usually occur for one or more of the following reasons:

• The original bricks were underfired and tend to crumble when exposed to moisture.

Diagonal bond brickwork, Belleville, Ontario, City Hall clock tower.

Frost action crumbles bricks in this Perth, Ontario, wall. There were no problems until new paving next to the wall caused splashing to saturate wall.

Once this 1880's brickwork in St. John's, Newfoundland, was saturated, frost action began to destroy it. Rather than repair the rainwater disposal system, coatings were added to the surface. They all failed.

Salt-induced damage to these soft bricks was made much worse by hard, dense portland cement-based mortar. Wind vortices and increased surface areas at the corner, make the salt concentrations larger.

- The brickwork has been saturated with water for prolonged periods, usually from leaking rainwater pipes or faulty gutters.
- Prolonged water saturation removes the mortar and the brickwork loses its cohesion.
- Water-saturated bricks suffer from freeze/thaw cycles and eventual shattering.
- Water-saturated brickwork develops ice lenses between the wythes or skins of brickwork, usually buckling or forcing off the outer wythe.
- Water-soluble salts form in or just below the brick surface as subflorescence or cryptoflorescence. Repeated cycles of hydration and dehydration of the salt crystals in the surface pores then lead to the crumbling or exfoliation of the brick surface. These phenomena may be associated particularly with prolonged saturation from leaking rainwater pipes; with chlorides from maritime environments; with deicing salts from the treatment of adjacent roads and sidewalks; and with rising damp from soils containing large quantities of soluble salts.

- Acid precipitation and air pollution may accelerate the deterioration of brickwork by dissolving lime or calcium carbonate from mortars; depositing water-soluble salts; and causing buildups of soiling which may be merely an aesthetic problem or may lead to actual damage occurring to the brickwork.

- Ties securing brick veneers break or corrode

The mortar has been totally removed from the brickwork of this Perth, Ontario, funeral home because of a neglected roof/gutter leak.

Salts from the repair mortar and the hardness of the Portland cement-based mortar have worked together to destroy more of the original brickwork at Sussex Drive, Ottawa, Ontario.

away, leaving the veneer unstable or even collapsing.

There is a second group of forms of deterioration which are associated with poor or misguided attempts at maintenance and restoration. The principal forms are as follows:

• When old pointing fails, rather than use the original type of semielastic lime mortar again, the misguided repairer uses a mortar which is based on ordinary portland cement. This change is based on the false assumption that if the mortar is denser, harder, and less permeable, it should be better. If the bricks expand, lime mortar will compact but portland cement-based mortar will not. In the lat-

ter case the result will be the crushing and spalling-off of the edges of the brick. If the bricks shrink, whereas the lime mortar will stretch somewhat but still adhere, the cement-based mortar may either crack away opening a crack for water to penetrate into the masonry; or worse still the cement-based mortar will pull the face clean off the original brick.

• The ordinary portland cement-based mortar may contain sulfate impurities which will cause salt contamination of the adjacent brickwork, leading to crumbling and exfoliation of original brick.

• When rainwater leaks have occurred apparently through the brickwork, attempts may have been made to treat the brick surface with paints and/or water-repellent coatings. In some cases these coatings may have caused the retention of water within the brickwork with consequent ice-damage or problems from water-soluble salts. A complete loss of the surface can result from changes in permeability caused by accumulations of such coatings or by the transformation of such coatings caused by reactions with ultraviolet radiation, atmospheric pollutants, and other chemicals.

• When the brickwork has been sandblasted in ill-considered attempts to remove soiling or paints and coatings, the bricks may have had their "fireskin" or outer surface removed, exposing the softer more permeable core of the brick. The original lime-based mortar pointing may also have been removed in this process. As a result the potentially more absorbent surface area of the brickwork is increased and opened to water penetration by the roughened brick surfaces and by the horizontal ledges which are exposed by the removal of the pointing.

The Conservation and Repair of Historic Brickwork

When the various forms of deterioration described above have taken place there is often little that can be done except to carefully cut out the worst affected areas and replace them with sound new bricks matching the original in dimensions, colors, textures, and physical characteristics such as modulus of rupture and thermal expansion coefficient. The new bricks should also meet the current ASTM standards for bricks, particularly with regard to water absorbtion, maximum saturation coefficient, and minimum compressive strength. These characteristics must in turn be related to "grades" which are related to "weathering indices" or some other system which correlates brick quality

1880's brickwork in St. John's, Newfoundland, shows how severe damage is related to water penetration and low frost resistance of dense bricks.

Sandblasting has torn the surfaces off these soft, locally made red bricks in Victoria, British Columbia.

This wall was sandblasted but did not deteriorate further after the joints had been well repointed.

with severity of climatic exposure. [See ASTM Designation C62-85A Standard Specification for Building Brick (Solid Masonry Units made from Clay or Shale) and ASTM Designation C67-85 Standard Methods of Sampling and Testing Brick and Structural Clay Tile.]

Where old bricks are recycled for repairs, representative samples should be tested for salt contents and for quality. Generally speaking recycled bricks should not be used for pavers, or in parapets, copings, sills, or indeed in any location where they will be exposed to excessive moisture and freeze/thaw cycles.

New mortar to be used with old brickwork should normally be lime-based and should be applied as dry as possible to avoid shrinkage. (See Mortar section in Chapter 7.)

In cases where historic brick walls have been sandblasted, if there is no direct evidence that the bricks are disintegrating, then the pointing should be examined first. In my experience water penetration through sand-blasted brickwork is often found to have occurred through the defective joints. Thus repointing is the first action to be recommended. Once this has been done, the wall should be carefully monitored over at least one winter to see if there is an accumulation of brick dust or flakes at the base of the wall because of ice or frost action on wet brickwork. If the failure is continuing in the bricks then coatings or water-repellents may be used or the bricks may be carefully cut out and replaced. In some cases the original brick was painted historically because it was known that the brick was incapable of withstanding the effects of the climate to which it was exposed. Subsequent overly efficient removal of paint accumulations may then have exposed brick which was not supposed to be exposed. In such cases the silicate-based coatings known as "breathable masonry coatings" may be used to replace original coatings which did not have the valuable quality of permitting water vapor transmission from behind.

Some severely deteriorated decorative historic brickwork might be a candidate for consolidation with synthetic resins. This topic is discussed in the next section.

TERRACOTTA

After a period from the end of the eighteenth century to the middle of the nineteenth century during which English terracotta, particularly Coade Stone, was imported to a limited degree, slowly a North American industry was established.

In the late nineteenth century and in the first three decades of the twentieth century, architectural terracotta was used to finish and decorate the facades of many great North American commercial buildings. As a material terracotta gradually ceased to be popular as designers moved to the use of reinforced concrete, glass, and steel.

Today, there is generally a poor understanding of what terracotta is, or was, how it was made, how it was fixed to concrete or steel structures, and how it behaved or misbehaved. All this strangely passed away—becoming almost shrouded in mystery to all but a few specialists. Generations of students of architecture and building construction have completed their courses without even hearing about terracotta, let alone learning how it was used or how it could be preserved. Failures of terracotta have been publicized in some quarters but often with little understanding of the reasons for such failures.

This section of the chapter should dispel some of the mysteries and help owners of terracotta-clad buildings and the architects, engineers, and contractors who work with them to understand, preserve, and maintain architectural terracotta for the enjoyment of future generations.

This raises the subject of terminology. There is a widespread but mistaken idea that all terracotta must be brown or "terracotta" colored; this is not so. To attempt to resolve any potential confusion, the term terracotta comes to us directly from the ancient Romans. It is derived from the two Latin words terra = earth and cocta = baked. In its simplest form using European clays, terracotta without additional colors or glazes has the pleasant warm red brown color which most term "terracotta color."

In parts of the United Kingdom an unglazed but fired clay body is referred to as "terracotta," while the term "faience" is reserved for glazed ware.

North American terminologies vary but one may safely refer to four types of architectural terracotta: "unglazed terracotta"; "glazed terracotta"; "fireproof terracotta" or "lightweight terracotta block"; and "polychrome glazed terracotta".

Architectural Terracotta

The term architectural terracotta is used to distinguish the masonry material used to form and decorate buildings from other forms of terracotta which have been and still are used primarily in domestic ceramics and in sculpture.

Architectural terracotta is a ceramic material which might be described as a close cousin to the more humble clay brick and clay tile. Like brick and tile, this form of terracotta is manufactured from a combination of ceramic materials skillfully selected and blended to produce a well-fired homogeneous material which if used correctly has a long-proven resistance to the worst excesses that weather and urban air pollution can offer. In the text that follows the term "terracotta" will be used to refer to architectural terracotta.

Terracotta has a long and respectable ancestry as a building material, having been used as early as 3200 B.C. in ancient Mesopotamia, in ancient Egypt, and subsequently in ancient Greece. The Etruscans, that mysterious ancient people who preceded the ancient Romans in central Italy, used terracotta extensively to decorate their temples and created some of the finest and largest terracotta statues and memorial groups ever made, for example, sarcophagi from the tombs at Cerveteri ca. 530 B.C. The Romans who continued with so many of the Etruscans' developments, also used terracotta extensively.

With the fall of the Roman Empire, at least in Europe the use of architectural terracotta largely faded away. Elsewhere, for example, in Central Asia, Persia and Turkey, gorgeously colored ceramic ornaments for buildings provide a separate chapter in the story, which lack of space excludes from this work.

Terracotta made a triumphal reappearance in the Renaissance Europe when the development of architectural ceramics was significantly advanced in Germany and Italy in the fourteenth century. In Italy the great master Lucca della Robbia (1400–1482) and subsequently other members of his family produced superb glazed polychrome terracotta panels and plaques for use as architectural decorations.

The polychrome glazing techniques, which were developed in fifteenth century Italy, offered not only the opportunity to decorate with brilliant colors but also gave otherwise permeable terracotta a glazed and much more water-resistant finish. This increased resistance to the penetration of water conferred increased weather resistance and hence made a much more durable product.

Glazed polychromatic wares were so extensively produced in the medieval Italian city of Faenza that they took the city's name and have given us the term "faience" which is sometimes used incorrectly to describe all forms of architectural terracotta. Italian master craftsmen reintroduced the craft to England in the Renaissance and unglazed terracotta was used by them in the sixteenth century, for example, to produce large sculpted medallions for the entrance front of Hampton Court in the reign of Henry VIII.

From this period, terracotta was used occasionally to decorate buildings or for sculptures, but it was in the eighteenth century in England that a new technological development led to a steady increase in the use of terracotta. This development was the invention of a form of terracotta produced under the proprietary name of "Coade's Material." After early production at Lyme Regis in the West of England, by 1769 "Coade Stone"

was being produced in large quantities in Lambeth, London. Coade Stone continued to be manufactured by H.N. Blanchard until about 1870. A somewhat creamier colored Coade Stone was manufactured by J.M. Blashfield between 1851 and 1875. The enormous popularity of Coade Stone was due to the fact that it could be used to produce what appeared to be stone statues, Classical Revival details, and other architectural ornaments very precisely, in bulk and at a fraction of the cost of hand-carved stonework. Coade Stone also had the additional good qualities of extreme durability and resistance to weathering. Even with the most expensive stonework it was not possible to guarantee to consistently match these good qualities, particularly in the increasingly sooty and polluted environment which was unfortunately associated with the growth of the Industrial Revolution.

Coade Stone was exported to North America where its durability and other qualities made it very attractive, particularly in Canada's harsh climate. Very early examples which still exist in Montreal include part of "Nelson's Column" in the Place Jacques Cartier and a series of plaques which decorated the first offices of the Bank of Montreal. Other early examples graced the Octagon House in Washington D.C.

In nineteenth century England, the architectural "giants" Ruskin, Pugin, Barry, and Eastlake all gave terracotta their approval and Victorians generally used terracotta enthusiastically for its cheapness, its attractive range of colors and textures, its plasticity, and ease of moulding to produce elaborate and finely detailed architectural decoration which could look exactly like stone; and above all for its resilience and durability in the increasingly soot-ridden and seriously polluted air of Victorian cities. Unglazed terracotta was first manufactured in North America in the 1860s and by the period 1870–1890 unglazed brown "structural terracotta" produced in factories in New York, Philadelphia and Chicago was being used for integral units in load-bearing walls and for ornamental detail such as string courses, capitals, and window surrounds in brick facades.

Chicago's disastrous great fire of 1871 provided both a major need to create new buildings and a requirement that they should have fire-resistant construction. Terracotta offered a solution to both.

Perhaps the most important role for terracotta was in the development of the skyscraper. In 1886 the Rookery, an 11-storey Chicago building by the architects Burnham and Root, had unglazed structural terracotta, brick, and granite facades covering its metal frame.

What is termed "fireproof terracotta" in the United States is a form of hollow unglazed terracotta block

Unglazed red terracotta of 1886, the Rookery, Chicago, Illinois.

extruded as tile-like units. These light-weight units were used between floor beams, as sheathing of skeletal iron or steel frames and inside walls and partitions.

The terracotta subflooring protected each level and helped to reduce the risk of vertical fire spread while the sheathing protected the structural members.

Its use encouraged by the development of city ordinances for the protection of buildings against fire, terracotta provided a primary method of protection against firespread and damage from the 1870s to about World War I when concrete was being produced sufficiently inexpensively for it to be brought into general use in North America. Although some American texts state that this form of terracotta was invented in the United States in 1871 by Balthasar Kruscher, it is clear that it is closely related to hollow pot flooring developed by Monsieur Saint Fart in eighteenth century France for use with wrought iron structural members and to similar eighteenth century English independent developments of terracotta. Examples of the uses of hollow, light-weight terracotta blocks in fire-resistant construction in combination with structural ironwork abound in late eighteenth and early nineteenth century Europe with significant examples still surviving in England, France, and Russia. Processes for the extrusion of such blocks from machines using helical impellors were patented as early as the 1840s.

The driving force behind the European developments was always the search for more and more fire-resistant construction. Some of the finest examples which are still in existance are in mills and warehouses where fires were a constant threat to the security of England's growing wealth from the Industrial Revolution.

Returning to North America, by the 1890s a slightly new form of terracotta had come into use for the cladding of steel frame buildings, largely replacing structural terracotta. "Terracotta cladding" units were hollow and approximately 4-in. thick overall. Thus they were thinner than structural terracotta units and unlike the latter required a variety of metal anchoring systems to tie them back to the structure behind. These units were also commonly colored with a white or cream colored slip and were glazed.

The first curtain wall skyscraper, the Reliance Building in Chicago, built 1891–95 and designed by Burnham and Root and D.H. Burnham and Co., was faced with vast expanses of glass set in white, glazed terracotta cladding over a steel frame.

In the opening decades of the twentieth century, many interesting imitation stone finishes were produced in terracotta. Examples include imitation granites which still often fool the casual observer from even a few feet away. Winnipeg's Curry Building of 1915 is a good example of this type.

In the 1920s the Gladding, McBean Company in California produced the last major development in terracotta. This development is known as "terracotta veneer." The units are much thinner than those of terracotta cladding being usually $1\frac{1}{2}$ to 2 in. thick. Ter-

Terracotta made to imitate granite in 1915 in the Curry Building, Winnipeg, Manitoba.

racotta veneer was often used for the increasingly streamlined and smooth-faced facades of the Art Deco, "Moderne," and International Style buildings. This last form of terracotta unfortunately showed up the disadvantages of the material when used in thin flat panels which tended to warp and have glazing problems. Since the panels were flat and plain there was no particular saving over the use of other materials; terracotta's major advantage had always been the precise high-quality reproduction of fine architectural sculpture and detail in three dimensions.

During this last major period of terracotta production, there were some interesting developments in surface finishes including lustrous metallic finishes resembling gilding.

Triumphs of terracotta work included such important examples as the Carson, Pirie, Scott and Co Store,

Chicago (Adler and Louis Sullivan, 1891–1904) and the Woolworth Building, New York (Cass Gilbert 1911–1913).

From 1720 to the 1980s there have been 420 manufacturers of terracotta in England and Wales. Now only two or three continue this long tradition. In just the Midwest of the United States alone well over a dozen terracotta manufacturers operated between 1870 and 1920, but none remained in business past the 1920s. Now in the whole of the United States less than ten produce terracotta.

Many people today mistakenly tend to think that mass production and prefabrication are products of our own times. The requirement to be able to look in a catalogue and select a complete building style, facades, and decorations and have the whole thing manufactured to suit one's space requirements in under a year—have it shipped across the Atlantic or even half way across the North American continent—would challenge any building material manufacturer today. Current catalogues simply do not exist to begin with. But in the late nineteenth and early twentieth centuries when steam locomotives still hauled the great bulk of America's and Canada's goods and passengers, such feats were not at all unusual. In fact much English architectural terracotta from such firms as Doulton was exported to Canada as late as World War I.

Terracotta Materials

The raw materials from which terracottas were (and still are) manufactured might vary considerably in type and proportions but generally consisted of a blend of argillaceous "rocks" such as marl (a mixture of clay and sand); ball clay (kaolin or china clay with organic matter and alkalis as impurities); fireclay; and a grog (ground semivitrified terracotta from previous firings). These materials were used to produce the bodies of the terracotta units. The finish on the bodies of slip-coated, glazed, semiglazed, and polychrome units could consist of applications of very finely ground selected colored clays or elutriated clays for the colors (elutriation processes separate very fine particles by differential settlement in columns of water). Glazes could consist of common salt, compounds of sodium, borax, boric acid, lead, or tin, or combinations of these. Other materials such as felspars were added as fluxes to make it possible to lower firing temperatures while at the same time avoiding the problems of underfiring.

Barium carbonate was added during milling and blending processes to combine with soluble salts in the clays and prevent them from crystallizing subsequently and causing problems. Manganese compounds and other metal oxides were added to produce colored

Terracotta veneer, Art Deco New York Delicatessen.

glazes or in the case of the former, to produce a more desirable self-color for the clay body. Coade Stone was manufactured from a kaolinitic clay containing titanium dioxide, felspar as a flux and quartz as a silicon or glass source.

> Analysis of a piece of Coade stone by the British Museum Research Laboratory indicated that the raw material was ball clay from Dorset or Devon, to which was added 5–10% flint, 5–10% quartz sand, at least 10% grog (probably crushed stoneware) and about 10% soda–lime–silica glass, which acted as a vitrifying agent. (Ashurst, J. & N., 1988).

The secret part of the Coade process which made the terracotta so durable was the addition of a grog of ground particles of previously fired terracotta. Chemical tests on randomly selected fired terracotta units carried out by the British Building Research Station in the period 1926–1928 found the following breakdown of constituents: silica 73.2%; alumina 10.0%; ferric oxide 3.4%; calcium oxide 1.2%; water 5.2%; organic material 6.5%; and traces of magnesium oxide.

Colors for Terracotta Cladding and Veneers

Although the Della Robbia family had produced colored glazed terracottas in the fifteenth century the modern North American production of colored glazed terracottas can be said to date from the introduction in 1885 of barium carbonate to neutralize soluble sulfates in the clays and prevent them from coating the surface of the terracotta units causing bond failures between body and glaze. By 1922 S.F. Laurence, in writing *Colour in Architecture*, described a wide range of colors then available for terracottas including "reds, ranging from pale pink to deep madder; blues from light sky blue to cerulean and deep indigo; greens from light emerald and malachite to grass greens and olive shades . . ." and so on, but particularly including white, off white, cream, and a spectacular range of colored imitations of polished stones. Typically, powdered metal oxides and other minerals were added to a glaze composition to provide a colored glaze. For certain colors the glaze might have to be fired twice. A typical glaze might be feldspar 46%; clay 6.4%; crushed flint 11%; white lead 21.3%; whiting 10.0%; and zinc oxide 5.3%. Colors might be formed as follows: iron oxide, cream and buff; cobalt, blue; copper or chromium, green; and a chrome/tin/lime combination, pink. Bright red, deep yellow, gold, and silver were among those colors which required a second firing at a lower temperature (Guest Ferriday, 1984).

Terracotta Manufacture

The manufacturing process for terracotta units is an extremely complex one with many applications of high levels of crafts' skills. As in any process of ceramics production the clay must first be selected and mixed to remove impurities and give a homogeneous mass. If the clay is too "plastic" it will shrink, twist, and deform as the moulded or formed object dries prior to the firing process. A better clay or marl may have to be found or fillers such as sand may be added to make the clay less plastic.

All the ingredients must be very thoroughly mixed, and all lumps, large air bubbles, debris, and organic remains removed. Grog (crushed and ground previously fired terracotta) could also be added to reduce shrinkage in overly plastic mixes and would also beneficially affect the clays' other properties of porosity, permeability, and elasticity.

Clays or marls were often excavated and then spread out on the ground in heaped layers to be "blunged" for a season or two. This English term refers to the natural process of frosts and rain breaking up the lumps and masses and mixing the materials. The weathered raw clays were then taken and sieved and "tempered" with water to give a plastic or moldable mass. During the weathering and sieving processes nodules or particles of iron pyrites (ferric sulfide) found in the clays were broken down and converted to hydrated ferric oxides such as limonite or are removed entirely. If they remained, pyrites could cause brown "rust" stains to appear and disfigure light surface finishes or at worst they could cause minor explosions to occur during the firing process leaving pits, blowholes, or craters in the surface of the units.

Today, electromagnets attached to the milling equipment also assist in this removal process. Barium carbonate and manganese compounds might be added at this stage. The former combines with water soluble salts and forms insoluble compounds, thus preventing them from reappearing and causing deterioration of body or finish at a later date. The latter improves body color. Once a satisfactory combination of clays and admixtures has been attained the next step is to pack the moist clay mixture into a negative mould made from plaster of paris or gypsum plaster. This mold has been cast from a clay model carved and modelled to represent the front and four other faces; only the rear of the unit lacks a mold.

When the final product is to be a great capital or a piece of free-standing sculptural decoration then the base or top might be the one face to lack a mold. The clay mixture is pressed into the mold by hand and then beaten into all of the smaller recesses of the decorated surfaces by a craftsworker called a "presser."

The clay model and hence the plaster mold are purposely created one-twelfth oversize to allow for the shrinkage which will inevitably result from the ensuing drying and firing processes.

The ultimate quality of the terracotta unit relies

greatly on the skill of the presser at this stage. If the presser fails to eliminate all air pockets and faults, or fails to compact the clay mixture into a homogeneous mass, then the fired terracotta may very well burst, crack, or delaminate in service, or the unit could explode in the kiln with serious consequences. The molds are frequently made of five separate pieces bound together for the pressing. If the final unit is to be very large, the model is often cut into units not larger than 18×24 in. to make installation easier. To save weight, facilitate drying, and ensure even firing the pressed units are hollow from the back. The exterior walls of the unit are usually $1-1\frac{1}{2}$ in. thick. Additional internal thin stiffening walls are added within the hollow unit to stiffen, strengthen and stabilize the outer walls. These internal walls are called "webs" or "straps."

The dry plaster draws moisture from the packed clay which then shrinks, thus releasing itself from the mould after about three days at room temperature. The clay body is now hard or stiff enough to support its own weight and is ready for "finishing" or "tooling." This process consists of smoothing what will be the exposed external faces with wooden or metal spatulae, rubber "kidneys," steel trowels, or scraps of leather, and according to the English authority John Fidler (1981), even the leather tongues from workers' shoes. This finishing process is akin to the burnishing which produced such fine durable surfaces on the pottery of some prehistoric cultures. Technically it induces a surface concentration of fine or even colloidal particles which when the units are fired produce a very fine vitreous integral surface layer known as the "fireskin." All traces of plaster mould fragments or particles are removed at this time and all the arrisses and reveals are cut clean. Any pinholes or imperfections are made good possibly by wiping over the surface with a damp brush. Construction holes, joggles, holes for anchors, and other details are also added at this point according to the shop drawings.

The units are now ready for a longer drying period which may last from a few days to several months.

Drying room temperatures of 86°F (30°C) cut down drying times to a minimum but great care must be taken to ensure that the blocks are indeed dry. Too rapid a drying process can cause warping but insufficiently dry terracotta will not fire properly and can even explode possibly destroying the kiln and its contents. The dried units can be coated with "slips" or "engobes" at this point or the bodies may be fired first to a "biscuit condition" and have such finishes applied at a second stage. A "slip" is a liquid suspension of very fine clay particles in water with a creamy consistency.

A typical "engobe" contains clay, a flux such as

finely crushed flint or felspar, and metallic oxides to provide colors. Both slip and engobe are brushed or sprayed onto the surface of the unit.

An additional glaze might be applied over a slip or engobe or they may all be applied singly or in combination. Glazes are liquid suspensions of finely ground minerals which melt to form a glasslike surface when fired. They are usually applied in two or three thin coats. Because the terracotta body shrinks in the process of firing in the kiln, surface finishes such as slips, engobes and/or glazes must shrink equally with it and with each other. Failure of all the parts to shrink at equal rates can cause surface damage immediately in the kiln or subsequently in service. The worst that can happen is that the entire surface finish spalls off the body or that only the glaze cracks away.

Lesser problems which may become serious later involve the swifter contraction of the surface finish resulting in a fine network of cracks in the slip and or glaze layer. This is called a "cracquelure." Such cracking may develop and become more serious in service. Ultimately water will penetrate down through the cracks to the body beneath and further losses of surface may result.

All such failures of body and surface finish to match thermal and moisture related expansion and contraction rates are termed "lack of fit."

Once prepared with surface finishes the dried units are carefully stacked in a kiln and fired usually at temperatures of between 1562° and 2192°F (850° and 1200°C).

Typical ranges for terracottas in the USA have been defined by pyrometric cones as follows:

| Range | Cone No. | Temperature in Degrees | |
		Fahrenheit	Centigrade
High	Cones 6–8	2232–2305	1222–1263
Medium	Cones 3–5	2134–2185	1168–1196
Low	Cones 01–3	2079–2134	1137–1168

Early historical terracottas which are described as "underfired terracotta" and Renaissance terracottas which were decorated with overglaze lustres and hard overglaze colors were fired at between 650° and 900° C. Fidler (1981) describes the chemical reactions which take place during the firing as follows: "excess water, carbon dioxide and other gases are initially driven off to be followed by the oxidation of carbonaceous matter and the burning out of sulfur from pyrites and other impurities. Ferrous compounds oxidise to ferric; the carbonates decompose and the chemically combined waters of various hydrated minerals are driven off. This process causes shrinkage, gradual re-

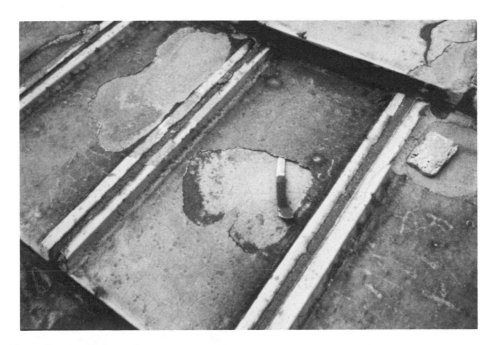

Craquelure and failure of terracotta glaze/slip layer, known as "poor fit", McLeod Building, Edmonton, Alberta.

crystallization and, if the temperature is high enough, vitrification, that is, the fusion bonding of clay by the sintering of its constituents.'' Expressed in these terms it seems that the process is a relatively simple one but as is often the case the apparent simplicity is deceptive.

The "sinter point" at which the particles of the various components begin to fuse together at their contiguous surfaces for a successful firing can easily be exceeded to a temperature at which all the particles melt and flow together in a large vitrified or glassy mass, the unit losing shape in the process. If all goes well, however, the final product has the following properties (McIntyre, 1929).

Coefficient of thermal expansion at 0–50° C, of 2 × 10^{-6} (broadly similar to stone)

Coefficient of elasticity (E) 2.34×10^{-6}–5.11×10^{-6}

Shear strenght 10.89 N/mm^2–16.2N/mm^2

Compressive strength 60.4 N/mm^2 (similar to a hard brick)

Tensile strength 5.7 N/mm^2

Some US standard data for terracotta are as follows (Berryman and Tindall, 1984).

Modulus of elasticity (E) 2.0–6.0×10.6^{-6} psi.

Compressive strength:

Typical 3000–7000 psi

High quality 8000–12,000 psi

Absorption: 7–9% average

Weight: average for hollow terracotta block with $1\frac{1}{2}$ in. thick walls and webs = 65–85 lb/ft³

Defects and Deterioration in Terracotta Building Systems

The deterioration of terracotta work is perhaps one of the most complicated forms of deterioration of building materials and systems which may confront us today. The problems can be concerned with any one or more of the following:

Faults in Units Related to the Manufacturing Process: So-Called Inherent Vices

A series of problems seen in terracotta units in buildings have their origins in the manufacturing process. The exposure of such faulty units in a building leads to an almost inevitable failure. These problems are discussed under the following five headings:

Underburning. Inadequate firing leading to undervit-

rification or failure to reach sintering temperature leaves the body open to water penetration and hence frost damage, surface loss, sulfate deposition (damage from efflorescent and subflorescent water-soluble salts), excessive thermal expansion, and a host of water-related defects.

Packing Faults. If the presser failed to fully compact the clay, leaving layers unbonded to each other with flat voids between the layers, these voids may fill with water which will freeze and cause exfoliation and delamination. Salts may also crystallize or go through hydration cycles along these planes, resulting in similar flaking and exfoliation in damp conditions. Structural failures may also occur if loads fall on these planes of weakness through units.

Glaze Problems. When the terracotta unit is removed from the kiln in a dry state, it takes up moisture from the surrounding environment and expands. This moisture absorbtion process is slow and may extend over two or even three years. To a certain extent the unit continues to expand and contract throughout its life in response to changes in temperature, relative humidity, and atmospheric pressure. Crazing, or the formation of "cracquelure" in the glaze layer may occur at this initial expansion and can get progressively worse throughout the life of the unit.

This problem occurs if the manufacturer has failed to achieve a proper "fit" or a close correspondence between the thermal and moisture expansion coefficients of the body and the surface finishes. Unless the fine networks of cracks extend right down through the glaze-slip layers to the body beneath, the crazing may not present a problem. If the cracks do go right through to the body, water and subsequently dirt may penetrate first downward to the body and then laterally. This can lead to a growing discoloration under the glaze, followed possibly by losses of glaze and slip layers. Soiling under the glaze may be impossible to remove without damaging the glaze layer and the surface of the unit generally. Glazes may be pitted by blowholes where minor explosions of steam or gas burst out through the finish from the body or slip.

Normally such units were rejected and did not get into a building but occasionally such flawed units did slip by and are found causing problems in facades. Such problems are often found in units with special colored experimental finishes such as imitation patinated copper or bronze. Glazes may also act as impermeable barriers trapping moisture within units where water has entered the system from above or from behind and has saturated the terracotta body. Once trapped thus, the water can freeze and the surface may be forced off as a result. J.& N. Ashurst (1988) note that lead glazes of the nineteenth century were fired at low temperatures and have been shown to deteriorate relatively quickly. This phenomenon has been noted elsewhere, particularly in the deterioration of stained or painted glass where underfired "paints" have deteriorated as metal ions are removed by acid precipitation and air pollution.

In terms of their microstructures, the least porous glazes are the least likely to accommodate the expansion of the terracotta bodies. Since obviously the manufacturer is attempting to obtain a glaze that is an effective barrier against water and dirt but at the same time trying to get a good "fit," the final result is always a balance between the two opposite extremes. Sometimes the balance falls a little too much to one side or the other.

Warping and Cracking. If the clay mix is too plastic the terracotta unit may warp, distort, or even crack during the drying process or during the firing process. Plasticity may be simply a characteristic of the clay or it may be the result of too high a moisture content in the body.

Seriously distorted units are normally rejected but occasionally they were actually used in construction. This problem is somewhat related to the next.

Problems of Dimensional Tolerances. As has been noted the initial clay models and hence the plaster molds for terracotta units must be scaled up one-twelfth to allow for inevitable shrinkages in drying and firing. Small variations in drying and firing temperatures or climatic variations during these processes can cause the shrinkages to be smaller or greater than the designed amount with the result that the units may be slightly smaller or larger than is required for the design. In the past oversized units were often cut down with saws or sharp chisels, or were even ground down to match their neighbors. This process often damaged the tough but brittle body, slip, and glaze combination, opening the body to water and dirt penetration at the edges of the unit. Modern diamond saws for cutting masonry have largely helped to ease this problem but there remains a definite risk of exposing the more permeable body or core of the unit.

Faults in Construction: Corrosion in Metal Armatures, Cramps, Dowels, and Other Fixing Details or Structural Supports

A second group of problems are related to faults in the construction of the terracotta masonry as a whole, to the connection between the terracotta and structural support systems. It is quite possible that examples from this group of problems will occur at the same time as problems in the first group.

Terracotta cladding and veneers rely on a system of metal anchors and ties to suspend them from structural steelwork or to tie them back to structural steelwork or backup masonry. Other terracotta units such as columns and ballusters may have steel armatures in the form of long vertical rods passing right through them to keep them aligned and in position. If water enters the hollow terracottawork, corrosion will commence in the steel with the accompanying expansion of the corrosion products. This expansion is quite sufficient to shatter the adjacent or surrounding blocks often leaving mere shards of terracotta hanging from the rusting steel.

In the typical case of the YMCA building in Winnipeg, such corrosion took place in steel T members which were cantilevered out of the main facade to carry the terracotta units of the entablature over the main entrance. The corrosion of these T members shattered the units so that their faces were totally lost. This problem can be expecially dangerous if the corrosion takes place in hidden steelwork which supports large overhanging cornices which may be more than 100 ft or 30 m above the sidewalk. In my experience this problem is all too likely to occur since the parapets or copings over these large cornices have often been poorly maintained and in some cases have even been found to have trees growing out of defective and open joints between terracotta units! While in some cases the original designs called for bronze rods, hooks, and armatures, most merely specified galvanized steel or even painted steel. In practice it seems that few bronze rods or other fixtures were used. The steel on the other hand is often found to have corroded.

The corrosion products take up many times the volume of the original metal and if the metal was tightly set, the expanding corrosion products will burst the masonry. Tell-tale rust staining will often occur in mortar joints, along the line of a crack, or down the surface of the terracotta units beneath a rusting tie, anchor or support. Although the corrosion of hidden steelwork can be one of the most difficult faults to diagnose, structural cracks through individual units or small groups of units associated with an outward bursting of the block or unit faces in the immediate vicinity will often be found to be linked to the formation of the thick layers of exfoliating corrosion on steelwork immediately behind the worst damaged area. The phenomenon is known as "oxide jacking" or "rust jacking." Hidden metalwork may be located with a magnetometer or other form of portable metal detector. Major corrosion may be located by equipment which detects the weak

Terracotta cornice with tree growing out of it, Edmonton, Alberta. Poor, or nonexistant maintenance has allowed the cornice to leak, threatening the hidden steel supports and anchors.

electrical fields which exist around corroding metals. I have worked on the conservation of terracotta work on a 1912 building in Vancouver where all the anchors were set in sulfur. Where rainwater and the chloride aerosols from the sea penetrated into the wall, the sulfur caused accelerated corrosion in the anchors and consequently massive shattering of the terracotta blocks.

Failures of Drainage Details

Unfortunately a number of details continued to be used over a long period despite that fact that they often failed with disastrous repercussions. One such detail

was the cornice with the hidden gutter in its upper surface. The water was supposed to be collected in this gutter and discharged by means of a pipe which ran back and down through the terracottawork to link up with an internal rainwater pipe. The pipes were often of cast iron which corroded and even split when water froze in them. The resultant leaks could cause severe damage which would often become critical before the problems were spotted and investigated. Other similar details consisted of terracotta parapets around small flat roofs or balconies where water could easily be trapped or where drains were often ridiculously undersized. Ice, dead birds, and other debris would swiftly block small drain pipes. Masses of ice or dammed up water could then smash the terracotta or lead to corrosion in hidden steelwork which in turn would lead to the same result. This problem is related to the next.

Cracking and bursting in terracotta associated with corrosion of steel structural frame, McLeod Building, Edmonton.

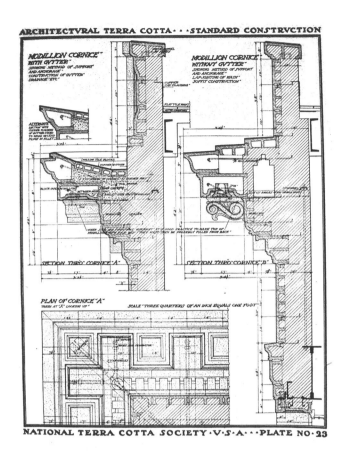

Typical terracotta cornice detail, National Terra Cotta Society 1927; note section on the left with potentially problematic concealed gutter with cast iron drain pipe running back and down through the wall.

Tanking or Ponding

In cases where water leaks into a terracotta system it may build up until the volume of the water is such that the load causes a structural failure and the terracotta crashes down to the street below.

Structural Failure Because of Overloading

A large group of failures can be related to the cracking of the rather brittle, comparatively thin-walled terracotta units under concentrated loads. One particularly common instance of this type of failure occurs when the brittle terracotta cladding becomes load-bearing as a result of differential movement between cladding and steel or concrete structural skeletons. A typical case

occurs where projecting string courses, band courses, or intermediate cornices have their hollow rear sections crushed between terracotta cladding of the walls below and above the projecting details. The cracking may be along the center of the front face of the projecting units or along the top or bottom just at, or behind the face. Overly large cantilevers can result in a tendency for the units to rotate and tilt outward, resulting in localized crushing of units above and beneath.

Severe overloading can be caused by the lack of provision of expansion joints. Very large areas of terracotta facades were often installed totally without any expansion joints. Thermal and moisture related movements in such areas can be very large and if the terracotta is restrained, stresses will build up leading eventually to catastrophic failure and the formation of cracks which may run through many units or even up through many storeys. This type of problem occurred on the 1913 Woolworth Building in New York.

All the usual causes of structural movements in walls, such as seismic shocks, road traffic vibrations, foundation settlement and rotation, or ground subsidence can lead to the overstressing and cracking of terracotta cladding or veneers.

Unsuitable Mortars

Mortars are used both to bed and set the terracotta units and to fill the voids in the back of the hollow units. These mortars often tend to cause problems for two reasons. The joints are usually $\frac{3}{16}-\frac{1}{4}$ in. wide (4.8–6.0 mm) and filled with a dense, hard, and brittle mortar consisting of cement and sand (1:3 p.b.v.) The joint profiles or cross sections are usually very nearly flush or slightly concave. If the units expand against the mortar in the joints the hard mortar tends to crush the edges of the units. If the units contract they tend to pull away from the mortar and open up a crack.

Once the gaps open, water penetrates behind the mortar which is then too impermeable and traps the water and dissolved salts behind it. The entrapped water can then cause a number of problems as has been noted. Occasionally the mortar, and particularly back-up mortar may contain impurities such as sulfates which can be transported by moisture into the units. This problem will tend to show itself first as staining in the centers of the faces of units and this will be followed by exfoliation of the surface caused by accumulations of water-soluble salts.

Damage Caused by Water-Soluble Salts

Anions such as sulfates, chlorides, nitrates, and phosphates occur as water-soluble salts and may contami-

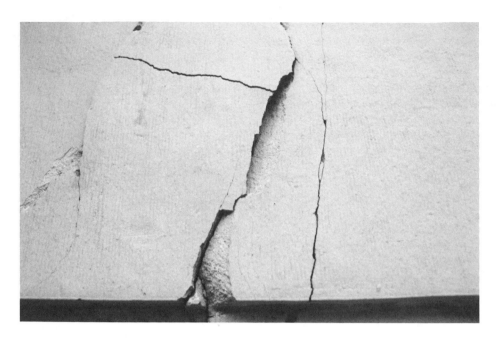

Terracotta cracking from overloading of block.

nate terracotta just as they do other masonry materials. The water-soluble salts travel in solution through the units until they reach a surface or a zone just beneath a surface where temperature and atmospheric pressure cause the water to evaporate leaving behind the salt in the form of crystalline deposits.

If the deposits form on the surface they are known as efflorescence. If they form beneath the surface in the pores and capillaries of the unit they are known as subflorescence or cryptoflorescence (crypto = hidden or secret). In the latter form the crystals are potentially most dangerous. Remaining packed into the confined spaces of the pores, capillaries, or microcracks in the body or between body and fireskin, or between body and glaze or slip, the crystals may undergo cycles of hydration and dehydration.

In taking up water from the environment around them the crystals may expand to many times their initial volumes and in so expanding can exert enormous pressures on the walls of the small voids in which they are concentrated. The crystals may also exert considerable pressures as they form from solutions. Such forces may be in the order of 20,000 psi (137,900 kPa). In buildings where limestone has unfortunately been installed over terracotta so that the runoff of acidic precipitation actually runs down over terracotta surfaces, dissolved calcium bicarbonate may be deposited on and in the micropores and capillaries of slips and glazes. Once in position the bicarbonates can react with oxides of sulfur and other pollutants to form harm-

ful salts and deposits of expansive sulfates for example. The exfoliation of glazes and slips may follow as an inevitable result.

External Forms of Deterioration

A third and final group of forms of deterioration are related to causes which are external to the terracotta and its immediate supports.

"Hang ons"

During the long life of terracotta buildings inevitably large numbers of signs, electrical service paraphernalia, and other items are attached to the surface of the terracotta units by means of lag bolts and screws set in holes drilled or smashed through the glazed and slip coated surfaces or fireskins. Every time that these surface finishes are perforated there is a risk of water penetration to the body behind or into the wall as a whole. The water may then cause a wide range of problems particularly including corrosion in metalwork and the deposition of water-soluble salts. Often the bolts or anchors themselves corrode and shatter the surrounding terracotta.

Biodeterioration

A large range of life forms ranging from trees at the macroscopic end of the scale to bacteria at the microscopic end can cause varying degrees of damage to terracotta units. Probably the most serious damage is caused by trees or shrubs which manage to become established in joints in horizontal surfaces of details such as cornices, copings, and belt courses. The roots are quite capable of penetrating deep into the masonry, prising the units apart and smashing arrisses. This damage is followed by more water penetration and further growth of vegetation. These most severe problems obviously only occur when terracotta masonry remains for long periods without even the most rudimentary maintenance inspections and cleanup work.

Bacteria, algae, and fungi may be responsible for unsightly discoloration of terracotta surfaces, but their major significance is that their very presence indicates that moisture contents in the terracotta have risen to dangerous levels where frost and salt damage are also likely to occur.

Pigeons and other birds may also soil terracotta with their guano causing an aesthetic problem. It should be noted that the guano may also be responsible for the deposition of harmful phosphates, nitrates, and other water-soluble salts.

Heavy accumulations of moist decaying organic debris on terracotta can provide a favorable environment for causing deterioration of glazes, slips, metallic and other colors, and furthering all forms of damage related to prolonged periods of wetness. The presence of birds on the building will often have led to the application of a variety of antibird devices which are usually distinguished only in the degree of their lack of success in deterring the birds, or in their success in providing more ways of damaging or soiling the terracotta. Prominent among these are old antibird gels and greases which have often attracted large quantities of dirt before hardening to the consistency and appearance of cold tar. Various plasticisers and solvents may also have migrated from these substances into the slip and body of the terracotta. The removal of the blackened, thick, and hard deposits which have become totally useless, can pose a major cleaning problem.

Erosion and Abrasion

The integrities of the fireskin and of glaze/slip combinations have been noted as being of great importance to the conservation of the terracotta as a whole. Erosion of the glaze particularly may result from the continuous impacts of high velocity dust and other particles.

Such problems will be found to be more severe where wind velocities are increased on very tall buildings and in areas of turbulence. This problem may be seen in Winnipeg, for example, where prairie dust is a constant factor and it is apparent from microscopic

Sandblasted terracotta, Ottawa, Ontario.

examination of glazed surfaces that they have been eroded by pitting and scratching. In consequence they have lost some of the original gloss from their glazes. In other cases severe damage to glazes and slips are found to have been caused by sand blasting by enthusiastic but woefully ill-informed attempts at cleaning the terracotta.

Acid Damage

In some cases glazed terracotta will be found to have a cloudy whitish "bloom" on the surface and the actual glaze may be seen to have been etched or even removed. After a little research it is usually discovered that the terracotta has been "cleaned" by somebody using a concentrated solution of hydrofluoric acid. In a dilute form this acid is the basis for many chemical cleaning products for acid insensitive stones and bricks. However, if it is used in a concentrated form it can actually dissolve silica and silicates in the form of glass or glazes. In concentrated form it has long been used for etching decorative patterns and lettering into glass. There have been some cases in North America where the concentrated acid was unfortunately used and the terracotta work was severely damaged leaving the characteristic whitish bloom or dribbles of redeposited colloidal silica on and below the etched surfaces. The nineteenth century terracotta faced Natural History Museum in London, England is one of the most famous examples of this problem. Once formed, these deposits are practically impossible to remove without damaging the surface of the terracotta beneath.

Inappropriate Repairs

Terracotta will often be found to have been repaired or patched with totally unsuitable hard portland cement based mortars, roofing tar, caulking compounds, and even galvanized steel sheet. These repairs are often difficult to remove but at least they must be carefully examined to ensure that they are not actually causing more damage to the terracotta. On one occasion I actually found that terracotta details high up on a building in Quebec City had been replaced with painted carved wood when they had shattered because of ice damage. The wood subsequently rotted and its corroding steel fixing screws presented a second generation of problems.

The Conservation of Terracotta Work

The conservation of terracotta is best considered under a series of major topics, many of which may have to be dealt with simultaneously or consecutively on any particular job.

Prevention of Water Ingress

Probably the greatest single cause of problems in terracotta work is the presence of water in or behind the terracotta, or causing corrosion in hidden metalwork. It follows, therefore, that one of the most important conservation measures is to prevent water getting into the terracotta via joints, through failing porous and permeable surfaces, via backup masonry, or from leaking drains and rainwater gutters.

All conservation inspections or surveys should concentrate particularly on locating any and all examples of this prime cause and then each example should be meticulously dealt with to eradicate the problem.

A second group of related problems may be associated with improper repairs which have blocked openings or waterproofed joints in the terracotta envelope which were designed to act as vents or drains. Some mortar joints functioned perfectly well in their original form although the mortar was permeable. In fact they functioned well exactly because the mortar was permeable and did not trap moisture or force trapped moisture to travel through the adjacent terracotta units where it could be trapped again and frozen causing damage.

Cleaning Terracotta

In many cases buildings which have for years been thought to have been black, grey or dingy shades of brown are found after cleaning to have been faced with crisp white, cream, rich red or even polychromatic terracotta. Happily, the heavy soiling can often be removed from glazed and slip finished terracotta by washing techniques using warm water, neutral detergents or surfactants and natural fiber or plastic hard bristle brushes or hard plastic scouring pads such as the Scotchbrite pads produced by 3M.

Unglazed terracotta can be cleaned with hydrofluoric acid based proprietory masonry-cleaning compounds. These are typified by the excellent products of ProSoCo of Kansas and Hydroclean of Hartford, Connecticut. Such formulations may include dilute hydrofluoric acid, phosphoric acid, sulfonic or sulfamic acid, chelating agents, and surfactants.

The product is usually diluted with water from 3:1 to 1:1 (water:product) and is applied with a large bristle brush. The diluted product is usually left on the surface for two or three minutes. This period is referred to as the "dwell time." Some products have been carefully formulated so that they are active for a few minutes but can then be left on the surface for hours without doing any damage. They loosen the soiling and then become inactive and can be rinsed off at any time. This feature is a decided advantage because other products may etch or "burn" the surface if they are inadvertently left on for too long because of delays in rinsing off. Delays can easily occur in practice, for example, when a hose breaks or a pump stops working.

The product is then rinsed off with a medium pressure spray of water. The rinse-off pressure is usually adequate at about 200 psi at a flow rate of 4 gallons per minute (gpm)(1379 kPa at 18 litres/min (lpm)). Pressures may in some cases be allowed to go as high as 600 psi at a flow rate of 5 gpm, but only when the terracotta is in good condition (4130 kPa at 22.7 lpm)

Many specialists are reluctant to recommend chemical cleaning of this kind for terracotta because of the very definite risks of forming colloidal silica "staining" or blooms. As has been noted such deposits of colloidal

Progress shots of cleaning terracotta using water and neutral detergent.

silica are almost impossible to remove. Unless chemical cleaning work is carried out strictly according to tests, with great care, and under constant supervision the risks are indeed too great.

It must always be remembered that hydrofluoric acid works because it dissolves the silicates of the surface of the ceramic unit at the interface between the soiling and the terracotta. The amount of material dissolved may be only a few micrometers thick, but it is a destructive method.

All cleaning work must be preceeded by careful testing on less important areas in the least visible locations in case any damage is inadvertently caused to the surface. All details of dilutions, dwell times, rinse-off pressures and flow rates, water temperatures, and actual products used must be carefully recorded so that they can be exactly reproduced. The chemical cleaners normally cease to function properly at or below about 50°F (10°C).

No work should be carried out when there is any risk of the rinse-off water freezing later in the masonry. It is generally recommended that no work should be carried out when there is any risk of frost before the wall has thoroughly dried out. No work should be carried out in strong sunshine because this will cause the cleaning solution to become more concentrated on the surface, possibly causing "burns" or patchy uneven cleaning and etching.

Some specialists recommend the use of poultices containing EDTA [ethylene diamine-tetra-acetic acid] and alkaline additives for the cleaning of unglazed terracotta. Ashurst and Ashurst (1988) give the following formula: in 1000 ml of water: 60 g ammonium carbonate; 60 g sodium bicarbonate; 25 g EDTA; 10 g surfactant disinfectant [such as Cetavlon] and 60 g carboxymethyl cellulose [or a cellulose based wallpaper paste]. Conservators might use various other poultice recipes substituting diatomaceous earth for the poultice medium and varying the other components. Diatomaceous earth is available in Canada as Celite (manufactured by Johns Manville in the United States). Fullers' Earth and kaolinite may also be used as poultice media.

Paint stains and similar deposits on terracotta can be removed by mixing appropriate paint removers based on organic solvents with the above poultice media to produce a thick paste which is then applied as a poultice and left to dry. Drying rates can be retarded, making the solvents more effective, by covering the poultice with a sheet of polyethylene.

No matter how attractive the prices may seem, on no account should sandblasting, cleaning with abrasive wheels, or "hydro-silica" cleaning be used on terracotta. These harsh abrasive treatments will remove or seriously damage the fireskin, glaze, or slip finishes

and will destroy the integrity of the surface. Hydro-silica cleaning uses a high-pressure water jet into which a stream of sand is introduced. The pressures are usually over 1000 psi (6895 kPa) with about 5% sand.

Chemical cleaning with alkali formulations based upon sodium hydroxide or caustic soda should also be avoided because there is a strong risk of the crystals of sodium hydroxide penetrating into and remaining in the pores and capillaries of the body of the terracotta and causing destructive subflorescence which will cause total breakdown of the surface.

It is a fundamental principle in conservation that the most gentle techniques and materials should be employed which will achieve the desired preservation of the resource. Thus if a small amount of low-pressure water and a little neutral detergent will clean soiled terracotta, then this combination should be used rather than large quantities of water and chemicals. Thus all cleaning tests should commence with the gentler methods and should only proceed to the more aggressive methods when absolutely necessary. As has been noted, once soiling has penetrated beneath the glaze it can not be practically removed without damaging the glaze or the glaze/slip/body interface.

The Preliminary Stages Before Restoration, Repair, and Maintenance

Before any restorations, repairs, or other interventions can be carried out on a terracotta clad structure it is essential that a full survey is carried out. The objective is to locate all the defects such as cracked or shattered blocks, blocks with rust stains on them, pollutant crusts and deposits; or structural movements and then to relate them all to their causes. The causes may include leaks, failed mortar joints, failed rainwater gutters or down-pipes, corroding steel armatures, corroding structural steel, or a lack of adequate expansion joints. All of the causes must then be remedied first before trying to treat the "symptoms of the disease."

The best technique for surveying and recording the locations of the terracotta problems is to examine all the building literally by hand, using "sounding" and other techniques to actually touch each unit. I use a heavy rubber mallet weighing about one kilo or just over two pounds. The blocks are struck with the edge of the mallet head and either have a sound "ring" or can be heard to be cracked or loose. Mortar joints are tested with a steel probe.

On large buildings I carry out surveys from the bucket of a crane. The best buckets or baskets are attached to pivots at the end of the crane's long telescopic boom. As has been noted baskets swinging at the end of a steel cable are not recommended even if they

A one kilo rubber mallet used for "sounding" masonry.

are permitted by law, because the basket tends to swing and rotate so much that it is very hard to work on the building. The basket may also crash into the building damaging the terracotta or the cable may actually tend to saw its way through projecting terracotta work such as a cornice over the basket. Terracotta work is frequently so delicate and brittle that severe damage can be caused by accidental impacts from cables or baskets.

Surveys carried out with binoculars from street level or from other buildings are simply not effective compared with working from a crane or better still from scaffolding.

The information derived from the survey is usually marked on photoelevations or largescale drawings using simple coding systems to distinguish between the various types of problems. A typical coded survey is shown on page 10.

The surveyor will normally make a photomosaic approximately to a scale of 1:50 ($\frac{1}{4}$ in. = 1 ft) or 1:25 ($\frac{1}{2}$ in. = 1 ft). I have such surveys laser printed onto transparent film and then set these transparencies into sheets of polyester drawing film. Very high quality prints are made from the resulting "reproducible" for marking up survey details or it can be marked up itself to form a basis for final contract documents. Slightly less sophisticated survey reports and contract documents can be prepared using color photographs in conjunction with blueline prints of original drawings. The problem with this latter approach is the reproduction

of the color photographs. Recent advances in laser printing have made this form of reproduction almost indispensible.

Individual blocks which are to be cut out are usually marked on the building with a large permanent marker or felt pen. Blocks which are not to be cut out and destroyed should not be marked in this way because it can be very difficult to remove the inks or dyes.

Searches for hidden ferrous metal reinforcement, supports, armatures, and other fixings can be conducted with metal detectors. Usually such searches are conducted in conjunction with the observation of cracks and rust staining or other clues to the presence of corroding metalwork.

Intrusive or destructive techniques of examination or exploratory work cover a broad range from using a chisel or steel probe to open up a failing joint and determine the extent of failures, right up to cutting out one or more blocks of terracotta to see the extent or cause of a particular problem.

One technique which is becoming increasingly popular is the use of the "borescope." A hole is drilled in the terracotta using a diamond tipped coring bit to give a hole of $\frac{1}{2}$ in. in diameter. The "borescope" is a bundle of optical fibers with a lighting system and a magnifying eyepiece so designed that the tip can be passed through the small hole and on into the interior of the terracotta work. Once the end of the borescope has been passed into the terracotta the interior of the block, mortar fill, corroded metalwork, and other significant features can

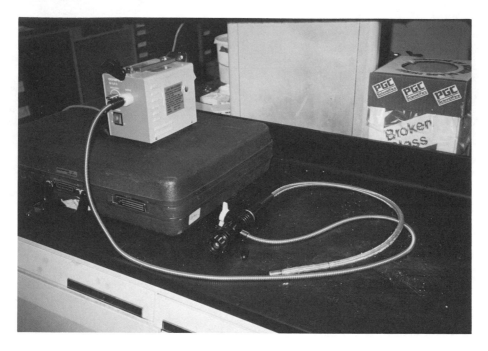

Olympus fiber-optic borescope complete with illumination source unit.

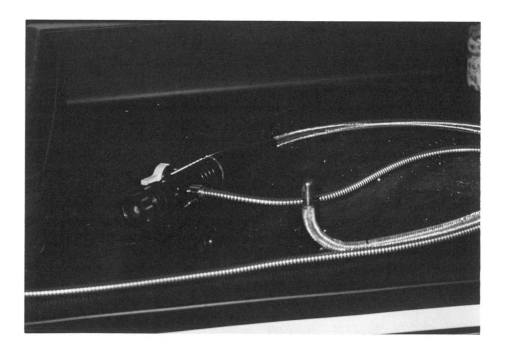

The working tip of the borescope here stands upright, controlled by the knob above the microscope on the left. The internal illumination arrives at the tip via fiber optics and can illuminate the interior of a cast iron column for example.

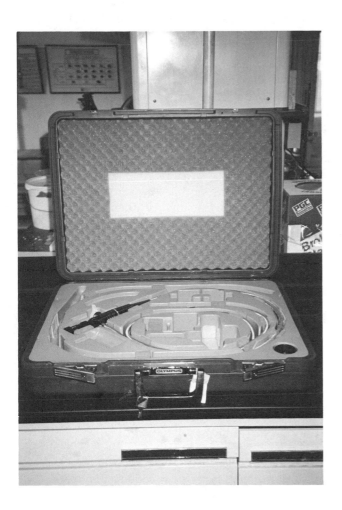

The Olympus borescope in its carrying case.

not only be seen but can be photographed by means of a camera which attaches to the outside end of the optical fiber bundle. Currently the major problem in this technique is the very high cost of the borescopes.

Where terracotta units or blocks have to be removed without causing damage to the adjacent blocks or the structural support system, small diameter diamond-tipped stone saws can be used to free the blocks by cutting first in the mortar joints and then if all else fails by cutting and sacrificing one terracotta unit in order to free the others.

In general when exploratory holes are being opened up it is a good practice to cut into terracotta units which are already damaged in order to get behind and release other units which are in good condition.

The drawings published by the no longer extant Na-

tional Terra Cotta Society of the U.S.A. in their *Architectural Terra Cotta: Standard Construction* in editions published in 1914 and 1927 are invaluable for the understanding of some of the most complex terracotta systems. They are particularly valuable in locating hidden metalwork or knowing what to expect within a wall. (See figure in "Failures of Drainage Details" section.)

Laboratory Testing and Analysis

There are three forms of laboratory work which may be useful to define problems in terracotta work sufficiently well for a conservation treatment to be designed or developed:

- Petrography or the petrographic analysis of thin sections under a microscope and scanning electron microscopy
- Chemical analyses
- Physical testing

Petrography

Petrography is the scientific term for the description and classification of rocks. A major form of petrographic analysis is carried out by cutting a thin slice from a rock or in this case a fragment of terracotta. The thin slice is stuck to a glass microscope slide and is then ground down to a transparent cross section only about six or seven microns thick. The very thin section can then be examined with transmitted light (light which passes right through the section) or with transmitted polarized light. The polarized light produces distinctive appearances for the mineral crystals and other components of the ceramic as it does for rocks. Thus the analyst can distinguish the size, form, and nature of the individual particles within the terracotta. The density of the terracotta can also be examined with the distribution and sizes of pores and voids.

Scanning Electron Microscopy

The scanning electron microscope (SEM) is an invaluable modern tool which is being increasingly used by conservators particularly to examine the microscopic details of the surfaces and interiors of stone and architectural ceramics. Watersoluble salts may also be extracted by boiling in distilled water and the solutions can then be subjected to standard quantitative and qualitative tests for anions using "wet chemistry."

Chemical Analyses

With an X-ray fluorescence microprobe the SEM can be used to establish what elements are present and in what amounts. The SEM will also show crystals of contaminating salts which have formed in or on the surface of the terracotta. Once consolidation treatments have been carried out on masonry materials the SEM can again be used to see exactly what the consolidant has done to the structure of the material.

Infrared Spectrography and X-Ray Diffraction

Known as IRS and XRD infrared spectrography and x-ray diffraction are two further forms of chemical analytical techniques which may also be used to characterize the chemical nature of the terracotta and its contaminants.

Physical Tests

Certain physical characteristics of the terracotta are of importance for the long-term preservation of the material. The primary concerns are:

- The compressive strength
- Shear strength
- Water absorbtion
- Thermal and moisture expansion coefficients
- Permeability through the glaze
- Glaze adhesion
- Saturation coefficient.

Compressive strengths vary widely for terracotta but as we have seen they may range from 3000 to 12,000 psi (20,685 to 82,740 kPa). Samples are cut from a damaged unit and are tested according to ASTM standard tests (American Society for Testing and Materials). The samples are loaded in compression and tested to failure, giving the average maximum load that the unit will carry.

Relative absorption of both glazed and unglazed terracottas is measured by immersing previously weighed dry samples in cold water for 24 hours and in boiling water for 5-hour intervals. After the immersions the samples are weighed again and the absorbtion is calculated as a proportion of the saturated to the dry weights. The saturation coefficient represents a ratio of the 24-hour absorbtio to the 5-hour absorbtion.

Thermal and moisture expansion coefficients are calculated by subjecting wet and dry samples to temperature cycles to which the terracotta might be exposed in diurnal and seasonal ranges. The samples are monitored throughout the process by means of strain gauges. By monitoring expansion rates of glazes, bodies, and complete units, potential problems of incompatibility between glazes and bodies and of expansion in complete terracotta veneers can be identified.

A simple physical examination of broken samples of the terracotta under a microscope at a magnification of about 30 times is particularly useful before and after each of the tests are carried out. All the data gathered from these tests and analyses can then be used to ensure that restoration and repair works are totally compatible with the surviving original work. Great care must be taken to ensure that new work does not cause the original to be overloaded or otherwise damaged.

Repair and Restoration

Once sources of water ingress have been blocked, terracotta repairs usually include the following:

- Reattachment of units to their backup masonry or to the structural framework of the building.
- The repair of spalled-off fragments and areas of slip and/or glaze loss.
- The repair of cracked terracotta units.
- The removal of corroded steel reinforcement and secondary supports and their replacement with noncorroding metals. Where sulfur has been used for settings this too should be removed.
- Mortar repairs both for rebedding and repointing.
- The replacement of damaged or missing units either with matching new terracotta or with substitute materials.

Cracked and/or detached terracotta units are normally repaired and reattached using threaded stainless steel rods and moisture-insensitive epoxy resins. The epoxy resins which are selected for exterior work on terracotta must not only be moisture-insensitive, curing in wet conditions or even under water, but they must also be resistant to ultraviolet radiation which can cause "yellowing" or other color changes and other forms of degradation. Cracked units which can be removed from the wall can be simply stuck together again with a sparing use of resin. If the units are still *in situ*, the resin may be injected by means of a veterinarian's hypodermic syringe.

Where units are loose or detached, but they cannot be easily removed without damaging them or the contiguous units, holes can be drilled though them using diamond tipped coring bits and then stainless steel rods are inserted and set in epoxy resin. Recessed or countersunk nuts can be threaded onto the rods to secure the errant blocks and the whole assembly can be concealed with a carefully tinted terracotta or stonedust composite patching mix.

Although some specialists use AISI (American Iron and Steel Institute) Type 304 Stainless Steel, I usually specify AISI Type 316 which has a much higher corrosion resistence.

In all cases where epoxy or other synthetic resins are being used for repairs, avoid splashing or spilling resin onto the surface of the terracotta. Once cured, resins may be very difficult or even impossible to remove. Depending on the situation barriers or separators to keep resin off surfaces can include vaseline or petroleum jelly, modeling clay, and polyethylene sheet.

Patented stainless steel fasteners may also be used. These employ capsules of resin which is released by striking the fastener a sharp blow when the fastener is in place in a drilled hole (e.g., Hilti HIT fasteners). Various other forms of stainless steel fasteners or anchors may be employed such as those manufactured by Hohmann & Barnard, Inc. of Hauppage, N.Y.

Pins or rods for attachment, location, or reinforcement may also be made from threaded nylon or Teflon rods, or from custom made glass-fiber reinforced polyester resin rods. Lightweight grouts using nonstaining portland cement may be injected under pressure to reattach terracotta units where the backup mortar has failed.

Where pointing and jointing mortars need to be replaced one must first establish the strength of the terracotta units so that the mortar mix can be made slightly weaker. J. & N. Ashurst (1988) recommend a series of mixes for repointing, bedding and filling:

- HTI powder : Lime : sand*/stone dust
  $\quad$ 1 $\quad$: $\quad$ 1 : $\qquad$ 3
  (HTI powder is prepared by grinding refractory bricks, the initials HTI stand for "high temperature insulation").
- Based on a coarse stuff of 1 part lime : 3 parts sand*
  Coarse Stuff : (nonstaining) white cement
  $\qquad$ 6 $\qquad$: $\qquad$ 1
- Hydraulic lime : sand*/stone dust
  $\qquad$ 1 $\qquad$: 3
- Masonry Cement : sand*
  $\qquad$ 1 $\qquad$: 5–6

* Note: The sand should be well graded down from a maximum sieve size of 1.18 mm. The mortar should be as dry as possible while still being workable. J. & N. Ashurst recommend that the lime should be in the form of putty; and add the pointing with waterproof caulking compounds such as mastics or silicone rubber should only be undertaken as temporary measures.

Pointing and mortar mixes for new terracotta recommended today by Gladding, McBean & Co. are as follows:

Setting mortar:
Mortar mix for setting ceramic veneer shall be as follows:
Portland cement, ASTM C 150-67, Type I or Type II. 1 ft^3.
Approved high calcium stacked lime putty screened and aged at least 20 days, containing not more than 4% magnesium oxide, $\frac{1}{2}$ ft^3 hydrated lime, ASTM C 206 or C 207, Type S. $\frac{1}{2}$ ft^3.
Clean Sharp Siliceous Sand graded from fine to very fine ASTM C 144. 4 ft^3.

Pointing mortar:
One volume of approved portland cement; $\frac{1}{4}$ volume aged high calcium lime putty or hydrated lime; three (3) volumes very fine sand; gauge with mix of one (1) volume Konset thoroughly mixed in six (6) volumes of water, or of Anti-Hydro or Suconem Red label or Tricosal or approved equal used in accordance with the manufacturers' directions.

It should be noted that the pointing mortar mixes which were used so successfully before the First World War did not include any of the additives listed above. In many cases these old pointing mortars have performed so well that they are still in excellent condition 80 years after installation even without any maintenance! Gladding, McBean, in their Notes to architects and specification writers suggest that "the Hydratite Liquid contributes better workability to the mortar and then after curing and drying out, adds a water repellent quality to the mortar backing. Other similar products, as specified by the architect may also be used."

Grout mix #1:
Grout for all vertical voids back of anchor-type ceramic veneer and handmade ceramic veneer shall be wet and sloppy composed of the following:

Approved portland cement	1 volume
Clean sharp sand	4 volumes
Top gravel well graded from fine to coarse	2 volumes

Grout mix #2:
Grout for all handmade ceramic veneer sills, copings, balusters, and rails, cornices, etc., shall be lean and composed of the following:

Approved portland cement	1 volume
Clean sharp sand	4 volumes
Top gravel well graded from fine to coarse	3 volumes

A specification published in *The American Architect*, May 9, 1923, p. 425, called for mortar composed of one volume of portland cement to three volumes of sand with lime "not to exceed $\frac{1}{5}$ of a sack of lime to a sack of cement" added.

Guest Ferriday (1984) gives mortar specifications for buildings in Portland, Oregon as ranging . . . "from four parts of lime for each part of Portland Cement to one part of lime for every four parts of Portland Cement. The ratio of lime and Portland Cement combined to sand was usually around one to two. Pointing mortar was generally of a different mix than setting mortar, with special sands or mortar stains producing colours compatible with the glazes."

No matter what the original mortar mixes were for bedding, setting, pointing or backing, it must be clear that mixes for repairs and restoration work must allow for the changed state of the old terracotta which is quite possibly no longer compatible with the original mortar mixes.

Surface Repairs and Coatings

In cases where there have been losses of very thin layers of glaze and slip finishes or the actual surface or fireskin from unglazed terracottas; and where craquelure or crazing has destroyed the integrity of the glaze/slip layer, I have seen excellent results produced by the careful application of breathable masonry coatings based on silicates. Two products with the essential very high vapor permeability ratings are currently available in North America, "Keim Granital" and Pro-

SoCo's Conservare "BMC." These coatings are available in limited standard ranges of colors but special colors can be mixed to order for an additional cost.

Such vapor permeable coatings are invaluable in restoring the weather-resistant qualities of units which have had their permeable bodies exposed by surface losses. Coating failures are usually associated with problems caused by moisture being trapped behind a coating which is not sufficiently vapor permeable.

Clear glazes are very difficult to replace or repair reliably but successes have been reported with ultraviolet stable polyurethane resins, which may also be tinted. Additional successes have been achieved with clear, nonyellowing epoxy resins and with acrylic resins.

There has been insufficient time for the long-range performance of these systems under real-life conditions to be properly evaluated. With the possible exception of the latest UV-stable resins, all synthetic resin systems have a tendency to powder, "chalk," and yellow or discolor in other ways with prolonged exposure to sunlight, urban pollution, and acid precipitation. J. & N. Ashurst (1988) quote a recipe for the consolidation of localized areas of deteriorated glazes, using "acrylic resins made up as a 10% solution in acetone and industrial methylated spirit (1:1)."

Epoxy/stonedust composites formulated for marble repairs have been successfully used for patching the white and off-white terracottas which were often originally designed to imitate marbles.

Terracotta with surface damage painted over with Keim Granital silicate-based paint blends in well with original surfaces.

Plastic Repairs or "Dentistry"

The terms "plastic repairs" or "dentistry" are used to describe processes which use composites of mortar materials, special aggregates, nonfading pigments, and small quantities of synthetic resins to make workable patching compounds which will harden as they cure. Where fragments of terracotta have spalled off, these patching compounds can be used to restore the surface, molding profiles, and other details.

Feather-edged repairs for large-scale losses should be avoided because the repair usually tends to fracture though the thin brittle edges and progressive failure occurs from these fractures. A thin diamond-tipped masonry saw blade can be used with its water cooling and lubrication to cut out a slightly undercut section from the terracotta to permit the insertion of a neatly squared-off patch. To avoid shrinkage in mortar repairs the clean, dust-free surface of the terracotta should first be thoroughly wetted with a hand spray to prevent excessive suction from the body of the terracotta. The mix should also be as dry as possible and an appropriate non reemulsifiable resin should be added to the mix to provide good adhesion.

Since all such cases are unique it is essential that tests are carried out using all variations of mixes and techniques in an inconspicuous place on the terracotta work.

Many specialists today prefer combinations of epoxy resin-based composites with stainless steel reinforcement to ensure that repairs are doubly securely bonded to terracotta units. This is especially recommended where such repairs are to remain without regular inspection high up to buildings above public thoroughfares and where an adhesion failure could result in a dangerous fall of heavy fragments causing injury or even loss of life.

The above cautious but sensible approach is similar to the conservative approach to structural adhesives for the attachment of terracotta veneers. A number of synthetic rubber-based adhesives are available for the attachment of terracotta and tilework but being aware of the serious consequences if a unit should fall, conservators usually employ additional stainless steel anchors. In polluted urban environments the provision of this additional security is particularly prudent.

Replacement with New Units

When terracotta units are shattered or otherwise severely damaged they have to be replaced. Such cases frequently occur where embedded steelwork has corroded and expanded shattering the terracotta. The best replacement is with new terracotta units which will require to be designed with great skill to match dimensions, surface patterns, textures, colors, and the requi-

site physical characteristics such as compressive strength and thermal expansion coefficients.

There are only about nine manufacturers and producers currently operating in North America and the currently increasing workload means that there are likely to be delays before they could undertake a project. The scale of a project may also limit the number of potential suppliers. Some projects might be too small for the largest manufacturers while others might be too large for the smaller producers. Even after a manufacturer has been found there may still be delays of as long as a number of years before the units can be delivered to the site.

A list of current manufacturers and producers is given at the end of this chapter.

Substitute Materials

Where there is no chance of obtaining actual terracotta for replacements or where more original material would be damaged unless action is taken immediately, there is a limited range of potential substitute materials which have been used with varying degrees of success. The most successful examples have been made from precast concrete, artificial stone, glass fiber reinforced polyester resin on a steel support frame, and cast aluminum. In certain cases compliance with building codes and other regulations have led to the use of lightweight replacements made of cast aluminum and glass fiber reinforced polyester.

The latter two examples have been most frequently employed for the replacement of severely deteriorated terracotta cornices which project far over urban sidewalks.

It is fair to comment here that there has been a great deal of semihysterical reaction to the risks of having overhanging terracotta cornices. The risks only occur if the cornices are never inspected or maintained. One thing which is very clear, however, is that there have been many disastrous examples where the terracotta cornice has been removed from a major multistorey building and as a result, the building looks as though it has been beheaded. The entire original design and rhythm of the building is ruined by such radical surgery.

It is tragic that probably in 90% of such cases there was no need to remove the cornice which could have been conserved or restored.

CONCLUSION

Some of North America's finest buildings have survived for our use and enjoyment because of the excellent qualities of the terracotta from which they were built three-quarters of a century ago. These buildings can be easily preserved for future generations by regular, skilled maintenance and careful attention to the well-being of certain critical parts of the building which are essential in keeping water out of the interior of the terracotta-faced walls. The glazed terracotta units also benefit from being washed down on a regular basis like the windows. Such regular cleaning prevents the buildup of potentially harmful deposits such as bird droppings and pollutant salts, thus ensuring the extended durability of the critical outer surface skin of the terracotta.

It is to be hoped that this section of the book will help in the preservation of these great and beautiful buildings for the enjoyment of future generations.

APPENDIX ON CURRENT MANUFACTURERS

The following list of current manufacturers and producers is derived from data published by S. M. Tindall in 1989 in the *Bulletin of the Association for Preservation Technology*.

- Boston Valley Terra Cotta
  Hamburg, New York
- Design Technics, Inc.
  New York, New York
- Gladding, McBean & Co.
  Lincoln, California
  Now a Division of Pacific Coast Building Products Inc. but established in 1875.
- Ludowici Celadon
  New Lexington, Ohio
- MJM Studios
  South Kearney, New Jersey
- Studio S Pottery
  Murfreesboro, Tennessee
- Superior Clay Corp.
  Ulrichsville, Ohio

Individual producers include:

- David Condon, Kilnworks
  San Pablo, California
- Robert Friedman
  Bethel, Missouri

REFERENCES

Ashurst, John; and Ashurst, Nicola (1988). *Brick, Terracotta and Earth. Vol. 2 Practical Building Conservation*. New York. Halsted Press a division of John Wiley & Sons, Inc.

Berryman, N. and Tindall, S.M. (1984). *Terra Cotta: Preservation of an Historic Building Material*. Chicago: Landmarks Preservation Council of Illinois.

Ferriday, Virginia Guest (1984). *Last of the Handmade Buildings*. Portland, Oregon. Mark Publishing Company.

Fidler, John A. "The Conservation of Architectural Terracotta and Faience". *ASCHB Transactions*. Vol. 6. 1981. London, U.K. (Association for Studies in the Conservation of Historic Buildings).

Gladding, McBean & Co. *Ceramic Veneer—Part 1. General Provisions*.

McIntyre, W.A. (1929). *Investigation into the Durability of Architectural Terracotta and Faience*. Building Research Special Report No. 12, BRS Tests 1926–1928. Department of Scientific and Industrial Research, UK.

CHAPTER 7

CEMENTITIOUS MATERIALS

MORTARS

When we look at an old masonry wall we are conscious of two things, the masonry units whether they are of brick, stone, or terracotta; and the joints between the units. Bricks, stones, and terracotta are laid in mortar and the units are arranged and overlapped in various patterns so that the wall is both strong and resistant to weathering.

The various ways of arranging the bricks or stones to provide single or double skins or wythes, veneers, or decorative patterns are called "bonds" or "bonding" and "coursing." Certain bonds and coursing patterns and the profiles of the joints are or were characteristic of the masonry of specific periods and regions or cultures. (See also Chapter 6.)

The actual appearance of the joint itself is determined by color, texture, and profile. Color and texture are controlled by the mortar materials used in the joint, while the profile depends primarily on a need to waterproof the joints and a desire on the part of the designer to produce decorative effects.

What we frequently see in the joints of old masonry is not the actual mortar in which stones or bricks are bedded but a secondary application of mortar known as "pointing." In North America it is sometimes incorrectly known as "tuck-pointing" which is an English term for a very specific type of pointing. The actual origin of the word "pointing" is obscure but one can speculate that the neat finishing of the mortar in the joints was usually executed with the point of a trowel or some other pointed tool.

In some cases the external appearance of the masonry was "improved" when, for example, inferior brickwork with irregular bricks and thick joints of varying widths was "tuckpointed" and made to resemble much higher quality work with fine thin joints and regular bricks. English bricklayers used the term "tuckpointing" in the eighteenth and nineteenth centuries specifically to describe a joint where, following normal finishing of the mortar in the joint, a second fine fillet or bead of pointing was tucked into a raked slot in the first layer of mortar. This gave the appearance of much finer work with fine joint lines and straight crisp edges to the units, particularly when paint was used to color over the coarse joint up to the fine raised line of the second pointing. Tuck pointing was frequently replaced by "bastard tuck-pointing" when the expensive double pointing operations were reduced to one operation carried out with a single slotted pointing tool. At a superficial glance the results looked similar.

In some cases, handmade or irregular machine made bricks were laid roughly and then the exterior wall face was painted and fine lines were painted on in a contrasting color to create the illusion of finely laid brickwork. This process was known as "striping" hence the painter who did it was called a "striper." The technique surprisingly was used even on quite large public buildings such as the City Hall of Victoria, British Columbia, Canada in 1878–81.

Mortar in old buildings can be characterized by three main ingredients; lime, aggregate (sand of varying grain sizes, shapes and colors), and hydraulic substances (which may or may not be present). Historical mortar mixes varied a lot in their minor constituents but were remarkably similar otherwise. Some typical historic mixes were (all parts by volume unless otherwise stated):

- Two measures fresh well-burnt lime to five measures of sand (Parliamentary Library, Ottawa, Canada 1870).

- One part lime to 2.2 parts sand (Redoute Dauphine, Quebec eighteenth century).
- One part lime to 2 parts sand (Halifax Citadel, Nova Scotia, Canada early nineteenth century).
- One part lime to 2 parts sand (Lower Fort Garry, Manitoba, Canada ca. 1831–1839).
- One part lime paste to 1.25–2.0 parts of sand (New York 1901).
- Vitruvius, the Roman military engineer whose books were widely referred to and whose formulae were actually used in America in the eighteenth and nineteenth century, recommended the following proportions: ". . . mix your mortar, if using pit sand, in the proportions of three parts of sand to one of lime; if using river sand or sea sand mix two parts of sand with one of lime . . . Further, in using river or sea sand, the addition of a third part composed of burnt brick, pounded up and sifted, will make your mortar of a better composition to use" (Vitruvius, 1960). We can now add to the recommendations of Vitruvius the comment that this mix with crushed bricks can produce a semi-hydraulic mortar with good frost resistance. Such mixes were used historically in North America with great success.

Having the original specifications for mortar may still leave the restoration architect or conservator with problems. As an illustration of this the 1870 specifications for the Parliamentary Library Buildings in Ottawa described the lime as being "best fresh burnt brown lime" to be mixed with three parts of "clean sharp pit sand, and the whole to be properly mixed together dry, and a sufficient quantity of water being added, the whole to be ground under edge runners or in pug mills." The specified pointing mortar was different and was "to be composed of one part best brown lime, one part sharp forge ashes, and one part iron scales mixed and ground under the edge runner to a fine paste as required for immediate use." (See page 142 for reference to "forge scale.")

Today we have little or no idea of the color of "best brown lime," let alone a mixture of this with "forge ashes and iron scales." The resultant mix could range from gray to black or even a buff with rust colored specks. As a further problem the specification makes no reference to the profile of the pointing. Heated debates occur on some buildings over whether the original nineteenth century pointing was tinted black and was formed with a quite large projecting semicircular beading. That may be the only type of old pointing now

left on the building but it could easily only date to say 1910. I have known many such cases which were simply impossible to solve with any certainty and where a simple slightly concave joint profile was adopted instead because it provided an excellent weathered joint without undue shadowing.

While historic mortar mixes may be established by modern analyses it is often academic and even inadvisable to use such mixes in repointing or repairing masonry which has survived the ravages of time and the environment in a weakened or deteriorated condition. The original mixes may simply be too strong for the old masonry units. When the stones or bricks take up moisture and are heated in the sun they expand and will compress the mortar in the joints. If the mortar is harder than the stone or brick, they will be crushed and the edges may spall off leaving the mortar in place.

As a general principle the mortar should always be slightly weaker than the masonry so that if anything has to fail, it should be the new mortar which has no historical value and is expendable. Mortar mixes for restorations and repairs can be selected from the accompanying charts on the basis of the type of exposure and the durability of the masonry units.

The final appearance of the selected modern mix can be adjusted to match the original by careful selection of aggregate particle sizes, configurations, and colors—possibly assisted by the addition of permanent nonfading mortar colors or pigments. These colors are based on natural "earths" and oxides which are in their most stable oxidation state and which will not undergo further chemical changes and therefore cannot change color.

Conservators generally prefer to obtain the colors of mortars by means of the aggregate rather than by the addition of pigments. Original aggregate particle size distributions can be matched by sieve analysis using a graduated series of brass sieves (see U.S.A. Sieve Series ASTM E-11-70).

The industrial classifications of particle sizes differ slightly from the geological classifications but if the particles are between 0.050–0.062 mm and 2.00 mm in diameter they are classified as sands. Below this diameter particles are classified as silts. Particles between 2.00 and 100.00 mm in diameter are classified as gravels.

The larger sizes of gravels upward from 64.00 mm may also be classified as cobbles.

Aggregate particle forms or configurations and colors are conveniently matched by examination of the original particles under a microscope at a magnification of between ×20 and ×40. the particles or grains may be simply described or classified under the following types:

Figure 53. Recommended mortar mixes.

	Internal Walls	External Walls			Paving
		Sheltered Exposure	Moderate Exposure	Severe or Marine Exposure	
Highly Durable eg: Granite Basalt Fully vitrified brick.	v vi vii	v vi	iv v	iii iv	ii iii
Moderately Durable eg: Many building limestones and sandstones. Well fired brick.	v vi vii viii ix	v vi vii viii	iv v vi vii	iii iv v	iii iv
Poorly Durable eg: Some calcareous sandstones. Some microporous limestone. Underfired brick.	vii viii ix x	vii viii ix	vi vii viii	v vi	v vi

(Right-hand arrow: Increase in durability and exposure)

The numbers i to xi refer to mortar designations given in Table of Mortar Types

• Sharp or angular, the so-called "sharp sand" or "pit sand." This is always called for as the best sand for mortars.
• Angular but with slightly rounded edges, a "river sand" from an immature stage of a river
• Round or rounded, a river sand from a mature stage of the river, so-called "soft sand"; sometimes specified for plastering sands.
• Lentoidal or shaped like long seeds or American footballs. Usually of windblown origin.
• Platey, usually grains or flakes of mica or slate.

It may also be worth noting the surface appearances of the grains which in some cases may have been selected for their high reflective value so that the aggregate imparted a sparkle or glitter. I have encountered just such an addition of sparkling aggregate in the parging or stucco mortar which was used in the 1920s for the facing of the Hogg family's famous residence at Bayou Bend, Houston, Texas. The mansion is now a museum containing the late Miss Ima Hogg's superb collection of Americana in its original setting and is a splendid part of the Houston Museum of Fine Art.

Particle surfaces may be described according to their lustre:

• Dull or earthy
• Vitreous or glassy
• Nacreous, like mother of pearl
• Adamantine, brilliant like diamonds
• Metallic, like pyrites or galena
• Silky, like some forms of gypsum and asbestos

Good overall color and textural matches can be obtained by using a simple method described by Morgan Phillips in 1978 (Phillips, 1978).

There has for many years been a tendency among contractors, tradespeople, and the public to assume that a hard inflexible mortar such as that produced by mixtures of ordinary grey portland cement and sand will produce the best durable finished product. This is emphatically not the case for work on old buildings. The addition of lime to mortars increases their flexibility, reduces damage to adjacent masonry units, and thus generally increases durability. Dense, hard portland cement and sand mortars also tend to be either

Mortar Designation	Type of Mortar Proportions by Volume:						Strength
	Cement: Lime: Sand	Masonry cement: Sand	Cement: Sand with plasticizer	Hydraulic lime: Sand	Lime: P.F.A.: Sand	Lime: Brick dust: Sand	
i							
ii	1 : 0.5 : 4 to 4.5	1 : 2.5 to 3.5	1 : 3 to 4				
iii	1 : 1 : 5 to 6	1 : 4 to 5	1 : 5 to 6				
iv	1 : 2 : 8 to 9	1 : 5.5 to 6.5	1 : 7 to 8				
v	1 : 3 : 10 to 12	1 : 6.5 to 7	1 : 8				
vi				2 : 5			
vii				1 : 3	2 : 1 : 5		
viii						2 : 2 : 5	
ix	0 : 2 : 5 *				3 : 1 : 9		
x						1 : 1 : 3	
xi	0 : 1 : 1 *						

* ix and xi should not be used where early strength or early resistance to frost are required. After J. Ashurst

(Strength arrow: Increasing Strength — Increasing Flexibility to accomodate movements e.g. due to settlement, vibration, temperature and moisture changes.)

Canadian Modern Cement-lime Mortars on the basis of Composition			
Designation of Mortar	Parts by Volume of:		Aggregate, Measured in a Damp, Loose Condition.
	Portland Cement	Hydrated Lime or Lime Putty	
M	1	1/4	For all mortars.
S	1	1/4 to 1/2	Not less than 2 1/4.
N	1	1/2 to 1 1/4	Not more than 3 X
O	1	1 1/4 to 2 1/2	the volumes of
K	1	2 1/2 to 4	cement and lime.

Sources: ASTM Specification C - 270. CSA Standard 179M - 1976

Figure 54. Mortar composition table.

impermeable or of very low permeability which means that when salts move towards the surface of the masonry in solution in water, the water cannot move through the joint and is thus forced to move into the masonry units on either side of the joint. This in turn means that the water evaporates from the surface of the stone or brick and leaves a steadily growing accumulation of salts behind in the units' surfaces. The phenomenon known as osmosis will then result in the accumulation of still more concentrated solutions in these areas and more and more salts will be deposited. Ultimately this means that the mortar remains projecting as a hard ridge and the masonry units are destroyed by the expansive cycles of hydration and dehydration. In cities with severe local air pollution problems coupled with long range acid precipitation this can lead to very

Berea sandstone blocks in chimney severely damaged by a combination of sulfates and a hard dense pointing mortar which forced the salts into the edges of the stone units.

severe damage being caused to permeable sandstones for example. I illustrate an example of this type of damage from the 1850–51 Church of the Ascension in Hamilton, Ontario.

The benefits of using lime today however are not quite that simple. Historically when limestone was "burned" to make lime for slaking and making mortars, the limestones were often selected because certain of their impurities, such as clays, actually made the final product semihydraulic, or to put it more simply, these limes produced mortars which would set faster and in damper conditions than pure lime mortars. These were termed "natural cements."

Today the hydrated lime which we can buy manufactured and packed in bags has had impurities removed and cannot simply be used, for example, in a 1:2 mix with sand just like the old mortars. We have to add a small amount of portland cement or some other pozzolanic medium to replace those missing and highly desirable hydraulic characteristics. We must also be careful that the portland cement does not contain sulfates or other impurities which can cause staining and efflorescence in the new masonry. For this reason, conservators usually specify nonstaining white portland cement or sulfate-resisting portland cement.

Alkali–Aggregate Reactivity

The hardening of cement is a chemical process which produces heat and liberates alkalies, particularly the hydroxides of calcium, sodium, and potassium. These hydroxides react negligibly with quartz, feldspar, calcite, and most of the dark silicate minerals and with rocks composed of all these minerals. There is, however, a group of siliceous minerals which, if present in the aggregate react chemically with the strongly alkaline hydroxides and produce alkalic silica gel. This gel absorbs water from the cement paste and develops extreme expansive forces which may exceed the tensile strength of the mortar or concrete and result in cracking and bursting of the surface with blister-like "popouts." The problem aggregates are opaline shale, opaline and chalcedonic chert, siliceous limestone; and siliceous cryptocrystalline rocks such as rhyolite, andesite, and dacite. These problem materials are not particularly rare or unusual. Andesite is a prominent historic building stone in British Columbia where it was quarried as Haddington Island Stone. Rhyolite was used in many buildings in Colorado. For example, a pink rhyolite was used for churches and other public buildings late in the nineteenth century in Denver. Sands or other aggregates formed from the parent rocks in these cases will be reactive with ordinary portland cements.

If these problem aggregates exist in a sand source which must be used in a restoration project there are two methods to avoid the destructive expansive effects. One is to specify a low alkali content cement with an alkali content of 0.6% or less, rather than the about 1.5% which is normal. The other possibility is to use a pozzolanic additive with the portland cement.

Other Forms of Mortar Deterioration

In North America today historic mortars are usually found to have deteriorated for one or more of the following reasons:

- The removal of carbonates from the lime by prolonged penetration of the masonry by large quantities of rainwater or snow melt water which is usually acidic. Mortars are thus reduced to wet sand and fragments of deteriorated mortar with little or no cohesive, compressive, or adhesive strength.
- The shattering of the mortar by the massive expansion of ice "lenses" or by repeated freeze/thaw cycles.
- The shattering of the mortar by the violent expansion of entrapped water as steam in case of fire.
- Despite frequent references in early specifications to the fact that all sands for mortars should be "clean" and free of clay, loam, and organic material, such materials did get into mortars and caused them to crumble.

The crumbling of the mortar is most commonly due to the expansion of clay minerals included in the original mix and later subjected to long periods of wetting. Clay minerals often have platey hexagonal prismatic crystals. When these are wetted the water enters the spaces between the plates and the crystals expand on their long axes. Because the crystals are randomly oriented the clay mineral mass expands anisotropically, that is, in all directions.

- The crumbling of the mortar caused by the presence and growth of masses of crystals of anionic salts such as chlorides, sulfates, and nitrates.

This problem can be related to the use of contaminated materials in the first place, for example, sea or beach sand with high chloride contents; or may be due to subsequent contamination, for example, by prolonged saturation with polluted rainwater, or by contact with soils with high natural sulfate contents.

Occasionally deteriorating mortars are found to be repair mortars which have been made with unsatisfactory mixes. Typically these cause failures because they contain too much portland cement and no lime. Associated problems are as follows:

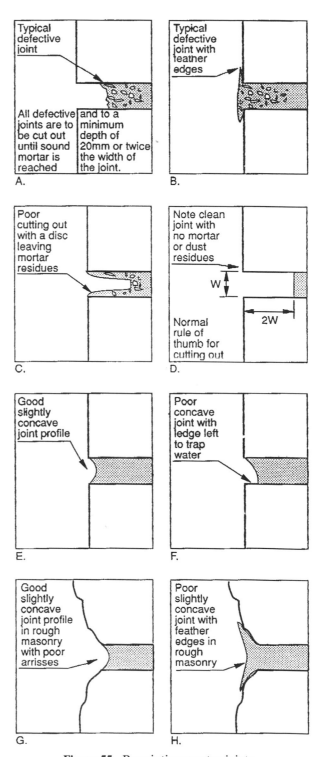

Figure 55. Repointing mortar joints.

• Joints will open and admit water because the mortar is inelastic and fails to allow for shrinkage in the masonry units.

• The edges of the masonry units are shattered by the hard mortar which will not compress when the units expand.

• Thin feathered edges of mortar may be brittle and crack away, opening joints to water penetration.

• Sulfate impurities from ordinary portland cement may damage the adjacent units and cause the joint to fail through loss of adhesion.

• Adhesion may be lost because of a reliance on the use of synthetic resins for adhesion of a repair mortar followed by the "reemulsification" of the resin when exposed to water. Many "bonding agents" are based on droplets of synthetic resins in suspension in water. These are often but erroneously described as "emulsions." Certain resins may be suitable only for use inside buildings where they will not be exposed to water. If exposed on the exterior of a building, when they get wet, the solid resins may return to solution, lose all strength, and even be washed away.

I have encountered just such a failure in mortar repairs high above the ground on stonework on Montreal's historic Windsor Station. During the investigation of the failure, residues of the problem resin were extracted with acetone reagent and were identified by infrared spectrophotometry as polyvinyl acetate. The PVA resin in question was then tested and found to be reemulsifiable. No additional noncorroding metal reinforcement had been used and when the resin broke down in rainwater the mortar patches had fallen off the face of the building.

Another typical problem results from the use of "dead" mortars which have been allowed to partially cure or harden and rather than throw them away and make a new batch, the inexperienced mason adds water to make them "workable."

This problem often occurs when workers are being asked to use lime/cement mixes which to them are unfamiliar. Improperly handled, such mixes crumble as they dry. When only small areas of mortar repairwork are being called for in various locations, there is often a tendency for the mason to mix too large a batch and then to try and stretch the use of that batch beyond its usefulness.

Mortars for Conservation

One of the most important features of mortars for conservation and restoration work must be resistance to the effects of freeze/thaw cycles and cycles of hydration and dehydration of water-soluble anionic salt crystals once a mortar has been formulated with lime and

Cementitious patch failure, Windsor Station, Montreal. Note the limestone surface failing under the patch. At least two generations of patches have failed because of poor preparation and lack of noncorroding anchors.

sulfate-resisting portland cement or pozzolanic additives to give the best combination of appropriate strength and elasticity. The requisite resistance to salt crystal expansion and freeze/thaw cycles may be obtained by one further modification of the mortar by air entrainment or ensuring that millions of tiny bubbles are enclosed in the mix.

Thus for any mortar which may be exposed to freeze/thaw cycles in a wet condition; sea salt from a marine environment; pollutants migrating out of old masonry; or deicing salts from streets—air entrainment is mandatory.

Intentionally entrained air bubbles are usually extremely small in size. About 90% of them are 100 μm or less in diameter and 60% are less than 20 μm. Some may be as large as 2 or 4 mm. For concrete mixes the recommended volume of air ranges from 3 to 9%, depending on the size of the aggregate, for example, with freeze/thaw cycles and deicing salts, with a 10 mm aggregate, 7–10% air content is recommended. For cement:lime:sand mortars for use in restoration work, experiments conducted by Parks Canada's engineers in Quebec have established that the optimum air content may be as high as 17%. It must be recognized that the presence of larger percentages of entrained air lead to a corresponding decrease in strength in the mortar. This may be relatively unimportant in work with older masonry units which require weaker mortars anyway.

Entrained air makes stiff or lean mortar mixes easier to work. This quality can be very valuable when the amount of water in the mortar mix is kept purposely low to avoid shrinkage problems. Entrained air may be obtained by two methods of which machine mixing is the most important, the other is by means of additives or air-entraining agents. In my experience mixing times are usually best at between $7\frac{1}{2}$ and 10 min. The mixing must be thorough so that the entrained air is evenly distributed throughout the mix. Mixing too small a batch or too large a batch will often result in reduced air entrainment. Worn blades and accumulations of old mortar residues in the mixer will also result in poorer air entrainment in a given time of mixing. Prolonged mixing gradually leads to further and further decreases in air entrainment. It may be necessary to add "air entraining agents" to supplement the amount of air which can be entrained by mixing. High alkali cements may entrain more air than low alkali cements using the same amount of air-entraining material. Masonry cements may already have air-entraining materials interground with the cement clinker during the manufacturing process. These materials must conform with the specifications in ASTM C226.

Commercial liquid air-entraining agents that will produce air void systems in the mortar during the mixing process are formulated from such organic materials as wood resins, sulfonated hydrocarbons, and synthetic detergents. Specified dosages of additive for concretes are usually in the order of 1% of the weight of the cement. I have known a number of cases where masons produced excellent air entrainment in mortars by means of adding small measures of the popular detergent Fairy Liquid. Laboratory testing of carefully made samples with measured additives and mixing times will enable a conservator to establish satisfactory combinations of materials and mixing formulae.

If mortars are to contain synthetic resin additives to increase bond these must very carefully specified as being specific products, suitable for exterior use and nonreemulsifiable.

Patching Mortars

Special composite mortars can be formulated for use in the restoration of stonework where small areas have been lost through spalling or other causes.

Missing sections of moldings are a typical application of this kind. Such repairs are sometimes referred to "plastic repairs" or "dentistry" (see Chapter 5).

Some of the most significant work in the development of patching mortars in North America has been carried out by the Center for Preservation Research of Columbia University, New York, and is illustrated by extracts at the end of Chapter 5.

Reinforcement of Repairs

Whatever formulations are used it is good practice to use noncorroding reinforcement to anchor the patch to the substrate of original material. I use stainless steel threaded rods of varying diameters set in epoxy in drilled holes in the substrate. The Center for Preservation Research commonly uses threaded nylon rods (see study at end of chapter).

Although the cost may apparently be high, the Jahn series of restoration mortars which are manufactured in the Netherlands offer excellent results for matching repairs on a wide range of masonry materials. These premixed and carefully formulated mortars give repairs which are generally salt-resistant and "frost-proof." The Jahn range is as follows:

- M40 and M50 injection mortars for stabilizing walls of brick or natural stone.
- M60 plaster mortar developed specially for the plastering or parging of existing interior walls with high concentrations of water-soluble salts or rising moisture.

- M70 stone restoration mortar developed specially for the restoration of natural stone elements such as beltcourses, cornices, balustrades, and statuary. M70 can be formulated to match sandstone, limestone, tuff, and shale of various textures and colors. After one week the hardened material can be chiselled carefully. After 28 days the M70 material can be worked in the same manner as the natural stone in question.
- M80 cast mortar developed specially for anchoring and dowel setting. M80 can be used for casting, and can be made up in liquid mixes for pumping and grouting.
- M90 concrete repair mortar developed for concrete repairs and especially suitable for repairing damage caused by the corrosion of steel reinforcement. M90 can be applied both horizontally and vertically and in any required thickness up to about four inches (100 mm). The reinforcement must be cleaned off and protected with a suitable paint or coating.
- M100 ceramics–terracotta–brick restoration mortar, developed for repairs to architectural ceramics such as terracotta and valuable brick ornaments. M100 can be delivered in any inorganic shade ie all iron pigments from ochre to red.

All of these products are available in North America and have been used with considerable success even in our very severe climatic areas (see end of Chapter for sources).

Grouts and Grouting

Masonry walls may suffer from mortar losses in their interiors because of prolonged penetration of acidic rainwater for example. They will thus develop large cavities within their cores and unless mortar can be reintroduced into these cavities the wall may fail under load. The art and rather inexact science of introducing liquid cementitious mixtures into voids in masonry, rock, and soils is called grouting. The liquid mixes are called grouts. The amount of grout which is "accepted" by the voids is called the "take."

Grouting may be carried out by three different methods:

- By gravity
- By pumping
- By vacuum

Gravity Grouting

This type of grouting involves introducing liquid mortar by means of hoses from small or medium sized reservoirs or "grout pans" which are raised about 12 to 15 ft (4 or 5 m) above the inlet point. The height of the reservoirs above the injection points allows gravity to provide the pressure. The inlet or injection points are a series of holes drilled into the defective masonry about 3 ft (1 m) apart horizontally and 18 in. (50 cm) apart vertically on a staggered grid. As the holes are drilled they should be flushed out with clean water.

Proceeding up the wall, as water is injected at the upper holes it should be allowed to flow down through the walls and out at lower holes until it runs clear. Where water flows out through open or faulty joints these should be noted and temporarily plugged with clay or tightly packed old rope. Work usually proceeds in 3-ft (1 m) vertical lifts at one time. A larger vertical lift will be liable to build up too high a pressure behind loose face stones which may then be forced out of the wall. The liquid grout is allowed to rise up in the wall until it flows out of the next line of holes above. These holes may be stopped off and the grout flow cut off to the wall. As the grout begins to cure, the next section of walling can be made ready. The temporary packing in the joints can be removed after the initial set to prepare the joints for subsequent pointing.

Very loose stones which may have dropped out of alignment may be realigned and supported in place with water-soaked hardwood wedges until the grout mortar has been placed and the stones are secure. As the wet wedges dry out they shrink, become loose, and can easily be removed. Being wet to start with they do not expand to push the stone out of alignment after it has been carefully positioned.

Pumped Grouting

Both hand- and power-operated pumps may be used to inject grout under pressure. Hand-operated pumps are preferred for delicate unstable masonry. The equipment consists of a mixer, a diaphragm pump, and hoses fitted with control valves. The same layout of injection holes is employed as was used for gravity grouting. The delivery hose is connected to the lowest injection nozzle, the pump is started, and the grout is allowed to rise within the wall. The rising level of the grout is observed through clear plastic tubes fitted in weep holes at intermediate levels up the wall. These tubes can be doubled over and tied off as the grout rises higher in the wall. When the top of the 3-ft (1 m) lift is reached at the next line of injection nozzles, the grout flow is stopped and the lower nozzle is closed off. When the grout has set the operation can be repeated.

Vacuum Grouting

Injection nozzles and holes are located as before and coupled to the grout hoses. The masonry to be grouted is then enclosed in a tough, air-tight, transparent polyethylene sheet. The air within the enclosure is evacuated with a powerful vacuum pump and the valve is opened to allow the grout to flow. The vacuum causes the grout to be sucked into the wall. The results are observed through the plastic and when the grouting is complete as shown by overflow from upper weep holes then the grout supply is cut off and the grout allowed to set.

Typical Grouting Pressures and Mixes

Typical gravity grout pressures for historic masonry may be 15–20 psi (about 98 kPa) while pumped grout pressures may be 145–215 psi (about 980–1470 kPa). These pressures may be compared with pressures of 100–350 psi (700–21,000 kPa) which are used for grouting fissured rock.

Mixes for grouting which are in normal use for civil engineering purposes may be much too strong for historic masonry. A typical mix for normal use is:

Portland cement:	220 lb (100 kg)
Alfesil (fly ash):	75 lb (34 kg)
Intrusion aid:	3.3 lb (1.5 kg)
Sand	variable
Water	variable

A mix used for grouting eighteenth century masonry in Quebec city's old fortifications was as follows:

Portland cement	53.3 lb (24.1 kg)
Sand	33.3 lb (15.0 kg)
Fly ash	17.1 lb (7.8 kg)
Intraplast N (Intrusion aid)	11.2 oz (317.0 g)
Water	35.4 lb (16.1 kg)

English gravity grouting mixes for ruins use (after Ashurst) One part by volume of portland cement: one and one-half parts by volume of water, or, one-half part portland cement: one-half part of very fine sand: one and one-half parts of water.

For very delicate ruins Ashurst has recommended the following grouts:

- a grouting operation in two stages with mix A and mix B (all parts by volume) mix A = 1 pbv hydrated lime: 0.20 pbv fly ash: 0.75 pbv water. Mix B used after refusal of A ("no take") = mix A + intrusion aid.
- 1 pbv prebagged (hydrated) lime: 1pbv fly ash: 1/ pbv bentonite.
- A higher strength grout is 1 pbv sulfate-resisting portland cement: 2 pbv hydrated lime: 1 pbv fly ash. Solids-to-water ratios are typically 1:3 or 1:4.

Conclusion

In any grouting operation the volume of the masonry must be calculated as must the approximate volume of the voids.

The volume of grout "take" must be constantly watched and if at any point the volume of "take" begins to exceed the likely void volume and especially the volume of the wall, then the grouting operation must be halted immediately and an investigation launched into the discrepancy.

Engineers and conservators who have worked on grouting operations have nearly all heard hilarious tales of the disappearance of large volumes of grout. I recall one in Turkey where truck-loads of grout were found to have filled a hitherto unknown subterranean cavern, and in Quebec a large volume of grout which disappeared into a fortification wall was found to have gone on to fill an old sewer!

Suppliers

HHO Jahn, Jahn Restauratietechnieken en onderzoek
Kloosterweg 34 3232 LC Brielle Netherlands.
POSTBUS 161 3230 ad Brielle, Netherlands
Jahn agents in the USA:
Dennis G Rude
Cathedral Stone Company,
2505 Reed Street NE, Washington DC
20018. (202) 832-2633

CONCRETE

Many ancient cultures including those of Crete, Egypt, Greece, and Rome used lime-based mortars in their masonry. Both the ancient Greeks and Romans were aware that lime mortars would not set under water or in very wet conditions and once set could be destroyed in very wet conditions.

They also knew that if certain materials such as volcanic earths, bricks, or tiles were ground up and mixed with slaked lime and sand then a "hydraulic" or "semi-hydraulic" mortar could be created which would be more or less resistant to water after setting and could even harden or cure under water. If larger fragments of broken brick, pumice, or volcanic rock were added to the hydraulic mortar, the result was the first concrete. The great numbers of Roman concrete structures which survive to our own day testify to the success of the Romans' development of concrete technology. The Romans knew that thorough mixing and compaction were important for the final quality and durability of the concrete. They also understood that rich mixes did not guarantee durability but that on the contrary they were more subject than lean mixes to shrinkage on drying or curing.

The massive Italian deposits of volcanic tuff rock at Pozzuoli, near Naples, were used extensively by the Romans and later cultures as the primary hydraulic ingredient in mortars and concretes. These deposits gave their name to pozzolan (or pozzuolan) which is the generic term for any volcanic material containing silica or a combination of silica and alumina which in itself possesses little cementitious value but which will in pulverized form and in the presence of moisture, chemically react with slaked lime (calcium hydroxide) at ordinary temperatures to form compounds possessing cementitious and hydraulic qualities. Semihydraulic lime mortars will not set under water whereas hydraulic cements will.

In fourteenth century Italy pozzolanic materials were again used to make hydraulic mortars after a long period of decline following the fall of the Roman Empire.

In the seventeenth century England, Holland, and Germany pozzolanic "trass" rock was used to make hydraulic mortars. Trass is a type of volcanic tuff which contains fragments of pumice and possibly fossils of leaves and plant stems. According to Gwilt's *Encyclopedia of Architecture* (1867), the rock was found at Andernach in Germany and in the neighbourhood of Liege. It was called "Dutch" because the lumps of rock were shipped down the Rhine from Andernach the principal source to Holland where they were pulverized and packed in barrels and exported as "Dutch terras" or "Dutch trass." According to nineteenth century dictionaries the word "trass" is derived from an old Dutch word "tiras," meaning cement.

The Development of Cements

In the eighteenth century, experiments were conducted in both England and France to discover materials which would form quick-setting, hard, hydraulic mortars for use in engineering works. In 1757 John Smeaton in England began a series of experiments in a search for a suitably hard, hydraulic cement which he could use for the rebuilding of the Eddystone lighthouse. The Eddystone rocks in the English Channel off the southwest coast of England had been the cause of a large number of shipwrecks and an earlier lighthouse had been swept away in a storm. Smeaton's work suddenly took the first great step in hydraulic cement development since the time of the Romans. He discovered first that despite the beliefs of traditional masons a pure limestone did not necessarily make a better cement; second that it was the presence of clay

in limestone which gave a hydraulic property to any lime produced from that stone; and third that a good hydraulic cement could be produced from a mixture of natural cement or semihydraulic lime and a pozzolanic material. He also discovered that the silicate material known as "forge scale" which flew off a mass of red hot iron when it was being hammered in a forge, could be used as a pozzolanic material.

In 1796 James Parker at Northfleet in Kent, England developed Parker's Roman or Sheppey Cement. This was a fast setting "natural" hydraulic cement manufactured by burning at calcining temperatures (1652–1832°F, 900–1000°C) a mixture of clay and limestone found in naturally occurring ovate or flattish masses of argillaceous limestone known as septaria which were found in the London clays and particularly at the Isle of Sheppey. It was expensive particularly if used with sand at a ratio of 1:1 as was recommended for the ordinary quality. If it was of the highest quality it could be used at a ratio of 1:2. Gwilt (1867) noted the fact that as early as 1840 it was bemoaned that "Sheppey Cement is now almost only a name" in consequence of the exhaustion of the septaria deposits. Parker's Roman Cement was however a superior waterproof and fast-setting hydraulic cement which was available until late in the nineteenth century. When first made it was a dark brown, so dark that it was sometimes called "black cement." Old Parker's Roman Cement when dry has a lighter brown or chocolate color. This cement was particularly popular for lining cisterns and forming waterproof rendering or parging.

Most sources agree that following research in France by Vicat, the main forerunner of modern portland cement was produced in 1811 in England by James Frost. The process involved roasting limestone and alluvial clay which had been first ground together 2:1 into a wet slurry and then dried. The resulting "clinker" was then ground again.

Joseph Aspdin is usually credited with the invention of portland cement and his first patent is dated 1824. The name portland cement came from the original cement's supposedly close resemblance to the famous English Portland oolitic limestone. This is of interest because it underlines the fact that early portland cements were much whiter than ordinary portland cements today.

Vicat published his work in France in 1837. This publication (Vicat, 1837) is significant because his extensive practical research led to the following conclusions:

- Intimately mixed clay and chalk could be burned to form a hydraulic compound.

- The proportions of the ingredients were very important to the durability of the cement.
- The strength of the mortar was directly related to the amount of water used for mixing.
- The silicate in the clay was the essential ingredient in the hardening process.

Isaac Johnson by 1845 was supplying a new high quality portland cement which had improved proportions of the clay/lime mix and was burned at a high temperature to produce vitrification.

Johnson had discovered that overburnt lumps of cement produced by the Aspdin process were actually better products and were slower setting. By the 1850s in England, portland cement was being produced by what are essentially the same methods as are used today, grinding limestone and clay together with water and burning the screened product at temperatures between 2372 and 2732°F (1300–1500°C). After firing the clinker is ground and gypsum may be added to lengthen setting time.

Portland cement was first brought to the United States in 1865 but by the late 1870s there was still hardly enough domestic production to compete with imports. Probably the first portland cement manufactured in the United States was produced at Coplay, Pennsylvania in 1872 by David O. Saylor.

Development of Concrete

After Roman times, the French author Philibert de Lorme in 1568 was one of the first to describe the use of a concrete based on what appears to have been a semihydraulic lime mortar mixed with small stones. In 1817 in London, Smirke's new Millbank Penitentiary was built in part with mass concrete foundations. Gwilt (1867) subsequently noted that concrete was sounder and stronger if it was allowed to fall from greater heights into the trenches. Smirke's concrete was thrown from a height and then rammed when in place. At Woolwich, Southeast of London in 1835 the Royal Engineers built an experimental mass-concrete casemate or bomb-proof vault within a fortification.

With advances in fire-resistant construction in the late eighteenth and nineteenth century cast-iron and rolled-iron beams were used in floor construction with brick jack-arches springing from them. Sometimes the iron was set in mortar. In the first patented fireproof floors such as that specified for the new Parliament Buildings in Ottawa, Canada in 1859, by Fuller and Jones of Ottawa and Toronto, the rolled-iron unequal flanged "I" beams were set in concrete which was poured on boards laid on the lower flanges. This practice preceded the essential knowledge that the alkaline concrete inhibited corrosion in the iron and that the expansion coefficients of iron and concrete were very similar. The British Royal Engineers subsequently

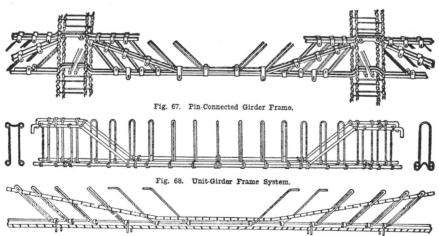

Fig. 67. Pin-Connected Girder Frame.

Fig. 68. Unit-Girder Frame System.

Fig. 69. Herringbone Trussed Bar Used as a Girder Frame.

Early designs for concrete reinforcement from Radford's Cyclopedia of Construction of 1909.

built their first massive concrete fortification at Newhaven, Sussex, England in 1865 after years of argument over the advantages and disadvantages of the use of concrete. In 1866 a 68 pounder gun was fired at the concrete and apparently this stringent test was passed. Subsequently the concrete cracked vertically elsewhere and following monitoring with tell-tales it was decided that seasonal temperature changes were responsible. As a result of these observations the first concrete expansion joints were designed.

Much deterioration of early concrete in the United States is found to be related to the fact that it was not made with a sufficiently good grade of portland cement. Cheaper or less hydraulic grades of cement which are encountered failing in massive fortifications are often termed "Rosendale cement." Rosendale cement is a term which is often used incorrectly to apply

to all "natural cements" in the eastern United States but in fact should only apply to a natural cement produced by burning a magnesian limestone from extensive sources near the town of Rosendale, Ulster County, New York. Other natural cements available at the turn of the century and published in a 1909 list by Radford's *Cyclopedia of Construction* (Radford, 1909) include Utica, Akron, Milwaukee, Louisville, and Fort Scott. In 1855, M. Lambot, a Frenchman, patented a reinforcement system which used wires and bars embedded in cementitious material, and in the same year another Frenchman, F. Coignet, patented a system for making concrete, or beton, from hydraulic lime. He followed this in 1861 by publishing a pamphlet advocating metal reinforcement and described various ways of applying it to strengthen concrete floors. Coignet's work was first really applied in 1869. One of the first uses of concrete building construction in the United States was in a house erected for W.E. Ward in 1872 at Port Chester, NY.

Although by 1900 there was general acceptance of the principle that the steel reinforcement could take all the tensile stresses while the concrete took all the compressive stresses, there was by no means general agreement on the design and location of the reinforcement. Some reinforcement was arranged in the catenary forms of suspension bridge chains or cables while others, such as Kahn trussed bars, might be arranged like miniature lattice girders embedded in the concrete. The latter were essentially long roughly "T" shaped bars which were placed at the bottom of beams and which had diagonal arms fixed to them and arranged symetrically to slope up and outward on either side of the center. Contemporary texts stated that the purpose of these diagonal arms was to hold the lower bar in position and stop it from deflecting downward. In research published in 1905 Professor Arthur N. Talbot of the University of Illinois, after carrying out a long series of tests on reinforced concrete beams stated that it was dubious whether there was even any benefit to be derived from the use of deformed bars. In the early 1900s in the first major widespread development of reinforced concrete there were three classes of bars—plain, deformed, and trussed. Plain bars were flat round or square in cross-section. Deformed bars were usually known by their form or by the name of the patent holder. Ransome's *Cyclopedia* in 1909 (Ransome, 1909) illustrated seven totally different forms of patented deformed bars which included the now familiar diamond bar, helical bars, and helical bars with round stud-like projections.

Trussed bars such as the Kahn bar or the herringbone trussed bar could have complex assemblies of bars which usually had a number of horizontal bars in

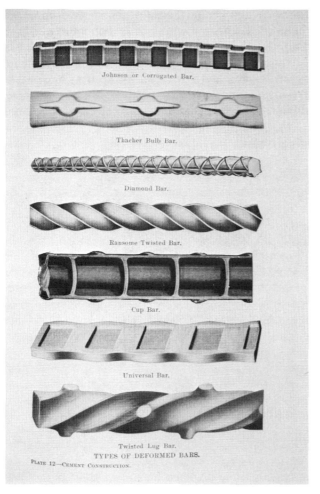

Early designs of deformed bars from Radford's Cyclopedia of Construction of 1909.

the bottom of the beam, a series of short diagonal arms, and perhaps a pair of long bars which descended from the ends of the beam down to the middle. Apart from the fact that it was believed that deformed bars were held better by the concrete, some early reinforced concrete from about 1895 onward may be found to have the bars very curiously distributed and even sometimes in concentrated bundles in the bottom of the beam.

Concrete Deterioration

The majority of concrete problems are related to the presence of water. Thus, large quantities of water penetrating through concrete may leach out calcium oxide and redeposit it on the surface of the concrete where it undergoes a reaction and forms sheets of crystalline calcite or stalactites hanging down from overhangs or from the underside of slabs. Such removal and redeposition of carbonates leads ultimately to a total breakdown of the concrete. Seepage accompanied by freeze/ thaw cycles and the formation of ice lenses can result in spalling, chipping, or general exfoliation of concrete surfaces, or of parging or rendered cementitious finishes. Day work joints or the joints between ''pours'' of concrete may act as lines of weakness along which ice action can cause movements of individual slabs by as much as 3 ins. The blocking of individual drains and of complete drainage systems have been known to lead

to water being trapped behind concrete masses and causing further deterioration.

Concrete copings in early concrete fortifications are particularly prone to failure along the horizontal joint between the coping and the wall beneath. Cracking in concrete can take many forms but the most common in early mass concrete work are the vertical cracks which are the result of initial shrinkage on drying or curing, and of thermal expansion and contraction in the absence of construction joints.

Where rolled iron joists are embedded in concrete as in mid-to-late nineteenth century slabs, initial cracking occurs along the lines of the iron joists and then leaking occurs along those lines. Eventually the iron corrodes and the concrete is forced apart along the line, or spalls in the immediate vicinity of the joist. Where very large sections of concrete are cast against smaller ones the differential shrinkage rates are usually quite sufficient to cause the two to crack apart. If a diagonal crack is otherwise hard to explain but honeycombed or crumbling concrete exists on either side of the crack, then sudden changes in concrete quality or excessive water content in the original mix may have been the causes of the deterioration.

In more recent concrete where steel reinforcement has been used, the shattering and spalling of the under-surface is usually clearly the result of the corrosion of the reinforcement. Often the reinforcement was poorly placed and was too close to the underside of the con-

Severely corroded early concrete reinforcement ca. 1900, Darnley Mill, Crooks Hollow, Ontario.

Heavy deposits of calcite from deteriorating concrete, Saint John the Divine, New York, NY.

crete. In some cases the reinforcement is actually showing through the surface. Iron or steel reinforcement or beams can only remain uncorroded in concrete in a highly alkaline environment of approximately pH 11–12. If this alkalinity is reduced toward neutrality or even to acidity the potential for corrosion grows steadily stronger. This undesirable change from alkalinity to neutrality and thence to acidity can be caused slowly by excessive amounts of water passing through the concrete, or much more quickly by the penetration of acidic precipitation into the concrete.

The processes of loss of alkalinity, consequent corrosion of reinforcement, and deterioration of concrete are collectively referred to as carbonation, the conversion of lime to calcium carbonate. Carbonation is usually detected by simple pH tests such as the phenolphthalein test.

Deterioration of reinforced concrete will also be dramatic in environments where large quantities of deicing salts are employed. The hydration and dehydration cycles of the salts may cause complete disintegration of the concrete or if chlorides are present they may result in severe corrosion in the steel accompanied by the expansion of corrosion products and the familiar problem of "oxide jacking" which pushes off the concrete surface in spalls or complete sheets. Studies at the Portland Cement Association reported on by Paul Klieger in 1980 show that continual exposure to the deicer solution and low concentrations of deicer are the most detrimental. Deicer scaling is usually not caused by chemical reactions, crystal pressures or thermal changes, or induced cycles of freezing. The damage is caused, as in normal freezing, by high hydraulic pressures created during freezing, the magnitude of these pressures depending on the distance the water must move for relief to an air void, the amount of water being displaced (9% of freezable water), and the permeability of the concrete paste through which the water must move. The actual mechanism is a facinating one. During freezing from the deicer solution, ice is formed and the concentration of deicer in the solution which remains immediately in front of the ice then increases. The process of osmosis ensures that salts will tend to move from a solution of low concentration to a high one. Thus a counter osmotic pressure is formed, drawing water into a zone where increasing pressure has already been created by the formation of the ice. These factors result in increased hydraulic pressure being required to drive the excess volume to an air void.

Other forms of concrete deterioration are commonly related to the presence of sulfates in the soil in which concrete is buried, or sulfates in groundwater, or sulfates in concrete aggregates such as clinkers. The sulfates react with the concrete to form gypsum which expands in the concrete and typically causes bowing or buckling of concrete slabs. The sulfates can also cause subflorescence and lead to a crumbling or scaling of the concrete surface. Alkaline aggregate reactions are described elsewhere in this chapter.

The Conservation of Concrete

The Canadian restoration architect Andrew Powter discussing concrete conservation in an article in the *Bulletin of the Association for Preservation Technology* in 1978, discusses three reasons why there are as yet no really satisfactory solutions to all the problems of concrete conservation (Powter, 1978). First, concrete simply has not been around long enough for conservators to be familiar with it as a material and to have

Severe damage to reinforcement in concrete beam carrying highway viaduct, Toronto, Ontario. The severity of the corrosion is due to a combination of acid precipitation and deicing salts.

any clear idea of the long-term effects of conservation media and methods. Second, conservation is usually concerned with materials which are contructed with units rather than in monolithic form. The problem of successfully conserving stucco is noted by Powter as being an interesting parallel.

Thirdly and perhaps most importantly, nineteenth and early twentieth century concrete structures were often poorly built without a proper knowledge of the propertics and characteristics of the materials and systems. Consequently deterioration may be extremely severe and the degree of intervention required from the conservator may be considered excessive.

Whole volumes can and have been written on the subject of the concrete repairs particularly involving the installation of new waterproof membranes to prevent the continued prolonged saturation of concrete and its consequent damage by ice and related phenomena. Badly deteriorated concrete structures may have severely corroded reinforcement carefully cut out and replaced with new stainless steel reinforcement. Cracked or partly shattered concrete may be consolidated by injections of moisture-insensitive epoxy resin. Epoxy consolidation of this type is a well-established practice in commercial and industrial structures in North America. Zones of totally shattered and defective concrete may be carefully cut out and replaced with air-entrained concrete with appropriate noncor-

roding reinforcement of, say, AISI Type 316 Stainless Steel. As is normal in good conservation practice, the cause of the deterioration should be very carefully established and the necessity for intervention should be evaluated. Particular attention must be paid to the use of high-quality materials and crafts skills, compatible materials; and the avoidance or minimization of shrinkage.

A primary focus will always be to attend to drainage problems first and then the removal of trees and heavy plant growth, because root systems can disrupt old concrete.

In conclusion, heritage concrete structures could perhaps be regarded as the "poor relations" of historic monuments. Unfortunately they are often ignored as being of little "historic" significance and in many cases they may even be swept away in ill-advised attempts to "clean up" sites.

PLASTER

Many of North America's historic building interiors were graced by delicately molded cornices and fine decorative ceiling centrepieces or rosettes made from plaster. All too often this plasterwork has been one of the first things to disappear in the frenzy of demolition of interiors which has unfortunately come to be a com-

Fine plasterwork of about 1860, Halifax, Nova Scotia.

mon companion to "heritage preservation" in the guise of building rehabilitation.

Although a quick glance at an interior ripe for conversion may reveal cracked plaster and details clogged with decades of paint accumulations, the plasterwork is well worth a second look.

Plaster in the eighteenth, nineteenth, and early twentieth centuries usually consisted of three or four principle materials which were applied in a series of layers to give a fine smooth final finish to interior walls and ceilings which could then be painted or papered according to the taste of the period.

Wood pegs assisted in attaching this mud plaster to the log wall of the Ukrainian house in Alberta. Although this example dates to about 1900 French Canadian examples date to the 17th century.

In the earliest European settlers' plasterwork a mud plaster was used or more usually a mud–lime mixture. Such simple but pleasant finishes can be found in Spanish missions in the American Southwest, the farmsteads of Quebec, and the log houses of settlers from the Ukraine.

Mud plaster consists of clay or earth which is mixed with water to give a "plastic" or workable consistency. If the clay mixture is too plastic it will shrink, crack, and distort on drying. It will also probably drop off the wall. Sand and fine gravels were added to reduce the concentrations of fine clay particles which were the cause of the excessive shrinkage.

Straw or grass were added as reinforcement sometimes with the useful cattle manure which not only provided fiber reinforcement but also natural protein adhesives. On a small scale the grass and straw acted just like the steel in reinforced concrete. Even if the plaster cracked and crazed, the fibrous reinforcement held it together.

With a bit of luck and some assistance from holes hacked in log surfaces or even small pegs set in the wooden walls, these early plasters managed to stay on the walls.

Lime for plasters might be made by burning limestone or sea shells in large kilns. When calcium carbonate is burned or rather heated to at least 880°C or better 1000°C, carbon dioxide is given off and calcium oxide or quicklime is produced. This may be "slaked" by adding small quantities of the powdered or lump quicklime to water, never the reverse or the mixture may explode, flinging caustic quicklime all over bystanders and producing serious burns. The slaking reaction is an exothermic one which means that a large quantity of heat is generated. Even with care and precautions, slaking can be a risky business and all workers are well advised to wear plastic safety goggles or face shields when mixing quicklime.

The lime was slaked and mixed with hoes in large wooden tubs or in pits and was left to mature under water in pits sometimes for as long as 10 years or more. (As long as the calcium or magnesium hydroxide remains under water it cannot harden. When exposed to the air the calcium or magnesium hydroxide takes up carbon dioxide from the air and forms calcium or magnesium carbonate.) If the mass of plaster was very thick the interior might still not have set two hundred years later. There are historical accounts of coal or coke fires being lit in braziers below freshly plastered ceilings and vaults. The idea was partially to dry out the plaster but it had also been noticed that what appeared to be the smoke and fumes from burning these fossil fuels somehow assisted the setting or hardening of the plaster. This was perhaps the first demonstration that the burning of fossil fuels and their derivatives produces carbon dioxide.

Such plaster was commonly reinforced with animal hair and was "tempered" with sand to prevent or reduce shrinkage. Some early plasters were mixtures of lime plaster and soil or clay.

Animal hair provided tensile reinforcement in early plaster but was sometimes poor distribution led to failures.

Typical scratch coat under layer of gypsum/lime plaster on rubble stone masonry, St. Raphael's church, Ontario, ca. 1840.

Lime plasters could be attached to the structure either directly by plastering onto a rough masonry surface or by plastering over thin strips of wood or laths nailed to vertical timbers. Some early settlers reverted to prehistoric techniques, plastering onto "hurdles" of split saplings woven to form a sort of heavy "basketwork" known as wattle. I have seen such techniques in seventeenth century Acadian houses in Nova Scotia and in nineteenth century houses in Mineral Point, Wisconsin.

The ancient Egyptians discovered that if you burned gypsum or alabaster you produced a powder which, if mixed with water, gave a creamy mass which would then harden. They had discovered gypsum plaster or plaster of paris. The second term derives from the fact that Paris lies on top of one of the largest gypsum deposits in Europe and thus became a major source for the plaster.

In England in the eighteenth and nineteenth centuries it was usual for $\frac{1}{2}$ in. (13-mm) layers of lime plaster to be reinforced with ox hair for coarse stuff. goat hair, specifically back hair, was used for finishing coats. In North America the type of hair used depended on the available animals but was often from cattle or even buffalo.

Gypsum plaster is formed by burning at about 320–338°F (160–170°C) and the reaction is as follows:

Gypsum or calcium sulfate dihydrate + heat =

calcium sulfate hemihydrate + $1\frac{1}{2}$ water

If one mixes the hemihydrate with water, the lost water is taken up and with the generation of some heat, the dihydrate is formed again and the plaster sets or hardens even under water. Gypsum plasters are somewhat soluble in water and will be seen to soften and "bubble" with the formation of masses of fine sulfate crystals wherever leaks occur in a building.

Getting the plaster to stay where it was put has always been a problem. Plaster is a brittle, not particularly sticky material and as has been noted the usual method of getting it attached to a wall or ceiling was to provide a physical connection by applying the plaster over a series of thin strips of wood or laths spaced about one quarter inch apart. The wet plaster squeezes through the gaps and expands out again on the far side. The tongues of plaster between the laths are known as "keys." When the plaster was applied to a masonry wall, the masonry was often prepared with a coarse plaster layer of "rough stuff" known variously as a "render," "scratch coat," or "brown coat." The surface of this underlying layer was allowed to harden slightly then was scratched or scored with the point of a trowel to produce a key for the finishing coat of finer plaster.

Most good quality historical plasterwork thus consisted of at least two coats—first a coarse sandy plaster and then a fine sand-free finishing coat. A variation on this had three coats: a render coat of about $\frac{3}{8}$–$\frac{1}{2}$ in. in thickness (a mix of 1 pbv lime putty to 3 pbv sand); followed by a "floating coat" about $\frac{1}{4}$ in. thick to level

Sulfates from rising damp destroying plasterwork in reconstruction of the governor's mansion, Fortress of Louisbourg, Nova Scotia.

out any major irregularities (same mix as render coat); and a final finishing or "setting coat" about $\frac{1}{8}$ in. thick was applied over all. The finishing coat was usually gypsum, or lime "gauged" with an equal amount of gypsum (1 gypsum:1 or 3 lime:2 sand).

The first and second coats of "coarse stuff" could consist of 1 pbv of lime to 2 pbv of clean sharp sand (always specified to be free of clay and loam) with long well-beaten ox-hair in the proportion of 9 lb of hair to 1 yard of mortar. When coarse stuff was applied over wood laths the render coat was often referred to as a "pricking up" coat. The surface of this coat was roughened or "pricked" with the end of a birch broom.

Examination of the lathing may help to date a particular piece of construction. Early laths were produced by splitting or "riving." Later laths were made by first sawing a thin board and then either splitting this board into separate laths or partially splitting the board from alternate directions to produce a zig-zag which was then pulled slightly apart and nailed into position. The latter form is known as "accordion lath." Early in the nineteenth century, the first completely sawn laths began to appear in the United States. The earlier saw marks are parallel straight lines perpendicular to the long side of the lath. Circular saw marks—a series of segments of circles of a diameter equal to that of the saw which caused them, do not appear commonly until the middle of the nineteenth century but the earliest dated example in the United States that I know of dates to 1813. The types of nails in the laths can also give

some indication of age, wire nails—of round cross section—being only manufactured from the latter part of the nineteenth century onward.

Ornamental plasterwork was moulded to complex forms using gelatin for moulds where details were un-

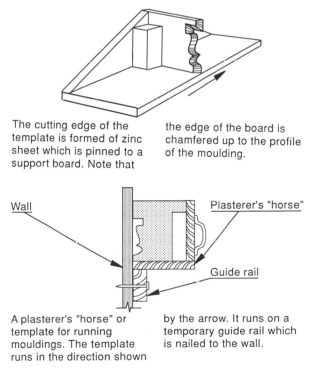

The cutting edge of the template is formed of zinc sheet which is pinned to a support board. Note that the edge of the board is chamfered up to the profile of the moulding.

A plasterer's "horse" or template for running mouldings. The template runs in the direction shown by the arrow. It runs on a temporary guide rail which is nailed to the wall.

Figure 56. Plaster moldings: plasterer's "horse".

dercut and thus could only be withdrawn from a flexible mould. Straight and curved sections of mouldings were formed by running a "horse" or wooden profile with its actual profile edge protected with a thin sheet of zinc, on wood battens nailed to the wall. Corinthian capitals and other decorative architectural details were often produced in gypsum and reinforced with coarse fibres or even loosely woven burlap or "jute scrim." Such details could be bought from catalogues very inexpensively in the last decade of the nineteenth century.

Failures in Plasterwork

Failures or faults in plasterwork are normally the result of the brittle plaster's inability to bend. The usual problem is that as the plaster bends on a sagging ceiling, the keys break, leaving large areas of thin unattached plaster.

Sometimes early laths were placed too close together and no plaster or very little squeezed through the gaps. With few or very thin keys such an area was very prone to damage. A second very obvious form of damage is that caused by water which may not only break down and soften the plaster but may cause rotting in laths and firring, and corrosion in fixing nails. If the original laths were of "green" or poorly seasoned wood they would later contract and that could lead to the cracking of keys and the detachment of layers. Sometimes the bond between finishing coat and scratch coat may fail as may the bond between scratch coat and masonry. If plasterwork is attached to masonry which may have been penetrated by water, take care to check that the attachment is still sound. Further problems are caused by the absence or poor distribution of hair reinforcement.

To test plaster surfaces, knock with your knuckles to detect the more hollow sound of detached areas and gently press surfaces with the finger tips to see if the plaster gives.

If there are fine cracks in the plaster and the edges of the cracks are at different levels try pressing the higher gently to see if it will move. If you can get at the back of ceiling or wall plaster test the individual keys with your fingers to see if the keys are still sound—in sound plasterwork the keys should not flex or move. Cracks in plasterwork may also be a useful clue to the existence of major structural movements in buildings. Obviously the causes must be traced and the problems eliminated before repairing the plaster.

Conserving and Restoring Plasterwork

Simple repairs of plasterwork are well described in a wide range of texts but difficulties may arise when the

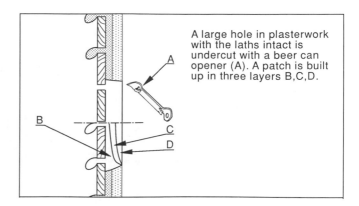

A large hole in plasterwork with the laths intact is undercut with a beer can opener (A). A patch is built up in three layers B,C,D.

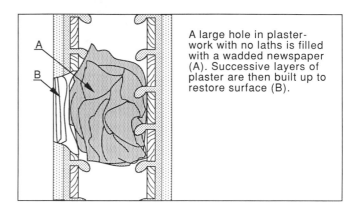

A large hole in plasterwork with no laths is filled with a wadded newspaper (A). Successive layers of plaster are then built up to restore surface (B).

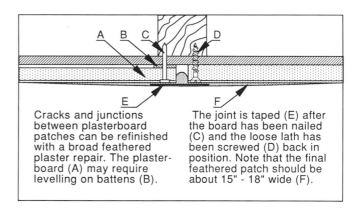

Cracks and junctions between plasterboard patches can be refinished with a broad feathered plaster repair. The plasterboard (A) may require levelling on battens (B).

The joint is taped (E) after the board has been nailed (C) and the loose lath has been screwed (D) back in position. Note that the final feathered patch should be about 15" - 18" wide (F).

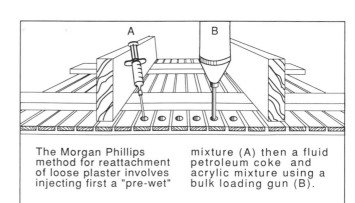

The Morgan Phillips method for reattachment of loose plaster involves injecting first a "pre-wet" mixture (A) then a fluid petroleum coke and acrylic mixture using a bulk loading gun (B).

Figure 57. Plaster repair.

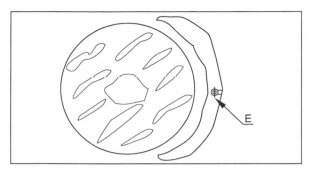

Figure 58a. Plaster medallion restoration: top view.

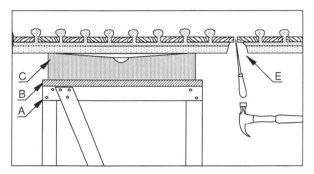

Figure 58b. Plaster medallion restoration: side view.

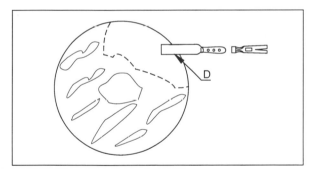

Figure 58c. Plaster medallion restoration: top view.

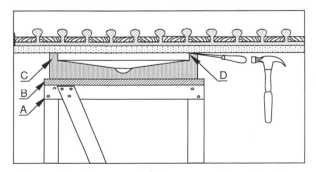

Figure 58d. Plaster medallion restoration: side view.

Taking down a plaster ceiling medallion: temporary support (A) holds up plywood sheet (B) and foam plastic padding (C). Sound medallions can be split off ceiling plaster by driving a putty knife into the plaster "slip" coat (D). Note that knife is driven tangentially not towards centre.

Delicate medallions are cut away with their backing plaster (E); the backing plaster is then carefully split or shaved off on a bench.

Legend for Figure 58.

conservator is confronted with major losses or areas where the plaster coats have separated from each other or from the laths or masonry behind. The conservation of as much as possible of the original plaster can be a very considerable challenge particularly when the back of the laths cannot be reached.

In this chapter I will examine repair and conservation methods for repairing detached or separated plaster layers and for the repair of moulded plasterwork such as ceiling medallions or rosettes.

It is important that the conservator should be familiar with all the traditional methods of forming decorative plasterwork since it may be necessary to use these same methods for repairs and reproductions.

Decorative work was commonly formed by two methods:

• casting in a mold
• "running" or "running with a horse"

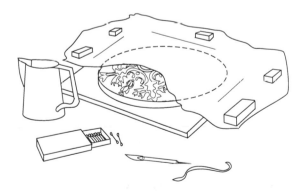

Water soluble paint layers are removed by placing medallion face up on a thick absorbent pad. The pad is wetted and then pad and medallion are covered with a sheet of polyethylene. After 24 hours the paint is softened and is more easily removed with scrapers and scalpels.

Figure 59. Plaster medallion restoration: paint removal.

New plaster moldings being made by "bench running".

Casting in a mold was the standard method for making rosettes, capitals, consoles, modillions, and other three-dimensional details which were repetitive in nature.

Running or running with a horse was the method used to produce continuous runs of moldings either *in situ* on a wall or on a bench. If the moldings were run on a bench they were lifted off when dry and then applied to the appropriate surface using plaster of paris as an adhesive. Joints between sections were subsequently made good with more plaster of paris.

Complex three-dimensional forms with major undercutting require flexible molds which will reproduce fine detail but which are sufficiently flexible to be peeled away releasing the freshly cast plaster. These moulds were traditionally made from gelatin which was supported by a natural fiber reinforced "mother mold."

The process for casting a small decorative rosette was, and in some traditional shops still is, as follows:

1. Form a temporary dam around the original plaster pattern on a work table which often has a marble top. The dam might be made from sheet zinc.

2. Paint a thin coat of shellac on the plaster.

3. Mix up 2 parts of stearic acid powder with 3 parts kerosene (by volume) warming them in a double boiler. Allow the mixture to chill and then whip it to the required consistency. The mix is then painted onto the pattern using pure bristle brushes which don't leave marks behind. The film of stearic acid mix which serves as a separator is very delicate and easily damaged. Any holes will mean that the gelatin may stick to the original pattern and tear off when the mold is removed, leaving flaws in the mold.

4. Gelatin is warmed in a double boiler to 165–180°F at which temperature it is poured over the pattern to form a mold.

5. When cool the mold is carefully removed and all traces of the stearate solution are removed using French chalk.

6. The new gelatine mold is then "tanned" using a saturated solution of alum. If this is not done the gelatin mold will blister.

7. Any alum crystals or other loose material are removed with a jet of compressed air.

8. The gelatin mold is given a thin even coat of the stearic acid and kerosene solution with no holes or lumps.

9. Casting plaster is then taken and any lumps are removed. The finely powdered plaster is added to a large pan of water until there is only $\frac{1}{8}$ in. of water showing on top, the plaster is thoroughly mixed, and then left to sit for three minutes.

10. The plaster is poured. Pouring would usually be in two operations. One shallow pour is made to cover the inside of the mold then fiber reinforce-

A gelatin mold being prepared to receive fresh gypsum plaster.

ment is added. A second pour covers the reinforcement and finishes the job.

11. When the plaster is set the back of the plaster may be scratched or scored to provide a key and the finished product is removed from the mold and taken to a drying room. The gelatin mold may be reused about six times but then it loses detail and is cut up and melted down again for reuse.

To take quick molds from fragments of old work in order to produce patterns for new work, latex rubber may be used with preshrunk bandage reinforcement. Generally rubber latex has been found not to last in storage and is therefore unsuitable for master molds. When master molds are required a silicone rubber is used such as Dow RTV E and less often Dow RTV G.[1] The highly flexible silicone rubber mold is backed with a fiber-reinforced plaster "mother mold" the purpose of which is to hold the silicone rubber rigidly and to prevent the mold being distorted.

It is essential that old plasterwork be clean before molds are taken for the purpose of casting replacements. I have seen jobs where molds were very carefully taken from old plasterwork which had all its details obscured by accumulations of old distemper or ceiling white. Naturally the new work which was cast

[1] Silicone rubbers for molding purposes are manufactured by: Dow Corning Corporation, Midland, Michigan 48686. 1-800-432-3220.

from these molds was totally incorrect and "blurred" in its details.

These accumulations of old water-soluble paints can be carefully removed using small quantities of hot water with sponges, rough cloth, and soft bristle brushes.

Running Moldings

Long lengths of moldings were traditionally run or formed by pushing a template cut out of zinc sheet through a mass of wet plaster. The zinc sheet is stiffened and supported by being pinned to a piece of board which is also cut out and chamfered to approximately the same profile as the molding. The board and template are fixed in a wooden support so that the support can be run along a temporary wooden guide rail in such a way that the profile is held vertically and at right angles to the wall. Circular moldings can be produced in the same way but with the "horse" pivoting round a center post.

The Reattachment of Loose Plaster

In 1980, Morgan Phillips, an architectural conservator with the Society for the Preservation of New England Antiquities published an article in which he described a method which he had developed for the reattachment of loose plaster (Phillips, 1980).

Unlike many of the traditional methods which some-

A highly flexible silicone rubber mold with and without its mother mold.

times might not work very well but could add a significant load to an already delicate system, the new method works well, is light in weight, and can be used ''blind'' to reattach plaster to inaccessible surfaces which are concealed by the plaster itself.

In essence the process is as follows:

1. The loose or partially detached plaster layer is supported with foam plastic padding, plywood sheet, and timber shoring.

2. If the lathing is exposed at the back of the plaster loose material is cleaned away with a vacuum cleaner.

3. Small holes are drilled through from the front of the plaster or from the back through the laths to the point where the plaster has detached from the

A lath and plaster test panel after injection of a mixture of acrylic resin, solvent, fluid petroleum coke, and glass microballoons. Note how the thixotropic mix is penetrating out through and sealing the finest cracks between the lath and the plaster.

lath or from its substrate or from a ground coat. Stops or collars are placed on the drill bit to ensure that it penetrates to the required plane and no further.

4. A "prewet" solution of diluted acrylic resin is injected into the holes with a hypodermic syringe of the type used by veterinarians. This prewet solution has the essential role of stabilizing or fixing any dust which exists in the hidden cracks or voids within the plaster. If this dust is not immobilized it tends to "roll" in front of the consolidating medium and form dams which then block further penetration.

5. A thixotropic consolidating medium is injected by means of a bulk loading gun with a modified tip for injection purposes.

As it was originally developed the consolidating medium consisted of a series of variations of a mixture containing an acrylic resin such as Rhoplex MC-76 (Rohm and Haas), chalk, and glass microballoons and a fine granular material called fluid petroleum coke.

The microballoons were Emerson and Cuming Microballoons IG-101, hollow glass spheres of 20–200 μm diameter. They contribute to the efficient packing of fillers, reduce the amount of liquid binder needed, and thereby reduce shrinkage. Being spherical they impart high plasticity to the liquid mixture, making it easier to inject, and being hollow, they reduce weight.

Fluid petroleum coke is a remarkable by-product of an oil-refining process whereby heavy hydrocarbon oils are converted to lighter fractions. The particles which are about 90% carbon, have a roughly spherical shape and are normally sieved or screened to remove particles larger than about $\frac{1}{32}$ in. (0.75 mm).

The remarkable quality of this material and the most important in this context is that when wetted by water or a number of other liquids, it releases larger volumes of gas than the volume of liquid absorbed. The gas is probably air.

In essence this means that fluid coke will provide a filler and an inert out-gassing agent which will foam the adhesive/filler mixture and cause it to fill voids. The filler thus simultaneously bridges the gaps and adheres firmly to the materials on either side.

A typical formula is as follows (all parts by volume):

2 parts powdered chalk
2 parts microballoons
2 parts fluid coke
3-3$\frac{1}{4}$ Rhoplex MC-76
Cabosil M-5 (pyrogenic silica) as a thickener if desired

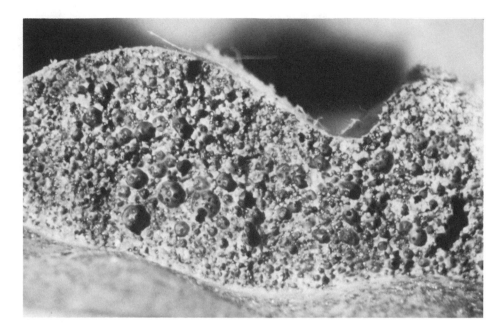

Close-up detail of section through cured fluid petroleum coke and acrylic resin adhesive/consolidant mix.

Other formulations use similar proportions but the acrylic resin is made up from 3 parts of Rhoplex M-76 to 1 part Rhoplex LC-67 plus $\frac{1}{4}$ part of water.

In a later case in Ontario where an historic wallpaper was on the plaster, the formula was modified to eliminate water, using 3 parts alcohol to 1 part acrylic resin (Rhoplex MC-76).

In other experiments with Ian Hodkinson I have used a prewetting formula with 10% isopropanol in water. This was tested for safe use on plaster to which oil paintings on canvas had been marouflaged (glued) in the Salon Bleu of the National Assembly Building of Quebec. Professor Hodkinson and I also experimented successfully with formulae using the fluid coke with other resins such as the acrylic resin Rhoplex AC 234 (Rohm and Haas) and the PVA Jade 403 (Talas, New York).

Some conservators have experienced difficulties in obtaining fluid coke which the oil companies often prefer not to handle in small quantities. They would prefer to deal in tank car loads! Happily there is a solution to this problem because it is available in 1 gallon and 4 gallon containers from the redoubtable Doug Adams' Conservation Materials Ltd of Sparks, Nevada.[2]

[2] Dorothy and Doug Adams, Conservation Materials Ltd., Box 2884, 340 Freeport Blvd., Sparks, Nevada, 89431 USA. (702) 331-0582.

REFERENCES

Ashurst, John and Nicola. (1988). *Stone Masonry, Practical Building Conservation. Vol. 1.* New York. Halsted Press a Division of John Wiley & Sons, Inc.

Gwilt, J. (1967). *An Encyclopaedia of Architecture: Historical, Theoretical and Practical.* London. Longmans Green and Co.

Phillips, M.W. (1974). On the Subjects of Analyzing Paints and Mortars and the Recreation of Moulding Profiles. Bulletin of the Association for Preservation Technology, Ottawa. Vol. X, No. 2, pp. 77–85.

Phillips, M.W. (1980). Adhesives for the Reattachment of Loose Plaster. *Bulletin of the Association for Preservation Technology,* Vol. XII, No. 2, pp. 37–63.

Powter, A. (1978). *Bulletin of the Association for Preservation Technology.*

Radford, William A., ed. (1909). *Radford's Cyclopedia of Construction.* Radford Architectural Company, Chicago.

Vicat, L.J. (1837). *A Practical Treatise on Calcareous Mortars and Cements.* London.

Vitruvius (1960). *The Ten Books on Architecture.* Translated by Morris Hickey Morgan. Reprint edition. New York: Dover.

PLASTER CONSERVATION CASE HISTORY

The following extract comes from a case history from the files of the Center for Preservation Research at Columbia University. It is included here to show the scope and detail which are included in a typical plaster conservation project.

Case Study: A Pedimental Sculpture

Following is an illustrated step-by-step record of the restoration of a Pedimental Sculpture carried out in May and June of 1989 by a team of conservators from the Center for Preservation Research at Columbia University in New York. The methodology and techniques discussed for this exterior stuccowork are applicable to the repair of general ornamental exterior. Installation techniques of exterior stuccowork can vary (the Pedimental stuccowork are was plaster of paris), the general techniques presented here are applicable for most situations. It is imperative, however, to properly identify the nature of the stuccowork before attempting restoration as different grouting and patching formulations are necessary for each stucco type.

STEP 1: DOCUMENTATION

Free-standing pipe scaffolding was constructed from which all inspection and restoration work was done. The pediment was divided into seventeen vertical divisions for the purpose of accurately recording existing conditions as well as sample and repair locations. Divisions were marked off using heavy nylon string secured at top and bottom with mastic. Sections were numbered with waterproof ink on waterproofed tape wrapped over the string. Existing conditions were documented photographically with 35 mm black-and-white and color film. Each frame included a color or gray scale as well as a dimensional scale. The numbered grid was transferred to several copies of a print made from an enlargement of a dot-screened rectified photograph taken in 1986. Existing conditions were recorded graphically onto these prints. These included conditions evident from visual inspection such as cracking, loss, flaking, and erosion. A survey of surface coatings identified seven separate repair campaigns. The locations of the different coatings were recorded graphically. The stucco was sounded with an acrylic hammer to determine detachment and voids. This information was recorded graphically, and showed over 50% of the sculpture to be detached and in danger of collapse or loss. Samples of the substrate and various stuccos and finishes were carefully removed

STEP 2: STABILIZATION

Strips of Japanese tissue torn by hand into approximately $\frac{3}{4}$ in. strips were used to temporarily hold in place numerous detached and cracked areas. These were adhered to the sculpture with a brush-applied solution of 10% B72 (a methyl acrylate-ethyl methacrylate copolymer manufactured by Rohm and Haas Inc.) in toluene.

STEP 3: CLEANING

The pediment was initially dusted clean using a number of soft nylon and natural bristle brushes. Several birds' nests were removed. Dirt and debris was removed from the cracks and voids by using compressed air and a final water rinse at very low pressure (about 25 psi) in preparation for grouting.

STEP 4: GROUTING

Since the original sculpture was plaster of paris it was decided to grout by injection through syringes with the same material modified with an acrylic emulsion (Rhoplex AC33, manufactured by Rohm and Haas, Inc.) for additional adhesion. Tests were run on possible retarders to increase working time, including various percentages of alcohol and acetic acid, but Rhoplex alone seemed to retard the set sufficiently to give a 20 minute working time in the hot, humid climate before the mix set to a point where it would not move through the syringes.

Detached open surfaces and blind hollow voids were marked with chalk for grouting after sounding. Blind voids were made accessible for grouting by drilling small holes ($\frac{1}{8}$ in.) with a portable variable speed drill. All voids were air-cleaned and flushed and prewetted with alcohol and water, administered through a squeeze bottle with a rigid bent spout that provided a fine stream of liquid. This not only removed internal debris, but served to reduce too rapid water absorption from the gypsum grout as well as reduce surface tension. Both enhanced the injectability of the mix once in place.

Trials revealed areas that needed damming to prevent the grout from escaping. Both cotton and potter's clay were used for this purpose. Although somewhat faster and easier to remove, cotton proved to be more time consuming to install. Clay, on the other hand, could be quickly packed over a hole or spread along a leaking crack.

The alcohol–water injection was quickly followed with a first injection of Rhoplex AC33, again using the needle-nosed squeeze bottle. Both dilute (10%) and full-strength emulsions were used depending on the degree of detachment.

Syringes were filled directly from the blender and injected into exposed areas and prepared holes, working from the bottom up to allow air to escape and monitor the amount of grout injected. The injection tip or cannula was inserted into the hole and held in place with a wad of cotton held tightly around to create back pressure, forcing the mixture into the cracks and voids. When completely filled, the hole was dammed with clay and the work progressed to the next hole marked with a small wooden stick for quick identification.

STEP 5: REINFORCEMENT

Numerous previous repairs and open cracks at the juncture of the eagle's wings, neck and the background suggested active movement and potential failure and detachment of these projecting elements. Quarter-inch stainless steel threaded rods were inserted into pre-drilled holes in the eagle's right and left wings and neck and tied back into the wall of the pediment. The rods were set at a downward angle 2 ft into the wall and secured at each end with epoxy.

Rebuilding with large amounts of mortar behind the wings and head done in association with the earlier replacement of the original iron reinforcements had exacerbated the repairs by adding tremendous weight on these projecting elements. Once this material was removed, the wings, which had been displaced the most, were returned (about $\frac{1}{4}$ in.) to their original position by rope straps and secured while the adhesive cured. Voids were then packed with the lightweight gypsum.

STEP 6: FILLING AND COMPENSATION

When the grout had thoroughly dried, usually the next day, the clay or cotton damming material was removed and the exposed gypsum undercut leaving a lip of the stucco layer exposed. This created a key into which the fill could be packed. All cracks, losses, and eroded details were filled with a natural hydraulic lime (Riverton hydrated hydraulic lime, available from the mix (1:2) applied with a painter's palette or micro spatula). This material was selected due to its compatibility with the extant natural cement stucco installed in 1850 and its overall durability and quick set.

STEP 7: LIME-WASH

The final step in the treatment was to coat the pediment with a protective water shedding lime-wash skin composed of:

1 part hydraulic lime (Riverton HH)
2 part water
$\frac{1}{2}$ part pigment (Rainbow cement color limeproof brown)
$\frac{1}{4}$ part Rhoplex AC33 (10%)

Four coats were ultimately applied. As the coats dried a laitance appeared on the surface, but was easily removed with a light water rinse. The final color was matched to the color of the 1850 natural cement stucco.

When all work was completed, several rubber snakes were placed on the sculpture to discourage pigeons from alighting and fouling the work. The snakes are not visible from below.

CHAPTER 8

CLEANING MASONRY

The cleaning of masonry materials is one of the commonest forms of conservation treatment today and yet it is depressingly often undertaken in a state of ignorance. There are a series of questions which must first be answered before any attempt is made to clean stone, brick, terracotta, or concrete, or any combination of these materials. It must also be realized that any attempt to clean the masonry units is also going to affect the mortar between them.

The combination of the science and art of masonry cleaning depend upon striking a balance between removing the undesirable material or "soiling" and not harming the masonry materials or "substrates." The first questions which must be posed and convincingly answered are as follows:

- Why is the masonry to be cleaned?
- Does it need cleaning?
- Will the masonry deteriorate if it is not cleaned?
- Will the masonry deteriorate if it is cleaned?

A classic case of improper masonry cleaning is when one removes old paints from historic brickwork only to discover that the bricks were underfired and were painted originally to make it possible to use them on the exterior of a building.

If the answers are satisfactory, particularly the answers to the questions on possible future deterioration, then one can proceed to the next stage. The cleaning of masonry is usually undertaken for two reasons: to preserve the masonry; or for aesthetic reasons usually connected with selling the building or rehabilitating it.

Whatever the real reason is for cleaning the masonry there is a basic principle of conservation which should be observed. This is that **the conservator should always use the most gentle techniques and the least possible degree of intervention to secure any conservation objective**. Simply put, this means that if feather dusting or vacuum cleaning will remove the soiling then those are the correct techniques. If a little water will do the job then there is no need to use a lot. If diluted chemicals will work then a concentrated chemical should not be used. Frequently several applications of a dilute cleaner are much more effective than one application of a concentrated one.

The selection of concentrated chemical compounds, high pressures, high flow rates, and other excessive techniques characteristically endanger the historic resource to an unacceptable degree and can also endanger the public and those engaged in the work.

CATEGORIES OF MASONRY MATERIALS

For the context of building cleaning, masonry materials can be divided into five categories:

- Stones composed entirely or partly of acid-soluble carbonates or chalky material. The correct term for these is "calcareous." The group includes limestones, marbles, calcareous sandstones, and sand lime bricks. These are normally cleaned with water and nonacidic chemical compounds.
- Stones composed of acid-resistant materials such as quartz or silica and silicate compounds. This group includes granite, andesite, most sandstones, and a whole range of hard, dense stones which the building trade groups as "granites" but which in

fact are not granites. Included in this latter group are gabbro, gneiss, syenite, and diorite. Although these stones are acid resistant certain acidic cleaners will etch and seriously disfigure their polished surfaces.

- Architectural ceramics. This large group of acid-resistant fired-clay products includes bricks and architectural terracottas. Again although these materials are acid resistant, certain acidic cleaners will seriously disfigure glazed surfaces.
- Cementitious products. Included in this group are lime mortars, "natural cements," lime and gypsum plasters and stuccos, and portland cement.
- Water-soluble or water-sensitive masonry materials such as adobe, clay block, terre pise, cob, sod, and alabaster.

Having thus roughly classified the masonry materials or potential substrates we must now examine the materials to be removed, and what binds them together or causes them to adhere to the substrate. The selection of appropriate associated cleaning materials and processes can then be made on the basis of proper knowledge rather than ignorance.

CATEGORIES OF MASONRY SOILING AND SOLVENTS

The substances to be removed are usually classified by their solvents and may be grouped as follows.

Water-Soluble Materials

Materials included in this group are "dirt" deposits consisting of carbon(soot) and other particulate matter such as carbonates, silicates, and iron, alone or held together by water-soluble salts such as calcium, sodium, or magnesium sulfates; and efflorescence or surface deposits of sulfates and chlorides.

Water, our commonest cleaning agent, has unfortunate disadvantages especially when used in great quantities. It can take millions of gallons or litres to clean a cathedral or a large office building. Water is well known as the cause of more deterioration in old buildings than any other single factor. If used in large quantities, water may soak deeply into masonry, penetrating to damage interior finishes and to create rot-producing conditions in hidden woodwork. Penetrating moisture may also cause corrosion in hidden iron and steel anchors, cramps, dowels, and other fixing details, thus giving rise to violent expansion of the corroding metalwork and the associated disastrous cracking and smashing of adjacent masonry elements. If masonry remains saturated when frosts occur then ice formation can cause masonry surfaces to spall off in thin layers, or on a macro scale it can cause whole sections of wall to be pushed out of position.

Deep saturation may also cause water-soluble salts to be liberated from the core of the masonry and to be transported to the surface where concentrations of these salts may cause subflorescence and associated damage to the surface. Water supplies, particularly in

Iron compounds in cleaning water contributed to the staining of the white marble facing of the building on the right, St. Patrick's Cathedral, New York.

large cities like New York or Montreal, may contain large quantities of chlorine and may run through corroding iron pipes. These can cause serious disfigurement and staining in masonry surfaces, particularly in light colored surfaces such as marble, limestone, and some sandstones. Water is generally best used in nebulous sprays discharging about 12 U.S. gallons (45 litres) per hour. If the fine or nebulous sprays are turned on and off for a hour or so at a time, the expansion of the dirt crust caused by the wetting is followed by contraction as it dries. The crust tends to crack away from the substrate which does not expand and contract at the same rate. There is also the advantage that less water is used, reducing the risks of penetration and long-term saturation. Fine sprays using up to 29 to 37 U.S. gallons (110 to 140 litres) per hour may also be used on less sensitive materials such as sound limestone.

To avoid over-saturation and associated problems in the masonry, nebulous sprays of water were successfully used in 1979 to clean the marble walls of St. Patrick's Cathedral.

All pipes and hoses used for water-cleaning purposes should be of plastic or other materials which will not corrode and cause staining of light colored masonry.

When light colored materials are being cleaned on a large scale it is worth obtaining analyses of the water supply to ascertain whether iron and other cationic or anionic contaminants are present in significant quantities. If there is too much iron, for example, the water used for cleaning may have to be run through filters.

After soaking with nebulous sprays recalcitrant deposits can be removed with natural fiber or plastic bristle brushes, or with higher pressure water jets. All pressure jet washing should be carefully tested in advance on the same materials and soiling in some less significant or less visible area. A whole series of variables must be exactly matched. Washing with a water jet under pressure involves a number of variables and an awful lot of nonsense has been spoken and written on this subject, some of it unfortunately in "official" standards and guidelines developed by well-intentioned people with insufficient practical experience. The principle variables which control the ultimate effect on the surface are as follows:

- Pressure, expressed in pounds per square inch (psi) or in kilo pascals (kPs). Today there are pumps which are capable of delivering a jet of water at a pressure of over 20,000 psi! Such pressures can produce a jet capable of cutting through inches of steel or stone. But such a pressure if used in conjunction with an oscillating sapphire head can produce a perfectly satisfactory cleaning system.

In practice I have often specified a certain pressure only to find that on the site the contractor has only one pressure gauge and that is on the pump truck, down on the street below. Even that gauge may have a needle which swings and vibrates wildly all over the dial. If the hose rises up through several storeys there will be considerable loss of pressure at the spray head or jet. Thus the pressure reading down on the street level may not mean very much. Pressures of 400–800 psi are usually satisfactory even for historic masonry but pressures of 200–300 psi may be quite satisfactory. The pressure should be measured at the gun or as close to the nozzle as possible.

- Flow rate, expressed in gallons per minute or litres per minute. A minimum flow rate of about 3 gpm is required but 4–6 gpm is more usually found to be satisfactory. Some contractors will try to use 10 gpm but pressures must be kept in the lower ranges when such high flow rates are used. A description of pressure means little or nothing without the flow rate. Thus we often see, for example, a water spray specified as say "800 psi at 5 gpm."

- Working distance, expressed in inches or millimeters as the distance between the nozzle orifice and the surface being cleaned.
- The size and configuration of the nozzle. Usually a stainless steel fan tip is recommended with a flat 25–50 degree wide spray. A needle jet will be liable to cut holes if left on the same spot for fractionally too long. A fan spray tip should not be less than 15 degrees.

All of these variables must be precisely tested and recorded to produce a series of sample "standards" usually of about 4′ × 4′, once the client, architect, engineer, and conservator have agreed on a certain sample as representing the degree of "clean" that is required. That sample area becomes a reference standard and is maintained until the end of the project. Every variable that it took to produce that precise finish must be meticulously recorded.

I have provided "expert testimony" in a number of court cases which would never have come to court if the "reference standards" had been produced and agreed to, and retained until the end of the project! To the uninitiated it seems unbelievable that the omission of such a seemingly small detail can cause so much trouble! Once agreement has been obtained the standard can also be photographed and the photograph becomes a vital legal document which prevents the unfortunate misunderstandings which will occur if the client comes back later and says that what has been produced is not at all what was expected.

The Use of Poultices or Leaching Packs

Water-soluble soiling and salts may be removed with the aid of leaching packs or poultices. Just as poultices are used in medicine to draw out toxins and other undesirable substances, they can also be used in conservation.

A thick paste is made up using water and an inert powder such as diatomaceous earth, kaolinite, fullers' earth, or atapulgite. The surface to be cleaned is lightly wetted and the poultice is applied as a thick paste with a trowel or wooden spatula. Poultices are usually from $\frac{1}{4}$ to $\frac{1}{2}$ in. thickness. The moisture at first soaks into the masonry and then returns to the surface to evaporate. When it returns to the surface it brings with it the undesirable water-soluble material which is left behind in the new "sacrificial surface" provided by the poultice. The now contaminated dried poultice material can

then be removed with a wooden spatula if it hasn't dropped off by itself. When poultices are being used on very porous and highly textured masonry surfaces a separation can be made between the masonry surface and the poultice using a Japanese tissue or a thin polyester geotextile in the form of a nonwoven needle felt of, say, 200 g/sq m. This will prevent the fine powder of the poultice from getting stuck in the pores of the masonry. If large areas of poultices are being applied they can be held in place with woven plastic mesh screening stretched on wooden frames. Polyethylene sheet can be used to cover the poultice to retard evaporation and enhance the removal process.

If the soiling to be removed is soluble in organic solvents then it is a simple matter to substitute them for the water in the poultice mix. Essentially a poultice is a mixture of a selected inert powder with a selected solvent.

The water-soluble salts and other materials which are to be removed must be identified before the commencement of poulticing. Tests on the used poultice material are then carried out at intervals to determine when the culprits are no longer present. The poulticing may then cease.

Materials Soluble in Organic Solvents

This group includes most paints and lacquers and certain types of deposit which are bound to the surface by or consist entirely of oils, resins, grease, and/or bituminous products.

Organic solvents have a number of problems associated with their use:

- Their cost.
- Health hazards, for example, may cause kidney and liver damage, heart failure, poisoning, and allergic reactions.
- Risks associated with flammability or explosion hazards.
- Risk of spreading stains into the masonry.
- Their volatility.

Ironically, it is the first problem which usually results in the careful and selective use of organic solvents only where they are essential. Some solvents are carcinogens, for example, benzene; others, like methylene chloride, are liable to be very dangerous to people with heart problems; others such as carbon tetrachloride may cause liver or kidney failure. Methanol or methyl hydrate may cause intoxication followed swiftly by blindness and even death. The dangers of all organic solvents should be fully understood and all appropriate working precautions should be taken.

Following pioneering legislation in California many of the solvents known as volatile organic compounds or VOCs may actually be banned for any large-scale use. It is most probable that many states and Canadian provinces will follow this trend. Organic solvents are usually selected on the basis of presenting the best combination of lower toxicity and solvent power. They are normally used in conjunction with leaching packs or poultices and this removes the risk of dissolved material spreading into and damaging the stone.

Dwell Time

The term "dwell time" refers to the period of time for which a poultice or any other application of chemical cleaning compounds is left on the surface to carry out its cleaning process. Poultices are usually left until they are dry at which time they crack and fall off the substrate. Cleaning compounds may also be based upon alkalies or acids and their dwell times may range from a few minutes to over 24 hours.

Materials Soluble in Alkalies

This group includes paints which have a linseed oil binder and "carbonaceous" or sooty soiling. These absorb fatty acids and may be neutralized and solubilized with alkalies. Alkalies such as potassium hydroxide and ammonium hydroxide neutralize acidic soiling and will saponify greasy materials which may thus be made water-soluble.

Alkalies have five problems associated with their use:

- The risk of efflorescence appearing after the treatment. The risks of later efflorescence are minimized by prewashing surfaces before alkali treatments and by extremely thorough rinsing off with water after treatments. In some cases post-treatment rinsing with "mild" acidic washes of dilute acetic acid may be used to assist in the neutralization of the alkalies.

- The risk of brown ferric hydroxide stains being formed in the presence of quantities of iron compounds in the stone. Ferric hydroxide staining is avoided by prewashing, working upward, and by not using alkalies on stones containing more than a small percentage of iron compounds. I would not use alkalies, for example, on a light colored sandstone with a ferrous compound content of more than 3%.

- The risk of severe alkali "burns," eye damage being a particular hazard. Injury from alkali (and acid) cleaning compounds can only be avoided if all operatives are fully aware of the hazards and if full protective clothing is worn whenever these products are in use.

Ferric hydroxide staining in sandstone which was incorrectly cleaned probably with sodium hydroxide.

New aluminum window frame attacked by alkaline masonry cleaner.

- The risk of damage to adjacent paintwork.
- The risk of damage to exposed aluminum. Concentrated alkalies attack aluminum and will rapidly corrode right through new aluminum window frames.

In a typical alkali-based cleaning operation the product is applied to a previously wetted surface as a gel. It is then left for a dwell time of perhaps 30 minutes. The gel is then rinsed off with a high-pressure water jet. Hydro Clean produces a typical limestone cleaning

Efflorescence on a recently cleaned limestone cornice in Montreal was revealed by pH test strips to have been caused by unauthorized use of alkaline masonry cleaners and subsequent failure to neutralize the alkalis.

product for which it is recommended that rinsing off be done with a high-pressure water jet using 1500 psi at 5 gpm.

Once the thorough rinse-off is complete the surface is treated with a mild acidic cleaner which is usually based upon acetic acid. This is followed by another and final rinse-off with water. The point of the acetic acid wash is to neutralize the alkali residues, and in conjunction with thorough rinsing with water, the acid wash helps avoid subsequent alkali efflorescence.

Materials Soluble in Acids

This group includes lime washes and lime deposits which may result from the redeposition of lime from dissolved mortars and cements. Deposits of calcium carbonate in hard layered crusts appear on masonry as a result of mildly acidic water dissolving lime within the masonry and redepositing it on the surface where it crystallizes with exposure to carbon dioxide in the atmosphere. Cleaning the deposits off the surface will of course do nothing about the deteriorated lime mortar or binder within the masonry.

The ubiquitous black carbon soiling on granites and other acid-resistant masonry materials such as brick and sandstone, is usually easily removed by chemically etching with acids. Acids clean by chemically reacting with the soiling material and by dissolving the interface between that material and the underlying stone or ar-

chitectural ceramic substrate. The most useful acid in this context is hydrofluoric acid which does not leave any water-soluble products in the stone and can thus not give rise to efflorescence.

Acidic cleaning compounds have the following associated problems:

- The formation of water-soluble salts and consequently efflorescence. Water-soluble salt formation can be avoided by making hydrofluoric acid the main active ingredient and eliminating the use of hydrochloric acid. This will also avoid the formation of yellow or rust colored ferrous and ferric chloride staining.

- The formation of yellow and rust colored ferrous and ferric chloride stains associated with the direct use of hydrochloric acid (muriatic acid). This problem and others associated with residual chlorides have led to the virtual abandonment of hydrochloric acid for cleaning masonry.

- The risk of injury from acid burns. Hydrofluoric acid will produce extremely severe chemical burns which are very slow to heal. It has the unusual characteristic of being able to penetrate through flesh to destroy the bone beneath. Even in small amounts it is very irritating and corrosive to skin, eyes and mucous membranes. Inhalation of the vapor may cause ulcers of the upper respiratory tract and is dangerous even for very brief expo-

Black soiling largely consisting of carbon and sulfates on brickwork on the Rookery, Chicago, Illinois.

Ferric chloride staining on Berea sandstone on a Montreal building probably caused by use of hydrochloric acid in an earlier attempt at cleaning the masonry.

sures. Skin burns may be followed by gangrene. Other acids which may be encountered in cleaning compounds include sulfamic acid, phosphoric acid, and sulfuric acid.

• The risk of damage to surrounding vegetation. Vegetation must be protected or better still temporarily replanted in another protected area.

• The risk of damage to exposed metalwork and glass in the vicinity. All exposed metalwork and glass must be protected with double layers of 6 mil polyethylene sheeting well taped down with duct tape to ensure that the acids do not penetrate behind them. Hydrofluoric acid is the acid used for etching glass and even brief accidental exposures

can swiftly lead to serious disfigurement of polished plate glass.

Peelable coatings such as Sure Klean Acid Stop may provide protection in specific cases but I have occasionally had difficulties in removing such coatings after the job was completed. The shelf life of such products should be checked in case a "peelable coating" has ceased to be peelable.

Recent environmental pollution control and safety legislation in both the United States and Canada has begun to restrict the use of acidic cleaners and particu-

ACID RESISTANCE									
NOTE	SUBSTANCE	*RATING	1	2	3	4	5	6	7
*A	Acrylic & Methacrylates							•	•
	Alkyds (modified)				•				
	Alkyds (short oil lenght)				•				
*B	Boiled Linseed Oil				•				
*C	Cellulose acetate butyrate		•						
	Cellulose nitrate						•		
*D	Chlorinated rubber							•	
	Epoxide (amino or phenolic resin blend)							•	
	Epoxide / fatty acid esters					•			
	Flourocarbons								•
*E	Neoprene							•	•
	Phenolic resins (methylon)								•
*F	Poly-propylene							•	•
*G	Polyesters							•	•
*H	Polyethylene								•
*I	Polyvinyl chloride (p.v.c.)							•	•
*J	Tung oil (polymerized)							•	

Notes:
* Rating 1—Very poor ranging to 7—Excellent
    Special Features:
    *A Poor resistance to concentrated oxidizing acids and fair only in organic acids.
    *B Slow drying.
    *C Poor resistance to organic acids, requires pigmentation and stabilizers.
    *D Poor heat resistance.
    *E Good in concentrated mineral and oxidizing acids, poor pigmentation and stabilizers.
    *F Poor resistance to concentrated oxidizing acids, requires in organic acids and solvents.
    *G Poor resistance to strong oxidants unless stabilized.
    *H Poor resistance to concentrated organic acids.
    *I Attacked by organic solvents and acids, needs u.v. absorber. Not favored by conservators because of long term instability and release of hydrochloric acid.
    *J May yellow.

Figure 60. General characteristics of binding media for paints and coatings.

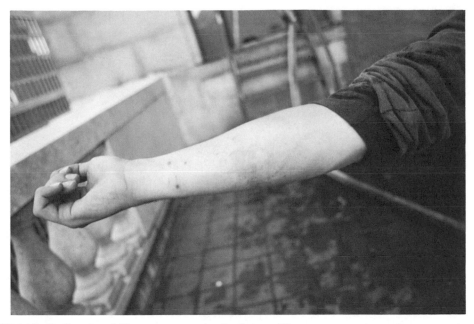

Slight hydrofluoric acid burns on an operative's arm. The man was not wearing any protective clothing.

Shrubs damaged by acid overspray and wind-drift during a masonry cleaning job, Royal Canadian Mint, Ottawa, Ontario.

Unprotected glass damaged by hydrofluoric acid during masonry cleaning job, Kingston, Ontario.

larly those containing hydrofluoric acid. The new legislation appears to take two forms; one states that pH levels of run-off and "spray back" must be neutral and the other limits the level of fluorides in the run-off to as little as 10 mgs/l.

The Use of Detergents or Surfactants

Before a liquid can dissolve a particular soil or "dirt" deposit it must wet it. Wetting can be achieved by the use of solvents or wetting agents. Solvents are described as being either polar or nonpolar.

Water is a polar solvent but most organic solvents, like carbon tetrachloride, are nonpolar. In polar molecules the centers of positive and negative charges do not coincide but in nonpolar molecules they do. The classic illustration of this is the orientation or "ordering" of water molecules in a meniscus where the two positively charged hydrogen ions adhere to the negatively charged walls of capillaries in stones and bricks.

Soils or dirt layers usually contain materials of both polarities but the polar ones which predominate are often bonded by water-soluble salts. It is usually found that polar substances are dissolved by polar liquids and nonpolar substances are dissolved by nonpolar liquids.

Surfaces with nonpolar materials are described as hydrophobic or water repelling and not easily wetted; and with polar materials they are described as hydrophilic or water attracting and easily wetted.

The differences in behavior between polar and nonpolar liquids is related to the large differences in surface tension between them. Water has a high surface tension and organic solvents have low surface tensions.

If it proves to be difficult to get a soil deposit into solution in water, the surface tension of the water can be greatly reduced by adding small quantities of soaps or detergents. These are known as surfactants—or surface active agents—and will make hydrophobic surfaces act as hydrophilic ones. The detergent molecules will cluster around soil particles and will help to reduce the forces of adhesion between the particles and the masonry, thus aiding in their removal.

Conservators normally specify nonionic or neutral detergents or surfactants. A typical example is Triton X-100 which is manufactured by Rohm and Haas Company. This is an anhydrous liquid consisting of water soluble octylphenoxypolyethoxyethanol. A 5% aqueous solution has a pH of 6.0–8.0. At 25°C Triton X-100 is soluble in all proportions in water, toluene, xylene, trichlorethylene, ethylene glycol, ethyl ether, ethyl alcohol, isopropyl alcohol, and most other solvents. It is, however, isoluble in kerosene, mineral spirits, and VMP naptha unless a coupling agent is used. Oleic acid, for example, is an effective coupling agent in systems based on kerosene. Contact causes severe eye damage and moderate skin irritation. Inhalation of vapor is harmful and Triton X-100 is harmful if swallowed.

Similar ethylene oxide derivatives or ethoxylate sur-

factants are manufactured by Union Carbide under the trade name Tergitol.

Metallic Stains and Chelating Agents

Stains and deposits on masonry surfaces may result from the corrosion of metals or the deposition of pollu-

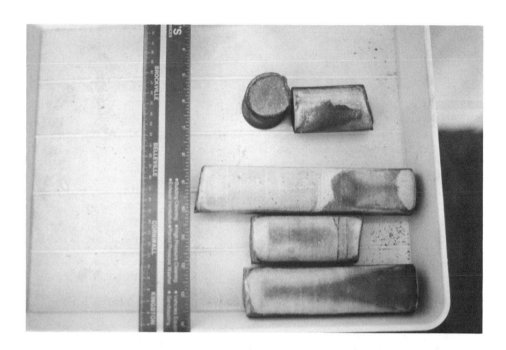

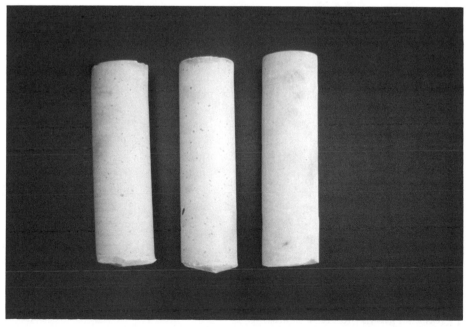

In a series of experiments, the ferric hydroxide staining on the andesite masonry of the Art Gallery of Vancouver was first matched on sample cores and was then removed by sodium dithionite poultices.

Soiling & Deposits → / Cleaning Methods & Materials ↓	Water Soluble Efflorescence: Sulfates, chlorides phosphates, nitrates soot crusts on limestones and marbles, light soiling on sandstone, brick, and terracotta	Hot Water Soluble Distemper paints, calcimine (kalsomine) paints, animal glues.	Acid Soluble Lime deposits, carbon on sandstone, granite, bricks, and terracotta.	Alkali Soluble Lime deposits, carbon on sandstone, granite, bricks, and terracotta.
Cold water washing	Yes		Yes	
Hot water washing		Yes		
Acidic cleaners (formulations of acids, surfactants and chelating agents)			Yes	
Alkali cleaners (formulations based on potassium or sodium hydroxide)				Yes
Dry ice packs or spray - on CO_2				
Hand removal with small tools or micro-abrasives			Yes	
Chelating Agents: Oxalic acid Citric acid				
E.D.T.A.				
Ortho Phosphoric acid				
Ammonia solutions				Yes
Poultices or leaching packs	Yes			
Naptha				
Lacquer solvent				
Acetone				Yes
Methylene chloride				
Paint solvent / varsol				
Ethyl alcohol				
Toluene				
Hydrogen peroxide				
Dilute aqueous sodium hypochlorite solution				
Herbicides Quaternary ammonium treatment				
Biocidal wash				
Bristle brushing	Yes	Yes	Yes	

Figure 61. Selection chart for methods compatible with substrates.

Soiling & Deposits → / Cleaning Methods & Materials ↓	Responding to physical effects in conjunction with chemicals					Metallic Stains		
	Bubble gum, chewing gum	Bituminous Products Tar	Heavy mortar and lime deposits	Ceiling tile and floor tile adhesive	Whitewash Limewash	Ferrous metals iron and steel	Copper, copper alloys: bronze, brass.	Vanadium salts
Cold water washing								Yes
Hot water washing								
Acidic cleaners (formulations of acids, surfactants and chelating agents)			Yes					
Alkali cleaners (formulations based on potassium or sodium hydroxide)								Yes
Dry ice packs or spray - on CO_2	Yes	Yes	Yes	Yes	Yes			
Hand removal with small tools or micro-abrasives			Yes		Yes			
Chelating Agents: Oxalic acid Citric acid						Yes		
E.D.T.A.						Yes	Yes	
Ortho Phosphoric acid						Yes		
Ammonia solutions							Yes	
Poultices or leaching packs		Yes						
Naptha								
Lacquer solvent								
Acetone								
Methylene chloride								
Paint solvent / varsol		Yes						
Ethyl alcohol								
Toluene								
Hydrogen peroxide								
Dilute aqueous sodium hypochlorite solution								
Herbicides Quaternary ammonium treatment								
Biocidal wash								
Bristle brushing						Yes	Yes	

Figure 62. Selection chart for methods compatible with substrates (continued).

tant metal particles from the air followed by corrosion. Such stains or deposits most usually originate from the corrosion of iron or copper and copper alloy building elements and the subsequent deposition of their corrosion products on the masonry by the runoff of rainwater. The stains may sometimes be removed by the use of leaching packs and chelating agents but long standing stains may be almost impossible to remove. Chelating agents are molecules which coordinate metal ions in two or more places. The metal ions are thus attached to the chelating agent, forming a metal complex which may be either soluble or insoluble in the solution. Since calcium and magnesium ions also coordinate with chelating agents, it is necessary to select one that is specific for the ions which are to be removed. The proper control of the solution pH is also critical to the efficient use of chelating agents.

Another major problems lies in the fact that the chelating agents do not selectively remove metallic stains which need to be removed rather than metallic "stains" which are the reason for the natural color of the stone. Ferric ions, iron oxide, or manganese colorants can be removed from say a sandstone and leave the stone with an unpleasant grayish bleached appearance.

In a typical masonry cleaning application the chelating agent ethylenediamine tetra-acetate (EDTA) might be used in a poultice with ammonium chloride and ammonium hydroxide to remove copper stains from marbles and limestones.

The general principle of removal of an iron stain is as follows:

- The stain is first reduced from the ferric to the ferrous state (from the insoluble to the soluble) by a reducing compound such as a bleach, or the "rust" may be disintegrated with potassium hexacyanoferrate.
- The iron is then removed in the soluble form by means of a chelating, complexing, or sequestering agent such as the alkali salt of an organic hydroxy

3 Soiling & Deposits / Cleaning Methods & Materials	Soluble in Organic Solvents						
	Paints				Bituminous products residues	Residues from selotape, masking tape, and scotchtape.	Chewing gum, bubble gum residues
	Alkyds and oil based paints	Graffiti spray lacquers	Latex paints	Shellac and resin varnishes			
Cold water washing							
Hot water washing							
Acidic cleaners (formulations of acids, surfactants and chelating agents)							
Alkali cleaners (formulations based on potassium or sodium hydroxide)							
Dry ice packs or spray - on CO_2							
Hand removal with small tools or micro- abrasives							
Chelating Agents: Oxalic acid Citric acid							
E.D.T.A.							
Ortho Phosphoric acid							
Ammonia solutions							
Poultices or leaching packs		Yes			Yes	Yes	Yes
Naptha							Yes
Lacquer solvent		Yes					
Acetone	Yes	Yes					
Methylene chloride	Yes		Yes				
Paint solvent / varsol					Yes		
Ethyl alcohol							
Toluene				Yes			
Hydrogen peroxide						Yes	Yes
Dilute aqueous sodium hypochlorite solution							
Herbicides Quaternary ammonium treatment							
Biocidal wash							
Bristle brushing							

Figure 63. Selection chart for methods compatible with substrates (continued).

4 Soiling & Deposits / Cleaning Methods & Materials	Biological Growths				
	Bacteria	Algae, fungi, molds, mildew	Lichens, mosses	Grasses, plants	Bird droppings
Cold water washing	Yes	Yes	Yes	Yes	Yes
Hot water washing					
Acidic cleaners (formulations of acids, surfactants and chelating agents)		Yes			Yes
Alkali cleaners (formulations based on potassium or sodium hydroxide)		Yes	Yes	Yes	
Dry ice packs or spray - on CO_2					
Hand removal with small tools or micro- abrasives					
Chelating Agents: Oxalic acid Citric acid					
E.D.T.A.					
Ortho Phosphoric acid					
Ammonia solutions		Yes			
Poultices or leaching packs	Yes	Yes			Yes
Naptha					
Lacquer solvent					
Acetone					
Methylene chloride					
Paint solvent / varsol					
Ethyl alcohol					
Toluene					
Hydrogen peroxide		Yes			
Dilute aqueous sodium hypochlorite solution	Yes	Yes			
Herbicides Quaternary ammonium treatment			Yes	Yes	
Biocidal wash	Yes				
Bristle brushing		Yes	Yes	Yes	Yes

Figure 64. Selection chart for methods compatible with substrates (continued).

carboxylic acid such as sodium citrate, sodium tartrate, or sodium gluconate; or EDTA in an alkaline solution.

An alternative approach is to remove the rust stain as a colorless soluble complex using hydrofluoric, formic, oxalic, or phosphoric acids at 5–10% concentrations; or with ammonium or sodium bifluoride. A 15% solution of sodium citrate mixed 1:1 with glycerol in a poultice or diammonium citrate may be more effective (Spry, 1982). I have removed deep rust staining and ferric hydroxide staining using a wash with a 15% sodium citrate solution followed by the use of a poultice with sodium dithionite (sodium hydrosulfite) which is one of the most powerful reducing agents known. Extreme care must be exercised when using sodium dithionite because although the salt is stable under perfectly dry conditions it is liable to become highly unstable when moist. If aqueous solutions are allowed to come into contact with flammable materials

such as textiles and are then permitted to evaporate to dryness, spontaneous combustion may occur. This material should only be used by experienced personnel under closely controlled conditions. If clothes are splashed with sodium dithionite solutions they should be immediately washed with large quantities of water.

POLLUTION CONTROLS

The conservator is increasingly finding it necessary to carefully collect all the runoff from the surfaces of a masonry building as it is being cleaned. The residues of old paints which were based on lead carbonate and the fluorides referred to above can all be collected in plywood troughs lined with polyethylene sheeting and the polluted liquid can be pumped into tanker trucks or drums for carefully controlled disposal. Acidic run off may be channeled into troughs containing lime or soda ash for neutralization. The resulting effluent may

Cleaning Method	Acid Soluble		Acid Resistant			
	Limestones, Marbles Calcareous sandstones, Sand - lime bricks.		Granites, Gabbro, Siliceous sandstones, Bricks, Andesite, Terracotta		Cementitious materials, Lime mortars, Natural cement concrete, Portland cement.	
	Soft	Hard	Soft	Hard	Soft	Hard
Washing: Pressure jet	No	Yes	No	Yes	No	Yes
Nebulous Sprays	Yes	Yes	Yes	Yes	Yes	Yes
Acidic Cleaners (formulations of acids, surfactants, chelating agents)	No	No	Yes	Yes	No	Yes
Alkalies*	Yes	Yes	Only after test application		Yes	Yes
Organic Solvents*	Yes	Yes	Yes	Yes	Yes	Yes
Poultices	Yes	Yes	Yes	Yes	Yes	Yes
Chelating Agents	Yes	Yes	Yes	Yes	Yes	Yes

*Note: Certain limestone and shales may contain organic residues of a bituminous or oily nature. Such materials should be carefully tested before using organic solvent and alkalies.

Figure 65. Selection chart for methods compatible with substrates (continued).

sometimes then be legally disposed of in a sewer. Collection and careful controlled disposal of toxic lead residues is commonly called for under many city by-laws and other pollution control legislation.

FUTURE DIRECTIONS

I am currently extremely interested in the apparently excellent performance of products such as the "Peelaway" range which combine selected chemical formulae, including low toxicity organic solvents, with poultice media and backing sheets which control or retard evaporation. These peelable paint removal systems then facilitate the safe disposal of the multiple layers of removed paint and the removal chemicals in one complete sheet. Increasingly stringent pollution controls are likely to make such systems almost indispensible.

REFERENCE

Spry, A.H. (1982). *Principles of Cleaning Masonry Materials*. Technical Bulletin 3.1, Published by the Australian Council of National Trusts.

CHAPTER 9

ARCHITECTURAL METALWORK

GENERAL INTRODUCTION

A wide range of metals have been and are used for structural and decorative purposes in architecture. Of these metals iron and steel are by far the most common, followed by aluminum, copper and copper alloys, zinc lead, and nickel. In the following parts of this chapter iron, steel, copper, and copper alloys are discussed in detail.

The more detailed discussions are prefaced by a brief introduction to the technology of metals generally. This is necessary in order to understand the behavior of metals in buildings and monuments and particularly to understand deterioration phenomena.

ORIGINS

Metals in their pure forms are elements which may be found naturally as "native" ores or may be produced by using energy in the form of high temperatures to smelt ores in which metal elements exist in compounds with other metals and substances such as silicates, sulfides, and carbonates.

CHEMICAL AND PHYSICAL DETERIORATION

Once formed, with the exception of the most noble metals such as gold, most metals undergo chemical deterioration processes or reactions with water, oxygen, and other substances in the environment in a process of reversion to a lower energy state back to the stable mineral compound or ore. This chemical process of reversion to the mineral state is normally termed "corrosion." The metal may also be referred to as having been "mineralized." The mineralized substances are referred to as "corrosion products."

Metals may also be subject to physical deterioration, the most common being a slow process of abrasion which can eventually wear the metal completely away. This physical form of deterioration is called "erosion." Other forms of physical deterioration may be related to hardening, embrittlement, and ultimate failure as a result of repeated flexing, bending, or other forms of loading or working. This is commonly referred to as "fatigue" or "work hardening." Yet another phenomenon is termed "plastic deformation under load" or more popularly "creep." In this case the metal undergoes slow deformation when subjected to loads and/or high temperatures. Lead is subject to creep. Cast lead statues therefore were typically formed with their limbs and other details modelled close to their sides, avoiding projections which would sag. Lead sheet also tends to creep down roof slopes unless detailed to avoid this problem.

Thus a sheet might commence with an even thickness but after 400 years on a steep roof slope if the sheet was too large in area to begin with, it would end up much thicker at the bottom than it was at the top.

QUALITIES AND ALLOYS

To select metals or improve metal qualities of hardness, strength, casting, and so forth to meet specific needs we may create metals by melting together a number of metals to form an "alloy." Alloys may consist

Metal Corrosion

Corrosion:

Chemical reaction of a metal with oxygen or other substances

Exposure to atmosphere, moisture, or heat, tends to revert element or pure metal to natural ores. (compounds)

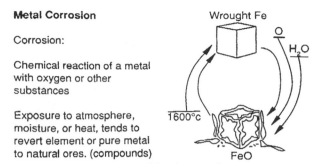

Figure 66a. Metal corrosion

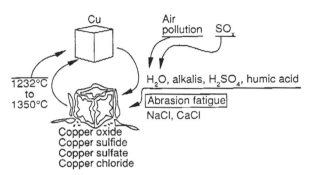

Figure 66b. Copper corrosion

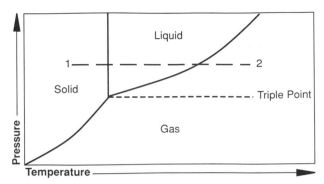

Figure 67. State of a pure metal vs. pressure and temperature.

of two elements—a binary alloy—or three—a tertiary alloy—and so forth.

To repeatedly obtain the same stable alloy which has all the desired properties and which does not rapidly corrode or fail in other ways, alloys are defined or described by means of "constitution diagrams." These diagrams plot percentage composition by weight against temperature assuming normal atmospheric pressure.

TEMPERATURE AND PRESSURE EFFECTS

Temperature and pressure control the state of "phase" in which a metal exists. Thus metals can exist as a solid, a liquid, or a vapor (gas). All common metals are solid at normal atmospheric pressure except mercury which is a liquid. All metals except arsenic change to liquid and thence to vapor as temperatures are increased. Arsenic changes directly to a vapor from a solid, a process known as "sublimation."

A "phase diagram" shows "regions" where a metal is solid, liquid or gaseous at various combinations of pressure and temperature. For a pure metal there is a certain point where all three states may coexist. This is known as the "triple point." Pure metals pass into the solid state or "freeze" at a constant temperature unlike alloys which freeze over a range of tempera-

tures. If one plots the changing freezing points of an alloy as temperature and composition are varied, the line thus produced is called the "liquidus." A line which denotes the temperatures at which freezing is complete is called the "solidus."

In the case of a binary alloy where the two descending liquidus lines intersect, an alloy of that composition freezes at a constant temperature at that point. It also has the lowest freezing point of any alloy in that system, that is to say, consisting of those two metals. Such an alloy is referred to as a "eutectic alloy." Eutectic

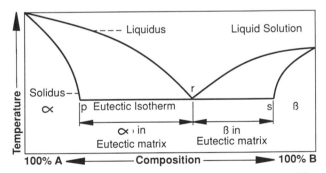

Figure 68. Constitution diagram for a binary alloy solidification: soluble in the liquid state and partly soluble in the solid state.

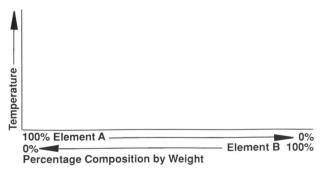

Figure 68b. Constitution diagram for a binary alloy (alloy of two elements) at atmospheric pressure.

is Greek for "most fusible." The point of intersection of the liquidus lines is called the "eutectic point." A "phase" is defined as a portion of matter which is homogeneous in the sense that its smallest adjacent parts are indistinguishable from one another, for example, solid copper is a phase. A solid solution of copper in nickel is another phase. A mechanical mixture of lead and copper represents two phases, for example, lead-coated copper as opposed to a lead/copper alloy. The number of phases that may be present in a given alloy is predictable if the alloy is in "equilibrium" with its environment at a certain temperature and pressure. Equilibrium is considered a dynamic condition of balance between atomic movements in which the resultant is zero. As we have noted, alloys are described by means of constitution diagrams or phase diagrams. These diagrams may also be called "equilibrium diagrams" because they show the combinations of temperature and pressure where a given alloy is in equilibrium.

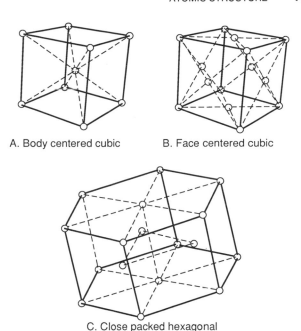

A. Body centered cubic   B. Face centered cubic

C. Close packed hexagonal

Figure 69. Metal crystal forms: unit cell structures.

ATOMIC STRUCTURE

When a metal is in a liquid state, atoms continuously enter and leave its surface creating a vapor pressure over the surface if the atoms leaving exceed those entering. When the temperature is raised to a point at which the vapor pressure exceeds atmospheric, then the passage of atoms from the surface produces a mechanical agitation of the surface known as "boiling." The arrangement of atoms within a liquid metal is random and changing.

As a liquid metal cools the motion of the atoms becomes slower and slower until the freezing point is reached.

In the solid metal the atoms are held together by the electrostatic attraction between the positive ions of the nucleus and the negative ions of the electron cloud. Since these forces are stronger in some directons than others, the atoms arrange themselves in geometric patterns or structures characteristic of the metal. Such structures are called "space lattices." Space lattices are formed by three-dimensional nets of straight lines which intersect. They divide space into equal prisms called "unit cells." Every intersection in the lattice and in the unit cell has an identical grouping of other lattice intersections about it. These intersections may be positions for atoms in the metal or they may be points about which more than one atom are clustered. There are 14 types of space lattices but the structures of most common metals follow one of three types. These three are "body centered cubic," for example, iron;

"face centered cubic," for example, copper; and "simple hexagonal," for example, zinc.

A crystal of metal normally contains many, possibly millions of unit cells located side by side and extending in all directions. As a cast metal cools from the liquid state, freezing occurs at the outside first and solidification proceeds toward the center. The crystals which form are commonly called "grains." In fast cooling grains grow from nuclei along the walls of the mold. The grains are long in directions perpendicular to the walls of the mold. If the mold has square corners, planes of weakness are produced where the long grains grown from adjacent faces intersect. The long grains are called "columnar grains." The weakness is caused by the failure of crystals to complete their space lattices where one group growing from one side meet the group growing from the adjacent side. All the grain

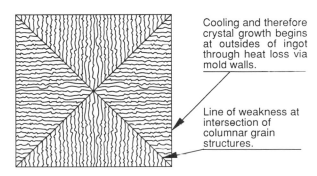

Cooling and therefore crystal growth begins at outsides of ingot through heat loss via mold walls.

Line of weakness at intersection of columnar grain structures.

Figure 70. Cross section of copper ingot showing columnar grains.

Sketch of typical dendrite which would be interlocked with hundreds of similar structures.

Figure 71. Dendrite structures.

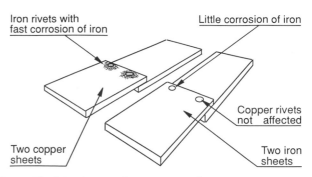

Iron rivets with fast corrosion of iron

Little corrosion of iron

Copper rivets not affected

Two copper sheets

Two iron sheets

Figure 73. Metal corrosion: same environment, same exposure time.

boundaries then align in planes causing a weakness in that plane.

If the heat is removed uniformly from all of the mass of liquid metal, "equiaxed grains" are formed. Nuclei are formed throughout the melt without special grain alignment. Grains tend to be the same size and are of nearly equal dimensions in all the principal directions, that is, "equiaxed."

A structure known as a "dendrite" or "dendritic structure" may occur in cast metals within both equiaxed and columnar grains. It occurs to some degree in most castings because of preferred directional growth. Such growth is a natural characteristic of metals since it is easier to add atoms to the unit cells in certain planes than in others.

The more rapid growth in the preferred directions results in the formation of a skeletal crystal system called a dendrite. The gaps between the skeletal ribs fill later with cooling melt. The freezing of the melt in the interstices is associated with contraction of the melt and this can lead to regions of microporosity being formed. Any impurities present may also tend to freeze around the outline of the dendrites. This phenomenon is known as "dendritic segregation" and is common in alloys. Microporosity and dendritic segregation tend to lead to somewhat reduced ductility in cast metal compared with the same metal treated thermally and mechanically for highest ductility.

Galvanic Corrosion:

An electrochemical action between two different metals in contact either directly or via electrolyte. They form a couple and there is a flow of electrons.

Galvanic corrosion will occur only if:

1. Two different metals have a potential difference and do not polarize rapidly.

2. There is contact so that electrons can flow.

3. There is an electrolyte so that ions can go into solution and travel from one metal to the other.

If the area of the more noble metal is very large compared with the baser metal, corrosion will be more severe.

Figure 74. Metal corrosion terminology

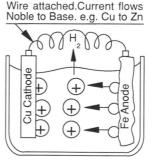
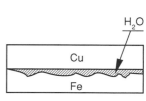

Wire attached. Current flows Noble to Base. e.g. Cu to Zn

Figure 75. Metal corrosion: galvanic series.

If metals are in contact then the metal nearest to the top of tables at right will act as the anode and will be consumed by corrosion.

Metals nearer the bottom of the tables will act as the cathode and will be protected. Metal from anode may plate on to metal of cathode.

Loss of positive ions from anode means metal becomes slightly negatively charged. More noble metal has a smaller tendency to ionize. (lose ions or become negatively charged)

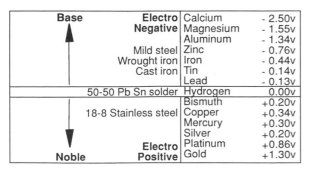

Base	Electro Negative		
		Calcium	- 2.50v
		Magnesium	- 1.55v
		Aluminum	- 1.34v
Mild steel		Zinc	- 0.76v
Wrought iron		Iron	- 0.44v
Cast iron		Tin	- 0.14v
		Lead	- 0.13v
50-50 Pb Sn solder		Hydrogen	0.00v
		Bismuth	+0.20v
18-8 Stainless steel		Copper	+0.34v
		Mercury	+0.30v
		Silver	+0.20v
	Electro	Platinum	+0.86v
Noble	Positive	Gold	+1.30v

Figure 72. Electromotive series.

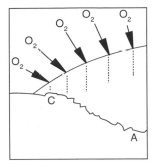

Oxygen transported faster via thin membrane than thick, thus area C becomes cathode and area A anode. Rust then builds up between C and A but does not interfere with reaction.

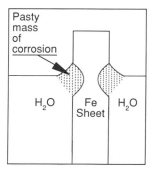

Immersed Fe sheet corrodes at water line. Pasty mass forms at water line with dark brown membrane on top.

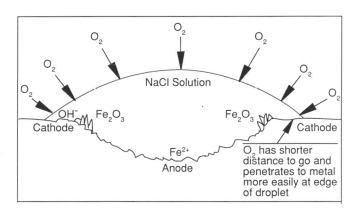

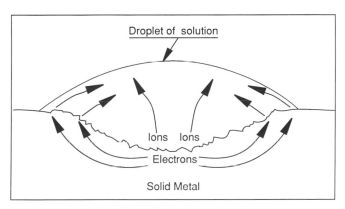

Figure 76. Metal corrosion: differential aeration.

GALVANIC CORROSION

Metals are customarily arranged according to their positions in what is known as the "electromotive series." The series of metals with hydrogen included, is arranged in the order of their electrode potentials. The series represents the order in which metals replace one another from their salts, rising from strongly reactive and relatively unstable metals with negative charges via zero up to highly stable metals with strong positive charges. Those high in the series replace those lower down. In the case of the architectural metals aluminum is at the bottom of the series with a charge of -1.34 V. Hydrogen is neutral at 0.00 V and gold is at the top of the series at $+1.30$ V.

The negatively charged metals are referred to as "base metals" while the high positively charged metals are referred to as "noble metals." If positively charged metals are exposed in contact either via an electrolyte or conductive solution with negatively charged metals then the former will act as an anode and corrode. This is called "galvanic corrosion." If one metal is higher than another on the series and the difference in potential is sufficiently large then galvanic corrosion may occur in the lower metal. There are three basic requirements for galvanic corrosion to occur.

Differences in electrical potential can occur on the

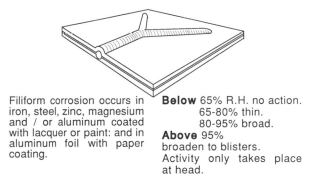

Filiform corrosion occurs in iron, steel, zinc, magnesium and / or aluminum coated with lacquer or paint: and in aluminum foil with paper coating.

Below 65% R.H. no action.
65-80% thin.
80-95% broad.
Above 95% broaden to blisters. Activity only takes place at head.

Figure 77a. Filiform corrosion

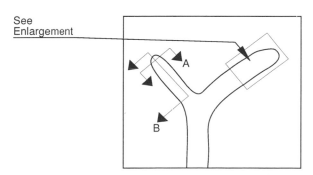

Figure 77b. Filiform corrosion: key plan.

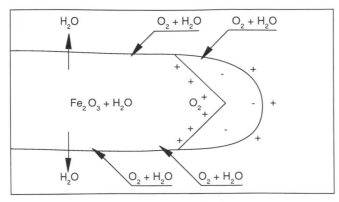

Figure 78. Plan view enlargement of tail or body.

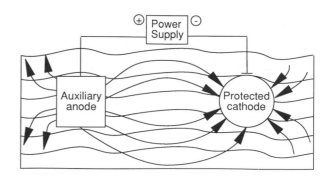

surface of one metal where by means of "differential aeration," more oxygen can reach one part than another. If this occurs in a moist or wet environment the difference in surface charges can result in an electron flow through the metal and an ion loss through the water or electrolyte on the surface. If the requisite conditions occur on a metal surface under a semi-permeable membrane the result may be "filiform corrosion" (Lat. filum: a thread; hence threadlike).

Humphrey Davy in 1824 described how zinc anodes could be used to protect copper hull sheathing.

Two forms of cathodic protection exist:

1. Power impressed.

2. Sacrificial anodes.

Sacrificial anodes are usually aluminum, zinc, or magnesium.

For calculation of weight of anodes required etc. see Shrier, L.L. (ED.) Corrosion Vol. 2. Corrosion control II : 30 Newnes - Butterworths. London Boston. 1979.

Figure 80. Cathodic protection: power impressed.

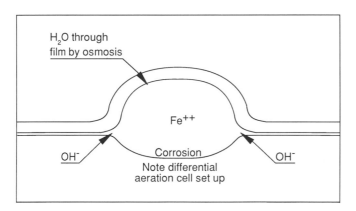

Figure 79a. Filiform corrosion: section A.

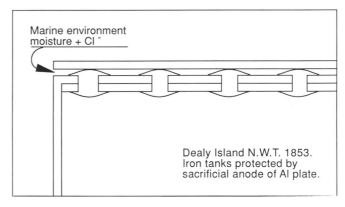

Dealy Island N.W.T. 1853. Iron tanks protected by sacrificial anode of Al plate.

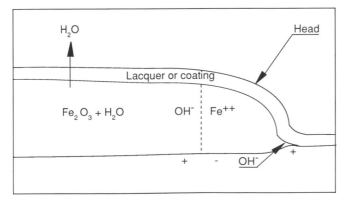

Figure 79b. Filiform corrosion: section B.

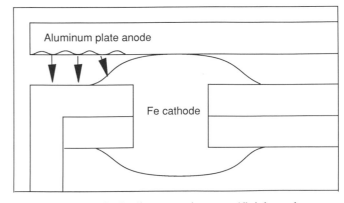

Figure 81. Cathodic protection: sacrificial anodes.

CATHODIC PROTECTION

In 1824 Humphrey Davy discovered that copper sheathing on ships' hulls could be protected from corrosion in seawater by zinc anodes. At first electrodes of zinc and later of aluminum, zinc, and magnesium alloys were used as sacrificial anodes to protect slightly more noble metals such as iron and steel.

In this way a steel bridge or an iron ship can be protected by making them into cathodes and connecting them electrically with good conductors to blocks of, say, an aluminum/magnesium alloy which then corrode preferentially as anodes. Two systems of cathodic protection can be employed. Sacrifical anodes may be simply connected to the cathodes as has been described.

An alternative which may be more efficient, is a "power impressed" system where an auxilliary anode is connected to a secondary DC power source and a current then flows from the anode to the cathode ensuring that ions always flow toward the protected cathode rather than away from it. Thus with no ion loss, corrosion is minimized if not eradicated.

FORMS OF CORROSION

As metals corrode they may progressively form films, layers, and then crusts of corrosion products. In an ideal situation the films or layers of corrosion products which form initially are even in thickness and distribution and are stable. Their stability can then protect the metal against further corrosion in normal environments. Such a form is referred to as "uniform corrosion." It would also be called a "patina," a term used for any desirable, stable, protective, and even attractive surface layer. In the corrosion of aluminum, a stable layer of aluminum oxide is formed which then tends to protect the metal against further corrosion. This layer is termed a "passivating layer."

Where the corrosion is not evenly distributed across the surface of the metal but instead occurs in comparatively deep holes which sink into the surface, this is termed "pitting." Electrochemical corrosion centering on impurities in metals frequently results in pitting such as can be seen in cross section.

"Selective corrosion" occurs when one metal is selectively removed from a alloy in corrosive conditions. Dezincification, the selective removal of zinc from brass, is the classic example of this type.

"Stress corrosion" is another form which occurs particularly where metals are under stress and exposed to localized corrosive environments. Examples of this type include brasses and bronzes under strain in ammo-

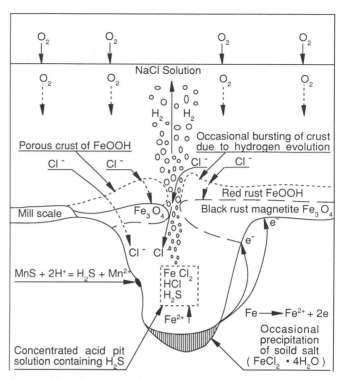

Figure 82. Electrochemical reactions in carbon steel when a pit is initiated at a sulphide inclusion. (After Wranglen, G., *Corros. Sci.* 14, 331, 1974).

nia solutions. The worst corrosion occurs in the most heavily stressed area.

IRON AND STEEL

In a pure form iron is a gray, relatively soft metal. It is tough, malleable, ductile, high in tensile strength, and can be magnetised.

Iron does not occur in the pure form in architectural uses but is found as cast iron, wrought (or rolled) iron, or steel. Cast iron is manufactured in two principal forms as gray cast iron or as white cast iron. Both are alloys of iron and carbon with silicon and traces of sulfur, phosphorus, and manganese. Their actual iron contents range from 90.42% to 92.335%. Gray cast iron melts at 1100°C (2012°F) and white cast iron melts at 1050°C (1922°F). The carbon occurs as microscopic flakes of graphite in a matrix of pearlite. Of all forms of iron, cast iron has the highest carbon content, usually averaging about 3.15–3.56%.

Wrought iron in contrast, in its most finished state, has a very low carbon content ranging from about 0.226 to 0.030%. In older buildings wrought iron is found either as hand wrought iron or as rolled iron.

From late in the eighteenth century wrought iron was heated to red heat and squeezed between profiled rollers to produce in "rolled iron" the forerunners of the structural steel members which are so familiar to us today. Wrought iron contains 99.59–99.95% iron, possibly as much as 0.109% silicon, and traces of phosphorus and sulfur. The silicon occurs as iron silicate in fine grayish lines known as slag lines which show up clearly in polished and etched cross sections of wrought iron. Wrought iron melts at 2732°F (1500°C) but below this temperature it takes on a pasty condition in which it can be readily welded, more readily than any other form or alloy of iron.

Steel, the last alloy is by far the most common. Steel is an alloy of iron and carbon with not more than 2% carbon.

The following list gives the carbon contents for various steels:

Low carbon steel up to	0.02% carbon
Mild steel	0.25% carbon
Medium carbon steel	0.25–0.45% carbon
High carbon steel	0.45–2.0% carbon

Steels may also be alloyed with or contain traces of any of the following: phosphorus, sulfur, manganese, nickel, silicon, aluminum, copper, titanium, and molybdenum. The presence of these other metals may be beneficial in that they can produce corrosion resistance, increase hardness or toughness, or other useful characteristics. All of the steels require differing degrees of heat treatment and mechanical working to attain their appropriate properties. Impurities such as sulfide inclusions, however, typically cause corrosion problems.

The Corrosion of Iron and Iron Alloys

Ever since prehistoric times when iron was first discovered in the Middle East and in China, it has confronted its users with a major problem. The metal iron corrodes if it is exposed to oxygen and water. There is a considerable difference between the corrosion of cast iron, wrought iron, and mild steel—the first being the least easily corroded, wrought iron being more easily corroded, and mild steel being the most easily corroded.

But here we are getting ahead of ourselves in talking about the corrosion of these different metals before we discuss their nature. It has already been noted that if they are unprotected, iron and iron alloys corrode or oxidize rapidly on exposure to moisture and air. At a relative humidity of 65% corrosion will be initiated but if acid precipitation, air pollution, or salt are present, much lower humidity levels may be sufficient for corro-

Late nineteenth century wrought iron "dog" spike from an industrial heritage site on a North Pacific beach below high water mark. The iron has been almost completely mineralized by the chlorides in the seawater, exposure to differential aeration, and galvanic corrosion because of the presence of other more noble metals in the water. Note the brittle layers of different corrosion products including black magnetite.

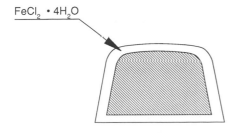

Iron corroded e.g. from burial in ground

Figure 83a. Iron corrosion.

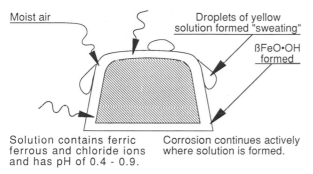

Moist air

Droplets of yellow
solution formed "sweating"

ßFeO•OH
formed

Solution contains ferric
ferrous and chloride ions
and has pH of 0.4 - 0.9.

Corrosion continues actively
where solution is formed.

Figure 83b. Corroded iron + H$_2$O.

sion to be initiated: some authorities say as low as 20% relative humidity. Oxidation processes or rusting, as they are commonly termed, involve a chemical reaction in which oxygen combines with the iron to form ferric or ferrous oxides. This initial reaction is followed by hydration processes forming hydrated ferric oxides, hydroxides, and ferric oxyhydroxides. The latter complex compounds are identified by Greek letters. Alpha is the yellow ochre colored goethite. Gamma is the bright orange red lepidocrocite. Beta is the dark red brown akaganeite. If other pollutants such as chlorides, carbonates, or sulfur are present these may react with the iron to form such corrosion products as ferric chloride, ferric oxychloride, or iron sulfide.

Red rust is usually the mineral hematite and black rust is usually the mineral magnetite. These are both oxides of iron but contain differing amounts of oxygen. Severely corroded iron which has been buried in the soil may contain the corrosion product ferrous chloride tetrahydrate.

If the corroded iron is then exposed to moist air, akaganeite is formed with droplets of a yellow solution on the surface. The formation of these very acidic droplets of hydrochloric acid (they have a pH of 0.4–0.9) is sometimes referred to as "sweating." Such corrosion is highly unstable and will continue actively wherever the solution is formed. The slag lines in wrought iron tend to retard corrosion and thus wrought iron will corrode less severely than say mild steel in the same environment. However, in seriously polluted environments corroding wrought iron may actually delaminate along the edges of the slag lines.

I am currently working on a midnineteenth century church where wrought iron cramps in stonework have in many cases corroded so badly that they have fallen apart into a series of thin layers which are defined by

Wrought iron 18th century anchor showing slag lines, Newport, Rhode Island.

A mid-nineteenth century wrought iron gate at Newport, Rhode Island corrodes in the salt sea air and the diagonal brace delaminates along the slag lines.

the slag lines. Cast iron usually forms a scale surface corrosion but is then fairly resistant to further corrosion.

However, in cases where cast iron is immersed in seawater or acid rain for prolonged periods a serious form of galvanic or electrochemical corrosion will occur. In such cases the graphite flakes in the cast iron act as cathodes and the pearlite matrix acts as an anode. As the process proceeds the pearlite is corroded away to a point where all that remains is a brittle black

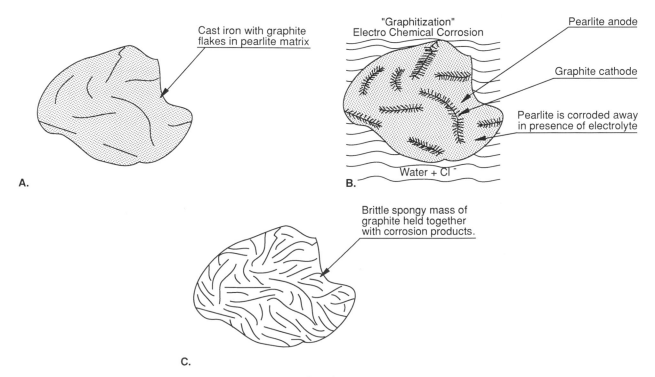

Figure 84. Cast iron corrosion.

spongy mass of graphite held together with corrosion products. The object retains its external shape and appearance but becomes much weaker and may even collapse.

Manufacturing or casting flaws in cast iron are sometimes mistaken for corrosion. Casting flaws usually take the form of bubbles, air holes, or even inclusions of moulding material or cinders. Cracks may be present as a result of stresses induced by uneven cooling or as a result of flaws caused by the cooling of the surface of the molten metal during poor or interrupted pouring. The latter defects are known as "cold shuts." Some of these flaws may subsequently become corrosion sites.

All of the ferrous metals which have been discussed above are subject to severe corrosion in the following environments: seawater; salt sea air; acids; soils, particularly soils containing chlorides or sulfates; gypsum plaster; magnesium oxychloride cements; ashes and clinkers; and many sulfur compounds.

Galvanic corrosion of ferrous metals will occur in the presence of water, metal impurities, and the following more noble metals: copper; brass; cupro nickel; bronze; aluminum bronzes; gun metal; lead; soft solder; stainless steel and chromium.

The corrosion of iron and steel and the formation of corrosion products involve a substantial increase in volume which may in turn result in the shattering of hollow cast-ironwork or the splitting or shattering of masonry in which the metal is embedded. In urban environments in Northeast America with long-range acid precipitation and local pollution, expanding iron and steel have caused and are causing millions of dollars worth of damage.

Removing or Stabilizing Corrosion Products and Conserving Iron and Steel

Having examined the nature of iron and its principal alloys and having seen how corrosion affects them, we may now proceed to see how corrosion products can be removed, stabilized, or chemically converted into new compounds which are stable and which will not damage the metal. Iron and steel structural and decorative work as opposed to thin sheet material may have corrosion removed from them by abrasive blasting in a jet of air.

Sandblasting is an appropriate treatment for removing corrosion products and defective paint residues from cast iron providing the cast iron is not excessively thin. Careful tests should be carried out to determine effective pressures, particle sizes, particle types, and working distances, that is, the distance between the nozzle and the surface being cleaned. It is sound practice to start with comparatively low pressures and fine particle sizes, for example, 200 p.s.i. and 70–100 mesh

This mid-nineteenth century wrought iron tank was buried in the ruins of a building for more than 60 years. The resulting corrosion has been so serious that in many areas there are only brittle layers of corrosion products left. The rivets and sheeting in this area proved to be intact under heavy scale.

Hollow cast iron ornaments shattered by the corrosion of the central railing, Governor General's Residence, Ottawa, Ontario.

may be obtained by using so-called soft abrasives such as crushed walnut shells at pressures as low as 30 psi (e.g., Shellblast AD68 from Agrashell, Inc. Los Angeles).

Other methods for the removal of corrosion products and paint include hand preparation, mechanical cleaning, flame cleaning, and acid pickling. None of these methods is fully satisfactory. Hand preparation involves the use of steel wire brushes, scaling hammers, and scrapers. Although the "cleaned surface" may appear to be clean the method is very inefficient and always leaves some rust, scale, and other undesirable residues in the pitted surface. Such techniques may also lead to scratching and scouring of original surfaces. Mechanical preparation with steel wire rotating brushes or even needle guns will produce better results

Sandblasting tests for the removal of paint and corrosion products from cast iron railings, Governor General's Residence, Ottawa, Ontario.

particles. Although silica sand may be used, good results may be obtained with crushed slag, for example, copper slag. If paint residues are also being removed great care should be taken to ensure that operatives are not exposed to highly toxic dusts from old lead-based paints.

It may even be wise to use a wet blasting technique in which the nozzle has independent controls for air, water, and abrasive. The fine spray from the "wet head" wets the potentially harmful lead dusts and knocks them down to be flushed away. Unfortunately the use of water sprays may lead to an increased risk of "flash" rusting occurring before the newly cleaned surface can be given a coat of primer. Wrought iron may often be too soft for some of the more aggressive abrasive cleaning treatments but successful results but undesirable residues are still left in pits and crevices.

Flame cleaning consists of using an oxyacetylene or oxypropane torch to heat the surface of the corroded metal. As the corrosion products are heated they expand at a different rate to the metal beneath and are detached. It is regarded as the most appropriate method for the cleaning of wrought iron but care should be taken when working on very thin wrought iron which may warp in the heat. Appropriate masks may be necessary for operatives to avoid risk of inhaling toxic lead vapor from old paint residues. Flame cleaning may also be used to remove "flash rusting" and to dry out areas of ironwork prior to the application of primers.

It is probably true to say that more ironwork corrodes because of paint and coating failures than for any other reason. It is also essential to note that there is no point in applying conventional primers and paint systems over unstabilized rust because the entire system will fail. The bond between the primer and the metal is the most critical since if this fails then the rest of the system, no matter how high the quality of the coatings, will fall off with the primer.

Some specialists prefer to "pickle" old ironwork by immersion in warm, dilute acids such as phosphoric acid. Not only will this result in removal of mill scale and corrosion products generally but the cleaned surface is given a protective layer of ferric phosphate. The problem with this treatment is that it requires the ironwork to be taken down from the building for the pickling to be carried out in a works. Commercially available "rust removers" which can be used without taking the ironwork off the building are usually based on phosphoric acid with an additive to provide a thick gel or paste so that the rust remover clings to vertical or overhanging surfaces. Additives include polymethyl cellulose and synthetic waxes.

REPAINTING

Once the decision is made to repaint a cleaned surface, it must be carefully checked to establish that it is free of rust, dust, oil, or grease, and that it is dry. It is then advisable to select a complete paint system from one manufacturer. All major paint manufacturers recommend specific combinations or systems of primers and finishing coats for specific substrates in specific environments. It is wise to use the entire system to avoid risks of incompatibility between coats.

Recommended primers include red lead if it is still available and its use is permitted, zinc phosphate, zinc chromate, or zinc dust primer. Since it is almost impos-

sible to avoid having pinholes in a single coat of primer it is well worth using two coats of primer. In fact this may well extend the life of the whole paint system which, as has been noted, relies on the primer for adhesion to the substrate. Some authorities note that zinc may react with most oil-based paints forming soluble salts under the film which can lead to embrittlement and loss of adhesion. Reputable manufacturers have designed their paint systems to avoid this risk.

It is strongly recommended that electrostatic paint deposition systems be used to ensure economic and highly efficient application. In my experience many failures of paint jobs on iron and steel occur because of poor or incomplete coverage and poor or improper surface preparation.

Other Methods of Approaching Corrosion Problems

Having considered the techniques of corrosion removal and repainting it is worth noting that there are now some interesting other possibilities which do not involve the removal of the unstable corrosion products but their conversion into stable compounds. The possibilities are:

1. The use of orthophosphoric acid-based rust converters to convert iron oxides into iron phosphates. The latter are gray-colored stable corrosion products.
2. The use of tannic acid-based rust converters which convert the iron oxides and other corrosion products into complex organo metallic compounds which include iron tannates.

There are two types of tannic acid-based rust converters currently on the market. One type consists of tannic acid, a small quantity of orthophosphoric acid, and a wetting agent with an organic solvent. The second type includes the above ingredients plus a synthetic resin in suspension. The resulting iron tannate compounds are blue black in color. The products which do not include the resin have the advantage that they can be applied again and again to react with any remaining or newly appeared corrosion products. Their pot lives and shelf lives are almost indefinite, they are of low toxicity and flammability, and their costs are not inflated by the high costs of the resins.

The resin suspension type products, of which Neutrarust is typical, are white or cream colored initially but react with corrosion products to form the familiar blue black iron tannate. Their pot lives and shelf lives may be limited by the life of the resin, they are more expensive because of the resin, and the coating of resin

Tannic acid-based corrosion conversion system used on iron hatch cover from the Royal Navy's 1901 Holland No. 1 Submarine after 69 years under the sea.

16th Century wrought iron strong box treated with corrosion converter based on tannic acid and a vinyl acetate copolymer.

may prevent subsequent retreatments from reacting with the corrosion products. All the tannic acid-based products produce a stable layer which should then be covered with a normal paint system. At the time that this book is being prepared the Canadian Conservation Institute in Ottawa is nearing the end of a long period of outdoor testing of a number of corrosion converters available in North America. Readers are encouraged to write and obtain data when they are released.

3. The use of silicate-based corrosion inhibitors which promote the silicate catalyzed formation of basic iron salts which convert into the stable compounds goethite and magnetite, and which restore the alkali conditions necessary for the continued stability and corrosion resistance of steel reinforcement in concrete and of steel stanchions in concrete casings. A typical product is manufactured in West Germany by the BAGRAT-Hans JAKLIN Company.

I have examined laboratory research reports on successful stabilization work which was carried out on corroded structural steel members embedded in masonry walls in an early twentieth century factory in West Germany.

The alkali silicate system was injected into shattered brickwork and concrete work. It is believed that not only were the masonry products stabilized but so were the corroding steel members. The stabilized steel has a shiny brown appearance but there is no apparent staining of the exterior surfaces of the masonry. The technique has had some success in applications in Canada.

Black staining is a possible problem associated with the use of the tannic acid-based products. These products will convert ferric and ferrous oxides into tannates no matter where they are and this may result in black tannates being formed in or on masonry surfaces. These tannates are relatively insoluble and may prove to be very difficult to remove.

All three of these conversion systems are designed to be protected by a normal paint or coating system of two coats of primer and finish coats.

A final group of possible solutions involves the use of acid pickling followed by electroplating or hot dipping. Late in the nineteenth century architects like Louis Sullivan frequently had cast ironwork electroplated with copper and even nickel on copper. Copper plating is still an attractive option and is much more resistant to corrosion than the zinc which is so frequently used. Zinc coatings can be a constant problem in polluted environments where they will corrode and form corrosion products which will lead to repeated paint failures. Traditional coatings for ferrous metals also included tin, lead, and Terne Alloy which is an alloy of 80% lead and 20% tin.

With today's long-range atmospheric pollution cou-

Acid precipitation and pollution from a nearby steelworks soaked into masonry in which this iron beam was embedded. The resulting corrosion was so serious that it could have led to structural collapse.

pled with urban pollution the lives of these traditional finishes may be more limited but they may still be used to provide authentic and good looking soft gray weathered finishes.

SHEET COPPERWORK

Copper like gold is one of the unusual metals which can be found in "native" or pure metallic form in nature. Conveniently found native copper was the first metal used by prehistoric peoples in many different parts of the world.

Copper is a beautiful and highly durable metal and will withstand corrosion to a remarkable degree even in some polluted environments. The earliest large-scale uses of copper occurred in Asia Minor where copper was first smelted in the fifth millenium B.C. In ancient China copper alloys reached superb quality by the Shang Dynasty (1523–1028 B.C).

Native copper was used by the ancient peoples of North America. A spearhead hammered out from native copper possibly 5000 years ago, was found on Allumette Island in the Ottawa River, Canada.

In ancient Europe copper was produced in a number of centers particularly in England, Wales, Italy, and Spain. Copper ore was mined and the metal worked extensively by the Romans in all of these locations. A considerable development of metallurgy in the Roman Empire was associated with the growth of the industry.

In 1566 extensive copper deposits were discovered in Britain but by an act passed in 1568 the exploitation was limited to agents of the crown. This somewhat repressive legislation was not repealed until 1689. Even with this restriction an extensive copper industry grew with major centers of production in Wales and Cornwall.

From the seventeenth century one of the greatest and longest continuing producers of copper has been at Røros in central Norway close to the Swedish border. This historic industrial center is now conserved as a World Heritage Site.

Traditionally copper sheet was produced by first smelting the ore and casting ingots. The ingots were annealed and then beaten with huge mechanical or "tilt" hammers powered by water wheels. The sheets thus produced were then cut with water-powered shears. The beating or "battery" of sheet copper began to be replaced by machine rolling from early in the eighteenth century. Subsequent eighteenth century developments included drawing processes which made it possible to form complicated profiles; and a machine which could stamp patterns and designs into copper

sheet. For decorative copper work the ancient hand technique of repousse, in which complicated relief is hammered out from the back of the sheet, has continued from the earliest times to today. Relatively thin copper sheets have been used for roofing purposes since Ancient Greece. The Parthenon in Athens is believed to have been roofed with copper shingles (Toner, 1988). In Germany and Scandinavia there are twelfth and thirteenth century roofs finished with copper sheets approximately one meter square. These sheets are joined together with standing seams at their sides and with double lock cross welts for the horizontal joints. An early example of sheet copper roofing on the Chapel of St. James's Palace in London has sheets 6 ft by 2 ft and 6 in. (1.8 m × 750 mm). These sheets were also joined together with standing seams and double lock cross welts.

In Philadelphia in 1795 the new Bank of the United States had its roof finished with copper sheets which were specified to be 4 ft by 2 ft and to weigh 8 lbs. It is interesting to note that this means that the copper weighed 1 lb or 16 oz/ft^2. This is still the standard weight for roofing. When the building was restored in 1974–1975 some of the copper was found still in position. The joints were formed as standing seams with single lock cross welts. The seams were folded over copper cleats which were nailed down with two cast-copper nails (Sweetser, 1977).

Only after the 1870s when improved rolling methods made it possible to roll thin uniform sheets did the standing seam cease to be the standard method. Unfortunately the wooden "conical roll," a wood batten of triangular cross section, jointing method which was used from this date through to the 1930s led to many practical difficulties at junctions. In more recent years many of these roofs have been found to have cracking at abutments and drips.

The so-called common roll system where the cooper was dressed up to a flat topped batten and covered with a separate copper cap strip was first used in the late nineteenth century but became very popular after the 1950s when the failures of conical roll systems were becoming only too apparent.

Copper as a Material

Freshly formed, uncorroded copper is a shiny pink metal, which is relatively soft and extremely ductile. Electrolytic copper, Industrial Alloy No. 110, which has a 99.90% minimum copper content, has a melting point of 1981°F (1083°C) and a density of 0.321–0.323 lb/in.^{3} at 68°F. The specific gravity is 8.89–8.94 and the modulus of elasticity 17,000,000 psi. The shear strength is 25,000 psi. The tensile strength is 36,000 psi but the yield strength (0.5% of extension under load) is 28,000 psi.

One of the most important characteristics of copper is its high coefficient of linear thermal expansion which means that the detailing of copper and sheet sizes must be designed to take this into account or the copper sheet will buckle and tear. The actual coefficient for Copper 110 is 0.0000098 meaning that a piece of copper 10 ft long when heated 100°F will become 10 ft + $0.0000098 \times 10 \times 100 = 10.0098$ ft long.

Copper is said to "work harden" which means that it becomes harder and slightly more brittle as it is worked by being rolled, drawn, or hammered. It can be returned to a softer condition by annealing, which is basically heating the metal to a certain temperature and holding it there for a time and then cooling it. Simple annealing will of course not restore copper which has become fatigued and has developed microcracking. Cracked or fissured copper would have to be nearly molten to restore it to a homogeneous state.

These characteristics of "work hardening" and associated embrittlement can cause cracking if the sizes of sheets are too large or if the gauge is too thin. A typical roof is usually fabricated with sheet copper weighing 16 oz/ft² in sheets 20 in. wide by 96 or 120 in. long with the standing seams $16\frac{3}{4}$ in. on centers.

If 20-oz copper is used the sheet sizes may be increased up to 24 in. wide by 96 or 120 in. long with the standing seams at $20\frac{3}{4}$ in. on centers. If the copper is to be lead-coated the 20-oz sheet should be used because the heat associated with the lead-coating process reduces the temper of the cold rolled sheet.

A sheet which is cut to the correct length and dressed up at the edges to form seams is termed a "pan."

Sheets which are too large or do not have joints which permit movement will eventually harden and crack from the effects of continuous flexure or bending back and forth. Large thin sheets which vibrate in strong winds may also suffer from the same phenomenon. The latter occurs most commonly on the lee slope of roofs where a wind blowing across the ridge will cause the formation of a negative pressure. The large thin sheets are consequently sucked outward then released in repeated cycles until the copper hardens and cracks. This type of failure is revealed by star shaped fractures and may also occur at gable ends and at just above eaves' level where negative loading can also occur.

If the copper is restrained frequently enough no large expansion can occur at any one point and thus buckling will be avoided. As a general principle it is best not to perforate copper sheet roofing with nails but to fix it by folding the vertical or longitudinal sheet edges around short strips of sheet copper which are

Star fractures caused by fatigue in copper sheet roofing, City Hall, Montreal. The sheets are too thin, too large, and vibrate in strong winds.

themselves nailed down to the roof beneath. These strips which are termed cleats are then covered and protected by the roofing sheet. In this way no holes are exposed to water penetration. Cleats are normally cut from the same sheet which is being fixed and are 2 in. wide by 3 in. long. They are fixed at 12 in. on center with two copper nails. A half inch strip of the end of the cleat is folded back over the nail heads. The free end is then folded into the seam or folded edge of the sheet. The weight of the sheet is directly related to the thickness of the sheet or its gauge. This means that there are in fact three ways of describing a sheet of copper.

The following table gives all the comparable figures for the seven weights of sheet currently manufactured in North America. (This and other data in this section are derived from the excellent booklet; Anon. *Copper Brass Bronze Design Handbook: Sheet Copper Applications*, produced by the Copper Development Associates Inc, Greenwich Office Park 2 Box 1840 Greenwich, CT 06836-1840. No date.)

Thickness or Gauge

Weight/ft² (oz)	Thickness (in.)		Nearest Gauge No. B & S
	Nominal	Minimum	
32	0.0431	0.0405	17
24	0.0323	0.0295	20
20	0.0270	0.0245	21
16	0.0216	0.0190	23
12	0.0162	0.0143	26
10	0.0135	0.0115	27
8	0.0108	0.0090	29

Sixteen-ounce copper sheet is used for a wide range of roofing and flashings. Expansion joints, lead coated copper sheets, gravel stops, hung and molded gutters, louver slats, and scuppers are commonly formed of 20-oz copper. The thickest, 32-oz copper, is usually reserved for built-in box gutters, edge strips, and sculptures.

In my experience the size of the sheet and the gauge or thickness are often the most critical features affecting the longevity of the roof. A close second to these as a potential cause of failure is the surface upon which the copper is laid. Copper sheet should be laid upon a stable substrate which is dry and smooth. The substrate should not be corrosive to the copper and should not stick to it. Typical failures which I have seen, have occurred where the copper has been laid directly onto rough concrete which has caused perforations at sharp high points, or on wooden boards which have cupped so that the copper has eventually torn over a series of upturned sharp board edges.

In another case a very large overhanging copper sheet covered cornice was constructed over a steel frame with galvanized steel sheet stiffening webs for the curved molding profiles. Acid precipitation penetrated into the interior and the steelwork and the zinc were in some places totally destroyed.

A good surface preparation consists typically of smooth wooden boarding with nail heads driven just below the surface, covered with a layer of asphalt impregnated roofing felt, then a layer of rosin-sized unsaturated building paper to prevent the felt sticking to the

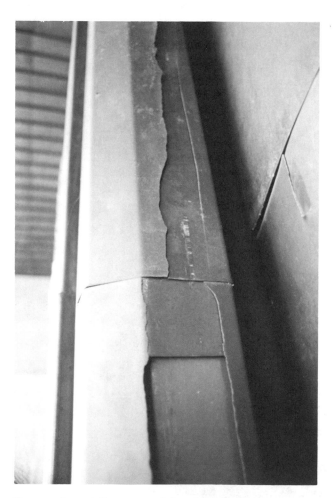

Copper sheet failure caused by differential expansion between rigidly secured copper and steel structural frame, Monument to the Enlighteners, Bakovski Tomb, Kotel, Bulgaria.

Copper cleats being used in the restoration of the copper sheet cornice of the 1913–23 Bell Telephone Exchange, Montreal Street, Montreal. Note the C.C.A. treated timber substructure.

Copper sheet roof on the East Block, Parliament Buildings, Ottawa. This old roof is failing because there are no proper underlays of felt or building paper and the boards beneath are cupping and tearing the copper.

1923 Montreal Bell Telephone Exchange copper cornice; note severe corrosion and poor repairs with steel nails and screws which have suffered from galvanic corrosion.

underside of the copper. The felt should weight not less than 15 lb/100 ft^2 and the paper approximately 6 lb/100 ft^2.

The softness of copper also exposes the metal to a risk of abrasion and erosion. The hardness of copper on the Rockwell F Scale is 60 (minimum) and on the Rockwell T Scale 25 (minimum). Copper sheetwork should not be detailed so that it receives constant concentrated streams of water or drips falling onto it from a height. Under these conditions, the water and waterborne dust or grit particles will erode the copper and will ultimately perforate the sheet. Constant rubbing by loose cables, ropes, and antennae, and excessive handling and abrasion from foot traffic will also seriously erode copper.

Corrosion Products and Patinas

Of all the metals commonly used in architecture, copper lies the highest on the electromotive or galvanic series. To understand the degrees of severity of corrosion which may be associated with galvanic action, the architectural metals are arranged in order starting with aluminum which has the highest negative charge and proceeding toward neutrality and thence to the higher positive charges. After aluminum which is the least durable, in ascending order of durability come zinc, steel, iron, tin, lead, and then copper. If any or all of this series of metals are exposed with copper in electrical contact with one another and linked by water or an electrolyte formed by salts dissolved in water, galvanic corrosion will occur and the aluminum will be the most severely corroded, followed by the other metals in slowly diminishing degrees. When exposed to the atmosphere copper forms thin layers of corrosion products. The nature, color and thickness of the corrosion product layers depend upon the gaseous and particulate matter present in the atmosphere either naturally or from anthropogenic or manmade sources. The speed and severity of the corrosion processes also depend upon relative humidity and the time during which the surface remains wet. Generally speaking higher humidities and longer times of wetness result in worse corrosion.

The colored layer of corrosion products is called a patina especially when the layer is stable and the color is thought to be attractive. The term patina is derived from the Roman copper or bronze dishes or patens which were often found in later periods with green crusts on them. When fresh copper is exposed to an outdoor environment it will change from its fresh metallic salmon pink to a dull brown in about three weeks or so. This shade then turns black or brownish black in rural unpolluted environments. In Edmonton, Alberta, for example, the 1915 copper roof of the Hotel Macdonald still retained some of the brown black color

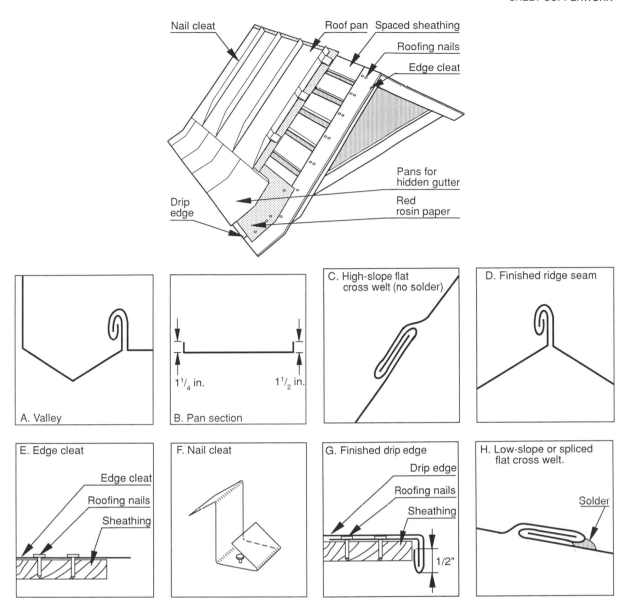

Figure 85. Metal roof details.

when the writer inspected it in the late 1980s. However, we are more familiar with outdoor copper finishes which turn green, greenish-blue, or bluish-green. Graedel et al. in a 1987 article published in the journal *Corrosion Science* discuss how in the eastern United States, whereas in 1890 it took about 20 years for the green patina to form, by 1960 it took only 8 years. They also quote similar data from Denmark where in Copenhagen it took 20–30 years for the green patina to form on copper roofs in the 1930s but dropped to 8 years in the 1960s (Graedel et al., 1987).

Chemically the first layers to form are cuprite or copper oxide which is brown. The black layer which forms next is copper sulfide. The slow transformation from black to green represents a chemical change from sulfide and oxides to sulfates. The sulfates may be blue or green or any combination of the two colors. One of the most common green colored sulfates, brochantite (pronounced broshantight), is a mixed sulfate–hydroxide salt of copper. The unstable salt antlerite is also a mixed sulfate–hydroxide salt of copper. Research in the 1930s showed that during the corrosion process which converts the sulfides, antlerite forms first and is followed by brochantite. Antlerite has been found in the blackish areas of the copper skin of the Statue of Liberty.

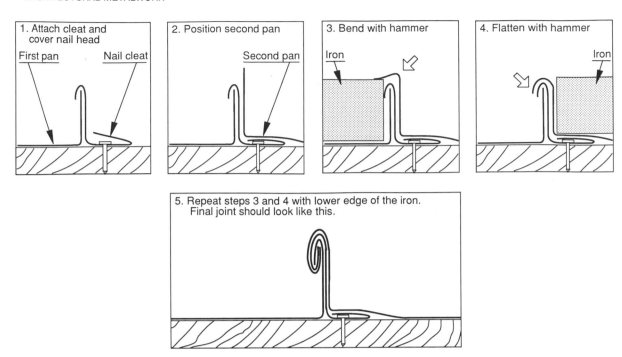

Figure 86. Turning a standing deam.

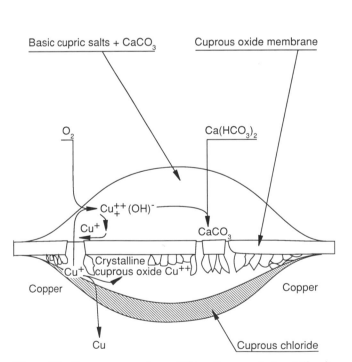

Figure 87. Copper corrosion: pitting of copper in hard (lime) water; a complete process. (After Lucey, V. F., *Br. Corros. J.* 2, 175, 1967).

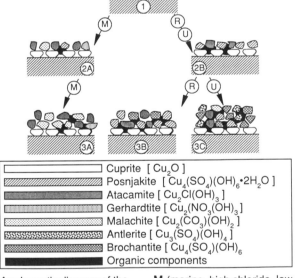

A schematic diagram of the processes involved in the growth of copper patinas. Individual crystals for the different minerals are shown. The letters on the arrows refer to the type of atmosphere within which patina formation occurs:

M (marine, high chloride, low acidity and reduced and oxidized sulfur), **R** (remote land, moderate acidity, chloride, and reduced and oxidized sulfur), **U** (urban, moderate chloride and reduced sulfur, high acidity and oxidized sulfur).

Figure 88. Copper patina growth.

Nielsen, among others, has suggested that the conversion of brochantite to antlerite is triggered by acid rain but Graedel et al. suggest that this is not the case and that the two crystalline salts probably form independently as a result of localized corrosion differences (Graedel et al., 1987). A third and final sulfate found in patinas is a hydrated basic sulfate known as posnjakite.

In marine environments, cities where chloride-based deicing salts are used, and in other locations where hydrochloric acid and other chlorine-based pollutants are present, then the basic copper chlorides atacamite and paratacamite may be found. Atacamite is soluble in weak acids and for this reason does not form a stable patina. It used to be thought that malachite, the beautiful green colored copper carbonate mineral which in its natural form has been used as a semiprecious stone, could be found as a major component of patinas. It has more recently been found to be either absent entirely from outdoor patinas or present as a minor trace only. The reason for this may be its solubility in acid precipitation. It is however known from indoor patinas. The similarly beautiful mixed salt of copper carbonate and copper hydroxide, blue azurite, has been reported as an ingredient of patinas.

Other corrosion products which may be less commonly found include the emerald green colored basic copper nitrate, gerhardtite, which may be found in outdoor and indoor patinas; green copper acetate known as verdigris; and copper oxalate. Copper oxalate which is gray in color has been identified by Italian research-

ers on the bronze Horses of Saint Mark's and is thought to be linked to chemical reactions with pigeon guano (Marchesini and Badan, 1977).

On some copper roofs and other sheet copper work small black spots may also be found on otherwise light green areas of corrosion products. The spots are usually less than one-eighth of an inch in diameter and are very hard and adhere well to the surface. Graedel et al. (1987) note that these spots contain phosphates, but also note that no rigorous analytical studies have been performed on them. Research at Columbia University has confirmed in 1992 that the black spots are copper sulfide.

Causes of Sheet Copper Corrosion Reviewed

As may be gathered from the corrosion products described above, they are directly related to the substances to which the copper is exposed and to complex combinations of other factors particularly including time of wetness. In moist air the copper oxidizes to form reddish brown cuprite. With moisture, carbon dioxide, carbonic acid, and/or carbonate dusts, copper carbonates and oxyhydroxides such as green malachite and blue azurite are formed. With moisture, sulfur dioxide, sulfur trioxide, and/or sulfuric acid, green brochantite is formed. In moist conditions with hydrogen sulfide, copper sulfides are formed such as black chalcocite. With moisture and chlorides, hydrochloric acid, or other chlorine compounds, copper chlorides

Copper sheet roofing on the right has been corroded by contact with organic acids from bituminous roofing compound. East Block, Parliament Buildings, Ottawa, Ontario.

Copper sheet flashing corroded by hydrofluoric acid-based masonry cleaning compound. Sun Life Assurance Building, Montreal.

and oxyhydroxides such as green nantokite and dark green atacamite are formed.

Copper may also be attacked by acidic runoff from some lichens and from new cedar, oak, some pine, and redwood shingles. Certain types of bituminous materials contain organic acids which will attack copper and leave it etched a brilliant metallic pink. Copper is attacked by alkalis ranging from fresh mortar and concrete, to ammonia and sodium and potassium hydroxide solutions which may be used for cleaning masonry.

Copper sheet roofing failing where nail heads have abraded through from underside. Repeated patching does not eliminate this problem on the Whittier Mansion, San Francisco.

Copper sheet cornice restored with Irish seams to permit thermal movement. Bell Telephone Exchange, Montreal.

Steel and ironwork should not generally be placed over copper work on roofs and in other exposed positions because the iron corrosion products will severely stain the copper rust color, dark brown, and even black.

Repairs

Copper sheet which has failed by buckling and cracking may simply be cut out and replaced but if the sheets were too large, too thin, or were fixed in such a way that they were not free to move, then these problems must be corrected. Too wide sheets, for example, can be cut apart down their centers and have a strip of new sheet inserted between the old sheets and attached to their longitudinal edges with folded seams. Similarly, large thin sheets which have vibrated or drummed until they developed star cracks can also have the affected areas cut out and a new strip folded in.

Fatigued or work-hardened areas may be reannealed but the temperature required for annealing is well above the ignition point of wooden boards, felt, and other roofing materials. For safety reasons it is normal for the copper to be taken off the roofs of historic buildings for annealing so that no fire risk is involved.

Some failures of copper sheet roof coverings may be due to secondary causes such as the corrosion of steel nails improperly used for securing cleats or the sheet itself; or the deterioration of wooden boarding substrates through fungal or insect attack or nail corro-

sion. Inspections of old copper roofs should locate any perforations of the sheet by nails which might be causing leaks. Other failures may be the result of the original copper sheet being unable to move or moving too much because it was improperly secured. Because of the geometrical problems involved in fabricating the end joints in complex cornice moulding profiles, the ends often tend to be improperly secured or may even be not secured at all. In such cases the lengths of sheet mouldings can start to vibrate and become looser and looser until they are torn off in the wind. This problem can be corrected by using so-called Irish seams at the ends. In such cases, the ends of the adjacent sheets are each folded back, usually half an inch, and a broad cover sheet strip is applied over them and folded and locked over the ends.

BRONZES AND COPPER ALLOYS

In recent years all over North America fine bronze statues and architectural bronzework have been severely damaged or even practically destroyed by well-intentioned but totally misguided attempts at cleaning or restoration. The average architect, property owner, or contractor may know virtually nothing about bronzes and their care. Good reference books and articles on this subject are not easily accessible and unfortunately many of them do not reflect the latest knowledge on the subject. Some even include methods which may actually harm the bronzes. The following section is an attempt to make the whole field less of a mystery and in so doing help to ensure that more of these great resources are preserved for posterity.

The Materials

As soon as we refer to "bronzes" we enter a world of confusion. Designers, manufacturers, artists, and contractors frequently use the same terms to describe totally different materials. The first point which all usually recognize is that bronzes are copper alloys. The first bronzes were an alloy of copper and tin. The actual proportions may vary considerably.

The bronzes of the ancient Greek horses of St Mark's in Venice have copper contents of 94.4–97.2% and tin contents of 1.2–3.6%. These famous bronzes also contain 1.0–1.7% lead and a trace of iron. Other early and more recent bronzes may contain 80–90% copper and 10–20% tin. It is probable that ancient man discovered by accident that a small amount of lead in the alloy greatly improved its casting qualities. Although at first lead may simply have been present in the copper and tin ores we can be sure that before long lead was being added on purpose. Today we have the following cast bronze alloy compositions among a host of others which contain other elements such as zinc, phosphorus, aluminum, and/or manganese.

Cast Bronze Alloys

Name	Copper (%)	Tin (%)	Lead (%)	Zinc (%)
Bronze alloy A	80.5	19		
Bronze alloy B	83.5	16		
Bronze alloy C	80.0	10	9.5	
Bronze alloy D	87.5	10		2

Data from H. Leidheiser, *The Corrosion of Copper, Tin and Alloys.* New York: Wiley, 1971.

In modern trade terminology "statuary bronze" contains 97% copper, 2% tin, and 1% zinc, while "architectural bronze" contains 57% copper, 40% zinc, and 3% lead. The high zinc content means that the latter is really a brass rather than a bronze. Brasses with lead added to them for improvements in casting qualities are referred to as "leaded brasses." Alloys of copper and zinc are known as brasses. The zinc concentration is typically in the range of 10–40%. A range of typical brasses is given below with their Industry Alloy Numbers. In North America a new Unified Numbering System has been adopted to identify metals in an orderly manner and to avoid confusion with names. In this new system for example, the old Industry Alloy No. 836 is redesignated C83600.[1]

Brasses

Brass Name	Industry Alloy No.	Cu (%)	Zn (%)	Pb (%)	Sn (%)	As (%)
Red brass	230	85	15			
Low brass	240	80	20			
Yellow brass	268	65	35			
Cartridge brass	260	70	30			
Medium leaded brass	340	65	34	1		
High leaded brass	342	65	33	2		
Admiralty brass	443	71	28		1	0.1*
Naval brass	464	60	39.25		0.75	

* Admiralty brass may contain 0.1% max. of arsenic or antimony.

Other historic "bronzes" include gunmetal and bell metal. In these two alloys there was always a struggle to achieve a balance between ease of casting, strength, less brittleness, and in the case of the bell metal, a pleasant sound when struck. Historic "brass" guns were actually cast in a bronze consisting of 88% copper, 10% tin, and 2% zinc (English Admiralty specification of the nineteenth century). Other gunmetal alloys were commonly used for bearings in nineteenth century and later steam engines, locomotives, and other engines. These bearing alloys might include more zinc and possibly lead. As an example of historic bell metal, the famous Liberty Bell contains 70% copper and 25–30% tin. This combination produced a potentially brittle metal but gave the best ring. Bells were occasionally melted down to make cannons but such ordnance was notorious for bursting when being fired.

There are four other groups of alloys which are sometimes described as bronzes. These are phosphor bronzes, aluminum bronzes, silicon bronzes, and cupro nickel or nickel silver alloys. Phosphor bronzes are used where combinations of strength, low brittleness, high ductility, and wear resistance are called for, for example, pumps, propellors, pinions, gears, and bearings for hardened steel shafts. Phosphor bronzes

---

[1] Readers who wish to have complete listings of all alloys with all numbering systems should refer to the most recent publications of the Canadian Copper and Brass Development Association and the Copper Development Association Inc. of the USA; e.g., *Copper and Copper Alloy Castings*, Publication No. 13, CCBDA. The numbering systems include: Industry Alloy Numbers; ASTM Numbers; SAE Numbers; AMS Numbers; US Federal Numbers, and US Military Numbers.

are often described by their tin contents, that is, 1.25% tin, 5% tin, or 8% tin.

Phosphor Bronzes

Industry Alloy No.	Sn (%)	Cu (%)	P (%)
502	1.25	98.7	0.05
510	5.0	94.75	0.25
521	8.0	91.75	0.25

Aluminum bronze might be typified by Industry Alloy No 612 which is 92% copper and 8% aluminum. Such bronzes may be hardened by heat treatments and are used for heavily loaded gears in machine tools and construction machinery. Silicon bronzes may have 97–98.5% copper and 1.5–3% silicon.

The silicon bronzes have the good general corrosion resistance of copper but can also be cast, rolled, spun, forged, or pressed. Common uses are for tanks, boilers, and stoves.

Cupro-nickel consists of 70% copper and 30% nickel (Industry Alloy No. 715). This alloy has excellent corrosion resistance and is used for tubing in oil fields and for marine condensers. Nickel silver is a very confusing term because the alloys contain no silver. Although these are white metals they may occasionally be slightly discolored green in highly corrosive environments. They may thus be mistaken for bronzes. Nickel silver has been extensively used for architectural decoration, ornamental metal grilles, food-handling equipment, tableware, and plated jewelery. It has good corrosion resistance and fairly high electrical resistivity.

"Nickel Silver" Alloys

Industry Alloy No.	Ni (%)	Cu (%)	Zn (%)
745	10	65	25
752	18	65	17
770	18	55	27

One further alloy which has been used for casting decorative architectural metalwork such as doors and panels is the beautiful Monel metal. Monel is perhaps the most important of the commercial nickel alloys which is produced by smelting a single natural ore and only removing impurities. All Monel alloys are extremely resistant to corrosion. These natural ores and hence the alloys contain roughly 68–72% nickel and 28–32% copper. Although Monel looks rather like stainless steel, it may have a greenish tint from the copper.

Durability and the History of Bronzes

Bronzes are generally resistant to corrosion and historically this has always been one of the most attractive features of these alloys and a major reason for their selection and use.

The ancient Chinese were arguably the master bronze workers of ancient times. Chinese history traditionally begins in a year corresponding to 2852 A.B. with the Age of the Five Rulers, but it is from the Shang or Yin Dynasty (1766–1122 or 1027 A.B. that we have a great mass of ancient Chinese ritual bronzes. Bronze was selected for its known durability. These vessels and furniture for sacrifices to gods and ancestors were buried with the rulers and notables of the period. It was from their tombs that later Chinese treasure hunters looted the bronzes with their gorgeous blue, green, and red patinas. The patinas are in fact the result of corrosion processes advancing infinitely slowly in the ancient tombs. The Chinese and subsequently collectors and museums all over the world came to treasure the bronzes not just for themselves and their age value but for the beauty of their stable patina—or "patina nobile" as the Italians term it. Artists and craftsmen may not only have admired a fine patina but they may have designed a work to have a certain patina and color. When we work with existing bronzes we must always take this into account and protect or carefully restore such surface finishes. In the growth of Western Civilization the Bronze Age had begun all over the Near East by 5500 years ago. The first uses were almost certainly in the highlands of Turkey and Iran where copper and tin ores occurred together. As in the East, bronze was treasured for its durability.

Most cultures have turned to bronze whenever there was a requirement for a durable material to commemorate deities, rulers, or other revered subjects for posterity. Sculptors in Ancient Greece and Rome produced some of the finest bronzes ever to leave a foundry. In Renaissance Europe bronze sculptures and superb architectural ornament were among the greatest creations of this period. Again and again in the seventeenth, eighteenth, and nineteenth centuries bronze sculpture and ornament enjoyed their own renaissances as artists and craftsworkers rediscovered the attractive qualities of bronzes. In the twentieth century stronger and more highly corrosion-resistant bronzes and related alloys have been added to the more traditional formulae.

Bronze Corrosion

Bronze like copper is highly resistant to corrosion in unpolluted environments. Even in twentieth century acid rain and urban air pollution bronzes can be among the most durable metals available to us. In outdoor

Severe corrosion in 1908 bronze lamp standard with green brochantite and black copper sulfide, Columbia University Campus, New York.

exposures bronze will form somewhat protective patinas following initial reactions with oxygen and sulfur compounds in the environment. In northeastern North American urban environments bronzes form first brown copper oxide then black copper sulfide and ultimately green or blue-green copper carbonate and copper sulfate. In seriously polluted environments where heavy local urban and industrial pollution combine with long range pollution in the form of acid precipitation, the black brown surfaces blacken further as dirt, dust, and carbon particles adhere to them combining with the copper sulfide. Areas of copper sulfide may react with acidic rainwater to form blue-green copper sulfate. This in turn may dissolve in acid rain and get redeposited as a green stain on light colored masonry surfaces beneath.

In all cases prolonged periods of moisture retention on the surface tend to lead to more severe corrosion damage.

Otherwise protective patinas may be attacked by acid precipitation and be made porous. The damaged patina can then act like a sponge holding harmful acidic moisture against the surface of the bronze. If patinas form slowly and evenly they can provide long lasting protection but if they form unevenly, have porous permeable areas, or are partially dissolved by acid rain or by contact with bird droppings, then the bronze beneath may suffer from selective corrosion and deep pitting will occur. Some alloys are particularly prone to the selective removal of one or more component metals in moist acidic conditions. Brasses and aluminum bronzes may suffer dezincification and dealuminification or the selective removal of zinc or aluminum in extremely corrosive conditions.

The great bronze doors of the Baptistry of Florence, Italy which were the work of the Renaissance master Ghiberti were intensively studied after they were found to be seriously corroded. It was noted that the protective patina had reacted with such pollutants as sulfur dioxide to become more soluble and porous. As acidic precipitation washed away parts of the patina it became more fragile and broke off more easily.

In all such cases where surface patinas and corrosion products become patchy, localized electrochemical corrosion is likely to occur. Typically in such cases surface corrosion may appear rapidly in the form of deep pitting and a combination of black raised patches and lower areas of light green color. Areas of bronze surface covered by black carbon-rich patches become protected cathodes and areas covered by green corrosion products such as copper sulfate become anodes. In moist acidic conditions ions are lost from the anodes and move to the cathodes. As a result, the black areas stand like islands while the green areas sink lower into the metal surface as they are corroded away. In this process the original patina and surface of the bronze are progressively destroyed. Deep pits beneath unstable patinas may also hold deposits of chlorides which will give rise to further corrosion outbreaks if they are not meticulously removed.

In summary, urban pollution and acid precipitation combine to present a serious threat to bronzes exposed outdoors. The most dangerous pollutants are oxides of sulfur and oxides of nitrogen. Acid rain which combines sulfuric acid, nitric acid, and hydrochloric acid is particularly dangerous. Additional threats may be posed by concentrations of decomposing bird droppings and other organic debris. Where dezincification of brasses is occurring not only will the zinc have been selectively removed leaving the brass with a spongy

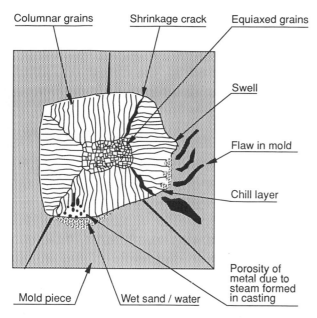

Columnar grains Shrinkage crack Equiaxed grains

Swell

Flaw in mold

Chill layer

Porosity of metal due to steam formed in casting

Mold piece Wet sand / water

Planes of weakness may result from pouring metal too hot or if mold extracts heat too quickly from the metal. Chill layer formed initially when molten metal hits cold mold.

Chill layers may be harder than the rest of the metal but may be accompanied by columnar grain formation with resultant planes of weakness.

Figure 89. Solid casting with typical flaws.

structure and an almost complete loss of tensile strength, but it may also be possible to note brilliant shiny pink patches of fresh electro-deposited copper on the surface.

Physical Deterioration of Bronzes

Physical deterioration of bronzes can take a number of different forms which can occur separately or may occur together with different forms of corrosion. The principal forms of deterioration are as follows.

Inherent Vices

These are cracks, holes, concentrations of air bubbles, inclusions of molding materials, flaws related to the crystalline structure, impurities in the alloy, inhomogeneities in the alloy (pockets of individual metals form rather than the metals being thoroughly mixed in a homogeneous alloy), and other features related to the manufacturing process. Bronzes may also be severely eroded because bronze is inherently a "soft" material. There are many cases of bronzes being worn away by no more than repeated handling by thousands of people over centuries or even decades.

Bronze statues which are easily accessible may be climbed on, sat on and otherwise abused. The 1903 "Alma Mater" by Daniel Chester French, at Columbia University, New York, is here totally buried by a group of students posing for a photograph.

Deterioration of Cores or Armatures Which Were Left in Hollow Bronzes Following the Casting Process

This problem is especially associated with the corrosion of iron or steel armatures or of "chaplets" which are pins used to support the core in a hollow bronze casting. Gray-white sulfate crusts may also form on the bronze as water moves from the remains of core material, bringing impurities out to the surface via tiny holes or cracks in the bronze. The corrosion of iron chaplet pins may cause rust staining or eventually localized splitting in the bronze.

Problems Associated with the Penetration of Water into the Interior of Hollow Bronzes

The penetration of water into the interior of hollow bronzes can lead to subsequent hidden corrosion or the freezing and expansion of the water with attendant risks of splitting the bronze. In this category can be included the formation of condensation in hollow bronzes in humid environments.

Problems of Surface Geometry and the Pooling of Water

The surface geometry of the bronze can provide pockets in which water can be trapped and where corrosion may therefore be particularly serious, or where ice expansion may cause problems. Such pockets are often most simply dealt with by drilling a drainage hole into the interior but at the same time ensuring that the interior is itself properly drained.

Structural Problems

There may be structural problems relating to the original design and the consequent inability of the structure of the bronze to support its own load or to carry wind and snow loads. Cases of problems related to thermal expansion can also be included in this group.

Cleaning and Conserving Bronzes

Following the damage done by corrosion in our polluted environments the next most serious form of damage is almost certainly that caused by ill-informed attempts at "cleaning" and the removal of corrosion products. An incredible range of chemicals and abrasives has been used indiscriminately on our valuable heritage of bronzes with serious damage occurring as a result. In New York, Washington, and Quebec,

Bronzes severely damaged by constant cleaning with mildly abrasive metal polishes; note green polish residues soiling stone surface. Royal Bank, Montreal.

bronzes have been assaulted by misguided individuals wielding sandblasting equipment and even steel wire brushes. The surfaces of the sandblasted and steel wire brushed bronzes have been reduced to pitted and scarred lunar landscapes bearing no resemblance to the original carefully chased and patinated surface. The artist and craftsworker's creations have been effectively defaced or even totally erased, and the damage is permanent.

In other cases, overzealous salespersons and woefully ignorant decision-makers have permitted epoxy resins to be used as "protective coatings" to "reduce further corrosion or to eliminate the need for costly maintenance" only to discover that the epoxy resin then commenced to change color, becoming darker and

DeMaisonneuve monument, Montreal, before cleaning and conservation. The corrosion was particularly severe because of chlorides from deicing salt and from the city water in the fountain.

darker shades of brown or even purple. When the color changes become unacceptable it is discovered that for all practical purposes it is impossible to remove the offending resin without causing further unacceptable damage to the bronze. Other bronzes have been assaulted with muriatic acid (hydrochloric acid) or battery acid (sulfuric acid), causing even more damage and leaving corrosive residues in the damaged bronze surface. Excessively hard abrasives have been used in many cases so that the bronze surface is scratched and even worn away.

It must be remembered that bronzes are relatively soft metals and that they will consequently be scratched and even lose their surfaces if materials which are harder than the bronze are used to clean them. Steel wool and steel wire brushes should never be used on bronzes. Not only will the steel scratch the surface but rust inhibitors commonly used with steel wools will cause brown stains to appear on the bronze. These stains may be extremely difficult to remove.

In approaching any outdoor bronze the conservator tries to obtain answers to a series of basic questions:

- Does the bronze really require cleaning? If so, why?
- Are there corrosion products on the surface of the bronze?

- What is the nature of the corrosion products and what is causing the corrosion? Is the cause still present?
- What was the original finish of the bronze?
- Did the artist or designer intend the bronze to be finished with a patina? If so, what was the color of the patina and how was it obtained?
- What will the bronze look like after it has been cleaned and will the client accept this appearance?
- What is the acceptable level of clean?
- Are the corrosion products occurring in patches or spots?
- Are the corrosion products stable or are they part of an active corrosion process?
- Is the surface of the bronze pitted or scratched?
- Might the bronze be damaged if no action is taken?
- Can the bronze corrosion be stabilized?
- Is the bronze physically stable?
- Is water getting trapped within the bronze or in pools on the outside of the bronze?

As a general principle the conservator adopts the treatment which will involve the least radical intervention using the gentlest possible techniques which will stop further deterioration or at least substantially re-

Winnipeg, Manitoba, bronze doors apparently damaged by thrown acid.

In some cases a lacquer coat may be protected with a cold wax coat. Many conservators today prefer to use pigmented waxes to reproduce the colors of patinated surfaces. There are a large number of chemical processes which can be used to produce artificial patinations. These processes, however, tend to be difficult to control in the field and usually employ very toxic chemicals. If the new patinas fail to adhere to the bronze surface when exposed to acidic precipitation—as many do—then the treatment may have to be repeated only to fail again. Repeated failures would of course be very costly and the bronze could well be damaged in the process. If the surface is badly corroded and pitted, a conservator with specialist experience in outdoor bronzes should direct the operations of the project. The conservator may remove thick black crusts with specially designed high-pressure water or microabrasive treatments.

Until relatively recently the latter have included glass microballoon or microbead peening. The beads are 75–125 μm in diameter and are blasted through a special pencil at as little as 30 psi or through a light duty suction gun at 80–100 psi. Alternative microabrasive treatments use crushed walnut shells, crushed corn cobs, or crushed coconut shells. A typical treatment used Agrishell medium AD 10.5-B, a graded walnut shell medium manufactured by MDC Industries of Philadelphia, at an air pressure of 20–30 psi at a working distance of 2–8 in. with an angle of impact of about 70 degrees to the surface.

Discussions between bronze conservators at the *Symposium Dialogue '89. The Conservation of Bronze Sculpture in the Outdoor Environment*, led to a general conclusion that crushed walnut shell treatments appear to give the best results. The symposium was organized by the National Association of Corrosion Engineers (1989). It was noted that peening techniques could actually "burr" bronze over the tops of pits, thus partly sealing off chlorides, for example, which could then act as centers for reemergent corrosion.

Anionic salts such as chlorides are removed from deep pits either by the use of highly localized microabrasive treatments or by means of poultices. Hard-to-remove crusts may also be removed using fine bronze wire wool or tough plastic abrasive pads with clean water or pharmaceutical mineral oil as lubricants. The conservator may also have to use carefully selected organic solvents to remove graffiti and old coatings which have failed or are discolored or peeling.

The wax coatings are used in areas where the bronze may be handled or slightly abraded by passing pedestrians. Most bronzes can be treated with a specially formulated lacquer known as Incralac. This lacquer

tard deterioration for a specific period. The gentlest possible technique may simply be to wash the bronze with clean water or even deionized water and to scrub off softened dirt with natural fibre bristle brushes. Oily or greasy residues from vehicle exhaust emissions and deposits mixed with wind-blown dust, grit, and carbon can build up to form hard-to-remove crusts. The addition of a nonionic detergent to the cleaning water, possibly plus the use of an organic solvent as a "degreaser" will usually solve this problem. The cleaned surface is then protected with a coating of a wax, a lacquer, or an oil. In excessively dusty environments clearly it could be unwise to consider the use of an oil which would remain slightly sticky and thus attract dirt.

Brown stains from steel wool remain even after cleaning this bronze test panel.

was designed specifically for the protection of copper alloys by the International Copper Research Association Inc. Incralac is based on a methyl methacrylate copolymer (an acrylic resin) with small quantities of benzotriazole (a corrosion inhibitor), ultraviolet inhibitors, plasticizers, and hardeners. Incralac is sprayed on using about 20 psi at a working distance of about 6 in. It is recommmended that Incralac should not be applied at an air temperature of lower than 60°F. Incralac is glossy but if a waxlike, less glossy finish is required, a polyethylene dispersion may be added.

Two or three coats of Incralac are necessary and

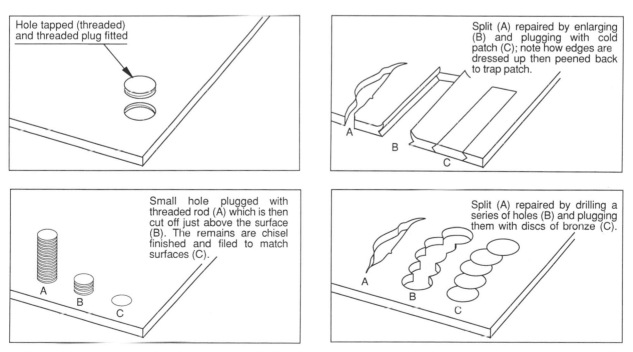

Figure 90a. Solid casting and flaws: conservation.

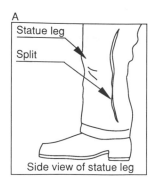 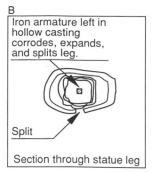 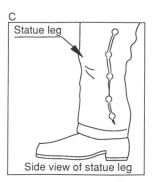 

Figure 90b. Solid casting and flaws: conservation.

Bronze statue representing Canada, by P. Hebert 1894, shows abrasion damage where people climb on her lap to be photographed.

about 20 minutes drying time is usually required between coats. The secret of successful application seems to be to keep the coats thin and not to allow any tears, dribbles, or spots to form.

Lacquer coatings may require replacement after one year of exposure in badly polluted environments, but may last three to four years in cleaner environments.

As has been noted waxes may be used by themselves hot, or over lacquers cold. The best waxes appear to be synthetic microcrystalline waxes blended with natural Carnauba wax to give a harder wax with a higher melting point than would be achieved with synthetic waxes alone. The waxes are applied by themselves as paste waxes and are usually applied to a heated bronze surface. Some conservators prefer to use a propane torch to heat the surface but others use infrared lamps.

The wax is usually applied to the bronze using a fairly stiff bristled stencil brush, taking good care not to damage the bronze with the metal ferrule of the brush. Short "jabbing" strokes are used perpendicular to the surface of the bronze. The surface is usually heated to about 380°F by means of a propane torch. The temperature drops off as soon as the torch is removed but remains high enough to keep the wax molten long enough to achieve good penetration. In comparison it takes about 30 minutes to heat a bronze surface to 224°F with a hot air gun. In the same period an infrared lamp will only heat the bronze to 180°F.

A particularly interesting wax coating has been developed in Canada. In addition to the microcrystalline waxes it also contains benzotriazole as a corrosion inhibitor. It might be noted here that benzotriazole has been identified as being a carcinogen. Since nearly all the organic solvents used in paste waxes are also toxic, this point may be somewhat academic. Normal precautions with respect to handling and disposing of these materials are of course obligatory.

Some synthetic waxes may have attractively high

Bronze doors and surround, Royal Bank, Montreal, have suffered from abrasion damage from users and over-cleaning.

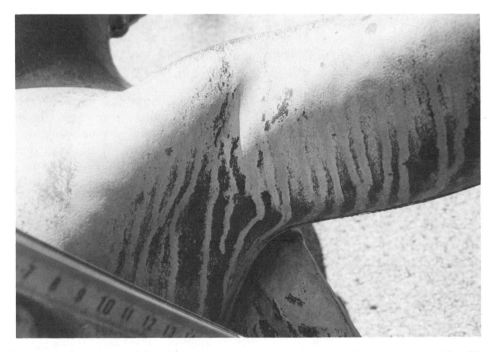

Dribble marks etched into the bronze are typical of acid precipitation damage on this 1894 statue "Canada", Ottawa, Ontario.

Extremely heavy corrosion of 1898 bronze flagpole base shows up different alloys where bronze plugs have been inserted following the removal of chaplets; Columbia University Campus, New York.

melting points which would mean that there would be no risk of them melting on hot sunny days. It is, however, worth noting that some of these waxes perform poorly at very low temperatures, crazing and detaching from the metal surface.

Bronzes which receive very high levels of handling have been successfully protected by thin coats of lemon oil or lemon grass oil mixed with high grade distillate paraffin oil (with a flash point above 350°F). A typical mix contains 5 oz lemon grass oil per gallon of paraffin. When oil is used it is recommended that once a protective film has been built up then the bronze should be oiled at least once every two weeks if it is in a heavy traffic area, for example, entrance doors. Bronzes in lighter traffic areas are oiled on a monthly basis.

In London, England, many of the bronze statues have been beautifully maintained for decades using mixtures of lanolin, paraffin, beeswax, and turpentine (a typical mix consists of 40% lanolin, 7% paraffin wax, and 53% white spirit). At least part of the success of such treatments must be ascribed to the frequency of the treatments. Easily accessible examples are cleaned off with organic solvents and the lanolin/wax treatment is repeated every three months. No examples are left longer than a year. The frequent cleaning and replace-

ment of the protective coating prevent harmful chemical buildups occurring on the surface and the water repellent coatings keep moisture away from the bronze surface, thus preventing any galvanic corrosion and other types of chemical attack.

It should be noted that with the exception of carnauba or Brazil wax, natural waxes are not generally recommended on their own because they can cause acidic reactions on the surface of the bronze if they are in place in moist environments for long periods of time.

Lanolin-based or oil coatings are similarly not recommended if there is any chance that they cannot be cleaned off and renewed at frequent intervals. Such coatings are slightly sticky and will attract dirt and metal particles which will build up on the surface of the bronze and give rise to corrosion problems.

Dealing with Physical Problems

Corroding iron or steelwork left from cores or armatures will have to be cut or drilled out and the bronze can then be repaired, usually with "cold" patching techniques. Hollow bronzes and others which tend to trap water can be drilled to provide proper drainage. Problems of a structural nature and problems caused

Before and after the waxing of "The Great God Pan," Columbia University Campus, New York. There appears to have been little if any cleaning away of corrosion products but hopefully the wax will help to prevent water and pollutants from getting at the surface of the bronzes and causing further corrosion. Unfortunately the pigeons are still leaving droppings all over the piece.

Before and after the waxing of "The Great God Pan," Columbia University Campus, New York (*continued*).

These bronze doors have been lacquered but the lacquer is failing. Selective corrosion is typically occurring along the lines of scratches and graffiti. In some areas faulty coatings are retaining moisture on the surface of the metal leading to worse corrosion (*continued on the following page*).

Lacquered bronze doors (*continued*).

Doors conserved by careful cleaning and by hot microcrystalline wax application.

by the partial or nonremoval of core material or iron chaplets may have to be solved by major "surgery" involving the removal of the bronze to a foundry or workshop where it can be cut apart to permit the removal of undesirable material and the insertion of reinforcement or repairs.

Once the repairs have been carried out the bronze can then be reassembled and the joints brazed. If the damage was extremely severe new sections of bronze may be specially cast. It is essential that the new work is cast in an alloy which exactly matches the original in composition. If an exact match is not achieved the new metal will not corrode in the same way as the original and the repair will be too obvious.

It is important to realize that while the day-to-day care and maintenance of bronzes can be comparatively easy, the cleaning, conservation, and repair of bronzes is a job for experienced conservators and craftsworkers.

REFERENCES

Graedel, T.E., Nassau, K., and Franey, J.P. (1987). Copper Patinas Formed in the Atmosphere, *Journal of Corrosion Science*, Vol. 27, 7, pp. 640 et seq.

Marchesini, L. and Badan, B. (1977). *Corrosion Phenomena on the Horses of San Marco* in *the Horses of San Marco*. Olivetti: Milan and New York. A book published in connection with the exhibition on the horses at the Metropolitan Museum of Art, New York.

National Association of Corrosion Engineers. *Symposium Dialogue '89. The Conservation of Bronze Sculpture in the Outdoor Environment.*

Sweetser, S. (1977). A Surviving Eighteenth Century Copper Roof. *Bulletin of the Association for Preservation Technology*, Vol. IX, No.2, pp. 10–15.

Toner, E.D. (1988). Traditional Copper Roofing. In Ashurst, John, and Ashurst, Nicola (eds.), *Practical Building Conservation: Vol. 4. Metals*. New York: Halsted Press, a division of John Wiley & Sons, Inc.

CHAPTER 10

PAINTS AND COATINGS

by FRANK G. MATERO

Painting, if not the chief, is as necessary a part of building as any other whatever, both for use and ornament, the doing of which well and often, being the surest way of preserving all the rest.

William Salmon, *Palladio Londinensis*, Second edition, 1738.

Architectural paints and coatings have had a long and continuous history in their use on both the interior and exterior surfaces of all types of buildings. As surface finishes, these materials provide protection as well as articulation and decoration for a broad range of traditional building materials including wood, stone, brick, plasters and stuccoes, and metals. Yet despite the aesthetic and functional significance of these materials, their historical usage and architectural relationship have been greatly compromised given their highly ephemeral nature. Easily obliterated by continual changes in taste and altered by environmental agents causing fading, darkening, and loss, architectural paints and coatings remain among the most misunderstood and misinterpreted of traditional building materials. As with other building trades, the practice of architectural painting in North America began and developed with the importation of European traditions, materials, and skilled labor during the seventeenth and eighteenth centuries. This involved the establishment of a well-developed network of manufacturers, suppliers, and retailers who provided the necessary range of raw materials and tools to the master painter and his apprentices for both the preparation and the application of paint.

By the midnineteenth century, however, technological changes led to the mass-production and marketing of "ready-mixed" paints and the establishment of large domestic manufactories and industries, thus changing the nature of the product as well as the trade. With the rapid growth of the petrochemical industry after World War II, a broader range of synthetic resin paints and related coatings became widely available. Yet despite these technological advances in the use of improved synthetic resin binders and more stable artificial pigments, and rapid mechanized production, modern architectural paints and coatings have remained remarkably unchanged in their basic formulation and use.

PAINTING MATERIALS

Paints, regardless of their usage, are composed of at least two basic components: the colorant and the medium or vehicle. These components individually and collectively determine the physical, mechanical, and chemical properties of the resulting paint systems as well as their application techniques. It is the function of the colorant to impart color, texture, and opacity or transparency to the system, while it is the role of the medium and vehicle to provide initial fluidity during application, subsequent adhesion, and durability of the film. Knowledge about the raw materials of painting and the systems they create was first discovered empirically and closely related to experiments in alchemy and medicine, and later to the science of chemistry.

PIGMENTS

Pigments (from the Latin *pigmentum*, meaning drug) are the actual coloring materials used in dry powder form to impart color and opacity to the paint. They are finely divided coloring materials which are suspended as discrete particles in the medium or vehicle in which they are used. Since antiquity pigments have been obtained from a wide variety of mineral, animal, and vegetable sources often classified as organic and inorganic. The inorganic pigments include both the naturally occurring clay earths such as yellow ocher, raw sienna, and raw umber and crushed minerals and ores such as azurite, orpiment, lapis lazuli, and hematite. These materials in turn can be further calcined or burned to extend the range of colors. In addition to these naturally occurring forms, manufactured substi-

Painting is an integral component of historic buildings and defines and articulates the architectural form according to the aesthetic and functional rules developed for a specific time and place. These restored Creole cottages in New Orleans, Louisiana, well illustrate the traditional painting practices popular in the area during the early nineteenth century.

THE PAINTER, AND THE GLAZIER.

A typical painter's shop of the early nineteenth century showing the activities of the master painter, window glazier, and lowly apprentice who continuously attended to the laborious process of mixing the paints by hand before the advent of manufactured commercial paints. [From Edward Hazen, *The Panorama of Professions and Trades or Every Man's Book,* Philadelphia: Uriah Hunt, 1839].

Spanish and American Segars.
Segar Tubes, long and short Pipes.
Corks, Dram Bottles.
Sweet scented and common Shaving Soap,
Ladies Wash Balls, Pomatum, Hair Powder.
Starch, Milk of Roses.
PAINTER's COLOURS, &c.
White Lead, Red do. Spanish Brown.
Spanish White ; spruce, stone, patent and
kings Yellow ; Yellow Oaker.
Venetian Red, Verdigrise, Prussian Blue.
Umber, Ivory black, Flake White
Drop Lake, distilled Verdigrise, Vermillion.
Rose Pink, India Ink, strewing Smalt.
Blue and green Frost, Red Chalk
Fine Copal Varnish, Spirits of Turpentine.
Turpentine Varnish, Linseed Oil, Rosin.
Putty, Chalk, American and English Glue
Deep and pale Gold Leaf per gross or dozen.
Silver and Dutch do. Gold Lackyer.
Painters Brushes.
Ground and unground Sash Tools,
Camels hair Pencils.
10 by 8, 7 by 9, 8 by 6 Glass.
Rotten Stone, Pomice Stone, Emmery.
Polishing Putty, Sandover, Spelter.
Gums for hard Varnish, Chelsea and Dutch
Lead Pots from No. 1 to 40, Crucibles.
Holland, English and American Powder.
Common and patent Shot, Lead, Flints.
A large assortment of Patent Lamps.
Best Spermaceti Oil.
Bailey's Cake blacking for Boots and Shoes.
Cephalic Snuff ; Salt of Lemons for remov-
ing iron mould from Linens, Muslins, &c.
Paper, Inkpowder, Cake Ink, Ink Pots and
Glasses, best Dutch Sealing Wax, Wafers,
Dutch Quills, black Lead Pencils.
India Rubbers, Liquid Blue.
DYING MATERIALS.
Coperas in tierces, Allum, Fustick.
Nicarague Wood, best Madder.
Ground Camwood per cask, Saunders.
Annatto Wood, Oil of Vitriol per Cary.
Blue Vitriol, Galls, Cochineal.
French, Spanish Flote and Carolina Indigo,
&c. &c.   Hartford, June 12.

ALLYN M. MATHER,
At his Store in *Windsor*, Broad-Street,

American newspaper announcement of imported painting materials from London listing the most typical supplies for the painters' trade at the end of the eighteenth century.[*The Connecticut Courant*, Hartford, July 10, 1797].

tutes such as vermilion or synthetic ultramarine were produced early on as well as other artificial pigments such as lead white, cobalt blue, and cadmium yellow to name but a few. Organic pigments, composed of carbon with oxygen, hydrogen, nitrogen, sulfur, and other elements, were traditionally derived from animal and vegetable sources producing often highly colored pigments and dyestuffs such as lamp, vine or bone black, madder, carmine, and indigo. In the latter part of the nineteenth century and well into this century, coal-tar synthetic colorants such as mauve and alizarin offered less expensive, more stable substitutes for the natural organic compounds. Other colorants such as dyes are soluble organic chemical compounds derived from natural sources as well as through modern synthesis which form true solutions.

Sometimes used directly in a paint vehicle, dyes are more frequently transformed into paint pigments called lakes or lake colors (from the word *lac/lacca* -a natural organic red dyestuff from India) by precipitating them directly onto inert carriers such as aluminum hydrate or calcium sulfate.

In addition to color, hiding power, and tinting strength, pigments possess other properties such as light-fastness, sensitivity to pH, as affected for example, by the acidity or alkalinity of the media or substrate, miscibility with other pigments, dispersion and wetting with the media, consistency of the paint through vehicle absorption, and the drying effect on unsaturated oils as observed with pigments containing lead, cobalt, and manganese. All these properties have been exploited to various degrees in the selection and continued use of specific pigments for specific situations throughout time.

THE VEHICLE OR MEDIUM

The medium or vehicle is usually the liquid component of the paint system which acts as the carrier of the pigment allowing it to be applied to the surface and in most cases, except for true fresco, to contain the binding material thus giving the paint its cohesive and adhesive film-forming properties. The medium is also responsible for a number of other properties including color, viscosity, pigment absorption, consistency or plasticity, shrinkage and tension, elasticity, and reversibility. The medium itself is often composed of two separate components: the binder or nonvolatile portion and the solvent or volatile portion. The solvent aids in the initial application and penetration of the system and later evaporates during film formation such as in the case of the evaporation of water from glue distemper paint or mineral spirits from oil base paints.

Most paints are generally classified by their medium either in terms of the vehicle, as in water- or oil-based; or of the binder, such as casein, oil, or synthetic resin-based paints. Many natural substances derived from animal, plant, and mineral sources have been used as binders for traditional paints. The majority of these have been replaced in recent years with modern synthetic film-forming resins such as alkyds, vinyls, epoxies, and urethanes. Regardless of their source or method of production, most binders, natural or synthetic, are classed as either aqueous or nonaqueous. The most commonly found aqueous binders for traditional architectural paints are proteinaceous

Two replication panels of traditional glue distemper limewashes and a glazed Prussian blue and white lead oil paint prepared from original period recipes and materials.

glues—gelatin in the pure form—obtained from the boiling and filtering of collagen from the skin, bones, tendons, and cartilage of mammals and fish; casein, a phosphoprotein prepared from skim milk; and to a lesser extent, plant gums, mucilaginous solutions of complex organic acids and calcium, magnesium, and potassium. Soluble mineral silicates such as sodium silicate (waterglass) and potassium silicate have also been used as inorganic aqueous binders, especially well-suited for exterior masonry surfaces. Nonaqueous binders have long been used for architectural painting because of their durability and water-repellent properties. The most commonly employed of these are vegetable drying oils derived from seeds such as linseed from flax and from nuts such as walnut. These oils possess the ability to form a solid, elastic film when exposed to the air in thin layers. Other oils such as fish oil, when combined with driers such as red lead, were often used as an inexpensive substitute. Plant and tree resins and exudates such as balsam, copal, and insect shellac were used alone or in combination with pigments or dyes to create hard protective varnish coatings often reserved for fine woods or as glazes over paints by dissolving them in distillates such as spirits of turpentine or heated oils. In addition, plant and animal waxes and coal and pine tars ("pitch") were used as hydrophobic vehicles for paints and waterproof coatings. With the increasing development of synthetic polymer resins after World War I, a large variety of highly specific paints and coatings have become available replacing the majority of the traditional binder systems. Alkyd resins, first introduced commercially in 1928, are one of the most widely used synthetic substitutes for linseed oil-based paints because of their faster drying time, better color retention, durability, and low cost. They are often combined in varying ratios with traditional oils creating long-, medium-, and short-oil alkyd paints, thus combining the best properties of both binders. Of the numerous high-performance solvent resins now available, two-part epoxide resins, first introduced in 1950, are perhaps the best known and widely used commercially for their excellent chemical and abrasion resistance and adhesion to wide variety of substrates. In addition to these, polyurethanes, used alone or in combination with epoxide resins, chlorinated rubber resins, and phenolic resins for metals and especially aluminum are now in common usage.

With increasing concern regarding the toxicity of the organic solvent component of these systems, and the restrictions regulating their use, waterborne epoxy and moisture-cured urethane paints have been developed as alternative high-performance systems. Perhaps the most important of the water-based synthetic resin systems to be used commercially for house painting are the so called "latex paints." First commercially marketed in 1948, these water-based latex emulsions quickly replaced the less durable glue-based distemper paints used for interior painting. The styrenebutadiene resin first used to create these emulsion paints has now been replaced by polyvinyl acetate and acrylic resins for better hardness, flexibility, gloss-retention, and permeability. Other ingredients, termed additives, account for the third and smallest class of components; yet these materials can impart a broad range of useful properties when employed as emulsifiers, extenders, wetting agents, driers, pigment suspension aids, preservatives, biocides, and freeze/thaw stabilizers. Sometimes, such properties can be imparted by the pigments selected such as Paris Green, a highly toxic copper aceto-arsenate pigment, used in the early nineteenth century for its brilliant color as well as for its biocidal qualities as a preservative paint for exterior wooden elements. Other pigments such as chalk, barytes, or China clay are still frequently added to extend or adulterate the body of the paint, often making it less expensive.

PAINT SYSTEMS

Regardless of the raw materials employed, all architectural paints are prepared by grinding or mixing the pigment and medium together into a paste or liquid. Originally done by hand using a slab and muller, this laborious process was eventually mechanized for increased production and consistency of product. Depending on the medium selected, all architectural paints and coatings can be classified into four categories or systems based on the mechanism of film formation and can be briefly define as follows.

1. Solidification by crystal formation. Unlike the other paint systems, this system does not employ an organic resin to create a film but rather relies on the curing of the substrate such as the carbonation of the lime (CaOH) substrate in true fresco or of a reactive component in the paint such as the formation of calcium silicates in cementitious paints.

2. Solidification by solvent loss. Film formation occurs by the application of a resin solution—be it natural or synthetic, aqueous or nonaqueous—and then the evaporation of the solvent leaving a hardened resin-pigment film behind. Paints formed exclusively by this process such as glue distempers can usually be reactivated by the application of the solvent.

3. Solidification by cross-linking. Related to solvent-based systems, cross-linked resin films form by the reaction of one or more resin monomers with a

Typical bristle brushes for common distemper (left) and oil (right) painting. Note the different shape and construction of each brush required for the unique properties and application of the paints.

Fancy bristle and quill brushes for fine decorative work and striping.

catalyst, such as epoxy-polyamide paints or with an external component such as oxygen in the case of linseed oil paints. Paints in this category are usually termed high-performance architectual coatings (HIPAC) as they exhibit great abrasion resistance and excellent resistance to heat, moisture, and strong acids and bases.

4. Solidification by coalescence. Film formation in this group is characterized by the creation of emulsions where the resin is suspended in water by emulsifiers which, upon evaporation of the water, cause the resin molecules to coalesce or form a thin uniform continuous film. Because of the tight flexible nature of this film, these acrylic and polyvinyl acetate "latex" paints provide great durability and easy safe application, avoiding the problems of toxicity encountered with other systems.

The unique characteristic of each paint system as well as the variety of decorative painting techniques employed in architectural work necessitated the development of various types of brushes and other tools. For common work, fine blunt bristle brushes or "rounds" were used to lay on oil paints while coarser tufted bristle brushes, rectangular in shape, were used instead for distempers. Fancy decorative work—graining, marbelizing, stencilling—required a huge assortment of specialized brushes, striping "pencils," floggers, dusters, stipplers, overgrainers, and combs to achieve the desired imitative and decorative effects.

PAINT FAILURE AND COMMON DETERIORATION MECHANISMS

As surface finishes, paints and related coatings are dependent on the overall condition of their substrate and their immediate environment. Therefore, paint failure is often indicative of other serious building problems such as water penetration through defective detailing or related deterioration and extreme exposures.

A wide variety of paint film failures can occur as a result of specific conditions related to:

- The composition of the paint itself or to its application methods such as poor surface preparation or application techniques.
- The chemical or mechanical incompatibility of different paint layers.
- Situations of extreme exposure such as maritime climates or heavy water-shedding elements on a structure.

As a result, concise terminology has been developed by the paint industry to identify unique conditions with specific mechanisms of deterioration. The most widely occurring conditions are described below.

Peeling and blistering rank among the most common deterioration problems affecting paints and related surface coatings. Characterized as a general loss of adhesion between layers or at the substrate interface, this condition may be caused by a variety of diverse factors including improper surface preparation, incompatibility between overlaying paint films such as oil and latex emulsions, and the entrapment and migration of water or water vapor behind the paint film.

Solvent blistering, a related condition, is not caused by external moisture but rather by the entrapment of the volatile component of the fresh paint as a result of too rapid drying of the paint film.

Wrinkling, another condition related to application, will occur if paint films are applied too thickly or before the previous coats have dried or if the paint is applied to too cold a surface. The resultant film will not only appear deformed but can result in a loss of gloss and color.

Crazing, checking, or surface microcracking result when paint films have become too brittle or thick and are no longer able to expand and contract in response to changes in the ambient temperature and humidity or dimensional changes in the substrate (ie., wood). Such failures may result from poor quality paint or insufficient drying time between coats.

Alligatoring is an advanced stage of the above condition resulting in deep open cracks and a discontinuous network of semidetached islands of paint. Once paint films reach this stage, their ability to protect the substrate and in particular to keep water out is severely compromised.

Chalking or powdering of paints is caused by the gradual breakdown of the binder in that film through photochemical degradation, usually from ultraviolet light, in combination with the overall composition of the paint itself. While chalking can help reduce paint buildup over time, rapid loss can cause staining to adjacent materials such as masonry and a significant reduction in the protective qualities of the surface film.

Staining and **discoloration** can be attributed to a wide variety of sources. Biological attack from microflora such as mildew and algae accounts for a great deal of black, brown, and green surface discoloration as well as staining from the substrate itself as in the case of the oxidation of metal supports or the bleeding of resinous knots in poorly prepared wood. Photochemical degradation of the pigments and media will also result in varying degrees of visual change depending on the composition of the paints. Light sensitive pigments can fade quickly or discolor depending on the pH conditions of the environment and certain media such as oils can darken through oxidation.

PAINT INVESTIGATION AND ANALYSIS

Over the last ten years significant advances have been made in the investigation and analysis of historic architectural paints. Moreover, their recognition as an important component of any restoration program has had far reaching effects in demanding that proper paint research be executed for a restoration project. These requirements have begun to establish standard methodologies in the examination, identification, and assessment of historic architectural paints and coatings. Because of the need to interpret often fragmentary evidence through historical as well as analytical inquiries, proper training and experience are the necessary prerequisites for such work. Generally paint research is undertaken to establish a structure's historic appearance at a specific point in time. While important, such results are not the only application of paint research. Through a comparative examination of a large number of samples, paint layer stratigraphies can be used to unravel the complex evolution which many structures undergo. This use of comparative examination as a relative dating device is often neglected in the physical investigation of a building. This is unfortunate since this technique can often give evidence of the most subtle alterations over time. Regardless of the purpose of the investigation, most paint research involves the methodical collection of a large number of samples from the site; processing these samples in a laboratory to record and assess layer structure and composition; and finally visual characterization by color matching to a universal standard such as the Munsell Color System. As the assessment and interpretation are only as effective as the samples collected, much depends on sampling techniques involving where and how many samples are taken. Accurate assessment of the paint stratigraphies and identification of the pigments and binders present in each layer demand a laboratory equipped to perform cross-section mounting and microchemical and instrumental analyses. Such work attempted on site is almost useless. Characterization of color, gloss, and texture is far more difficult as the aging and deterioration of these paint films usually alters their visual characteristics. Fading of pigments and yellowing or blanching of media greatly affect the overall appearance of the paint, making direct assessment difficult. The investigation and analysis of any painted finish must begin with an understanding of the overall structure in terms of its historical context. Information

Test exposures of eighteenth and nineteenth century interior decorative wall painting from a house in Havana, Cuba. Such complex superimpositions of painting campaigns are common occurrences in architectural contexts making examination and conservation extremely difficult and unique.

on such seemingly unrelated factors as client/architect background, geographic location, and construction date can provide many clues for the interpretation of the actual findings as they relate to broader architectural questions. For this reason, it is best that the sampling and initial analysis be performed by the same investigator and guided by the existing documentary sources. In addition to processing such specific site-related information, the investigator must possess a broad knowledge of architectural history and of traditional painting materials and techniques in order to properly interpret the findings. Too often this is ignored, resulting in restorations which claim to be archaeologically correct but in fact make little sense when compared against known historical traditions. Because of the large number of samples required, given the size and complexity of a building, sample collection is often preceded at the site by a preliminary examination technique known as "cratering." This allows the quick characterization of paint layer sequences or stratigraphies by cutting through and exposing the layers using a small utility knife or scalpel and polishing them with a wet abrasive, usually water or mineral spirits and various grades of grit papers. "Craters" prepared in this way can be viewed under low power magnification (10–40) and areas determined useful for

further investigation may be sampled by hand with a scalpel or coring bit. Regardless of the technique used to extract samples, the paint substrate such as wood or plaster must always be included in order to orient the sample and ensure a complete stratigraphy. Removed samples are examined in the laboratory first under reflected light using a stereobinocular microscope in both mounted and unmounted states. Samples mounted in acrylic or polyester resin cubes allow for precise cross-sectioning by hand or with a low-speed microsaw followed by accurate recording of the paint stratigraphies. Mounting also affords greater ease in manipulation and permanent storage. Examination and retention of portions of unmounted samples are useful in observing layer surfaces obliquely and phenomena such as fracturing.

Pigment and media identification are difficult and time-consuming activities; however, the information gained can often be of invaluable significance for historical as well as visual interpretation. The combination and type of pigments and media determine the visual appearance of the paint and their identification can often suggest whether alteration has occurred. Moreover, knowledge of the pigments employed can sometimes contribute toward establishing general time frames based on known dates of pigment introduction

THE

DECORATIVE

PAINTERS' & GLAZIERS' GUIDE;

CONTAINING THE MOST APPROVED METHODS OF IMITATING

OAK, MAHOGANY, MAPLE, ROSE, CEDAR, CORAL,

And every other Kind of Fancy Wood;

VERD-ANTIQUE, DOVE, SIENNA, PORPHYRY, WHITE VEINED, AND OTHER MARBLES;

IN OIL OR DISTEMPER COLOUR;

DESIGNS FOR DECORATING APARTMENTS,

IN ACCORDANCE WITH THE VARIOUS STYLES OF ARCHITECTURE;

WITH DIRECTIONS FOR STENCILING, AND PROCESS FOR DESTROYING DAMP IN WALLS;

ALSO A COMPLETE BODY OF INFORMATION ON THE

ART OF STAINING AND PAINTING ON GLASS;

PLANS FOR THE ERECTION OF APPARATUS FOR ANNEALING IT;

AND THE METHOD OF JOINING FIGURES TOGETHER BY LEADING,

WITH EXAMPLES FROM ANCIENT WINDOWS.

THIRD EDITION,
WITH CONSIDERABLE ADDITIONS.

BY NATHANIEL WHITTOCK,

ASSISTED BY THE MOST EXPERIENCED PRACTICAL ARTIZANS IN EVERY DEPARTMENT OF
DECORATIVE PAINTING AND GLAZING.

LONDON:
PUBLISHED BY SHERWOOD, GILBERT, AND PIPER,
PATERNOSTER ROW.
1832.

Title page of Nathaniel Whittock's *The Decorative Painters' and Glaziers' Guide . . .* of 1832, illustrating the diverse information included in such trade books of the period.

Assorted nineteenth century decorative painter's stencils and stencil patterns, pounce templates, and designs for decorative wall and ceiling painting. (Emanuel Nickel Collection, Albany Institute of History and Art).

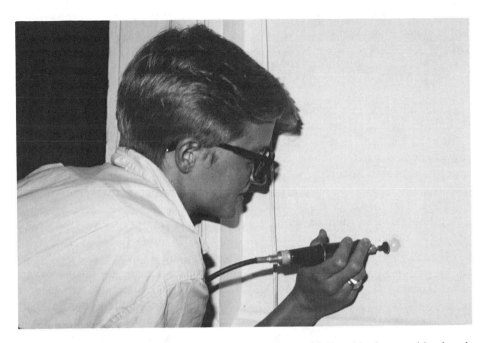

Preliminary *in situ* examination by exposing paint layers with the aid of a portable abrasive tip drill can greatly aid in the initial investigation of a building's painting history.

Polyester mounted cross-sections of paint samples removed from a site and examined with a light microscope can reveal much information about the various painting campaigns, the materials and techniques of painting, and fluctuating attitudes toward taste and technology over time.

or use. Paint materials can also give some insight into the social and economic status of the owner, occupant, building, or region, or the technological factors governing paint selection. To what degree this information is collected often depends upon time, budget, and significance of the project.

Pigment and media identification can be performed using a variety of techniques including optical microscopy and instrumental analysis such as x-ray diffraction (XRD), energy dispersive x-ray fluorescence (EDX), electron beam microprobe, infrared spectroscopy, and gas chromatography (GC) to name a few. Polarized light and ultraviolet fluorescence microscopy in conjunction with microchemical or microcrystalline spot tests nevertheless offer the most versatile and relatively inexpensive means of general identification and

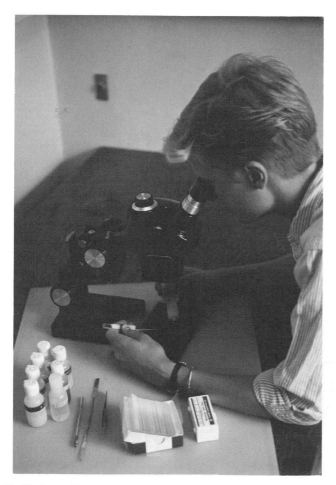

Preliminary identification of paint composition can be performed using standard microchemical tests before more advanced instrumental analysis is attempted.

are well-suited to handle the large number of samples required. Where necessary, instrumental techniques can be called upon to answer specific questions or to identify more complex substances such as organic binding media.

RESTORATION AND CONSERVATION TREATMENT TECHNIQUES

Conservation practices for historic architectural paints include a wide array of techniques for the removal as well as the retention and replication of historic fabric depending on the specific situation. While areas of decorative painting such as free-hand or stencil work, graining, marbleizing, and other fancy finishes demand techniques that focus on the retention of as much of the original as possible, most architectural surfaces that have experienced years of paint accumulation require removal of this accumulation to prepare the surfaces for proper repainting and often to reveal lost or blurred architectural details.

REMOVAL METHODS

Techniques for large-scale paint removal include chemical systems employing organic solvents, alkali salts such as potassium and ammonium hydroxide, and various detergent and enzyme preparations; heat systems such as electric heat plates or forced air heat guns; and abrasive techniques utilizing a wide range of abrasives and pressures. All three systems have their advantages and disadvantages depending on the nature of the substrate and the type, age, and thickness of the paints to be removed; however, in general, several points for comparison should be made.

First, heat as a removal method is effective only for paints which will soften upon exposure to high temperatures such as oil or emulsion films. While this method can be used safely without volatilizing toxic lead and other metals in the films, it can run the risk of burning vulnerable surfaces such as wood, or even worse, ignite flammable materials within walls. Commercial chemical strippers such as those based on organic solvent and alkali preparations are toxic and difficult to contain and dispose of, and in the case of alkali-based strippers can raise the grain of wooden surfaces and leave harmful residues in all absorbent materials such as wood and masonry. Commercial chemical poultice systems offer improved methods of application and removal; however, by increasing contact time, the chemical residue from these systems can be difficult to effectively remove or neutralize. Mechanical removal, and in particular, abrasive techniques, can be very effec-

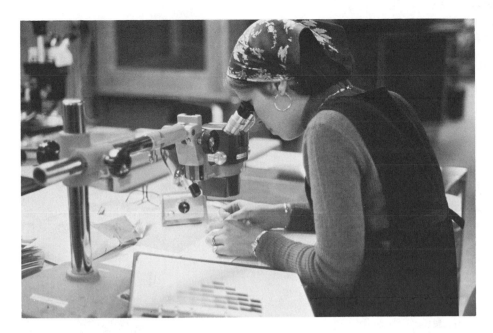

Visual color matching of the selected historic paint layer is often performed using a universal color standard such as the Munsell Color Notation System. Such techniques, although standard, depend greatly on the survival of the original finishes as well as the accuracy of the investigator.

Chemical removal of overpaint from the original wall stenciling of the Connecticut State Capitol. By carefully selecting the ingredients and dwell time of the formulations, great control can be achieved in the removal of individual paint layers to the desired level of exposure.

tive methods. However, they can cause severe damage to the substrate or the surrounding elements if the proper aggregate and pressure are not controlled. Hardness, particle shape, volume flow, pressure, and application distance all play a role in the success or failure of abrasive cleaning.

RETENTION METHODS

Where techniques to stablize and clean extant paint films are required, standard procedures borrowed from smaller scale fine arts conservation practices are often adopted. The basic criteria guiding such interventions are the use of stable materials of low toxicity and the ability for retreatment at a later time. While a wide variety of materials and techniques developed by individual conservators exists, basic procedures for reattaching flaking and detached paint, consolidating powdering surfaces, and general cleaning can be summarized.

REATTACHMENT

Until the early 1930s, only natural products—many found in the original paint films—were used for conservation purposes, such as dammar, mastic, beeswax, drying oils, gum arabic, and gelatin, to name a few. Today there exists a wide range of available synthetic materials which have to a great degree replaced many of the traditional materials; however, both classes of materials are still used alone and in combination.

Where single or multiple layers of paint are flaking or detaching, a fixative must be chosen which will satisfy the following general requirements:

- They should provide reinforcement of the adhesion of the paint layer to the substrate.
- They should provide reinforcement of the cohesion of the individual layers.
- They should facilitate the reestablishment of the original plane of the surface.
- They should display effective but not excessive adhesive and cohesive strength.
- They should have good penetration and compatible flexibility with the surrounding paint.
- They must be colorless and transparent and not produce excessive gloss.
- They must be resistant to biological attack and atmospheric pollutants.
- They must remain soluble, have low toxicity, and not encourage dust accumulation.

Synthetic organic and, to a lesser degree, synthetic inorganic resins account for the majority of treatments involving the reattachment and consolidation of flaking and powdering paints.

Examples of the inorganic resins include the alkali- and fluorosilicates, silicon esters, barium hydroxide, and lime water solutions. Synthetic organic resins, applied as both aqueous solutions and emulsions, and organic solvent solutions usually containing 4–10% solids include: polyvinyl acetate, acrylates and methacrylates, polystyrene, polyethylene and polypropylene, polyacetal resins, cellulosic derivatives, polyglycols, and microcrystalline waxes. The selection of one

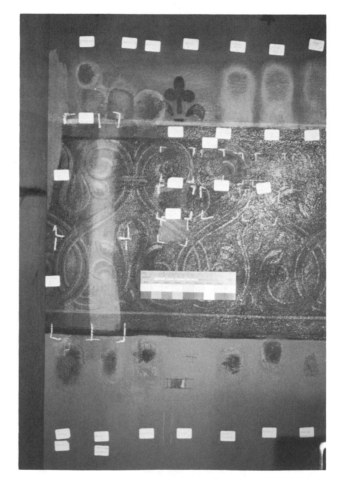

Prior to any conservation treatment, a testing program of commercial and prepared products is designed and applied to establish comparative results. Here a wide variety of wet cleaning methods including organic solvents, gels, detergents, and other reagents are being tested to remove later varnish coatings and overpaint from a late nineteenth century decorative border.

or more of these materials depends on the nature of the paint films and substrate, degree of detachment, surface orientation, and exposure. Application is usually by brush, spray, or injection and is often accompanied by heat and pressure if the films have become deformed or out of alignment.

CLEANING

The cleaning of loose and chemically bonded surface grime and degraded discolored coatings accounts for a large portion of the conservation techniques employed for architectural painting. While the materials and methods vary significantly depending on the nature and age of the paint film, a broad variety of dry mechanical,

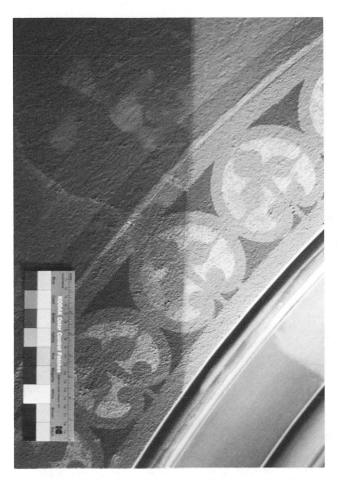

Dry cleaning with soft abrasive pads often provides adequate cleaning of distemper paints where "wet" methods cannot be used.

and aqueous and nonaqueous organic solvent-based cleaning systems exist simultaneously. Given the large-scale nature of most architectural work and the recent legal restrictions curtailing the use of volatile organic solvents, modified solvent gel systems, detergents, and enzyme preparations have been developed recently and applied with great success as alternative cleaning systems.

REPLICATION AND COMPENSATION

Unlike the conservation of most painted museum artifacts such as paintings and sculpture, the restoration of historic structures often involves the replication of their painted surfaces for full interpretation, or at best a combination of conservation and replication techniques where original finishes survive. While the concern and methods for conserving architectural paints is now finally being addressed, replication is still the principal restoration activity. Visual replication by matching color and gloss is no easy task and in fact depends heavily on the historical as well as the analytical data collected. Considering the probable alteration of the paint over time as well as the lack of specific knowledge concerning the exact appearance of these finishes, it is understandable as to why the replication process is difficult. Color matching using a standard universal color system such as the Munsell or Plochere Color Systems provide some framework for visual comparison and documentation and improved instrumental techniques such as microspectrophotometry allow for more objective color measurement. While color is perhaps the most significant physical characteristic for replication, other aspects such as gloss, texture, and transparency are also important for historical accuracy. In these cases, traditional painting materials and techniques have been employed in a number of restorations in an effort to reproduce characteristics not obtainable with modern paints. Such literal reproductions can sometimes cause difficulties due to the toxicity of the materials and the instability of the pigments and media resulting in fading, darkening, and irreversibility. Visually accurate modern substitutes complying with legal as well as historical requirements have been attempted in recent years with satisfactory results. Where decorative painting is to be replicated, every effort must be made to carefully duplicate the original quality of the work.

Improvement or creative modification of the original work is outside the requirement of proper historical replication. Where retention of the original surface is preferable to replication, inpainting allows for the visual reintegration of damaged or missing areas of origi-

Where it is desirable to retain original finishes, paint loss and other surface damage are generally in-painted with paints prepared from stable reversible materials. In this example, an early nineteenth century grained door and marbleized wall are being in-painted after cleaning while the baseboard below has been totally repainted using commercial housepaint matched to the color of the original white lead oil paint.

Historic replication in the laboratory or studio prior to full-scale reproduction is often required especially when the original techniques are complicated or unusual. This replication test of the original imitation copper finish found on the exterior plaster frieze of Frank Lloyd Wright's Dana House well illustrates the complete process from analysis to replication in order to achieve the correct historical appearance.

The most successful restoration work recognizes the varying approaches often needed in dealing with historic architectural finishes. At the United States Military Academy's Cullum Hall, the restoration of the interior of the Great Hall was achieved by cleaning and stabilizing the surviving original painted decoration of the ceiling and mouldings while at the same time recreating the marbleizing and bronzing on the damaged and overpainted walls.

nal painting. This is always done with materials of high stability and reversibility as in other conservation treatments. New coatings based on reversible nonyellowing synthetic resins used alone or in combination with more traditional resins are often applied either as replacements for original varnishes or glazes or as new protective surfaces for fragile decoration. On large expansive surfaces, coatings should be selected which will not attract dust and atmospheric pollutants.

BIBLIOGRAPHY

Ashton, H.E. Paint—What is It? *Canadian Building Digest*, No. 76. Ottawa: National Research Council, April 1966.

Banov, Abel. *Paints and Coatings Handbook for Contractors. Architects. Builders and Engineers*. Tenth printing. Michigan: Structures Publishing Co., 1973.

Candee, Richard M. Preparing and Mixing Colors in 1812. *Antiques* (April) 1978. Includes reprint of Hezekiah Reynolds' Directions for House and Ship Painting. New Haven, 1812.

Candee, Richard N. Materials Toward a History of Housepaints: the Materials and Craft of the Housepainter in Eighteenth Century America. Master of Arts Thesis, State University of New York, College at Oneonta, Cooperstown, May 1965.

Feller, R. (ed.) *Artist' Pigments. Vol. 1*. Washington D.C.: National Gallery of Art, 1986.

Gettens, Rutherford J., and Stout, George L. *Painting Materials. A Short Encyclopedia*. Second ed. New York: Dover Publications, 1966. (Unabridged reprint of 1942 edition.)

Harley, R.D. *Artist's Pigments c. 1600–1835*. Second ed. London: Butterworth Scientific, 1982.

Little, Nina F. *American Decorative Wall Painting 1700–1850*. New York: E.P. Dutton & Co., 1972.

Masschelein-Kleiner, L. *Ancient Binding Media. Varnishes and Adhesives*. Rev. ed. Rome: ICCROM, 1983.

Mora, L. and Mora P. *Le superfici architettoniche, materiale e colore*. Note ed eperienze per un approccio al problema del restauro.'' in Il Colore nell'Edilizia Storica. Supplemento No. 6 del Bollettino d'Arte del Ministerio per i Beni Culturali e Ambientali, 1985.

Mora, L. and Mora P. *Materiali tradizionali e modalita di intervento*. In Il Colore nell'Edilizia del Borgo Pio di Terracina: Piano del colore del centro storico in declivio e pianura. Ministerio per i Beni Culturali e Ambientali, Istituto Centrale per il Restauro, Regione Lazio, Comune di Terracina, November 1986.

Moss, Roger. *Century of Color. Exterior Decoration for American Buildings 1820–1920*. Watkins Glen, New York: American Life Foundation, 1981.

CHAPTER 11

ARCHITECTURAL GLASS

Although glass has been used since the second millenium B.C. in Egypt for the manufacture of decorative and ritual objects and subsequently domestic wares, glass was not used for architectural purposes for windows until the Roman period. The ancient Egyptian glass is often referred to as faience, somewhat confusingly since strictly speaking faience or fayence is a tin-glazed earthenware made famous by the sixteenth century products of the city of Faenza, Italy. More accurately, the Egyptian product should be called glazed siliceous ware. The manufacture of such products involved the use of "frits" which were glassy powders formed by heating the raw materials, raking them, and pulverizing them. The fritted silica was mixed with small amounts of calcium oxide and sodium oxide, shaped by hand in an open mold and heated. The resulting product consisted of frit grains fused together at their surfaces. The objects thus formed were often coated with a mixture of finely powdered frit with complex copper compounds and then were refired to give a colored glaze. The colors ranged from green to dark blue.

The development of the use of colored or stained glass for church windows is somewhat hazy but it is recorded that by the sixth century A.D. St. Gregory had the windows of St. Martin of Tours, France, glazed with colored glass. It is also recorded that in 675 A.D. Gallic or French glaziers were employed at Monkwearmouth Abbey in the North of England. Some of the early windows included thin cut and polished slabs of alabaster or crystalline gypsum which transmitted a beautiful golden-amber light. The use of semitransparent polished alabaster for windows is well known in ancient Rome and Byzantium. Possibly the earliest example of pictorial stained glass was found in archaeo-logical excavations at Lorsch Abbey, Germany, and dates from the ninth or tenth century. The story of the development of stained glass in medieval Europe is beyond the scope of this work but is well discussed in such works as *Stained Glass* by Lee, Seddon, and Stephens (1976).

The earliest plain glass for windows in North America was imported from England and can be dated with certainty to the 1620s in New England. Dutch imported stained glass was used as early as the 1630s in the Hudson River community, and in 1638 Evert Duyckink established a family company of painters, glaziers, and glassmakers in New Amsterdam. Despite these early beginnings, probably the earliest major use of American-made stained glass is not until 1845 when sixty large stained glass windows were installed in Holy Trinity Church, Brooklyn, New York.

GLASS MATERIALS AND MANUFACTURE

To manufacture glass, a carefully designed combination of materials are melted and cooled in a certain way to produce a supercooled liquid that is so stiff and of such high viscosity that it has most of the qualities of a solid.

The main ingredient in all glasses is silica which may be derived from sand, quartz crystals, or flint. However, a temperature of about 3100°F (1704°C) is required to melt silica. Thus pure silica has only been used comparatively recently to form high temperature-resistant glasses. Early furnaces were capable of reaching 1000°C in the second millennium B.C. Only since about 1850 have furnaces been capable of exceeding 1200°C. The Romans discovered that if one mixed lime and soda with the silica its melting point was lowered and it became cheaper and more practical to make glass. In fact the melting point is lowered to 2700°F (1482°C), but the addition of metallic oxides such as lead oxide also had the effect of lowering the melting point and hence the working temperatures still further.

In these early formulae soda ash is usually referred to as the "flux" and limestone as the "stabilizer." A flux is any substance which can be used to lower the melting point of another material and reduce viscosity. Broken glass known as "cullet" can also be used to lower the melting point of new mixtures. Stabilizers such as calcium or magnesium oxide improve the chemical durability of a glass and prevent crystallization or disintegration of the glassy mass.

GLASS

When glass is in the various states between being plastic and molten it can be pressed, molded, floated, blown, drawn, cast, and rolled into a multitude of forms. The glass normally becomes plastic, that is, workable, at temperatures above 900°C.

The final stage of manufacture is the carefully controlled cooling. If molten glass is left alone it cools rapidly and stresses may develop between the rapidly cooled and solidified exterior and the still molten interior. To prevent the buildup of stresses, new glass is "annealed" or reheated and only permitted to cool slowly. Glasses with built-in stresses may shatter unexpectedly.

Glasses of differing compositions have different annealing points, "softening points," and "working points," and thus have different "working ranges." The working range is the difference in temperature between the working point and the softening point. The softening point occurs when the glass reaches a viscosity similar to that of Cheddar cheese. The working point is at a viscosity considerably stiffer than molasses. For a modern soda–lime glass the annealing point is at about 500°C; the softening point at about 680°C; and the working point at over 900°C.

COLORED GLASSES

Glass may be colored accidentally, for example, by the inclusion of small quantities of iron compounds, in which case the glass has a greenish color. Small quantities of iron being ubiquitous in sands, most glasses have a greenish color especially if one looks through the glass from the edge and thus through a greater thickness of glass.

In simple terms a metal is said to be "oxidized" when it combines with oxygen to form an oxide. The oxide is in turn "reduced" if it loses the oxygen when heated with charcoal, for example, and returns to a metallic state. Different states of oxidation produce different colors in glass. Ferrous oxide, for example, produces a blue color in the glass but if the glass is heated in an oxidizing atmosphere and the iron is in the form of ferric oxide then the glass has a brown or yellow color. The green color referred to above is the result of mixing ferric and ferrous iron.

Other colored glasses may be formed by mixing small quantities of mineral oxides with the silica and other ingredients. Copper and cobalt compounds, for example, produce beautiful blues; gold produces ruby red; manganese produces purples; and chrome and strontium produce yellows. Because the mineral compounds may be very expensive a very thin layer of colored glass may be laid on over a plain glass in the process known as "flashing." The intensity of the colors permits the flashed glass layers to be much less than one millimeter in thickness.

Colors in the glass may be of two basic forms, that is, when the metal oxides are dissolved in the glass as above; or when the metal is dispersed through the glass as minute particles in what are known as colloidal dispersions. In the latter glasses beautiful effects may be obtained, for example, by mixtures of colloidal gold and silver, where the glass appears to be an opaque green when viewed in reflected light but a transparent wine red when viewed with transmitted light.

GLASS TYPES

Glasses may be classified according to two systems—by silica content or by composition. Using the first system arranged by diminishing silica content the glasses are as follows: fused silica; window glass; container glass; fluorescent tubing; neutral glass; hard borosilicate; lead glass tubing; television tubes and screens; textile glass fiber; glass wool insulation; and superfine glass wool.

By composition glasses may be listed as follows: soda-lime, glass; lead glass; borosilicate glass, for example, Pyrex; and phosphate glasses. Soda-lime glasses are used for window glass, plate glass, bottles and glass bricks, and so on. Historical window glasses have the same general composition except that oxide contents may be higher as might levels of impurities. A typical soda-lime glass may contain:

| Silicon dioxide | 70–75% by weight |
| Aluminum dioxide | 0.5–2.0% |

Sodium oxide   12–16%
Magnesium oxide   0–4%
Calcium oxide   8–12%

FORMING THE GLASS

Historic window glass could normally be produced by one of three methods. The glass could be cast onto a sheet of iron and then after separation from the iron, if necessary it could have its surface polished to remove irregularities and to improve transparency. This is known as plate glass and was first used in North America in the 1830s. In Europe plate glass was first produced for large mirrors and subsequently for large shop windows. Plate glass could be further refined by having the edges bevelled by grinding and polishing.

The two other methods involve using an iron tube or blowpipe to pick up a "gather" or blob of "metal" or molten glass and to blow a globular or cylindrical vessel which is then converted into a flat sheet. When a globular vessel is blown the glass blower rolls the gather on a "marver" or flat sheet of iron. The first marvers were of stone or marble—marbre in French—hence the term. Once a blown globular vessel of sufficient size is formed, a solid iron "pontil" or "punty" rod is attached to the end opposite to the blowpipe and then the vessel is detached from the blowpipe. The cooling vessel is returned to the mouth of the furnace and reheated. The original neck is cut away with a pair of shears and the glass blower spins the semimolten vessel until centrifugal force extends the glass into a flat round sheet known as a "crown." The center of the crown was known as a "bull's eye" or "bullion" and contrary to some popular opinion was regarded as poor material. As such it was usually thrown back into the batch and melted or was smashed and used for the production of cullet. Crown glass might be produced in sheets which were as large as 48–49 in. in diameter and were known as "tables."

The table was subsequently cut up with great care to produce the maximum possible number of rectangular panes or of diamond-shaped "quarrels" or "quarries." The latter term is said to be a derivative of quarrel = a crossbow bolt, the head of which had a similar diamond shape. But the word may ultimately be derived from the Old French and diminutive Latin terms for square.

The third early method for making flat sheets was the so-called "cylinder" or "muff" glass. In this technique a sausage-shaped vessel is swung back and forth at the end of the blowpipe in a pit while it is being blown. In this way gravity helps to increase the length of the vessel. When the desired size has been obtained,

the vessel is detached and taken back to the furnace and reheated. The sides of the vessel are cut lengthwise and the ends are cut off with shears. The resulting two half-cylinders are then reintroduced into the furnace entrance and allowed to relax into flat sheets. In the twentieth century some very large cylinder glass sheets were produced by blowing the initial vessel with a compressed air hose rather than by mouth.

A fourth but much less common form of glass was produced from the 1830s until the early 1900s. This was known as "pressed glass." Small, often colored, panes were produced for special purposes including windows for boat interiors, screens, and secretary desks. This type was actually made in a mold and was often highly decorated in bas-relief with such designs as leaf and vine motifs, steamboats, Gothic tracery, and fine geometrical patterns.

19th century pressed glass panes.

GLASS DETERIORATION

Glass can react with water or with aqueous solutions with chemical changes occurring first at the surface and possibly spreading right through the thickness of the glass. The seriousness of the deterioration depends particularly on the chemical constituents of the glass and the pH of the liquid. It is believed that water molecules diffuse into the glass and react with free oxygen atoms to form hydroxyl ions which then migrate out with the alkali cations from the glass causing what is known as "alkali extraction." A hydroxyl is a radical containing hydrogen and oxygen. Radicals are fundamental atoms or groups of atoms which normally form parts of compounds but which remain unaltered during the compound's ordinary chemical changes. The hydroxyls react with the silica dioxide in the glass and form a silica gel. Eventually all the alkalis are leached out and only separated silica layers remain; the glass becomes irridescent and loses transparency. The irridescence is caused by rays of light being reflected from thin alternating layers of air and weathered glass.

The removal of the alkali cations causes a loss of volume in the surface and the depleted surface cracks off the body of the glass as the former shrinks. This causes multilayered effects. The extracted alkalis can build up to form an alkali-rich surface layer above the depleted layer and if the former increases its alkalinity to above pH 9 then the silica will be attacked and the whole structure of the glass will disintegrate.

GLASS FORMULAE AND THEIR EFFECTS ON DURABILITY

In the early 1970s it was noted that some medieval stained glass deteriorated badly while other glass of the same period exposed in the same environment did not. But at the same time comparisons of their formulae did not provide any obvious reasons for this. During this period T.M. El Shamy showed that the traditional way of calculating formulae for analyses did not work. He demonstrated that they would not show why one glass was deteriorating in a polluted environment when another was not, when analyses of their two formulae were based on weight percentages. Formulae had to be calculated on the basis of the number of molecules of each compound rather than their weights. The analytical results based on mol percentages showed that there was a tendency for crusts to form if the silica content dropped below 66 mol percent. Calculated in this way it was suddenly also found that there were many more actual molecules of calcium and magnesium oxides than had been thought. Although the addition of some

calcium or magnesium oxide will produce a durable glass from what would otherwise be an unstable potash glass, the tolerances are quite narrow. Five mol percent lime is too low and the glass is unstable, 10–15 mol percent is highly durable, and 20 mol percent or more gets increasingly less stable again.

Some medieval glasses have an exceptionally high lime content and comparatively little silica (less than 50 mol percent). In wet conditions breakdown of the silica occurs readily and a highly alkaline crust develops which retains moisture to fuel the deterioration reactions. Subsequent hydration of the alkali-depleted surface layer can lead to its subsequent expansion and further exfoliation as a result.

CRIZZLING AND WEEPING GLASSES

"Sick," "sweating," or "weeping" glass has an excess alkali content and is deficient in lime. Such glass develops a slick surface with droplets of moisture in humid conditions. Water vapor combines with chemically uncombined alkalis to leach them out of the glass and form the droplets. High lime contents of above 15 mol percent also lead to rapid reductions in durability of glasses. Some medieval glasses which contain 35 percent of calcium oxide are now in very poor condition.

In the 1950s it was noted that often the use of potash fluxes rather than soda seemed to lead to the formation of "crizzling" and weeping surfaces. Crizzling is characterised by the development of networks of microcracks followed by sweating or weeping and ultimately disintegration of the glass. It was subsequently found that the high potash contents were associated with either no lime or magnesia contents or a lime or magnesia content in excess of 30 percent. Again it was the lime and magnesia molecules which were critical.

Underfiring of glasses and glass "paints" can leave oxides in a vulnerable state if they are exposed in wet polluted environments. If, for example, the glass was melted at relatively low temperatures leaving small quantities of unreacted magnesium oxide and if the glass was then soaked in water containing sulfate ions, a reaction could occur forming high-volume disruptive salts such as complex hydrates of magnesium sulfate. If these salts form in the surface the outer layer expands and crumbles away.

LEAD GLASSES AND THEIR DETERIORATION

Lead glasses which contain substantial amounts of lead oxide as the flux, are characterized by high density, high refractive index (high luster), high cost, relative softness, and ease of working (for engraving and grinding and/or polishing bevels, etc.). They are of moderate to low durability being corroded by prolonged immersion in acidic solutions. They are used for cut glass, tubing for forming, for example, neon light tubing and laboratory tubing, electrical seals, and for optical glass. In the last use they are also known as "flint glass" from the crushed flint used as a source for their silica.

INCREASES IN OPACITY

When crizzling occurs it may be accompanied by the penetration of oxygen, moisture, and acids into the glass. Electrons are stripped from elements such as iron and manganese which were used to color the glass and new dark brown or black oxides are formed which tend to be insoluble. Such color changes may make the glass opaque.

THE DETERIORATION OF PAINTING ON GLASS

The paint layers that were used to trace outlines and details or an additional background tone called "grisaille" are liable to be attacked by pollutants. These paints are composed of metal oxides (usually of copper and iron) plus a finely powdered and highly fusible lead glass (frit) to lower the melting point of the paint. The paint is applied to the glass and then the painted glass pieces are placed in a kiln which is heated to a temperature sufficiently high to melt and fuse the paint mixture onto the glass but not high enough to melt the piece of glass. If the glass paint does not form fully cohesive or evenly melted layers which are evenly bonded to the glass substrate and form coherent films then problems will occur and the paint layers will fail. Improper flux mixtures usually also cause problems by not permitting the glass to melt and the metallic oxides are left accessible to leaching.

DESCRIBING DIFFERENT FORMS OF DETERIORATION

Cox et al. (1979) describe different forms of deterioration which had been found on some 200 pieces of medieval glass from York Minster. Their system is of interest both as an example of the range of problems which may be encountered with any major sampling of architectural glass, and as a typical defect classification system which might be employed in other contexts. The series were as follows:

- Unweathered but not bright and shiny.
- Half pitted and half quite weathered.
- Pitted, for example, micropits 0.2 mm in diameter at a frequency of about 100/cm², up to 4 mm in diameter pits on both sides. In some cases pits penetrated through glass.
- Pitted and crusted.
- Crusted with a uniform crust of opaque white or brown. Actual remaining glass beneath might be paper-thin.
- Surface fractured. Spalling at concave fracture lines with sides of shallow depressions showing conchoidal fracture marks.

To make this list slightly more comprehensive we might include:

- Crizzled and weeping or sweating glass.

LEADED GLASS

Stained glass and polished and bevelled glass are normally leaded, that is to say, the pieces of glass are set into lead strips of a cross section like the letters H, I, or C. These strips are known as "cames." Being made from lead they are subject to plastic deformation under load, or creep. Thus leaded windows and other glasswork may be found to have crept and sagged so that they are no longer properly supported and so that the glass may be loose. In polluted environments the lead may be seriously embrittled or corroded after 80–100 years. The cames in turn are attached at intervals by means of twisted copper wire ties to horizontal wrought iron or bronze "saddle bars." In severely polluted environments lead, copper, and iron may all have corroded and caused the sagging, distortion, or even collapse of the window.

To properly weatherproof a stained glass window a soft cement or putty compound is prepared and rubbed into the leads, sealing the gaps between the leads and the glass. The traditional mixes for such putties included white lead, whiting, Japan driers, linseed oil, and kerosene and lampblack. These putties embrittle with age and exposure to pulluted environments.

DURABILITY OF GLASSES IN THE BUILT ENVIRONMENT

Many European medieval stained glass and early window glasses have been found to be severely damaged by exposure to air pollution in the presence of prolonged acidic moist conditions. The glasses in question have high calcium and/or magnesium oxide contents and/or high potash contents but generally have a different composition from those used in North American art and architecture. The use of the former glasses in similarly polluted environments in North America would of course result in similar problems. The major problems in North America may be summarized as follows:

- The exposure of poorly fired glass paints to polluted exterior environments.
- The exposure of tinted or colored glasses which were not fired at sufficiently high temperatures and in which consequently mineral oxides may be liable to leaching in polluted environments with the associated formation of porous layers in the glass.
- Failure or collapse of the glazing structural system due to problems with lead cames or glazing bars; corrosion in iron or steel reinforcement and supports; failure of putties or glazing compounds; and rotting of wooden window frames—all of which may be directly or indirectly related to exposure to acidic precipitation or air pollutants.
- Alkali solutions, hydrofluoric acid, and phosphoric acid all actively attack and corrode glass and support systems. All of these substances are used in commercial masonry cleaning formulations and could thus cause damage in localized pollutant spills, wind-born overspray, or contaminated runoff incidents.
- Since the process of glass forming requires fairly rapid cooling after the glass has acquired its desired shape and before it deforms to an undesirable shape, strains are set up in the glass due to the relatively large thermal gradient in the glass as it "sets." These strains must be annealed out to prevent breakage or shattering. This is normally accomplished by placing the glass in a special furnace or "lehr" in which the glass is brought up to just below its deformation temperature and then is slowly cooled to prevent the reintroduction of strains. If this process has not been carried out or has been improperly carried out then associated microcracking may result in pollutant damage making worse what is already a bad situation.

THE CONSERVATION AND RESTORATION OF GLASS AND GLAZING

The conservation of seriously deteriorated glass is highly specialized and should only be attempted by a trained and experienced glass conservator. No conservation or restoration work should be attempted without a detailed site inspection being carried out.

Peter Gibson (1989) writing on the conservation of architectural (stained or leaded) glass gives a useful list of recommended equipment for the inspection including the following (his text is part of a book which is essential reading for anyone who wishes to know about glass conservation):

- Ladder to give access to all parts of the window.
- Wooden "strainers," or timbers which can be attached to the top of the ladder to transfer the load of the top of the ladder onto the adjacent mullions or frame members.
- Ropes or some other means to attach the strainers to the ladder.
- A dusting brush with 3 in. long soft hairs for dusting glass, stonework, and metalwork.
- Stonemason's hammer and chisel for testing mortar in glazing groove in stone masonry.
- Single lens reflex camera and tripod to take daylight photographs rather than flash.
- Long cable release so that shutter can be triggered from floor avoiding vibration.
- Powerful flashlight.
- Measuring tapes and a surveyor's folding rule.
- If survey is being carried out after vandalism or accidental damage to the window then emergency repair and stabilization tools and materials may be required, including glazing tools, spare leads, butyl mastic, hardboard, and suitable saws.

As is usual with other conservation surveys, arrangements should be made to ensure that the architect and all other interested parties should be present at least for part of the time of the inspection.

Attendance by a laborer or contractor may also be required to adjust or move ladders and scaffolds, or to assist with temporary repairs and stabilization work. Telephone numbers are essential to locate other relevant persons, emergency services, and other agencies in case of accident or access difficulties.

Where the leadwork and the other metal supports are severely corroded, the window may have to be carefully taken out and removed to a studio or workshop for releading. The window should be recorded by photography before removal. In some cases loose or flaking paint layers may require temporary stabilization with reversible consolidants before moving the glass. This process is normally carried out by the glass conservator. There is some divergence of opinion on the subject of the reuse of old lead from melted-down cames, but the general opinion seems to be that cames made from new lead should be used. The glass conservator may require the architect or architectural conservator to specify and install new saddle bars and other structural supports for the conserved and releaded windows.

Cox, G.A, Heavens, O.S., Newton, R.G., and Pollard, A.M. (1979). "A Study of the Weathering Behavior of Medieval Glass from York Minster." *Journal of Glass Studies*, **21**, 54–75.

Lee, B., Seddon, B., and Stephens, B. (1976). *Stained Glass.*

Newton, R. and Davison, S. (1989). *The Conservation of Glass*. London: Butterworths.

CHAPTER 12

FOUNDATIONS AND FOOTINGS

THE NATURE AND PROBLEMS OF OLD FOUNDATIONS AND FOOTINGS

A foundation may be defined as the base or substructure which supports a building, whereas a footing is the lowermost part of a foundation. The footing may simply be the lowest widest base course or a series of stepped courses which begin at the bottom three or four times as wide as the wall of the superstructure and gradually reduce to the width of the wall in about three or four steps.

The proper construction and the condition of a foundation under an old building depend on a number of factors which may be considered under four headings:

- The nature of the site upon which the structure was built.
- The nature of the materials of which the foundation was built.
- The influences to which the foundation itself, or its immediate surrounding or bearing materials are subjected or have been subjected.
- The nature and extent of the building or structure erected upon the foundation and hence the loading on the foundation and on the soil or rock beneath the foundation.

Newton's Third Law of Motion has important applications to the performance of foundations. It states as follows: To every action there is an equal and opposite reaction.

In the simplest possible situation when a structure is placed upon the ground the mass of that structure tends to move downward toward the center of the earth under the influence of gravity. If the downward movement or action of the structure is not resisted by an equal and opposite upward reaction then the structure will continue to move downward or settle until such time as the downward action is matched by an upward reaction.

In practical terms this means that for an old foundation to be stable if it was placed on soft compressible soil, then that soil would have compressed to a point at which it resisted further compression. The structure then remains stable at least until the load is increased or decreased, or until the bearing capacity of the soil is changed.

C.B. Crawford, in writing "Foundation Movements" for *Canadian Building Digest* 148 in April 1972 noted that "the Palace of Fine Arts in Mexico City has sunk ten feet into the ground since it was built 60 years ago (Crawford, 1972)."

This classic example occurred because despite advice to the contrary, the architect designed the foundations so that the force which they exerted exceeded the bearing or reactive capacity per square foot of the soil. Happily this case is very unusual in its magnitude. However, much smaller movements can still result in serious damage being caused to a structure.

Since the loading upon a foundation and hence on the soil beneath is rarely totally even, there is a tendency for unrestrained foundations to slowly rotate in the direction of the heavier load.

Beneath foundations, a weakening of the soil resulting in a lowering of its compressive strength may cause the whole previously stable supported structure to commence to move downward until sufficient resistance is gained to provide the requisite reaction. Such a weakening will occur when subterranean water removes fine material from the soil, creating voids; or when organic material such as wood in the soil decays and creates similar voids.

Movement in unstable foundations does not necessarily have to occur downward. A decrease in load or an increase in the reaction from beneath may both result in an upward movement of the structure. Soils may swell because of the growth of water-soluble salts; the swelling of clay mineral crystals when wetted; or because of the freezing of moisture in the soil.

A soil which has been heavily loaded may "rebound" moving upward if the load is reduced by the removal of part of the structure, for example by the removal of part of a wall. Foundations may also be gripped by expanding ice in the soil and moved upward in a process known as adfreezing.

To understand more about upward and lateral movements of old foundations a second phenomenon must be noted. The forces delivered by the foundation are not simply transmitted downward but radiate outward in such a way that lines of equal pressure or stress in the soil can be plotted as a series of bulbs seen in vertical cross section. Thus forces from a heavily loaded foundation may actually result in strong lateral forces and even upward forces being transmitted through adjacent soil. The curved lines of equal stress due to footing loads are often referred to as "bulbs of pressure." In a typical case the line of stress increase equal to 10% of the applied load extends to a depth twice the width of the footing.

When a tall new building is placed next to an old one, the foundations and particularly the soil between the foundations of the old building may be thrust upward.

Some 15 years ago I examined the foundations of a church in New England during the erection of an adjacent multistorey tower and it was possible to see that the floor between the massive piers in the crypt had deflected upward by as much as a foot. The foundation walls of the crypt had also deflected inward because of lateral forces from adjacent foundations.

At least part of the problem may also have occurred when the excavations for the adjacent building partially caved in, causing lateral soil movements and the fracturing of city sewer and water mains. The water flowing through the soil also helped to reduce the bearing capacity of the soils and may have allowed the heavily loaded piers to sink further into the ground.

In cases where fine grained soils are full of water the soil will tend to act like a liquid, displacing as the basement of a building is placed in it. In such cases a building with a watertight basement may actually float like a concrete boat moving up and down as the subterranean water levels change.

A second type of problem may be associated with excavations for new buildings adjacent to old ones. If the soil can move into or toward the excavation, for example, because of a failure of sheet piling, then the bearing capacity of the soil beneath the foundations of the old building may be catastrophically reduced. A sudden reduction can cause equally sudden settlement and cracking in superstructures and in buried sewers and other services.

If a series of narrow footings are installed close together the bulbs of pressure intersect and the influence on the ground is deeper than would be the case for an isolated footing.

PILING

Piles have been used since the time of the ancient Romans not only to carry foundation loads to deeper and more solid strata but also to gain resistance from friction on the sides of the piles. Early piles were always of timber and might consist of a series of round tree trunks driven deep into the ground in closely set rows capped with one or two layers of 3- or 4-in.-thick planks. Early piles were driven by heavy weights which were hauled up by gangs of men or teams of horses and dropped down timber guides onto the head of the pile. Patents for the application of steam power to pile driving date to as early as 1806 to William Deverell of Blackfriars in London, and in 1842 and 1843 to James Nasmyth, the British inventor of the steam hammer.

In the middle of the nineteenth century a typical specification for piling called for

> (pine) 10–15 inches square, nice staight grown sticks, free from shakes and in all respects sound and perfect. They must be properly shod with iron and pointed, and the tops squared and fitted with wrought iron rings or collars, to prevent splitting by driving . . . When all are thus driven to the proper depth the tops of the piles are to be carefully squared to a uniform level throughout and the upper timberwork fitted. Longitudinal half timbers five to seven inches wide and 10–14 inches deep, are first bolted to the piles, notched down upon shoulders cut for them (the shoulders were one third the width of the top of the pile). These constitute the walings and serve to bind the whole pile-framing together. If the piles are sufficiently near to each other [say not more than two feet from centre to centre] the . . . planking, which is rough, and three or four inches in thickness, may be spiked at once down on the surface formed by the piles and waling. If the piles are further apart it will be necessary to fit transverse sleepers, say six inches by six inches on the walings, in order to

receive the planking which is to be spiked down upon them (Dempsay, 1851).

Competing proposals for the timber piling beneath the foundations of the massive stone walls of the new Engine House for the Hamilton, Ontario, Water Works in 1854–1855 called for "spruce piles in alternate double rows, capped with six inch by twelve inch oak planking covered in concrete"; or "ten to fourteen inch diameter hardwood; foundations to be laid on two layers of three inch pine planking spiked to heads of piles which are in four rows at two inch intervals."

Such elaborate timber pilings and cappings continued to be built under large masonry walls well into the twentieth century, but many architects and engineers today tend to be totally unaware of their existence until settlement occurs and investigations reveal traces of deteriorated timbers.

I encountered a typical case recently where a lowering of subterranean water levels in Winnipeg, Manitoba, led to the decay of two layers of 3-in.-thick oak planking under the stone footings of a nineteenth century church. As the wood rotted it compressed under the load of the heavy masonry walls above and they settled evenly into the ground. At the same time the masonry piers which supported the central floor beam moved upward because of the expansive effects of concentrations of water-soluble sulfates in the soil beneath the piers. As a result the floors of the church were bowed upward 4 in. in the middle of the building. The explanation for this case in Winnipeg is that the wood piling and capping under masonry footings will often cause major structural problems when subterranean water levels fall. The wood is perfectly safe while it remains in water or clay sealed-off from the air. Wood decay fungi cannot grow or cause decay in wood unless they have access to air. A drop in water level can allow air to get to the wet wood and the decay attack may be very swift and disastrous for the wood and consequently for the masonry it supports.

SOILS AND ROCK

From the foregoing discussion it can be deduced that the most desirable support for a foundation is an impermeable and dimensionally stable rock. A good solid granite should be ideal. Some apparently solid limestones and shales, however, contain materials such as pyrites (iron sulfide) which may react with acidic subterranean water to form gypsum (calcium sulfate dihydrate) which can then cause the expansion of the rock surface and heaving or upward movement in foundations and ground slabs.

The least stable soils upon which foundations are sometimes found to have been built, are fine grained compressible clays, peat, and some types of man-made fill. Such soils may continue to react, expanding and contracting as they take up and lose water, for the whole life of the building. Round grained sands in wet conditions where water actually flows through the soil may also have a tendency to move away from beneath foundations in the direction of the flow unless the sands are contained or restrained. Unstable soils which exist in sloping strata and which are thus liable to solifluction (or soil flow or sliding) present particularly difficult problems. The problems of foundations in peats and bogs or swamps are so complicated as to require a separate special work all to themselves.

The best normal soils to support foundations are those which have a wide distribution of particle sizes well packed and mixed with few voids and which lack clay minerals and organic material.

DIFFERENTIAL SETTLEMENT

Uniform settlement usually poses few problems but it is comparatively unusual. Differential settlement is unfortunately much more common and can occur for one or more of the following reasons:

- Differences in thicknesses of compressible soil layers under the foundations.
- Variations in soil compressibility.
- Differences in foundation loading.
- Differences in footing sizes and pressures.
- Variations in the moisture content of the soil.
- Differences in the depths of footings.
- Variations in the depth and location of freezing and thawing phenomena in the soil under and around the foundations.

Classic examples of differential settlement include the leaning Campanile Tower of Pisa, the Washington Monument, in Washington DC, and the not so famous Empress Hotel in Victoria, British Columbia, Canada. In each of these cases the loads were fairly uniform and differential settlement resulted in the structure tilting on a plane.

In the case of the Washington Monument the tilt became obvious during construction and the foundations were extended all round the monument to spread the load to match the compressive strength of the subsoil under one side of the structure.

In the case of the Empress Hotel the building is built on 50-ft timber piles which rest on gravel at one end of the building but only penetrate to the middle of a compressible clay layer at the other end. Sixty five years after construction the building was found to be still slowly tilting. At the clay end the maximum settlement was more than 30 in. Annual measurements taken since 1912 shortly after the building was completed, show that as is often the case, much of the settlement occurred during the first five years but the movement still continues much more slowly.

We have just discussed three cases where the structures have tilted evenly and where as a result no serious cracking has occurred. Obviously if the structure continues to lean until a point of instability is reached, as is now apparently the case with the relatively slender Campanile of Pisa, then overstressing of the masonry materials, cracking, and even collapse may result.

However, a much more common cause of structural cracking and even collapse results from differential settlement due to differential foundation loading.

Perhaps the simplest case to consider is that of a great triumphal arch like the Arc de Triomphe in Paris. The foundation loads are concentrated under the piers on either side of the arch. The archway itself being a void has no load but to avoid the evils of differential settlement of the piers leading to cracking and consequent failure of the great arch, a continuous foundation joins the two piers. In compressible soils it may even be necessary for an inverted arch to be constructed in the foundation to transfer the upward forces from the soil under the arch over to the bases of the piers. These upward forces are easier to comprehend if one considers that the parts of the heavily loaded foundations under the two piers are compressing the soil beneath and moving downward while the foundation under the central arch has no superimposed load and does not move downward except under its own load.

The differential loading on the long foundation results in an effective upward force being applied on the central section resulting in an upward deformation which is termed "hogging." In more normal masonry structures this problem is seen at window and door openings where stone sills may be bent upward and may fail with cracks tapering downward from the centers of the sills. In a multistorey building the long lines of window openings one above the other can reduce the loads on the foundations under those windows by a very large factor.

Traditional masons knowing of the inevitable initial foundation settlement resulting from the compression or consolidation of soils under foundations, set stone sills so that they spanned clear over the masonry under a window or door and thus no upward movement could be transmitted to the sill causing it to be bent and broken.

In great medieval cathedrals and in more recent structures built along similar lines the great central towers can produce extremely heavy forces on the foundations causing the center of the foundations to sag in relation to the extremities. This is the opposite of the hogging described in sills and floors between heavy piers.

THE EFFECTS OF TREE ROOT SYSTEMS

One of the commonest causes of foundation settlement and consequent structural cracking and failure is the action of tree roots in clay soils. Deciduous or broad leafed trees such as oaks, maples, and poplars in long dry summers may remove such large quantities of water from subterranaean clay layers that they can cause those clays to shrink substantially. Where the clay layers penetrate beneath the foundations the latter may bridge over the shrinking layers only to collapse later into the voids thus formed, or the foundations may deform downward gradually keeping pace with the shrinking layers.

Structural cracking in the superstructure is then associated with the foundation movements. It is common to find that storm sewers, drains, and even gas mains are also fractured by such root-induced shrinkages. While the clays will swell again as water returns to the soil in the fall the fractures remain, slightly closed it is true but there nevertheless to act as permanent hazards. The water and the sewage leak into the soil and possibly penetrate into basements via cracks caused by the same shrinkage. The leaking gas of course presents a threat of explosion. The leaking water may even cause the same tree roots to grow toward the source and then into the pipe, sometimes totally blocking the pipe.

In order to assess the potential risk of foundation damage from trees near buildings we must ask how far the root systems extend around the trees. The general rule of thumb is that the roots extend out at least as far as the leafy canopy of the tree but I have noted roots from maples extending 60 ft away from the trunk of a tree when the leaf canopy extended only some 30 ft. In the latter case the roots were passing under a church basement floor about 15 ft below grade. The downward extent of root penetration has been measured to a depth of at least 20 ft.

THE RESTORATION AND RENEWAL OF OLD FOUNDATIONS

The first part of this chapter described the nature and problems of old foundations and footings. The second

Structural cracking in an Ottawa building where tree roots are removing moisture from clay under foundations causing shrinkage followed by settlement.

part examines the various techniques which are available for the restoration of deteriorated foundations and for the reinforcement and upgrading of unsatisfactory foundations.

The selection of a particular method depends to a large extent on the exact nature of the problems affecting the stability of the foundations or footings. It may be worth systematically listing the causes of the defects so that the associated treatments can be discussed with them:

- Excavations both from the surface and underground in the proximity of or under existing foundations, for example, excavations for new buildings, tunnelling, and mining operations which may lead to settlement, subsidence, or lateral move-

ment. Countermeasures include continuous underpinning with RC beams.

- The transmission of vibrations or shocks through old foundations, for example, caused by the installation of machinery in old buildings, pile driving or blasting operations in the vicinity, or heavy bus or truck traffic on adjacent streets. Countermeasures include the installation of vibration dampers and isolation systems if the vibrations are expected to continue.

- Rises, falls, or sudden variations of subterranean water levels causing differential shrinkage or expansion of soils beneath the footings. Countermeasures may include controls on water use and drainage.

- Falls in subterranean water levels exposing tim-

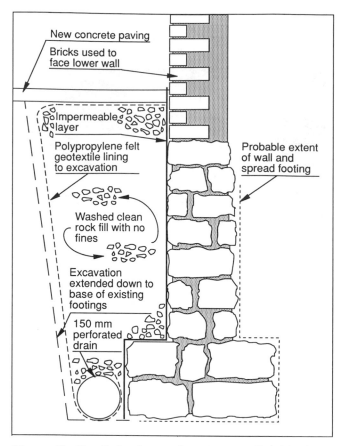

New concrete paving

Bricks used to face lower wall

Impermeable layer

Polypropylene felt geotextile lining to excavation

Probable extent of wall and spread footing

Washed clean rock fill with no fines

Excavation extended down to base of existing footings

150 mm perforated drain

Figure 91. Detail for base of masonry wall with damp problems.

ber pile caps and leading to rotting and subsequent settlement. Countermeasures include temporarily lowering the water level to permit capping of the timber piles with reinforced concrete caps followed by allowing the water level to rise again so that it completely covers the remaining timbers.

- Changes in loads on foundations caused by alterations and additions to the structure; or the redistribution of loads caused by, for example, the failure of the bond mortar between two wythes of a thick masonry wall, leading to concentrations of loads on one or the other wythes and eccentric, loading on foundations. Countermeasures are largely concerned with the stabilization and restoration of the superstructure.

- The deterioration of materials and structural systems in the foundations, for example, the deterioration or total removal of mortars and the softening of stones. Countermeasures include continuous underpinning and piled underpinning.

- Movements of foundations caused by landslides which may be of natural origin or may be caused

by man. Countermeasures include land stabilization with the use of complex piling systems.

- Seismic activity ranging from small earth tremors up to major earthquakes. Countermeasures include attempts at upgrading the seismic resistance of foundations using reinforcing beams, isolators, and vibration dampers.

It is essential to recognize that all old buildings have reached a state of equilibrium which may be delicate or even precarious.

When any intervention is called for to stabilize a foundation or to restore a structure where problems have been caused by foundation movement or failure, the first concern must be to preserve that state of equilibrium. The goal should always be to restore or increase lost margins of safety rather than to abandon the original construction scheme which should be treated with respect.

There is a fundamental difference between the construction of a foundation for a new structure and the strengthening of one which is already in existence. In the former case the functions of the designer and of the site engineer are normally quite separate. In the latter case the functions tend to come together and may even be combined in the same person. Also in the latter case any questions of deterioration and consequent restoration of the foundations must be dealt with in exactly the same way as similar questions on the superstructure. The principal requirement in all such work is that the responsible practitioners have the fullest possible amount of experience in this precise field.

It is essential that no intervention is made without having first established who is to be involved, that all members of the team can work closely together without any problems, and how the work is to be carried out. The team should not be changed without very careful consideration being given to the reasons for such a change.

Once the team and approach have been established the fullest possible examination of the existing conditions of the structure, the underlying soils and the relevant macro and micro environments must be carried out in the field.

The available methods for the conservation of foundations and the restoration and improvement of lost safety margins may be described as follows:

- continuous underpinning
- piled underpinning
  - paired piles
  - staggered piles
  - jacked piles

- root piles or *pale radici*
- cantilever underpinning
- injection or consolidation techniques
- seismic isolation retrofitting

No matter which of the above techniques are used it must be realised that although in the past the restoration and reinforcement of foundations was usually entrusted to skilled craftsmen, in the period since the Second World War this has become a modern applied science. There are however still the essential requirements for experience, intuition, and inspiration of the practitioner who will direct the project. That person must also be directly involved in the project on site.

UNDERPINNING

Underpinning may be defined as the process of transferring the loads from a foundation in such a way that the foundation may be repaired, renewed, or relocated. Underpinning is carried out when:

- excessive settlement of a foundation has occurred
- to permit the level of adjacent ground to be lowered
- to increase the load-bearing capacity of the foundation or to express it another way, to reduce the load on a soil which has too low a compressive strength

CONTINUOUS UNDERPINNING

Of all the forms of underpinning this is perhaps the most common or certainly has been until now.

The process is relatively simple and is carried out as follows:

First stage: A series of pits are excavated against the base of the wall and down to a predetermined level below the base of the existing footings. Each pit is then extended under the footing. The pits are usually about 4 ft wide and are excavated about 8 ft apart.

Second stage: A reinforced concrete pad is cast in the bottom of the pit and left to cure. The underside of the footing is cleaned off, removing all dust, dirt, and fragments of mortar. A new foundation wall of brick or stone masonry is then built up working outward from the back of the recess first. The wall is built up to about $1\frac{1}{2}$ in. below the underside of the footings and then the mortar is left to cure

Third stage: When the mortar has cured, a dry mortar mix of one part by volume of sulfate-resistant port-

land cement and one part by volume of sand is packed into the remaining space. The mortar should be just wet enough to adhere to an inverted trowel but not wetter. The dryness of the mix assists in avoiding shrinkage. Traditionally pieces of roofing slate were placed in the gap with the mortar to reduce the total thickness of the mortar and thus also to assist in curing and reducing shrinkage. This was specially useful when lime was used as part of the mortar mix. The mortar should be firmly packed home and can even be hammered in using a short section of board and a large mallet.

Fourth stage: Once the mortar has cured, the first stage is then repeated with a new excavation immediately next to the first one. The process is repeated until the whole wall has been underpinned.

Critics of this system quite correctly point out that there is a risk of a general relaxation of the structure above and that this can lead to cracking. It is also difficult to obtain sufficient compaction of the soil beneath the new footing to avoid subsequent compaction and settlement. Further problems are encountered if the water table is reached. It may also be dangerous to dewater in order to reach deeper levels. In very rare cases the underpinning has actually been carried out by hand by a diver working under water in what has at times approached liquid mud. This is of course appallingly dangerous work. One such case was the underpinning with concrete of the foundations of Winchester Cathedral in England. The cathedral contains a memorial to the divers who carried out this work for about five years from 1905, placing bags of cement in total darkness under water and right under the suspect foundations. Very similar but uncommemorated work has been carried out more recently in Canada by Mr. Charles Ross in the freezing dark waters of the Ottawa River under the foundations of the piers of a vintage bridge.

PRESTRESSING AND PRETESTING

To avoid the problems of subsequent settlement of footings as the soil beneath compresses, the soil can be prestressed or preloaded by means of jacks. If we return to the first stage of the continuous underpinning process we can carry out the excavation and place a pad in the bottom of the excavation. Then we take a precast concrete beam and place it against the underside of the cleaned-off footings. A small amount of concrete is placed between the beam and the footing, a jack is inserted into the gap between the pad and the beam, and then the beam is gently pressed against the underside of the footings and left to cure. When the concrete has cured, the load of the structure above is calculated and then that load may be applied on the jack. Until the load is reached the jack will press against the concrete above and will compress the soil beneath. Carefully done, this means that the soil beneath can be compressed and compacted up to the load that it will have to bear. Once the load is reached and movement ceases the ends of the precast concrete beam are pinned up with masonry which is left to cure. Once that masonry has cured the jacks can be removed and the missing masonry filled in.

Much of the preloading or precompression of soils today is carried out with the aid of Freyssinet flat jacks which are typically 16 in. in diameter and $1\frac{5}{8}$ in. thick with a rated load of 380 kips (1 kip = 1000 lb).

Another system used in continuous underpinning is the Pynford system invented and developed for wide use in the United Kingdom. The system uses the Pynford patent stool which is rather like a very short miniature dead shore consisting of an upper and a lower steel plate held apart by short steel tubular legs. Larger stools can have plates of 1.2 to 2.0 in. in thickness and legs about 31 in. long. Each is capable of carrying loads of up to 100 tons. Once they have been set in cutout pockets and have been pinned up using expanding grouts, the masonry on either side can be cut away and new foundation beams can be cast into position around the stools with the reinforcement passing right through them.

Critics of continuous underpinning quite justifiably point out that it is not totally reliable and that it cannot exactly duplicate conditions which have taken decades or even centuries to establish themselves. Loads, for example, do not necessarily fall on the foundations exactly as calculated from the apparent centers of gravity of masses of superimposed masonry.

A classic of continuous underpinning occurred during the building of the Washington Monument in Washington D.C. The building of this gigantic obelisk was commenced in 1848 with the placing of a huge stepped rubble masonry footing 80 ft square (6400 ft²) and 23 ft, 4 in. thick. Work ceased because the funds ran out when the obelisk was 190 ft high. Work commenced again in 1873 and it was immediately discovered that the footings were settling. The first stage of the underpinning consisted of placing a new concrete ring footing 126 ft, $5\frac{1}{2}$ in. square, 41 ft, $2\frac{3}{4}$ in. wide and inserted about 18 ft under the outer edge of the old footings. The new concrete ring footing was constructed in a series of 4-ft-wide trenches, each being filled with concrete which was allowed to cure before the next one was excavated. In a second step a series of concrete buttresses were set into slots cut into the side of the old stepped rubble masonry base. When these were cured the inter-

vening spaces were filled with a second series of concrete buttresses set into similar slots. This second ring was set about 6 ft into the base of the stepped footing. The new footings increased the total bearing area to approximately 14,100 ft². Construction was then continued and the monument was completed without further settlement or other incident.

PILED UNDERPINNING

Paired piles and staggered piles are basically the same method but with the piles located in different patterns. In this method a pair of piles are driven on either side of a wall which has been found to be supported by unsatisfactory footings or foundations. A hole is then cut in the wall and a reinforced concrete needle is inserted through the hole and connected to the caps of the two piles. In this way the load of the structure is transferred to the needle and thence to the piles. In paired piling the needles are set perpendicularly to the face of the wall and each pile supports the end of only one needle. In the case of staggered piling the needles zig-zag along the wall passing through holes in the wall at a series of diagonals in plan. Each pile supports the ends of two needles.

JACKED PILING

In jacked piling the actual piles are made up of short sections which are built up under the base of the old structure as follows: first an excavation is made beneath the footings and a reinforced concrete pad is placed against the underside of the footings and left to cure. A short pointed section of pile is placed upright in the bottom of the excavation and a jack is then placed on top of the pile. Short sections of steel beam are placed on top of the jack and the jack is then operated so that it pushes the pile down into the ground using the mass of the structure above for a reaction. When the first section of piling has been completely driven, the jack is backed off and a new section of pile is positioned. The jacking operation is then repeated. The weight of the structure must provide sufficient load to provide the necessary reaction to prevent the jacks from pushing the wall up and causing hogging and cracking.

ROOT PILES OR *PALE RADICI*

The *pale radici* method was invented by the Italian engineer Fernando Lizzi. The term means "root piles." *Pale radici* or root piles are also known as micropiles. Lizzi applied for the first patents on 11.3.1952 (No 497736) and on the 29.12.1952 (No. 502416).

The first *pale radici* underpinning was carried out in 1952 on the A. Angiulli School in Naples. The piles had a nominal diameter of 4 in. (10 cm) and an average length of 43 ft (13 m) for an assumed working load of only 10 tons per pile. Since that early work, this remarkably successful method has been used on thousands of buildings all over the world including the foundations of the Ponte Vecchio in Florence, the Ducal Palace in Urbino, and the fifteenth century church of Tourny, France.

The method is simple and consists of boring a pair of holes down through the foundations and on into the soil beneath. The holes are drilled at an angle of about 70 degrees alternately from either side of the wall. A reinforcing rod is inserted in the hole and a high-strength concrete is injected down the hole under pressure. Compressed air may also be used during the placing of the pile in the hole. The final result is a pile which has expanded laterally into softer more compressible strata producing a rough cross section which provides excellent friction with the surrounding soil and therefore good adhesion to it.

- For soils of average consistency 66-ft (20 mr) piles are sufficient.
- For very stiff soils, pile lengths of 33–50 ft (10–15 ms) are sufficient.
- For gravels and sands which are more or less compact the limit varies from 20 to 33 ft (6–10 ms).
- For clays the lengths can vary from 33 to 50 ft (10–15 ms).

The concrete is normally 1323–1764 lb/35 ft³ of cement (600–800 kg/m³) of sieved sand. A single reinforcing rod is used for the 4-in. piles but a multirod frame or a tube is used for larger diameter piles. Because they cause so little if any disturbance to the old masonry, root piles are one of the most satisfactory answers to the problem of stabilizing old and delicate foundations.

CANTILEVER UNDERPINNING

In this technique a pair of piles are sunk next to each other on one side of the defective foundations. A hole is cut through the wall and a reinforced concrete needle is inserted into the hole and attached to the caps of the two piles. When the concrete has cured the now cantilevered needle is pinned up to take up the load from the wall.

There are a wide range of injection or consolidation techniques which rely on injecting fluid cementitious grouts which may or may not be effective and can add very considerable loads.

The success rates may be wildly varied because success depends on the uniform spreading of the grout beneath the footings. Since soils and various stata may be very different degrees of peremeability it is difficult to ensure this uniormity. Also clays and silts which are among the most problematic soils may not be injectable at all.

SEISMIC ISOLATION RETROFITTING

In this category belongs the technique known as base isolation which has been pioneered for heritage buildings by the engineers John Kariotis of Kariotis and Associates Pasadena and Eric Elsesser of Forell/Elsesser of San Francisco, and the architects of the Ehrenkrantz Group, San Francisco, working on the seismic upgrading of the Salt Lake City and County Building, Utah. The building was built 1890–1894 and was an unreinforced masonry structure of five storeys with a 250-ft-high central clocktower. The technique finally used on the foundations was as follows:

- The foundations are isolated from the building by the use of large "bearings" which are about 17 in. square by about 15 in. tall. Each bearing consists of a sandwich of alternating layers of steel and rubber with a lead core. The lead core prevents building motion due to wind loads but yields and provides inelastic viscous damping to absorb earthquake energy during a seismic event, which in turn helps to control horizontal deflections.
- The steel plates which are bonded to the rubber prevent the rubber from spreading outward under vertical loading, thus making the bearings very stiff in the vertical direction.

The method is applied as follows:

- New concrete side beams are poured on each side of all masonry walls. The walls are notched out 4 in. on each side of their bases to receive these beams.
- Posttensioning rods are placed in holes drilled right through the walls and are tightened to "clinch" the masonry material of the wall between the beams.
- The isolators are positioned in specially cut pockets in the base of the wall.

- Concrete cross beams are then cast so that they link the two side beams, and transfer the wall loads from the side beams to the isolator bearings.
- Wide flange steel beams are used welded together as grillages to spread the loads from the isolators to the footings so as not to endanger the latter.
- A new concrete floor is added above the isolators to act as a rigid diaphragm connecting all the side beams and linking all the isolators so that they will act as a system.
- After all these steps are completed the mortar joint below the side beam is cut away and the building weight is thus finally transferred to the isolators.

BIBLIOGRAPHY

This is an enormous subject which cannot be dealt with in any great detail in such a short section. Further interesting reading is to be found in:

Lizzi, Fernando *The Static Restoration of Monuments* Genoa: Sagep Publisher, 1982.

Bailey, J.S. and Allen, E.W. Seismic Isolation and Retrofitting Salt Lake City and County Building. *APT Bulletin*, Vol. XX, No. 2, 1988, p. 32–44.

Pryke, J.F.S. A New Method of Underpinning. *Concrete and Constructional Engineering*, February, 1956. This article describes the Pynford system. Further data on the Pynford system and other works of this famous British firm can be obtained by writing to: Pynford Information Services. 105 Fonthill Road, London. N4 3JH United Kingdom. Telephone 01-263-1383.

REFERENCES

Crawford, C.B. (1972). Foundation Movements. *Canadian Building* Digest 148, April.

Dempsey, G.D. (1851). *Builder's Guide: A Practical Manual etc*. London: Atchley & Co., pp 7–9.

CHAPTER 13

RESTORING SLATE ROOFING

Slate has been used as an extremely durable roofing material for hundreds of years, but in recent decades many slate roofs have been replaced using other materials because of a lack of knowledge of the nature of slate and of the preservation of slate roofing systems. In many cases the original roofs could have been saved but were not because of a combination of a lack of contractors capable of doing the work and the owners' negative reaction to initial high costs. This section may at least help to dispel some of the apparent mystery about slate roofs and help designers and owners to appreciate the fine qualities of this beautiful natural material.

APPROACHING RESTORATION

A systematic approach to the problems of restoring a slate roof should include finding the answers to the following questions:

- What is the nature of the slate itself both chemically and physically? Does the slate itself have any "inherent vices"?
- What is the nature of the slate roofing system? How are the slates fixed to the roof and in what condition are the fixings or attachments?
- What are the nature and conditions of the underlay and substructure?
- What are the dimensions, textures, patterns, types, and colors of the original slates? What are the current sources for matching slates of requisite quality?

THE NATURE OF SLATE AND SOME INHERENT PROBLEMS

Slate is metamorphic rock which is transformed from shale by enormous heat and pressure in the earth's crust. The parent rock is itself formed by the long-term petrification or hardening of clays or mud rocks. All slates share the most useful property of splitting into thin flat sheets which characteristically have a high modulus of rupture compared with other stones. This means that they are comparatively strong in bending. Slate is a microgranular crystalline rock characterized by perfect cleavage quite independent of original bedding.

The essential mineral components are clear mica (mainly muscovite or sericite) and silicon (quartz). Secondary components are biotite (black mica), chlorite (a complex form of magnesium silicate), and hematite (ferric oxide). Minor components include carbonates, magnetite, apatite, clay, andalusite (a silicate of aluminum), barite, rutile, pyrite, graphite, feldspar, zircon, tourmaline, and carbonaceous material.

Generally the mineral components of slates tend to be in stable states and do not react with water or acids in the environment. Indeed some slates are so resistant to acids that they were used for early laboratory benches and sinks. The lack of durability of certain slates is related to their chemical and physical structures; and particularly to their content of certain minerals which react with acids found in polluted environments.

The ASTM Standard Specification for Roofing Slate, ANSI/ASTM C 406-58 (Reapproved 1976) notes that "the process of weathering, which affects a large part of our domestic slate, results from (1) chemical changes in certain mineral impurities and (2) a physical effect arising from the chemical weathering. Slates so affected contain considerable amounts of calcite, pyrite, and carbon, all interspersed as fine particles throughout the material. In the presence of moisture and oxygen, a reaction takes place between the pyrite and the calcite that converts the calcite to gypsum. Because the gypsum product requires more space than the original calcite particles from which it was formed, a swelling action results which brings about deterioration of the slate.''

The observation of these phenomena led to the development of the ASTM Standard Test Method for Weather Resistance of Natural Slate ANSI/ASTM C 217-58 (Reapproved 1976) which involves shearing or scratching grooves in slates before and after soaking for seven days in 1% sulfuric acid. This was one of the first standardized scientific tests used to establish the effects of acid precipitation and air pollution on building materials. Useful as this test is, it does not fully reflect the effects of current polluted environments. I have recently tested the effects of various combinations of sulfuric acid, nitric acid, and hydrochloric acid in proportions and at concentrations which resemble those encountered in acid precipitation. It was found that slates resistant to sulfuric acid alone deteriorated when exposed to certain combinations of acids.

With this in mind it is worth reviewing the reactions with acids of some of the typical minerals found in slates. Pyrite (ferric sulfide, commonly known as "fools' gold") for example is regarded as insoluble in hydrochloric acid but is readily soluble in nitric acid and gives off fumes of sulfur dioxide when tested. Thus it can be seen that a slate containing substantial inclusions of pyrite crystals could be liable to severe deterioration in today's polluted environments, particularly in the Northeast of North America. The breakdown of the pyrites could lead to secondary reactions with carbonates in addition to the creation of holes where pyrites existed. Some slates contain carbonates such as calcite (calcium carbonate) and rhodochrosite (manganese carbonate) which are both more readily soluble in the combination of acids than in sulfuric acid alone. However, apatite (calcium fluoride phosphate) is readily soluble in sulfuric acid as are biotite and chlorite; and thus in these cases the related ASTM standard test C 217 supplies useful data.

Once the chemical reactions have taken place the structure of the slate is weakened and its permeability is increased. It is an unfortunate coincidence that the Northeast of North America not only has some of the highest levels of damaging atmospheric pollution but also has long severe winters. Increasing amounts of water can get into the structure of the slate and the risk of damage from freezing is enormously increased.

The visible forms of the damage will usually be delamination in which the very thin layers of the slate peel away; general softening and crumbling; the development of holes; or the cracking apart of slates along lines of weakness.

Imperfections which are found in slates and which are described by the ASTM Standard Specification include the following:

- curvature, which should not exceed $\frac{1}{8}$ in. in 12 in.;
- knots, knurls, or "pins" which are rounded defects or "swirling grain" inclusions projecting more than $\frac{1}{16}$ in. from the face of the slate and which may cause projections preventing the slates from lying down flat;
- "ribbons" or bands of soft, often carbonaceous material, which may weather out or cause nails to shear out.

In addition to the use of ASTM C 217-58, the physical state of the slates may be tested by means of the following ASTM Standard Methods of Testing:

ANSI/ASTM C 120-52 (Reapproved 1976) Standard Methods of Flexure Testing of Slate (Modulus of Rupture, Modulus of Elasticity)

ANSI/ASTM C121-48 (Reapproved 1976) Standard Test Method for Water Absorption of Slate

Slates are classified in three grades which are based on the expected length of service. Grade S1 slates are expected to have a service life of 75 to 100 years or more. Grade S2 slates are expected to have a service life 40–75 years; and Grade S3, 20–40 years. All grades should have a minimum modulus of rupture across the grain of 9000 psi (62 mPa). Water absorption percentages should be a maximum of 0.25% for Grade S1; a maximum of 0.36% for Grade S2; and a maximum of 0.45% for Grade S3. The maximum depths of softening from the weathering test (C 217-58) should be 0.002 in. for Grade S1; 0.008 in. for S2; and 0.014 in. for S3.

FAULTS ASSOCIATED WITH QUARRYING, TRANSPORT, AND LAYING

When slates are found to be cracked and slipping from their positions on the roof, it is possible that they were cracked when they were laid or were cracked after laying by roofers or others walking on them or placing loads on them. Slates may be cracked before they reach the site either by blasting in the quarries or by poor transporation. Uneven movement of settlement of old roof boarding or structures may also cause cracking in slates.

FAILURES IN SLATE ROOFING SYSTEMS AND FIXINGS

Many failures of slate roofs are found to be caused by the corrosion of the fixing nails rather than any failure of the slates themselves. The fixing nails should be of copper with a large flat head and annular rings to promote grip in the wood battens or sheathing beneath. The recommended lengths of the nails are $1\frac{1}{4}$ in. for slates up to 18 in. long; and over; and 2 in. for hips and ridges. For slates thicker than the standard $\frac{3}{16}$ to $\frac{1}{4}$ in., the increased nail length is twice the thickness of the slate plus 1 in. Stainless steel nails may be used instead of copper but steel, galvanized steel, and copper-coated steel nails should never be used. Other systems of fixing slates traditionally included the use of hardwood pegs and wire hooks which may also have rotted or corroded. Other failures may be caused by nails being driven right through the slate or being left projecting so that the slate above breaks over the head.

UNDERLAYS AND SUBSTRUCTURES

Slates were traditionally laid on 1×2 in. wood laths or battens spaced at appropriate intervals, or on boarding 1 in. or more in thickness. In current practice the boarding is covered with asphalt saturated rag felt weighing 30 lb/ft^2 for slates up to $\frac{3}{4}$ in. in thickness. Under thicker slates a 50 lb felt is recommended.

The felt functions as a useful cushion and spreads loads, preventing breakages especially in the thicker and heavier slates. Failures of the slate roof will occur when the laths, battens, or boards are attacked by wood destroying insects and fungi, collapsing or ceasing to give any purchase to the fixing nails.

RESTORATION CRITERIA

When slates are found to have been destroyed by chemical and physical deterioration the next step is to replace those slates while salvaging sound slates for reuse.

DIMENSIONS

The restorer must first establish the dimensions of the original slates, and then try to find a source which can supply the requisite slates to those dimensions. Slate dimensions are given as follows: Length in inches × width in inches × thickness expressed as a fraction of an inch. "Lap" and "exposure" dimensions are also required. "Lap" describes the amount by which a slate is covered by the next but one course above it. "Exposure" describes the portion of the length of a slate which is actually exposed to the weather. A formula for calculating lap and exposure in standard slate roofs is as follows:

If L = the total length of a slate, the lap = 3 in. and

$$\text{the exposure} = L - 3 \text{ in.}/2$$

Thus for a 24 in. long slate, the lap is 3 in. and the exposure should be 24 in. minus 3 in. = 21 in. divided by 2 which gives an exposure of $10\frac{1}{2}$ in.

The sizes are also described by a wonderful series of historic British terms which are the delight of quiz program and crossword puzzle enthusiasts. These terms describe sizes which rise from the diminutive "Singles" which are from 10 to 12 in. in length and from 5 up to 10 in. in width. The sizes progress upward from Singles to Doubles; Small Ladies; Large Ladies; Small Viscountesses; Viscountesses; Countesses; Small Marchionesses; Marchionesses; Duchesses; Princesses; Empresses; Imperials; Queens and Rags. The largest British sizes of Empresses 26 × 15 in. Imperials 30 × 24 in.; and Queens or Rags 36 × 24 in., are not normally found in North America.

In rural buildings in Cornwall, Wales, and the old English counties of Northumberland and Cumberland, and in parts of Central Western Norway even these sizes were exceeded and roofs might be finished with huge slabs of slate which might be as large as 72 × 48 in. Such vast slabs were naturally of much greater thickness than the smaller slates, that is $\frac{3}{4}$ to 1 in. or more. The thicknesses of slates might be as little as $\frac{1}{8}$ in. for the smallest slates but average about $\frac{3}{16}$ in. for medium sizes and $\frac{1}{4}$ to $\frac{5}{16}$ in. for the larger common slates. The slates which exceed 24 in. in length might be as thick as $\frac{3}{8}$ in. or more.

Since slate is a natural material which is usually handsplit along natural cleavage planes there is liable to be a wide range of variations in thickness. The writer has had at least one case recently where the failure of a restored slate roof was found to be partially due to some of the slates being too thin. To avoid such problems in cases where old roofs are at low angles and the slates are long, the writer specifies a minimum thickness of, say, $\frac{1}{4}$ in. In Canada and parts of the northern United States where heavy snowloads are likely, slate thicknesses are usually from $\frac{3}{16}$ to $\frac{5}{16}$ in.

In the United States slate is sold by the "square" or sufficent slates to cover an area 10 × 10 ft (100 ft²) with a 3 in. lap. In Britain slate might be sold by the square or by the "thousand." Like the "bakers' dozen" the slaters' "thousand" was inflated. In both Britain and France the "thousand" or "mille" might actually number 1200 slates plus 60 to allow for breakages.

TEXTURES, FORMS, PATTERNS, AND TYPES

Surface textures and any special forms should also be noted. Surfaces may be basically smooth or rough, depending on the natural cleavage and structure of the type of slate. Special forms include a wide range of shapes and patterns, such as hexagons, octagons, variegated, diagonal, American cottage style, and fish scale or rounded. There are several methods of laying slate which may be found in North America. These are the "standard slate roof" which uses slates of uniform sizes and of an average thickness of $\frac{3}{16}$ in.; the "textural slate roof" in which rough and smooth surfaced slates are mixed and thicknesses and lengths may also be varied; and the "graduated slate roof" which involves the use of a wide range of thicknesses from $\frac{3}{16}$ in. up to as large as 2 in. in exceptional cases but not uncommonly $1\frac{1}{2}$ in. The slates are carefully graduated starting with the thickest and largest at the eaves and gradually reducing in even courses up to the thinnest and smallest at the ridge. "Dutch lap" slate roofs are laid with regular slate on shingle lath or tight sheathing, but with a single thickness of slates with each slate lapped at its head and on one side by 3 in. The laths are commonly laid at 17 in. centers; "open slating" was described as being especially suitable for barns and other buildings where ventilation was required. The slates were laid 4 in. apart horizontally and were lapped 3 in. with an exposure of about $8\frac{1}{8}$ in.; the last type is the French method which employs 12 × 12 in. or 14 × 14 in. slates laid diagonally and with their lower corners cropped to form hexagons. A course of rectangular slates measuring say 20 × 9 in. were laid horizontally at the eaves and the ridges to cover the remaining triangular spaces.

COLORS AND SOURCES

The next feature which will require matching is that of color. The basic slate colors are:

Black; blue black

Dark gray; gray; light gray–silver gray

Dark purple; purple; light purple; variegated purple

Green; gray green

Red

Mottled purple and green

"Freaks"—combinations or variations of the above colors with browns. Freak colors available from U.S. quarries include "opals," "bronzes," and "buffs." The variegated purples are predominantly purple but are spotted and streaked with green. Some varieties weather to pleasant shades of brown.

The following schedule gives the various colors with their common sources:

Blue gray: Lehigh-Northampton Counties, Pennsylvania; Esmont, Buckingham and Fluvanna Counties, Virginia.

Unfading gray: Northampton County, Pennsylvania.

Gray: Vermont and Washington County, New York.

Gray black: Vermont and Washington County, New York.

Blue black—hard vein: Chapman Quarries and Northampton County, Pennsylvania.

Unfading black: Peach Bottom, York County, Pennsylvania; Maryland and Piscatsquis County, Maine.

Unfading green: Western Vermont and Washington County, New York.

Weathering green: (weathers to soft brown, buff and gray colors) Western Vermont, Washington County, New York.

Unfading purple: Western Vermont, Washington County, New York.

Unfading mottled green and purple: Western Vermont, Washington County, New York.

Variegated purple: Western Vermont, Washington County, New York.

Unfading red: Washington County, New York.

In Canada some slate roofs were made with Canadian slates from quarries in Madoc, Ontario (a blue black slate) while others such as the original roofs of the Parliament Buildings in Ottawa were made from slates from Melbourne, Quebec. The latter roof did not last and had to be replaced. Apart from some limited workings in Newfoundland and British Columbia the Canadian slate industry is currently inactive.

Blue black and dark gray slates are currently being

imported into North America from Italy, and gray and gray green slates from Spain. I recently examined one of the Italian slates and found it to contain many pyrite crystals about $\frac{1}{8}$ in. in diameter. Other examples appeared to be excellent and strongly resembled good quality Pennsylvania and Vermont blue gray and gray black.

Slates may also be imported from the United Kingdom. Slates from Cornwall in the West of England are a beautiful gray green and light gray. Welsh slates are usually blue black or dark gray and the slates from the North of England are usually various shades of purple.

French slates are principally quarried in the Ardennes and the Angers districts.

CHAPTER 14

SYNTHETIC RESINS, POLYMERS, AND PRESERVATION

Once regarded as cheap substitutes for "real" materials, synthetic resins and plastics have now been largely recognized for their values and for the fact that they can often be used where natural materials cannot.

Many of today's plastics and synthetic resins are derived from a single source—petroleum. Crude oil is broken down into simple molecules made up of hydrogen and carbon atoms and then these molecules can be used like fibers in a thread to form long molecular chains or macromolecules.

The field is bewilderingly large and some of the names of the materials are so long and complex that many nonscientists seem to have a permanent mental block to understanding or learning about them.

Many of the new materials are used in the science and practice of conservation to arrest or retard the deterioration of natural materials and to reinforce and repair them and systems in which they are used.

This chapter is offered in an attempt to demystify the materials and as an introductory guide to their nature and use.

PLASTICS

In the broadest sense, a "plastic" is defined as any nonmetallic material that can be molded into shape. In practice the definition is narrowed to include only a certain number of natural and synthetic resins and their compounds which can be molded, cast, extruded, or used for coatings, consolidants, and films.

Most of these resins are of an organic nature, being macromolecular compounds with hydrogen, nitrogen, and oxygen atoms bonded to and grouped around carbon atoms.

A common classification of plastics divides them into two groups, thermoplastic and thermosetting. Thermoplastics are those which when heated soften even at temperatures as low as 140°F (60°C) and can then be molded without any change in their chemical structure. Thermosetting resins undergo chemical changes when molded and cannot be reshaped by softening them by heating. Selections of common plastics are given below for each type:

Thermoplastic	Thermosetting
Acrylics	Alkyds
Cellulosics	Epoxides
Fluorocarbons	Furan
Natural:	Inorganics
Shellac	Melamines
Asphalt	Phenolics
etc	Polyesters
Nylon	Silicones
Polyethylenes	Ureas
Polystyrenes	
Polyvinyls	
Protein substances:	
Casein	
Soy	

NATURAL AND HISTORIC SYNTHETIC RESINS AND POLYMERS

Not all polymers are new or synthetic. Wood includes a number of natural polymers, lignin, cellulose, and hemicellulose. Cellulose is defined as an amorphous carbohydrate polymer with the formula $(C_6H_{10}O_5)_x$.

The history of plastics might be said to date from early beginnings in 1833 when Braconnot nitrated starch xyloidine and 1838 Pelouze nitrated paper, both in France. In 1845 and 1846, respectively, Schonbein of Switzerland first nitrated cotton fibers and then patented cellulose nitrate in the United States. In 1851 collodion was used commercially and in 1862 A. Parkes displayed celluloid objects at a fair in London, England. In 1865 Parkes obtained a patent for cellulose nitrate objects in England. In 1866 commercial manufacture began in England.

In 1863, John Wesley Hyatt, a printer in New York, set out to discover a substitute for ivory to be used in the manufacture of billiard balls. This was not an early example of animal conservation activism but was inspired by a hefty $10,000.00 prize offered by the U.S. billiard ball makers Phelan and Collender. The result of Hyatt's tinkerings was "celluloid," the first of a long line of American synthetic polymers or plastics. The result was unfortunately too brittle to be used for billiard balls but was found to be almost perfect for gentlemen's detachable shirt-collars and cuffs, and for ladies combs.

The first person to drop a burning cigar or cigarette on his celluloid shirt front found to his horror that the new material was almost explosively flammable! Celluloid was produced by treating cellulose with nitric acid. The resulting substance was referred to as "nitrocellulose" and was closely related to gun-cotton, a powerful explosive known as pyroxylin or trinitrocellulose which was invented in 1845 by Schonbein. It was manufactured by treating the cellulose fibers of cotton wool with nitric and sulfuric acids.

Just six years after Hyatt invented his new material it was discovered that if camphor was added to it, the resulting polymer was much less brittle and was indeed resilient enough to make billiard balls. In 1872 Hyatt patented the name celluloid in the United States.

Although the addition of camphor as a plasticizer reduced brittleness, with the passage of time the camphor was lost because of its high vapour pressure. Thus the material became more brittle and unstable with age. Unpigmented cellulose nitrate is not stable to light or ultraviolet radiation and will become acidic, brittle, lose tensile strength, turn yellow, and shrink.

In the nineteenth century, it was discovered that like its natural cousins the cellulose nitrate resin could be thinned with a solvent and could be used as a coating or clear lacquer. Solvents include organic esters, ethyl acetate, butyl acetate, amyl acetate, and ketones like acetone and diacetone alcohol. Celluloid is now a trademark for a specific compound of nitrocellulose and camphor. Like many other synthetic resins celluloid is colorless and flammable. One of the major uses of celluloid was in the manufacture of early movie film which had an evil and well-deserved reputation for becoming unstable and bursting into flames. Before the introduction of more suitable modern resins, despite its problems, celluloid in solution in a solvent of equal parts of amyl acetate and acetone was used by conservators to consolidate friable old stone and ceramics (Plenderleith, 1956).

Nitroglycerin, a thick pale yellow liquid polymer with the formula $CH_2NO_3 CHNO_3CH_2NO_3$, again infamous for being explosive on concussion or on exposure to sudden heat, was so dangerously unstable that it has even collected its own factual and fictional literature. It can also be used as a vasodilator in medicine.

Early versions of plastics tended to consist, like celluloid, of chemically treated natural substances. In 1907 Leo Baekeland, a Belgian born chemist working in New York, took a new direction in creating a truly made-to-order new material. In searching for a substitute for shellac he mixed and heated together two chemicals derived from coal, phenol and formaldehyde. When his glassware cooled down he found that he had created a new synthetic resin or plastic. This was the first truly synthetic resin and was named Bakelite in honor of its inventor (patented in 1908 in the United States).

Since Baekeland's epoch making discovery, chemists routinely make large molecules consisting of carbon atoms surrounded by groupings of other atoms such as hydrogen and oxygen linked in the form of chains. These large molecule chains are called monomers and by means of heat or pressure these chains can be caused to align and link to form polymers. Denser structures and cross links between the chains can be produced by subjecting the polymers to high-energy radiation.

From this somewhat unlikely excursion into the worlds of billiard balls, detachable collars, explosives, and medicine we have been introduced to the whole gamut of positive and negative features of the new resins. We can see that the synthetic resins were often designed for one purpose but proved to be better suited for others. Many were not only flammable but might even be explosive in certain conditions. Many tended to be unstable, changing their color or form as they got older and as they were exposed to high temperatures, for example. Undesirable characteristics could sometimes be removed or desirable ones conferred by the addition of various other substances.

But with aging, additional substances such as plasticizers and stabilizers may leave again with dangerous consequences. All of these characteristics and others still affect synthetic resins and the ways in which we can use them. Many resins which were not designed for use in conservation are now so employed despite the fact that they may often have features which make them unsatisfactory for such specific uses.

RESINS PLUS WHAT?

A resin may be used by itself to form a coating or it may be thinned with a solvent. The resin gives the plastic compound its name and it is the cohesive and adhesive agent which provides rigidity and binds together the other materials in the plastic.

Fillers, which are usually inert fibrous or powdered materials, are used to reduce cost by reducing the total amount of expensive resin. They may also be used to improve impact strength, temperature resistance, chemical resistance, electrical resistance, and a host of other desired characteristics. Fillers have ranged from wood and rock flour or powder, to ground mica, paper, talc, carbon, glass fibers, and powdered metals.

Plasticizers are liquids with high boiling points (200–400°F) used to improve flow of resins and to make finished materials more flexible or less brittle.

Lubricants are used to prevent moulded products from sticking to the moulds or to provide self-lubricating surfaces, for example, for gears. Lubricants include graphite, lanolin, and metallic soaps.

Colorants include dyes, toners, and pigments selected not only for their particular color or shade but also for their own long-term performance, for example, nonfading, and their effects on the final plastic product, for example, effects on curing rates and electrical properties.

Catalysts (or hardeners) are used to control the rate or extent of polymerization of the resin.

Stabilizers (or inhibitors) are included to extend the pot life (time between mixing and the use of the mixture) of a material or to prevent color changes or other forms of aging-related deterioration.

RESINS AND PLASTICS IN CONSERVATION

The major resins and plastics in use in conservation are the acrylics, epoxides, polyesters, and silicones which may be used by themselves for fillers, adhesives, water repellents, and consolidants. A number of others such as alkyds, polyvinyls, and phenolics are used in paints and coatings.

ACRYLICS

This group of resins is still very popular with conservators in many areas of cultural resource conservation.

The acrylics were invented before the Second World War and their industrial development has been credited to Otto Rohm of Darmstadt. Chemically the acrylics are close relations to the vinyl resins. Solid resins can be made from acrylic and methacrylic acids but the esters of these acids have been found to produce the most useful resins. In the latter group is that made by the polymerization of methyl methacrylate. The product is a hard, clear, strong resin which is familiar to us in solid form under the trade names Plexiglas, Lucite, or Perspex. Other methacrylic ester polymers include ethyl, n-propyl, isobutyl, and n-butyl methacrylates. The latter polymers are commercially important as coatings and lacquers. The acrylics tend to be light and ultraviolet stable and develop good adhesion to most surfaces. Solvents include acetone and toluene, the latter giving the lowest viscosity for polymers. Their solubility can mean that they are to a certain extent reversible.

CELLULOSICS

Cellulose nitrate has already been described in some detail and has been referred to as being unstable and with strong tendencies to yellowing in sunlight and shrinkage on curing. Cellulose acetate, on the other hand, in a low viscosity form produces excellent lacquers. An alkyd resin such as glycol phthalate is used with cellulose acetate in the combined role of resin and plasticizer. Resulting cellulose acetate products are light and ultraviolet stable, of low flammability, and with aging, retain flexibility and remain neutral. The last feature is in strong contrast to cellulose nitrate which becomes strongly acidic as it ages. Cellulose acetate is perhaps most familiar as "dope" for heritage aerophane wing fabrics. Cellulose nitrate is most familiar to conservators as a "nightmare" material from which some nineteenth and early twentieth century artifacts and early movie film stock were made. Such artifacts may become acidic, unstable fire hazards and have been known to destroy finishes on adjacent surfaces by giving off solvent vapors. By 1927 all new United States cars had cellulose nitrate-based paint finishes.

POLYVINYLS

Apart from being used in vehicles for pigmented paints and coatings, polyvinyls have also been applied in the form of vinyl copolymers as water repellents.

EPOXIDES

These resins are used on a large scale in paint manufacture and as adhesives. They are produced by polymerization of epichlorhydrin with phenolic compounds such as diphenylol propane (bis-phenol) in the presence of an alkali catalyst. Variations in the proportion of the two reagents determine the extent of further polymerization, thus forming a variety of epoxy resins. Resins may vary from very low viscosity liquids to solids which may be thermoset by reaction with other resins such as polyamines, polyamides, and phenolic resins. Epoxies were introduced in the late 1940s and some varieties have been found to age badly, changing color, yellowing or even turning purple with exposure to ultraviolet radiation. Other varieties may be "water clear" and provide excellent adhesion for repairing such materials as glass and stone.

A major problem for conservators is that epoxies are practically irreversible. This means that once an epoxy has been used it may be impossible to remove it without seriously damaging or even destroying the parent material. Accidental splashes and leakages must be removed immediately, before they harden and become impossible to shift. Epoxy resins are manufactured like polyesters with two components which are mixed to exact proportions immediately prior to use.

They cure or harden by chemical reaction rather than by solvent loss and thus do not shrink. The manufacturer's recommendations should be closely followed in selecting clean-up solvents which may include toluene and acetone. These solvents are toxic and highly flammable. King (1989) recommends dimethylformamide (DMF) as being a better solvent for use on resin leakages on masonry because DMF is fully miscible with water and can be washed and flushed away. Some epoxies will not cure in contact with moisture and in such conditions "moisture insensitive" epoxies must be used.

Moisture insensitive epoxies are frequently used for repairs to stone units which cannot be effectively and totally dried *in situ*. Epoxies are also commonly used with steel bars and plates for repairs and reinforcement of deteriorated wooden structural members. Specially developed methods of wood reinforcement using epoxies include the WER Method (wood-epoxy-reinforcement) developed by P. Stumes (1979) in Canada and the BETA System developed by D. Klapwijk in the Netherlands.

Epoxies are also used with sand or stone dust aggregate for "plastic repairs" and as grouts for setting anchors and dowels in the restoration of historic stone masonry. Epoxy resin composites can also be formulated as flexible filling compounds (Phillips and Selwyn, 1978).

POLYESTERS

Polyester resins have seen extensive use with stone dust and other fillers in the fabrication of thin cross-section reproductions of large stone and terracotta cornices and other details.

SILICONES

This is the generic name used to describe a class of polymeric organosilicon compounds which, for example, might be built up starting with a silicon atom with an alkyl group on opposite sides linked to oxygen atoms on the other two sides. The oxygen atoms form the link to further silicon atoms with more pairs of alkyl groups and so on in a long chain. In such compounds, the carbon to carbon chains known in other synthetic plastics are replaced by the equally stable silicon–oxygen–silicon–oxygen chain. Silicones in solution may have water-repellent characteristics when applied to masonry but the longevity of the effective water repellent depends on the alkyl group used and hence the resistance to alkaline conditions, and to such variables as ultraviolet exposure, and moisture content of the masonry when the silicon is applied. Many of the silicone water repellents have been found to have broken down with exposure to ultraviolet radiation and moreover they did so irregularly and unevenly so that moisture could be admitted through one part of a surface and held behind a residual coating in another area. The invisible remains of such old partially failed coatings often cause serious problems of exfoliation in old masonry and can seriously complicate attempts at cleaning the treated masonry even 20 years afterwards when all details of the original treatment have usually been forgotten. The remains may have to be removed with specially formulated paint and coating removers before any other cleaning can commence.

SILICONATES

These are products which can be diluted with water or with water–alcohol mixtures. Once applied to masonry they react with carbon dioxide in the atmosphere, with the masonry materials, and with themselves to form a polysiloxane resin. Siliconates may be used in water–glass (potassium silicate) mixtures to form injectable barriers against rising damp and as binders for pigmented masonry paints.

SILANES

With smaller molecules than the silicones and siliconates, the silanes can penetrate more deeply into masonry. They can be used with a wider range of solvents which include anhydrous alcohol which means that they can be used on masonry where bitumen and plastics such as polystyrene are present without fear of solvents damaging them. Silanes require moisture to react and form a useful water repellent. Some may also require catalysts for their reactions, reacting well with alkalis but remaining totally inactive in neutral materials such as brick. Applications can be problematic also because if reaction rates are slow much of the silane may evaporate before it has a chance to penetrate and react.

To achieve acceptable reaction rates and hence water-repellent qualities, German specialists recommend alkylmethoxysilanes rather than alkylethoxysilanes. An American specialist has suggested alkyltriethoxysilanes and alkyltriisopropoxysilanes (private communication).

Paradoxically the final product with silanes will only be alkali resistant and tend to be durable when long alkyl groups are used. Methyl silanes are totally unsuitable for imparting water repellency.

OLIGOMEROUS ALKYLALKOXYSILOXANES

If a small amount of water is added to a alkylalkoxysilane during manufacture the resulting product is an oligomerous alkylalkoxysiloxane. It has all the good qualities of silanes but unlike them is not subject to evaporation. Catalysts and other additives ensure that good water repellency is achieved within five hours of application and that the resulting product is alkali stable. With these modifications, concentrations can be reduced and thus costs are effectively cut. High concentrations of silanes of 20–40% are used to compensate for possible evaporation losses while oligomerous alkylalkoxysiloxane concentrations need to be no more than 6–8%.

POLYMERIC ALKYLALKOXYSILOXANES

These products are produced in the same way as the oligomerous alkylalkoxysiloxanes but more water is used in the manufacturing reactions producing a long chain polymer. While the resulting product is initially as effective as a silicone, dropping water absorbtion from 6.7% on an untreated sample to 1.6% on a treated sample, the resins tend to remain tacky for long periods and thus treated surfaces tend to get dirty.

SILICIC ACID ESTERS

Silicic acid esters may be used by themselves or with the addition of a water-repellent siloxane to consolidate deteriorated stones which have lost binding material. The lost binders are replaced by silicon dioxide which is formed after a period of some weeks. Successful reactions are dependent upon a complex combination of moisture conditions in the stone, surface evaporation rates, and atmospheric humidity.

CONCLUSION

Synthetic resins may provide a solution to many difficult conservation and renovation problems but they can be extremely expensive to apply and may require regular replacement forever after! All their positive and negative features should be carefully considered prior to deciding on their use. Resins may be irreversible or virtually impossible to remove without causing unacceptable damage; however, at the same time they may also be unstable and may change their nature and appearance, making it necessary to remove them.

Those who use synthetic resins may be exposed to toxic, flammable, explosive, corrosive, or allergenic combinations of resins, hardeners, or solvents. The strongest precautions must be taken at all times with full use of protective clothing, masks, appropriate filters, and fire and explosion controls.

Even after all this, synthetic resins may still offer the only means of preserving an old building material. There are those who object to the use of synthetics on historic stone and woodwork thereby creating new composite materials. In some cases they may be justified but in many cases the alternative is the total loss of the original and here the use of the resins comes into its own.

REFERENCES

King, E. (1989). *The Use of Resin (Polymer) Products in the Repair and Conservation of Buildings: Wood Glass and Resin*. English Heritage Technical Handbook, Volume 5. Aldershot: Gower Technical Press Ltd.

Phillips, M.W. and Selwyn, J.E. (1978). *Epoxies for Wood Repairs in Historic Buildings*. Washington D.C.: Heritage Conservation and Recreation Service, US Department of the Interior.

Plenderleith, H.J. (1956). *The Conservation of Antiquities and Works of Art*. London: Oxford University Press.

Stumes, P. (1979). *W.E.R.-System Manual: Structural Rehabilitation of Deteriorated Timber*. Ottawa: Association for Preservation Technology.

FURTHER READING

Gettens, R.I. and Stout, G.L. (1966). *Painting Materials: A Short Encyclopaedia*. New York: Dover Publications, 1966.

Roth, M. *Comparison of Silicone Resins, Siliconates, Silanes and Siloxanes as Water Repellent Treatments for Masonry*. Reprinted from Wacker-Chemie GmbH, Munich, Germany, ND. Conservare Technical Bulletin 983-1. ProSoCo, Inc. Kansas City, KS.

SIKA Technical Literature. SIKA Chemical Corporation. PO Box 297, Lyndhurst NJ 07071. Particularly for epoxy resins.

Weber, H. *Stone Conservation-Planning and Execution*. ND. Conservare Technical Bulletin 483-1. ProSoCo, Inc. Kansas City, KS.

CHAPTER 15

HISTORIC WALLPAPERS

Wallpapers have been used to decorate interiors since the sixteenth century in Europe and since the seventeenth century in North America. The Chinese had hand-painted nonrepeating scenes on large sheets of paper long before this and their papers first found their way into Europe among the packing materials used for Chinese export porcelain in the seventeenth century. By the early eighteenth century these papers were being exported to the West and were sold in relatively expensive complete sets to make scenes. Usually these were of three types, flowering trees with butterflies and insects; landscapes; and procession groups. Early papers in Europe were wood-block printed on single sheets no larger than 22 × 32 in. A typical French eighteenth century paper was 14 × $20\frac{3}{4}$ in. The reason for this was that the size of the individual sheet was controlled by the size of the mold and "deckle" which were used in the manufacture of paper. The paper maker typically prepared a pulp from mashed up rags, water, and other ingredients and then placed an even layer of the pulp on the wire mesh in the bottom half of the paper making mold. The upper half of the mold, a frame or "deckle," was then pressed onto this to hold the pulp in place in a thin layer as it dried out. In some processes the mold with its wire mesh screen was lowered into the vat of pulp, then raised with a even layer of pulp on the screen. A large mass of wet pulp on a large screen was very heavy and awkward to handle. This also tended to place limits on the sizes of sheets for hand manufacture. The screen left a fine grid pattern in the paper which can be seen as a watermark. The deckle left an irregular edge around the sheet where the thickness tapers off. This is still known as a "deckle edge" and has been artificially reproduced on

imitations of handmade paper sold as expensive notepaper.

The product was dried further, pressed under a large screw press or even stood upon, then finished. The sheets could then have patterns printed upon them using large wood blocks and water-soluble paints with an animal glue or size vehicle. In some cases part of the pattern was block printed and other parts were stencilled on.

Although the first small sheets were applied to the walls individually, by the mid-eighteenth century the small sheets were pasted together into rolls before being printed upon.

Block printed papers can be recognized by a close examination of the paint areas where the surface usually shows what are known as "sunburst" effects and bubble craters. When the paint-coated wood-block was pressed straight down onto the paper the paint tended to be squeezed outward from the center of each design element producing radiating "sunburst" patterns. Air was also trapped by the descending block and tiny bubbles were forced into the paint. The bubbles burst when the block was lifted, leaving tiny circular craters.

"Endless" paper rolls were first made on cylinders in 1799 in England and in 1817 in America, but for some reason the new paper-making machines were not really used for wallpaper manufacturing until 1820 in France, 1830 in England, and 1835 in America. In the 1840s wallpapers began to be made on steam-powered machines using patterned cylinders or rollers to produce the design. Typical rollers were of wood with the outlines of the design motifs formed of brass strips which were hammered into the wood. Within the fence-like brass borders the body of each motif was formed by densely packed felt. The fresh paper roll was fed into the machine and rotated on a very large central drum. As the paper travelled around the drum it was brought into contact with the raised surface patterns on the revolving rollers each of which printed a part of the pattern in a separate color. Each roller was continuously recharged with paint by a moving belt from a trough.

Machine-printed papers which date from 1841 at the earliest can be identified by a close examination of the paint layer. The fine brass borders of the patterns on the rollers produce a clear line round the edge of the pattern elements; and the paint within the pattern elements tends to be streaked in one direction parallel to the length of the roll and the way it went through the machine.

Although machine-made paper widths were supposed to be standard in each country by the 1850s, that is, in France, 18 in., in England, 21 in. (but 20 in. when hung), and in the United States 20 in., in practice widths varied widely and might range from 18 to 40 in. Papers suspected of being old handmade papers should be examined to see if they are in small individual sheets and to see whether they have the marks of the wire screen in them. To do this you take the sheet and hold it up to a strong light so that the fine rectangular grid pattern of the wires shows up as a water mark. Other manufacturers' water marks may also show up in the transmitted light.

A royal monogram GR and crown stamp in black line on the back of the sheet could indicate that the paper was printed and taxed in England prior to 1832 when the relevant tax laws were repealed. The French also had stamps to record the payment of taxes.

From the earliest times European papers most frequently seem to have imitated textiles such as the expensive silk hanging which decorated the houses of the rich, and subsequently fine imported textiles with delicate floral patterns from China and India via the East India Company. Thus a paper would have a printed floral motif plus a second fine line motif which imitated the texture of fabric. The ones which imitated the fine floral patterns were termed "caffaw" or "caffy" papers, these terms being possibly derived from "Cathay" or China.

In the seventeenth and eighteenth centuries, English paper "stainers," as wallpaper makers were known, imitated rich damask-woven textiles using flock papers. In such a paper the outlines which were to be "flocked" were printed onto the paper with plain varnish or less commonly animal glue or size. The paper was then passed over a "flocking trough" which was a long shallow box with a flexible drumskin stretched across its underside. Boys with long thin canes beat on the drum-skin raising a cloud of fine grated wool or silk particles which rose and stuck to the sticky printed outlines.

Similar techniques were used from the eighteenth century onward to apply metallic powders to imitate gold, and powdered mica to give glitter effects.

Late in the eighteenth century and in the early years of the nineteenth large panoramic papers became very popular. Typical scenes were made up of many separate rolls which were applied vertically to join up to form a long panorama which might extend 20 or 30 ft in length. The subjects included scenes from the Voyages of Captain Cook; classical ruins; Italian scenes; and scenes in Constantinople. In the 1820s and 1840s such panoramas were often accompanied by "architectural" papers which consisted of printed ballustrades to place on the dado panel below the chair rail; and columns, capitals, entablatures and swags of draperies which could be used to frame the view, and give the impression that the viewer was in fact in a sort of open loggia gazing out at some exotic scene.

During the nineteenth century a typical wall was divided into a series of separate areas, each of which could have different wallpapers. In the middle of the century, the French often divided their walls vertically into panels above a dado, but for most of the century the wall was divided horizontally. Working up from the base of the wall, immediately above the baseboard one might have a narrow "border paper" 2–4 in. wide followed by a dado paper which extended up to the chair rail. Above the chair rail might be another border paper and above that the main area of wall. The latter area was covered with a "fill paper." Above the fill paper might be another border paper framing the main wall area. Finally, the top of the wall would be finished with a deep "frieze" paper which could be 15–18 in. wide.

During the 1820s the Zuber factory in Alsace developed new techniques which made possible the printing of superb wallpapers in the styles known by the French terms "irisée" and "ombré." The irisée or rainbow papers were particularly beautiful and inspired many copies which never approached the beauty of the genuine article. All these papers were inspired by rich shiny silk brocades and satins hanging in full folds, and they succeeded remarkably in creating an almost three-dimensional illusion of the real thing.

In about 1850 the use of cheap wood pulp for making paper was successfully introduced into England and then after about five years into America. By the 1880s such papers had taken over the mass market and the products were unfortunately of low quality. It was not until the 1920s that a method was found to successfully remove the acidity caused by the presence of lignin in the wood pulp. As a result of this acidity many of the later nineteenth century papers are typically brown or "yellowed" and are so brittle that they tend to fall apart.

Even a brief historical introduction to historic wallpapers such as this would be incomplete without mention of the impact in America of the new English stylized flower patterns praised in Charles Eastlake's popular book published in England in 1868, *Hints on Household Taste*.

These patterns in the 1870s rapidly swept away much of the French influence which had been felt in North America from the eighteenth century. For much of the last quarter of the nineteenth century wallpaper designs were influenced by such English master designers as William Morris, Cristopher Dresser, and Walter Crane.

In the 1880s American wallpaper manufacturers again followed English "aesthetic" taste and introduced exotic designs inspired by Japanese and Middle Eastern motifs. These designs became known as "Anglo-Japanese" and "Moorish." The last decade of the nineteenth century saw a deterioration in American wallpaper designs although some of the more avantgarde designers did import Art Nouveau wallpaper from England and Europe.

A number of variations on the wallpaper theme were developed from the 1870s onward. The first was Lincrusta Walton, a heavy, linseed oil impregnated and linen backed paper, rather like linoleum but thinner and which was patterned in high relief. It was sold in both colored and plain forms and the latter could be colored and perhaps highlighted in "Dutch metal" or artificial gold, just before or just after it was applied to the wall. This product was manufactured in Connecticut from 1882 onward. A second close relation to Lincrusta Walton was Anaglypta, a much lighter, less solid bas-relief paper.

Japanese "leather papers" were imitation leathers with low relief patterns made from oil impregnated paper pulp which was beaten onto wooden moulds with small wooden mallets. These relatively expensive papers were of very high quality and were so realistic that many believed they were actually leathers. The illusion was often augmented by the application of painted "faux" or imitation finishes and glazes.

A further technical development was the invention of the ingrain paper which was made from mixed cotton and wool rags which were dyed before pulping so that the final unbleached product had a textured "ingrained" coloring. A similar process produced what were known as "oatmeal" papers. In the twentieth century particularly since the 1940s fine expensive wallpapers have been produced by silk screening. A silk screen is formed with an extremely intricate stencil which is carried on and supported by a very finely woven silk textile. The textile is stretched over a wooden frame and this forms the screen. Silk screen printing involves laying the screen down over the paper and then very carefully applying the paint onto the back of the screen so that it passes through the extremely fine holes in the textile but only in the open parts of the stencil pattern. Silk screen printed papers can be detected by examining the pattern under a microscope. The edges of the pattern have tiny "teeth" or steps which occur where curving lines pass across the regular fine grid pattern of holes in the textile.

THE ATTACHMENT OF WALLPAPERS

Early wallpapers in England were actually nailed to the wall with small tacks and there are records of this being done in America in 1741. The lines of tacks were often covered with paper or textile borders which were also tacked to the wall. From the beginning of the eighteenth century it was common to paste papers to the wall after "sizing" the wall. Size is a refined animal protein glue which was applied thinned with water. Papers were occasionally mounted on fabric or canvas before hanging. Wallpaper paste was commonly made with flour, water, and a small quantity of alum all mixed up and boiled until it formed a thick paste. Borders were often pasted on over the papers to cover over poor junctions between sheets, cracks in the wall, and other defects.

THE CARE AND PRESERVATION OF WALLPAPERS

The problems of old wallpapers can occur in one or more locations in a system of "layers" or levels which can be considered starting at the bottom at the support and working outward to the surface. First comes the support, substrate or surface to which the wallpaper is attached; this may be plaster, boards, or stretched canvas. The substrate may be cracking, moving, suffering from insect and fungal attacks, or it may be detached from its own supports which may also be under attack. To illustrate this, plaster may be both cracked and separating from its supporting lath system which in turn may be attacked by insects and fungi. Stretcher frames for textiles to support papers may also have been subject to insect and fungal attacks and tacks may have corroded causing the textile to fall off its frame. The textiles too may have deteriorated.

The paper is attached to the substrate by the next level of the system which may be tacks but is usually a flour paste. The paste is water soluble and will support mould growth when damp. It may also become dessicated, or at the opposite extreme, be totally removed by moisture, causing the paper to separate from the substrate. The paper may then peel right off the wall or it may blister in what is termed "blind cleavage," where the conservator cannot get access to the edge of the detached area. The paste may also be eaten by insects such as cockroaches and silverfish.

The paper itself is the next layer. Here we must consider the fibers from which the paper is made; ingrain dyes; fillers which give the paper body and make it smooth; and residues of animal protein-based size as well as residues of bleaches used in the manufacture. One of the worst problems of the paper itself is that of acidity which may be related to manufacture from wood pulp containing lignin or to acids moving into the paper from damp boards in the substrate.

Many major conservation problems relate to the de-acidification of the papers since they are the principle support of the pattern or design; and when the paper fails, the design is lost.

The next level in the system is the paint layer which may in fact consist of many layers of different colors on a colored ground. A colored ground consisted of a layer of colored paint which was brushed onto the entire surface of the sheet to provide a background upon which the design was then printed. All the paints are commonly water soluble with a pigment; possibly an extender such as powdered chalk to provide covering power; and glue size as a binder. Occasionally oil-based or resin-based media were used to produce glossy finishes and even ground colors but these tend to be unusual. An exception to this are the so-called "sanitary" papers which were produced from the end of the nineteenth century for bathrooms, kitchens, and nurseries. These papers were deliberately designed to be washed or at least wiped with wet cloths so that they could be kept clean.

The paint layers are often found to be thick and chalky with a tendency to be brittle and to detach from the paper particularly if the paper has buckled, been rolled, or been folded. Pigments may have faded and metallic pigments may have corroded. If the glue size becomes damp, fungi may also grow on the paint layer. At best the paint layer may simply be dusty or lightly soiled. At worst the surface may have been varnished so that the delicate powder pigments are embedded in a yellowing varnish which may be very difficult to dissolve. Historic wallpapers should not be varnished or lacquered in modern misguided attempts to "conserve" them.

Often papers which have been torn have been "repaired" by well-meaning persons with pressure sensitive tapes, Scotch tape, rubber cement, or cellulose nitrate based cements. It will usually require the services of a skilled conservator to remove such repairs but they must be removed or they will ultimately destroy the paper. The adhesives may harden and become less soluble; and parts of them may "bleed" and migrate out away from the tape to provide sticky traps for dust and dirt. The tapes themselves may also yellow until they are no longer clear or "invisible."

Repairs and the reattachment of papers should only be carried out with the purest of wheat starch-based pastes which can be easily removed if necessary and which do not harm the paper. Repairs to the paper itself may be made with relatively strong fine Japanese tissues attached with the same starch paste. Patterns can then be in-painted over the patch. Repairs to holes may also be made by an expert paper conservator using "leaf-casting" or similar techniques which actually rebuild the paper using pulped fibres and relatively weak binders such as methyl cellulose.

In the majority of cases old papers simply require careful cleaning. This is often done by first protecting and supporting the surface with a fine nylon screening textile and then gently vacuuming through it. Dust may also be removed slowly and delicately with soft camel hair brushes. Slightly more difficult to remove dirt may be cleaned off using dry cleaning techniques with various types of draftsman's erasers such as a "Pink Pearl" or a vinyl cleaning pad. All residues should be carefully removed with soft camel hair brushes.

Old wallpapers are particularly subject to damage from moisture and light. Interior humidity levels should be carefully studied and ideally should not be above 50% relative humidity. Temperatures should ideally be around 65–68°F (18–20°C). Artificial lighting should be limited to incandescent light kept to a level of no more than 15 foot candles. No direct sunlight should fall on wallpapers and all windows should be covered with ultraviolet-filtering Plexiglas. A recommended maximum level for ultraviolet radiation is 75 mW/lumen. If old valuable wallpapers are found to be severely damaged with tears, major paint losses, and other various forms of deterioration then the advice and aid of an experienced professional conservator should be sought.

THE REPRODUCTION OF OLD WALLPAPERS

A number of firms produce reproductions of old wallpapers and in some rarer cases old firms are still producing or reproducing some of their old patterns. In cases where the original paper is no longer produced then silk screened versions can be produced by such firms as Bradbury and Bradbury in California.

FOR FURTHER READING

Anon. *Trois Siècles de Papiers Peints*. Paris: Musée des Arts Decoratifs, 1967.

Frangiamore, Catherine L. *Rescuing Historic Wallpaper: Identification, Preservation, Restoration*. Nashville: American Association for State and Local History, 1974.

Frangiamore, Catherine Lynn. *Wallpapers in Historic Preservation*. Washington: Technical Preservation Services Division, USDI, 1977.

Greysmith, Brenda. *Wallpaper*. New York: Macmillan Publishing Co., Inc., 1976.

Lynn, Catherine. *Wallpaper in America from the Seventeenth Century to World War I*. New York: Barra Foundation and Cooper Hewitt Museum. WW Norton and Company, Inc., 1980.

Nylander, R.C., Redmond, E. and Sander, Penny J. *Wallpaper in New England*. Boston: The Society for the Preservation of New England Antiquities, 1986.

Various authors. *Journal of the American Institute for Conservation*, Vol. 20 Nos. One and Two, Fall 1980 and Spring 1981. Washington 1981. American Institute for Conservation. Number 2 is a special issue devoted to wallpaper conservation.

Some Firms Producing Reproductions of Historic Wallpapers

In the USA

Bradbury and Bradbury Wallpapers, Box 155, Benicia CA 94510.

Brunschwig et Fils, Inc., 979 Third Ave., New York NY 10022

A.L. Diament and Co., 2415 South Street, Philadelphia PA 19146.

Scalamandre, 977 Third Ave, New York NY 10022

F Schumacher and Co., 919 Third Ave, New York NY 10022.

In Europe and the United Kingdom

Cole and Son (Wallpapers) Ltd., 18 Mortimer Street, London W1. UK.

Sanderson & Sons, Ltd., 53 Berners Street London W1. UK.

Societe francaises de Papiers Peints, 60 Balagny sur Therain, Oise, FRANCE.

Marburger Tapetenfabrik, 3570 Kirchhain, Hessen, GERMANY.

Zuber et cie, 68 Rixheim, FRANCE.

INDEX

NA 105 .W43 1993 40641

Weaver, Martin E., 1938-

Conserving buildings

DISCARD

The fine for this
item when overdue
is 10¢ a day.

GAYLORD MG